A·R·A·B
FOLK-
TALES

A·R·A·B
FOLK-
TALES

Translated and Edited by

Inea Bushnaq

Pantheon Books, New York

Library of Congress Cataloging in Publication Data
Main entry under title:
Arab folktales.
Bibliography: p.
1. Tales—Arab countries.   I. Bushnaq, Inea.
GR268.A73A73   1986   398.2'927   85-9569
ISBN 0-394-50104-7

*The royalties from this book have been tithed to support
the New York Public Library.*

Book design by Susan Mitchell
Manufactured in the United States of America
First Edition

*For
Nadya,
Elise,
and
Rick*

Contents

Djinn, Ghouls, and Afreets
TALES OF MAGIC AND THE SUPERNATURAL
∴ 63 ∴

Magical Marriages and Mismatches
MORE TALES OF THE SUPERNATURAL
∴ 153 ∴

*Beasts That Roam the Earth
and Birds That Fly with Wings*
ANIMAL TALES
∴ 209 ∴

Famous Fools and Rascals
STORIES OF DJUHA AND HIS KIND
∴ 249 ∴

∴ ∴ ∴

∴

∴ *Embroidery with Word and Thread* ∴

Arab village women walking home from the spring, heavy water jars balanced at a slight angle on their heads, long gowns swaying with the movement of their stride, can well be likened to date palms and gazelles and sugarcane and young mares, as they are in these folktales. Strong and straight, even the most ragged of them steps with the proud gait of a queen, a graceful carriage being essential to the job.

A popular love song begins,

> *Ya hamila al jarra min fen* . . .
> O water-bearer, from where, from where
> Do you carry your jar of earthenware?
> O let your glances stray
> This way, this way . . .

A more observant songwriter might have guessed by her dress from what cluster of houses on what hill she came. For in the otherwise plain setting of their lives, the Arab women of the eastern Mediterranean have taken pleasure in decorating their clothes. Embroidery is one of their arts, story-telling another.

In days when travel was mostly on foot and distances therefore much longer, each village and hamlet developed as a separate community. In each place the women sported their own designs in finely stitched embroidery distinguishable from that of their neighbors. For the outsider it is enough to know that the modest gowns of black, indigo, or bleached homespun were generally decorated in the same parts. A panel covering the chest was the most richly patterned. Down the flanks, vertical strips of color accentuated the swing of the hips, and across the back hem an eye-catching panel drew the attention of anyone chancing to look after her to the neatness of the wearer's heels, often stained a coquettish rose with henna dye.

Regional differences can also be read in the trim of a dress. Where the soil is rich and rainfall permits more than one crop, where women help in the work of the fields, embroidery on their dress will be as sparse as their free time. Where the young girls are set to mind the herd, their dresses are crowded with colored thread, for they can stitch while their cattle graze. And gold thread, striped silk, and rich velvet set apart the wedding gown—sometimes called the "royal"—worn to be admired by the whole community.

Like the dresses that the women wear, the stories they tell are similar in outline. The jealous stepmother will plot against her husband's children whether she lives in Morocco or Iraq. But in one place she may float them down the Euphrates on a raft, in another leave them in the desert to starve. The differences lie in the details. Universally, the prince is so impressionable that he falls in love to the verge of illness on seeing some token of the heroine; whether it is a fine clog, an anklet, or a jewel will depend on local fashion.

"Tent of the pasha," "tree of life," "sugar on the plate," "eye of the camel," "bottom of the coffee cup" are some of the names given to the patterns in peasant embroidery. They could well be titles to the fairy stories. Indeed, like a commonly told tale, the decoration of a dress displays a number of well-known elements, unchanging and recognizable by name, but arranged and combined according to the taste of the stitcher. In the stories the action may begin with an order from the sultan for a curfew. Patrolling the city in disguise at night, the sultan inevitably discovers one house where a light burns despite his orders. But one teller may place three frightened spinsters around that light, another a bold weaver who cares nothing for the king and his orders. Or the starting point may be a girl alone in the house with no fire to cook on. She sees a light in the distance. Some tales have her beg an ember off a friendly spirit; in others she is lured into danger by a hungry Ghoul.

The embroidery designs are generally geometrical—parallel lines in the "comb" pattern, triangles in the "amulet." But sometimes one comes across what the peasants call the "chain of boys." Nestling among curly foliage is a row of putti copied from some foreign book or altar cloth. In the same

way, the reader of a tale may suddenly recognize Odysseus under an Arab name escaping from the cave of a blind Ghoul by strapping himself to the undersides of three sheep.

∴ *Storytellers, Private and Public* ∴

Stitching and talking are both for the pleasant evening hours when the day's work has been done, as one popular opening formula suggests:

> *Kan ma kan*
> *Bidna nihki*
> *Willa innam*
>
> There was, there was not,
> Shall we tell stories
> Or sleep in our cots?

Darkness is the best time for fiction. To spend the good daylight hours spinning tales is ill-omened. The superstition lingers still in parts of Iraq that whoever tells stories in the daytime risks growing horns and having his gold turn to iron. The Berbers of North Africa seem to have a similar association between horns and ill-timed storytelling. In their lore the sin of the teller would be visited on his children, who might be gored by some horned beast.

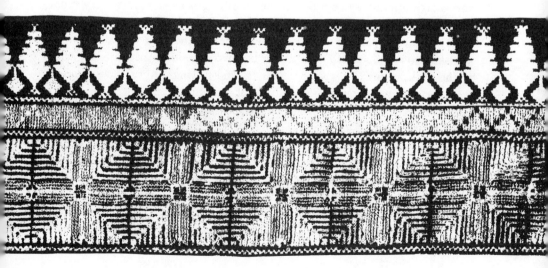

Kan ma kan. "There was, there was not." To an Arab the words evoke memories of winter evenings with a roomful of women stitching, their tired servants and sleepy children held in thrall by an old lady whispering of giants with teeth of silver and teeth of brass, of princesses like cypress trees whose brows shine clear as the Pleiades, of lovelorn heroes pale as the crocus ailing for the affection of such princesses. Or they might conjure up the endless hot nights when Ramadan falls in the summer. After the long day's fast, the evening is a time to revive; sundown breakfast parties become festive gatherings of kin. The wait is long until the drummer makes his round just before dawn prayers, warning that now is the time for a quick bite and last sip of water before the next day's fast begins. On some flat rooftop high enough to catch a cooling breeze, the hours are pleasantly spent in company, sometimes listening to the playing of a lute, often telling stories.

Such was the entertainment of the women and the children. Theirs were the household tales about princes and princesses, about Djinn and Ghouls and magic rings and hidden treasures, about younger sons and daughters despised and ill-treated who triumph in the end. They told them to one another or begged the most fluent among them to display her art.

The men met outside their homes. In the days before the cinema, the coffeehouse was the liveliest resort for males. With its mirrors and decorative tiles, and its bank of shining water pipes wound with colored cords and tassels, it was a veritable pleasure dome. As smells of charcoal embers mixed with coffee scented the air, the sprightly click of dice, ivory on wood, sounded from the backgammon boards. In smaller hamlets with no such elaborate amenity, the men might simply boil a brew of coffee and share tobacco in the village guesthouse or meet on the threshing floor, always an airy spot chosen where the wind will blow away the chaff.

When talk of politics and markets and luck in the hunt runs down, the well-known anecdotes of Djuha might be aired once more, or some new tale of the tricks of men or women might be told to laugh over. But the most welcome diversion would be the advent of the professional storyteller. This itinerant reciter of lengthy romances whose heroes predate Islam, of the exploits of Abu Zeid and the love of Antara and Abla, carried his stock from village to village, offering it to coffeehouse audiences in return for his keep. Ramadan was his richest time. With his only prop a stick used to wave or beat on the ground for emphasis, he could earn food and a corner to sleep in for several days as his listeners hung on his words or stopped him to debate some point of conduct, dividing into factions for this hero or that.

The blind Egyptian writer Taha Hussein opens his autobiography with a first memory: a reed fence in the Nile village of his turn-of-the-century childhood. His greatest pleasure was to feel the cane beneath his fingers and, when the sun had set and the people had supped, to grope his way along the fence until it led him to the poet's sweet singsong reciting the old sagas about Abu Zeid and Khalifa and Diyab to the listening men. What misery then to be carried off by a sister to bed, to lie on the floor under his quilt in terror of the Afreets. For nightly with the darkness, the spirits arose from their underground abode and filled the corners of his room.

In the *suqs* or markets of large cities the professional teller of tales might set up shop on a mat lit by a kerosene lamp. Occasionally he can still be seen today in a corner of a slow-paced city like Fez. With a listening crowd around him he will break off his narrative at some cliff-hanging moment to sip from a glass of tea. Like the pay television in an airport lounge, he will resume the tale when a sufficient shower of coins nudges him to action.

∴ *The Pillars of Islam* ∴

From the Atlantic coast of Africa to the Indian Ocean, from the Sahara to Samarkand, Moslems the world over turn their face toward the same place five times each day as they recite their prayers. Wherever they are, they stand as if on the invisible spokes of one great wheel whose hub is the holy city of Mecca. There in the early seventh century the angel Gabriel dictated the Koran to the prophet Mohammad. Upon this book, and the traditional accounts of the life of the prophet, the religion of Islam is based. With a minimum of ritual and no organized religious hierarchy, Islam permeates every aspect of Moslem life. The devout turn to the word of God for guidance not only in spiritual matters but over everyday practical details.

To become a Moslem requires no ceremony. A man simply needs to declare his belief that there is no God but God and that Mohammad is His prophet. This profession of faith is the first of what are called the "five pillars of Islam." The second is the observance of the five daily prayers. At dawn and at noon, in the middle of the afternoon, at sunset and at night, the Moslem day is punctuated by the stirring call intoned from the tops of the minarets. Any place is regarded as suitable for the worship of God, though a prayer rug not used for any other purpose ensures an unpolluted setting, as do the ritual ablutions before prayer. A ditchdigger on hearing the call to prayer will spread his coat by the side of the road and, heedless of the surrounding traffic, turn to Mecca and pray.

The mosque is where the community meets to pray together at noon on

Friday. Usually the finest building in the town, it is open and accessible to all. Any day in one of the holiest shrines of Islam, the Dome of the Rock in Jerusalem, one may come upon a party of village women sitting companionably after their prayers while their infants crawl at their feet. In the recessed windows of the mosque, students unable to read in peace in their crowded homes pore over their books in the calm of the vast space.

Until fifty years ago, education for most Arab youths meant attendance at a *kuttab*, or Koranic school, either in a schoolroom attached to the mosque or at the foot of one of the pillars inside. Sitting cross-legged on a low chair, the sheikh taught his students to recite the verses of the Koran correctly. A graduate of the *kuttab* is one who is able to repeat the entire holy book by heart.

In rural villages a teacher might be engaged to instruct the children in the Koran for a salary of wheat and olive oil and a lamb in season, as in the story "A Lost Shoe of Gold." The religious sheikh or elder, distinguished by a white turban, will have studied the Koran and the Sunna, the traditional account of the way of life of the prophet. Especially revered are sheikhs from the ancient theological university at the Al Azhar Mosque in Cairo.

It is usual for a learned sheikh to preach the Friday sermon, but any man may do so. There is no priesthood in Islam, so that any Moslem may lead the prayers in the mosque as *imam*, sound the call to prayer as *muezzin*, and even perform a marriage.

In the shadow of the mosque stood not only the school but also the *shari'a* or Koranic law court. Its judge or *qadi* still settles family disputes according to Islamic law. The tale "Justice" portrays such a court in session, but more often one finds sheikhs and *qadis* in stories not of justice but of trickery and knavery, like "The Girl Outwits Three Men," "The Judgment of the *Qadi*," and "Si' Djeha and the *Qadi*'s Coat," where they are foolish and corruptible.

Though authority is mocked in the tales, the caliph or prince of the faithful, in whom rested the highest political and religious leadership of the nation of Islam, is a shining folk hero. He is the Harun al Rasheed of *The Arabian Nights*, forever reaching for a purse of gold to reward a deserving subject and always game for an adventure with his favorite, Ja'far al Barmaki, or that notorious rascal, Abu Nuwas.

Social welfare and care for the poor are the responsibility of the faithful in Islam. The third of the five duties or pillars of Islam is the fast, and one of its purposes is to remind Moslems of the plight of their less fortunate brothers. For the whole of the lunar month of Ramadan, the devout abstain from food and drink from first light until sundown. In a hot country this is an especially taxing discipline. Travelers, the sick, and nursing mothers are exempt, but should provide food for a poor person for each day of the fast that is missed. When the fast is broken at the end of Ramadan, all are obliged to donate food to the poor. Almsgiving or *zakat* is the fourth religious duty of the Moslem. He is expected to give to God *lillah*, a portion of his income or work.

∴ *The Hajj* ∴

Before the automobile, for most people in the Arab countries a visit to the nearest town meant a walk of several hours, not undertaken very often. Only the landowner or well-to-do merchant maintained horses and camels. Robbers and the fearsome *dhabi'*, a hyena believed to have the power of mesmerizing the lonely traveler and luring him to its lair, were further deterrents. And yet from every community in the Moslem world people undertook, or hoped to undertake, a journey of thousands of miles at least once in their lives. This was the Hajj—the pilgrimage to Mecca—the last of the five duties of Islam, an obligation for every Moslem with the necessary means and health.

Every year in the month of Dhu-l-Hijja—the month of the pilgrimage—the faithful have converged on Mecca in Saudi Arabia by thousands and hundreds of thousands. There in seamless robes of white, king and pauper, dark Nubian and fair Circassian, men and women together bow and worship God. Since the seventh century and the days when men came walking and riding into Mecca, the Hajj each year has made real the unity of the people of Islam.

The pilgrim returning from Mecca is addressed with the title Hajji, or Pilgrim, So-and-So. His homecoming is an event to celebrate with family and friends. Whether his house is a single room of mud brick or a stone palace in the city, it will be marked with lively decorations boasting of his return. Above the doorway is painted the name of Allah with the shrine of Mecca in black flanked by two green cypresses, and on either side of the door, handprints in indigo for luck and a scattering of flowers and naïve designs. At a house that has electricity, strings of light bulbs festoon the roof and terraces.

Sheep are killed and divided among the poor for the feast of sacrifices at the close of the pilgrimage. Well-wishers crowd the house. Traditionally the pilgrim brings back presents of dates from Saudi Arabia such as the prophet might have eaten, as well as gifts of prayer beads, prayer mats, and for the women, cheap silver rings and *kohl*—powdered antimony of a silvery black. Applied to the rim of the eyelids, *kohl* is valued as a medicine. It is also worn by women as their chief cosmetic and on special occasions, by men also.

This is the time to listen to the new Hajji tell of his journey, probably the greatest experience of his life. As they say, *al hijje furjje,* "a pilgrimage is also a spectacle."

The adventure of the Hajj begins in the *khans* and caravansaries of the stopping places along the way. There a man meets fellow pilgrims from far places who have different turns of phrase but share the language of the holy book. In the words of the Koran, "We have sent it down, a Koran in Arabic, that ye may understand." Along with life histories and news of their home-lands, the pilgrims exchange their best-remembered folktales.

Indeed, in reading through the wealth of stories that have been collected from the oral tradition over the last hundred years, one is more impressed by the number of motifs and whole tales common to Syria and Morocco, Iraq and Algeria rather than by marked regional differences. It is as though the distances between these countries were not the barrier they appear on the map. For example, the simple fable "How the Monkey Got His Shape" was recorded in Palestine in 1911 and collected in Libya in almost identical form during the 1930s. "Sheikh of the Lamps" and "The Fair Foster Child of the Ghoul" were both told at the end of the last century. Their close similarity is astonishing when one considers their widely separated sources—Damascus and Tunis. And the same tale is found in modern collections from northern Syria.

Themes appealing to the folk imagination are not unlimited, of course; story types recur in different corners of Europe, Africa, and the New World. Nevertheless, the common culture of Islam and the Hajj, peculiar to the Moslem and Arabic-speaking world, must have been instrumental in spreading stories found so far apart. Military campaigns and the slave trade no doubt aided the importing of tales from country to country. Anecdotes about Djuha traveled along the merchant routes deep into Russia. Yet the yearly Hajj, with its weeks in the company of like-minded fellow travelers, seems ideally suited to the traffic of folklore. Night after night, the mood is one of happy expectation and there is little to do but wait for the morning. If one short journey between Southwark and the shrine of Thomas à Becket yielded *The Canterbury Tales,* may not twelve centuries of the Hajj have played a similar role for Arab tales?

The Tiller of the Soil, at Work and at Rest

Whether he bends over a sickle and short-handled mattock in the rich soil of river plains, or walks behind his plow on stony hillside fields, the life of the Arab peasant is one of steady toil and exertion for a bare subsistence. Relief from the strenuous round of labor is provided by family celebrations, religious holidays, and seasonal events in nature.

Family and clan are by far the most important fact of Arab social life. In life as in the stories, everyone is addressed as "uncle," "brother," or "son," depending on his age, for the family is the foremost point of reference. Cousin marriage reinforces the ties of kinship. Weddings therefore are the prime occasions for making merry, the times when the family puts on its grandest show. The bath of the bride and the painting of her arms and feet with henna patterns become excuses for the women's parties mentioned in the stories. There is music, men and women dance (in separate gatherings), and for everyone there is good food in plenty.

Other days on which there are meat and fancy sweets (with names like "mouthful of the *qadi*" and "hair of the maidens") are the two Moslem festivals. The Great Feast, or feast of the sacrifices, falls in the month of the pilgrimage, and the Lesser Feast celebrates the end of the fasting of Ramadan.

There is also the variety of weather and seasons. In February the almond blossoms, and the wild cyclamen appears in the crevices between rocks. Women and children are lured to venture beyond the plowed fields. Tender cyclamen leaves and fresh thistles taste good with rice and they are free for the plucking. If the rains have been plentiful and the *wadi* running full, a picnic in sight of the flowing water will be suggested, as in "Sheikh of the Lamps." For the men and boys, hunting is the preferred diversion—quail and rabbits and, on a lucky day, perhaps a gazelle.

Such are the bright moments of the Arab year. They stand out in the memory as the princes and princesses stand out in the tales, ideal, luxurious, and happy. Fairytale princes wear no ordinary gowns but gold gossamer so fine it can fold into a walnut shell. When they journey, it is not over mere roads but through the seven layers of the earth and across the seven seas. Theirs are no humdrum errands but quests for magic fruit and horses of the Djinn. They are blessed with many children, both boys and girls, as fine as golden birds.

If such royalty seems strangely well informed on matters of pasturing sheep or irrigation, like the prince in "Jubeinah and the Slave" or in "The Fair Foster Child of the Ghoul," remember that these are tales told by hardworking and unlettered tillers of the soil. What do they know of the protocol of palaces? Like country folk everywhere in preindustrial days (and much of rural Arab life continues at such a pace), the setting of the *fellahin* is of the plainest.

While the peasant storyteller may not have been familiar with the ways of princes, he was able to describe the common folk in detail. The poor and the hungry are many. The woodcutter scavenges thornbrush and dead twigs to sell as firewood; the fisherman stands on the shore at dawn and mutters a prayer before he casts his net. In the towns, weavers work through the night to make a living, falling asleep over the loom, and apprentice bakers dream of fortunes to be earned as seasonal harvesters. Merchants and guild masters are the heroes of urban success stories. Through the stories walk worried jewelers and sharp-tongued bathhouse keepers, polite cloth merchants and starving bird catchers—not very different from those who might have trodden the fields and the streets.

Particulars of farming life—how an ox is shod or a millstone moved, when ripe dates are beaten down from the date palms—are described as a matter of course. Thus the tales outline and color in a picture of the skills and the trades and the difficulties that filled the storytellers' days.

Excitement comes, though, not in hearing the mundane details of the workaday world, but in listening to the wonders that might befall the most ordinary of men. In the stories a cobbler climbs the minaret as usual to sound the call for prayer, and suddenly a giant bird snatches him into the air, flies with him beyond the mountains that hold down the edges of the world, and drops him into a harem of Djinn maidens each as beautiful as a houri strayed out of paradise. A weary laborer decides to give up the struggle against hunger and lay his burden in the lap of God, when look! there comes his donkey with both saddlebags full of gold. Or the carder who fluffs the wool with which the mattresses are filled after it has been washed each year is suddenly able to fluff beauty into a dry old maid.

As if to bring such dreams a little closer, the characters of the stories rarely have a name, or when they do, it is as common as Hasan or Mohammad or Hussein. There are nicknames only for the ill-treated victims, like Jubeinah (Little Face White as Cheese) or Juleidah (Little Leather-Covered One), and the rascals, like Smemi' an-Nada (Little Boy Who Hears the Dew When It Falls). A hero might be distinguished by being called Clever Hasan or Clever Mohammad.

Peasant Dialects and Learned Journals

In villages today the women continue to enjoy evenings together over scented tea and roast melon seeds, but more often now they meet in the house of the happy owner of a television set. With their sleepy children they watch the latest drama from the Cairo studios, or "Peyton Place" with subtitles.

It is a wistful moment when interest in recording an oral tradition awakens. It means that that tradition is well past its finest days, since it is the fear of losing it altogether which first motivates the collector to preserve the oral legacy in an uncharacteristic form, mechanically taping or writing it down.

As early as the eighth century, Arab philologists of the Abbasid era, who were centered in Baghdad, combed the tribes to write down the old poems still recited by the *rawis*, or professional bards. From generation to generation they had passed on orally the poetry of the time of the prophet and before. The collectors' purpose was to equip themselves with all the knowledge to be had about the prophet's times, the better to write scholarly commentaries on the Koran. In doing so they saved for all generations some of the finest poetry in the language.

In modern times, as increasing literacy, radio, and cinema began to supplant the Arab oral tradition, the preservation of the folk culture met with a peculiar obstacle: the language itself. In Arabic there are two distinct languages: the written, which is the language of the Koran, and the common vernacular. The difference is marked. Spoken Arabic has its own vocabulary

not found in the dictionary, and has streamlined some of the unwieldy gram-
matical forms. Moreover, it varies from region to region. A Moroccan and an
Iraqi can read each other's newspapers, but they need time to attune themselves
to each other's spoken idioms. In the center of a small town sits the scribe in the
shade of his black umbrella with a typewriter on his knees. People able to read,
and to write shopping lists, balk at composing a whole letter in the written
Arabic. Even a schoolboy's plea to his mother for a package of sesame cakes
sounds stilted and formal by the time it is written down.

Contemporary novelists wanting to convey realism face the question of
how to render conversation in classical Arabic. At the same time, folklorists
are working on new phonetic forms to represent spoken sounds not found
in the corresponding written language. This language barrier firmly divides
the colloquial tradition, however quaint and worth preserving, from the
serious matters couched in classical Arabic and printed in books.

Furthermore, modernity and the twentieth century, arriving full-blown
in a largely preindustrial world, have threatened with extinction a way of
life valid only one generation ago, thus elevating into "tradition" recent
usage and popular customs. A mother who as a child cradled a rag tied
round two sticks buys her daughter a Barbie Doll in pink plastic with yellow
nylon hair. What are now looked upon as "folk arts" and "old-fashioned
ways" were, a mere thirty years ago, regular everyday objects and the normal
way of doing things. Women did not pause to admire the colored basket as
they looked for the freshest bunch of thyme to buy, any more than they ate
bread that was not kneaded at home. The same generation which welcomed
the comforts of modern living introduced during colonial times has also
found itself grasping for a remembrance of the fast-eroding "ethnic" and
"national" culture of its childhood.

Beyond individual nostalgia, some see a direct link between the 1952
revolution in Egypt and official interest in the culture of the common people,
and the growth of institutions of preservation has continued steadily since
that time. By 1964 the Folklore Archive in the Ministry of Culture in Cairo
was publishing a magazine and building up a library of tapes. Since 1969
a folklore magazine has been published monthly by the Folklore Centre in
the Ministry of Information in Baghdad, each issue containing several folktales. Similar publications began to appear in Amman in 1973 and on the
West Bank in 1974. No doubt the renewed national pride of the Arab
countries as they gained independence from colonial rule, the establishment
of dozens of new colleges, and an awareness of the speed with which age-
old traditions are falling victim to Westernization have each contributed to
a surge of interest in local folklore.

Anticipating the Arabs' own attention to their oral heritage by almost a century was that of a number of Western scholars. Around the 1880s a range of foreign diplomats, teachers, and students of antiquity on official missions or on vacation recorded stories dictated by their unlettered servants or acquaintances, often with the help of an Arab friend. The example of the Grimm brothers may have inspired this scholarly activity, as well as the colonial administrations' need for grammars of local languages. Gaston Delphin, a professor at Oran, Algeria, says in the introduction to a grammar of spoken Arabic published in 1891: "No people appreciates beautiful language more than the Arabs." He offers his grammar to help Frenchmen "express themselves correctly and avoid shocking the customs and the ears" of the local people. He recorded a number of animal and trickster stories from illiterate sources to use as examples.

In 1900 Enno Littmann, an archaeologist on an American expedition, spent his free time in Jerusalem collecting stories through an Arab friend, who transcribed his own mother's tales in Arabic as she spoke. Littmann published the stories in the vernacular in the hope "that these texts may prove to be one step forward in the nowadays very slight movement to arrive at a literary Arabic language which will be nearer the spoken language." Hans Schmidt, working with the German Protestant Archaeological Institute in the Holy Land, spent the twelve days of Christmas, 1910, with a schoolmaster in the town of Bir Zeit to find out "what still lived in the mouths of the peasants by way of folktales." The resulting publication with co-author Paul Kahle of two hundred tales and narratives in a careful rendering of the spoken language in Latin letters is treasured by the folklorists of Bir Zeit today. In Tunis in 1889, Hans Stumme; in Damascus in 1897, Johannes Oestrup; in Iraq in 1878, Albert Socin; in Morocco in 1901, Bruno Meissner made their own collections. One can imagine these dignified academics intently hanging on the words of aged whitewashers, fifteen-year-old Nubian servants, middle-aged folk poets, construction workers, cooks, porters, and the other storytellers whom they cite as their unlettered sources. Their efforts, and those of many others listed in the bibliography, produced a rich haul of texts in the language of the people of an age when storytelling was a far more vital form of entertainment than it is at present.

Their collections appeared in French, English, German, and Italian academic journals and bulletins, intended for the Arab specialist and linguist. The texts of the stories were printed in Arabic script or phonetically transcribed into Roman letters, usually accompanied by a translation and commentary in the language of the journal. Supplemented today by more recent studies, especially publications in Arabic by Arab folklorists and folk archives, they provide a representative survey of stories, recorded as nearly as possible as they were spoken. A number of collections of folk stories recast into classical Arabic have also been published in different Arab countries in the last thirty years. While they are very useful in furnishing the plots of many tales, they lose much of the grain and the humor of the unimproved folk narrative.

The raw material for the present volume comes from all three of these classes of printed sources, as well as from a number of tapes I made myself in the villages north of Jerusalem and the desert near Beersheba. Using a selection of text materials for each story, whether in Arabic letters or in Arabic printed in the Latin alphabet, I translated some stories entire as they stood and spliced others together from several variants. Throughout, my aim has been to present the English reader with a story as colorful and comprehensible as possible that is at the same time true to the spirit of the teller.

It is many years since I heard some of these stories myself as a child. The evenings seem shorter now, and the pace has changed. There is less room for either embroidery or telling stories. But Arabic remains a magic language and the power of its words continues strong. For the poor especially, there is sometimes little else that has as golden a shine.

In the bare, hilly countryside of Palestine, the earth is a rusty red and the rocks stick out white like bones. The cloudy olive trees are sometimes grey and sometimes green, and the thorns underfoot are bleached by the sun. Walking there once, some companions and I happened on a hovel of tumbled stone with a sheet of tin for a roof. A few hens scratched in the dust. Hearing us, the master of the house emerged, an ancient man with holes in his robe. We knew it was Nayif al Badawi, Nayif the Beduin, who survived on alms, having no sons to provide for him.

Greeting us, he inquired whether we had eaten. When we assured him that—Allah be praised—we had, he shook his head regretfully. "Had I known," he said, "that you would honor me by walking this way, I should have strewn the path between your house and mine with mint and rose petals!"

G l o s s a r y

Afreet   A demon or spirit from the Djinn world, of great strength and cunning; often a snatcher of women.

Caliph   A successor of Mohammad as one of the spiritual and political leaders of the nation of Islam. The best-known in the tales is the 'Abbasid caliph of Baghdad, Harun Al Rasheed.

Diwan   The court or council of a ruler; also, the hall where the court meets.

Djinn   Invisible beings created by God out of smokeless fire. They can be good or evil, and appear to humans in many disguises.

Fellahin   Literally, "tillers" or "plowmen," these are people who work on the land, as opposed to city dwellers or Beduins.

Ghoul   A fabulous desert monster that lies in wait for the unwary traveler and devours human flesh. Though the word is feminine, in the tales "Ghoul" refers to a male monster, "She-Ghoul" (*ghouleh*) to his sister or mother.

Hammam   A bath. In the tales it means the public bath, especially the women's bath, which is presided over by a keeper called a *hammamjiyeh*.

Ins   A human being created by God from potter's clay. The word is used in the tales to distinguish humans from spirits, as in the frequently asked question "Are you Ins or Djinn?"

Khan   An inn built around a large courtyard where animals can be stabled and wares stored. It is a frequent stopping place for caravans and merchants.

Qadi   The judge of an Islamic court of justice. In the tales, he is often called upon to settle disputes.

Saluki   A desert greyhound, used for hunting.

Sheikh   Literally, "one who is old," therefore a venerable patriarch. A Beduin sheikh is the head of the tribe; a religious sheikh is a scholar learned in the Koran.

Sultan   An absolute ruler or king. "Sultan" is the title of the Ottoman rulers, and is used in the tales interchangeably with "king."

Suq   A market or bazaar. Covered *suqs* appear all along the streets of big cities, and are organized into specialties—goldsmiths, spice vendors, butchers, vegetable sellers, and so on.

Wadi   A riverbed, steep valley, or ravine where water rarely flows because of the arid climate.

Wazir   A minister or chief courtier.

Yammah   In direct address, this means "O Mother!" It is also used as an exclamation of fear. Other forms: *Ya Ummi, Ya Yimma.*

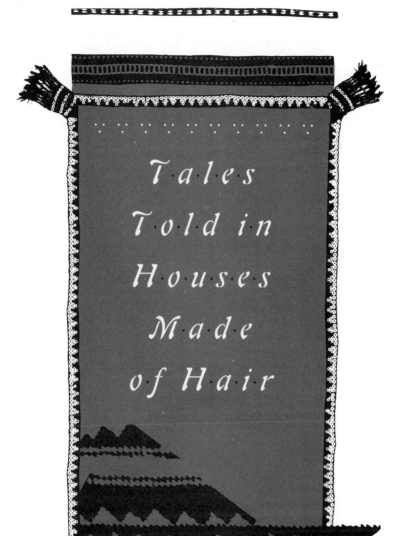

T·a·l·e·s
T·o·l·d i·n
H·o·u·s·e·s
M·a·d·e
o·f H·a·i·r

Beduin Tales

∴

T

he reader who has not sipped cardamom-scented coffee in the breezy shade of a goat-hair tent—in Arabic, *beit shaar,* house of hair—will glimpse in this section a way of life which dates back over a thousand years. With only slight changes it continues to the present day.

The Arabs themselves look upon the Beduins—the *baduw* or dwellers of the *badiya,* the wilderness—with a nostalgic pride. The spareness of their ascetic existence, coupled with the chivalrous code governing it, represent an Arab ideal of nobility. In tent and village, generations have grown up on romances like that of Antara the desert hero, brave and magnanimous and a poet to boot. The Beduins refer to themselves simply as *al 'Arab, the* Arabs, for the true Arab is the desert nomad. His is the purest form of the language. Around the thornbrush fires of his encampments was spoken some of the most inspired of Arabic poetry as long ago as the Jahiliyya—the Time of Ignorance, before the prophet Mohammad became the messenger of God. Later when Islam had spread as far as Spain, the sons of the rich were sent back from the outposts of the empire to the Island of the Arabs, which is now Saudi Arabia, to learn their native tongue at the wellspring of their culture.

The wilderness of arid rock and earth beyond the gardens and plowed fields of river valley and oasis, and outside the sand deserts like Rub' al Khali or the Empty Quarter, where nothing lives and nothing grows, is the range of the Beduin wanderings. The greater part of the Arab world lies in such terrain. From Morocco to the borders of Iran the landscape is dotted with the rectangular tents of desert dwellers. In every country the two societies—of *fellahin,* or tillers of the soil, and *baduw*—exist side by side. They vary less from land to land than they differ between themselves.

Wherever there is scrub and thorn enough to feed a few camels, the Beduin will stretch his black tent cloth and stop to graze his animals. When the sparse growth gives out, he folds his tent and moves on to fresh pasture. On the well-being of his beasts depend his life and that of his family. The milk of the camel, fresh or soured, feeds them; its flesh on occasion feasts them. The roof over their heads is of camel's hair, as is the long robe which protects them from the sun. Where there is no brush, dried camel dung fuels a fire. More important yet, the camel, who endures thirst longer than

all other pack animals, carries tent and tent holder over the waterless stretches between one well and the next.

   For most of the year the sun beats down relentlessly, sucking color and life from every growing plant. Then, when the cattle have become thin on the hard, dry stalks surviving the summer's heat, at last the rain clouds blow in from the west. Songs are sung of these clouds, and girls are named for them. In their wake the desert bursts into life. From horizon to horizon wild flowers streak the earth with bands of color. The camels, their herds reflected in the shallow pools of rainwater, browse on grass so brightly green that "it seems to want to speak." For the children it is a holiday to run about gathering fresh herbs and tender roots to eat. Then the Beduin camps are pitched deep in the desert until, as suddenly as it appeared, the fleeting bloom turns brown and vanishes. But the pleasures of that brief flowering are so vivid that the first caliphs, grandsons of the desert, walled in their capital Damascus, pined for its memory. For themselves they built hunting lodges, graceful palaces in the wilderness just where the rainpools collect and draw the game birds and gazelles to water.

   Constantly on the move, the Beduin carries no excess luggage. Beyond his tent, his weapons, and his cooking pots, his wealth lies in his herds. If he belongs to one of the great clans, like the 'Aneza or the Shammar of Syria, or perhaps the Sirhan or Bani Sakhr farther south, these will be camel herds. Goat keepers and sheep breeders among the nomads are not as highly regarded, for they live closer to the settled people who are tied to their fields.

Yet even the largest camel herd can be decimated in a season by drought or plague. Where so little is certain, the personal virtues of a man and his name, not his possessions, give him fame.

Though blood-relationship and kinship are matters of jealous pride, the rank of sheikh (literally, elder of the tribe) is not inherited. A leader among peers, each sheikh has to make the title his own. The opening of the tale of "The Boy in Girl's Dress" lists the qualities of a sheikh and describes the replacement of the hero's father by another leader. "Successor to the Sheikh," which is a folk rendering of a fragment of a familiar epic, demonstrates the necessity of winning the loyalty of the tribesmen in order to become their sheikh. For a Beduin tale to end on a satisfying note, the storyteller has to be able to conclude with a sentence like "So it is when men are noble!" amid the murmured approval of his listeners. What keener pleasure than to hear of a man justly acclaimed for qualities like his courage or greatness of heart? A happy ending to the sound of wedding drums pales beside this. That is why, in the story "The Jewel in the Sand," the finding of the fair owner of the jewel is but a preparation for a finale in which the two heroes compete with each other in generous behavior. And in the love story "The Boy in Girl's Dress," beyond the two lovers the listeners thrill to the grand gesture of the heroine's cousin, who forgoes his right to her. The story ends not with the wedding of Husam but with the ample reward of the noble cousin: "The men said, 'By Allah, that is just, and you deserve it all!' And they drank coffee and each went to his tent."

Generosity, first and foremost, is the hallmark of the nobleman of the desert. A man's worth is counted not so much by what he owns himself as by what he gives to others. If the poor and the hunted grasp his tent peg in their need, if his guest tent is many tent poles wide to accommodate the numbers that throng to eat under his roof, if his guests walk away praising his openhandedness, then he feels wealthy indeed, even if he and his family are reduced to feeding on milk and a handful of dates.

In "The Foreign Wife," though the third and favorite son is rejected because his maternal ancestors are not known, his name is kept alive alongside the names of respected men when his mother sets up a guest tent and offers hospitality on his behalf. Again and again in the stories the message is clear: generosity and hospitality are qualities to distinguish a hero; see, for example, "The Last Camel of Emir Hamid" and "Two Mothers Mourning." And if there is a moral to the story "Atiyah, the Gift of God," it reads: "Only he who is narrow-hearted and ungenerous is the enemy of God and man."

Though every tent holder is bound to feed the traveler at his door—to deny food and shelter in a treeless, waterless country could be denying life itself—it is the pride of the clan sheikhs to regale their guests on so grand a scale that Beduin hospitality has become legendary. The mound of coffee grounds outside an encampment marks the sheikh's tent; happy testimony to the number of his guests. To this day a Beduin host will boast of the extent of his hospitality, taking pleasure in reckoning the number of his guests over a year by the number of herds he has slaughtered for them in that time.

The arrival of an honored guest is soon made known throughout the encampment. The servants stand at their four-foot wooden pestles pounding out rhythmic improvisations as they crush the coffee beans in the carved wooden mortars. This signals to the men of the tribe that it will be their pleasant duty to show respect for the guest of their sheikh by sharing the banquet being prepared in his honor. When all have filed into the guest tent, several men carry in a vast metal tray on which the flesh of a young camel or a couple of lambs is heaped over a bed of rice or thin, flat sheets of bread. The heads of the animals—one animal killed for each guest of importance—crown the dish. Eating from this communal platter, the men use their hands, deftly tearing off bread and meat in neat mouthfuls to toss into their mouths without touching fingers to lips. Ten men at a time reach into the food, making room for the next ten till all are sated and the tray is carried out for the women and children to pick clean. When the servant with the water ewer and basin has made his rounds, then is the time for talk. As the small coffee cups are filled and refilled with a spiced, unsweetened brew, a professional entertainer may recite poetry, accompanying himself on the one-stringed *rabab*, or tell the stories of old wars and bygone raids.

Traditionally the period of Beduin hospitality is three and one-third days: the first being devoted to *salaam*, or greeting, the second to *ta'aam*, or eating, and the third to *kalaam*, or speaking—for it is boorish to worry a guest with questions upon arrival. After the third day, the hours between sunset and the morning star's rising are spent in preparing for departure. Any guest who lingers beyond the drying of the dew is as welcome "as the spotted snake." But for those three days the host is responsible for his guest. So binding is the guest-friendship that even an enemy, once he has eaten salt under a man's roof, will be protected as his guest. That is why in the story of "The Boy in Girl's Dress" the heroine hurries to feed her lover before the return of her father, whom he has offended. In the animal fable "The Duty of the Host," a guest is robbed; the moth is so ashamed of having failed in hospitality that she throws herself into the nearest flame, as do her descendants, still choosing death over such disgrace.

A valued guest is accompanied by his host and a few riders until he is out of sight of the encampment. This formal escort is a compliment to the guest's importance; it also ensures his safety while he remains in the tribe's territory. Tribal wars are fought over the control of grazing grounds and wells, and a sheikh who cannot guarantee the safety of his people or his guests in his "quarter" of the desert loses all standing. Sometimes a weak tribe pays "brotherhood money" for protection by a strong neighbor, reducing itself to the state of a vassal. Members of such a tribe are looked down upon, and no powerful clan will permit marriage ties with its vassals.

Besides the wars between the tribes, *ghazu* raids are mentioned in several of the stories. These are plundering expeditions undertaken by the youth of the tribe in a spirit of adventure to test their mettle and increase the wealth of their people. Such a raid, if well conducted, can net a rich haul of camels. If any young men die, however, blood feuds result that can continue for generations, since deaths have to be avenged. In Beduin stories a hero who is disguised as a lowly servant or a girl often reveals himself by defending a camp single-handed from raiders who appear in the absence of the men of the tribe.

To cheer the menfolk on to battle, Beduin women stand together sounding their high-pitched trills and letting loose their long black hair. In one of the stories, raiders refuse an appeal to give up some of their booty, saying, "What will we tell our women who ground the wheat for our travel rations?" No doubt the women would have to be reckoned with if the men returned empty-handed. Praise is sung for one folk heroine because she turned a rout into victory by running into the battle, shouting, "If our men have become women, we women must become men!" It is striking how often the women in the stories are treated with a consideration both tender and chivalrous. In "The Beduin's Gazelle," for instance, how gently the husband breaks the bad news to his wife! And in "Successor to the Sheikh," rather than accuse his wife of cheating, Ghanim plays a trick to make her admit the truth. Even in the case of the bold sheikh's daughter who creeps into the hero's bed in the story of "Atiyah, the Gift of God," both the hero and the girl's cousin, her betrothed, take elaborate pains to extricate her from a compromising discovery.

Where the family is the most important social unit, ancestry and birth become significant. As in the rest of the Arab world, there is a preference among Beduins for cousin marriage, to ensure a pure line and strengthen and extend clan loyalties. When the girls of the settlement begin to grow dreamy in the presence of the handsome Atiyah, the elders are concerned. "Where shall we hide our beards when their first cousins come to claim them?" and Atiyah is sent away to avoid scandal. In the tales the convention of a promised hand provides a touch of added drama, for the heroine, inevitably betrothed to her first cousin at birth, remains unattainable until the happy ending. On his part the cousin is offered a gallant role when he bows before the claims of true love and waives his rights.

  Altogether, there seems to be something fuller-blooded about the love theme in the Beduin tales than in the household stories. The frank interest in Atiyah shown by all the girls who catch sight of his face differs from the more stylized emotion of the household tales. The stories set in the desert are rooted in the romantic epic cycles recited in the gathering places of men, whether coffeehouses or guest tents. These cycles tell of the passions and adventures of historical and legendary heroes, and the action depends less on magic than on the wit, courage, and idealized human qualities of the characters. There may even be some echo of pre-Islamic poems, in which a melancholy reminiscence of some past love was a common set piece. Even those who cannot read carry with them rich hoards of poetry, not to mention the Koran, by heart. Compare "When Husam awoke and saw the abandoned site of his neighbor's tent, he told his father, 'I cannot live where Halima has been, now that my eye cannot see her,' " with the seventh-century lines,

> Has Layla filled you with longing
>   Departing amidst her tribe?
> Yes indeed and the tears came flooding
>   In streams over my breast
> He wept at traces of a woman's camp
>   Who had travelled to faraway lands.*

"Full-Moon-of-the-Night" is a Beduin version of "The Maiden of the Tree of Raranj and Taranj." In the desert story it is the hero's sharp observation rather than a magic ring which leads him to the maiden whose camels are black as a moonless night. She, of course, is beautiful beyond words, and somehow more convincingly so than the supernatural houri who emerges

---

* *Diwan* of Qais Ibn Al-Khattim, tr. Ilse Lichtenstadter, from *Introduction to Classical Arabic Literature* (New York: Schocken Books, 1976).

from the fruit of the Tree of Raranj and Taranj. After all, her camel herder works for her the year round and counts himself adequately rewarded merely to be granted the privilege of bidding her good morning.

The same story opens with a lively encounter between the hero and a young woman balancing her water jar on her head. The daily round of the Beduin woman permits her to meet the youths of the camp out of sight of the elders. Foraging for firewood or pasturing the cattle, the girls are less restricted than their sisters in the towns and villages, and they may find opportunities for a little flirtation and romantic banter. Yet the rules are clear if the lone shepherd girl stitching embroidery as she walks behind her goats, her long black gown billowing in the wind, should bring dishonor on her tribe. There is no mercy. If she does not kill herself, her kin will do so, and kill her seducer as well. "The Prince in the Pit" and "The Good Neighbors" spell out the code: only blood will wash away the stain that tarnishes the honor of a clan.

It is the pride of the nomad to be free of the trammels of the settled state, independent and self-sufficient. Living far from the mosques and courts of Islamic law, the Beduins have a common law of their own, the *'urf*, or law of custom and convenience. In the tales there are several instances of a man falling out with his people. The desert is wide, and rather than suffer his kin, he will move his house and cattle elsewhere to live as he chooses. In matters of religion, too, the Beduin is less punctilious than townsman or villager, even if, as the stories show, the son of a sheikh is taught not only horsemanship but also the Koran. The tribes of northern Arabia say of themselves that the angel Gabriel bears them a grudge for their neglect: they did not study as carefully as they might the holy book that he dictated to the prophet Mohammad. They explain the harshness of their desert climate by saying that Gibrin, or Gabriel, whose work it is to round up the rain clouds into herds and drive them across the land, lingers over the plowed fields of the *fellahin* till they are drenched. But whenever he is over Beduin territory, he swings his camel goad so hard that it makes a roar in the sky, hurrying the clouds and allowing them no time for more than a few meager showers. Nevertheless, the desert Arabs are a noble breed well able to survive where lesser men might perish.

The following impromptu composition was sung fifty years ago by one of the sheikhs of Beersheba during the entertainment of a government official. It sums up the ideal Beduin life:

O God, shaper of the trees and fruit,
Maker of the sun,
Grant me the ten things I ask for.
No man can wish for more while he lives.
Stand, O Lord, and write them into my destiny.

First, I pray for a large and shade-giving tent,
A tent that is open all the day long,
To which the people are happy to come.

Next I pray for a woman to be my wife,
Beautiful of face and remarkable in her ways,
A wife who is quick to set her hands to cooking
As soon as she sees a guest.

Third, O God, preserve my honor from shame.
Let no man blacken my name.

Fourth, I wish for a red mare who runs fast under the hot sun,
And in my hand a gun that never misses the mark.

Fifth, give me goats and sheep in flocks so large
That the work of the shepherd is hard:
Much meat for my guests to eat their fill.

Sixth, I wish for camels with udders full of milk—
Drink to offer any man who passes this way.

Seventh, I pray for men brave and true,
A loyal band to ride by my side
And keep safe the lands of my quarter.

Eighth, give me leave to make the pilgrimage to Mecca
To visit my friend Mohammad.

Ninth, after a life that is long,
Help me, O God, to answer the Angels of Death,
Both Naker and Nkeer,
When they question me in my grave.

And tenth, save me from the fire of hell;
Let paradise be my lot.

The Last Camel of Emir Hamid

Saudi Arabia

There was a wealthy prince whose name was Emir Hamid. He had much gold and he owned much cattle. But his heart was spacious and his hand was open and he freely gave to all who came both food and drink. Indeed, such was his liberality with the multitude of guests who ate in his tent that eventually he had nothing left at all, neither gold nor cattle. One she-camel only remained to him.

Now, it chanced that the sultan and his minister were traveling in those parts dressed like two dervishes so none would know them. Toward evening they arrived at Emir Hamid's tent. He bade them enter and rolled out matting for them, and they sat. Then the emir turned away from them toward the screen that divides the women's quarters from the rest and signaled silently to his wife to bake a couple of loaves for the guests. The woman answered out loud, "There is nothing for a man's jaws to close on in this tent!" So the emir said, "Go to your neighbor and ask her to lend us a basin of flour so we may offer our guests a meal."

The woman went to her neighbor and asked, but the neighbor said, "I am a poor woman, I have nothing. Let whoever wants to be generous prove his hospitality with the she-camel in his own house." The woman returned and repeated the neighbor's words to the emir. He drew his sword and cut down his camel. He pulled off the hide and sliced the flesh into pieces, heaping it into the cooking pot. When the guests saw what he was doing, they shouted, "Stop, O sheikh! This is the camel who carries your tent when you move!" But the emir replied, "No, this is the camel to feast my guests. Allah will send another to take its place." And they dined together.

When they had done, the sultan asked, "What is your name?" "Emir Hamid," said their host. "Go down to the mosque on Friday," the visitor told him. "The sultan will give you the price of your she-camel."

When it was Friday, Emir Hamid walked to the mosque for the noonday prayers. He asked among the worshippers where the sultan was. The people said, "There he is, kneeling with his hands uplifted. He is asking for God's blessing." To himself Emir Hamid said, "No, he is praying to God for a she-camel to give me. I am able enough to ask for myself!" And he left the mosque, and on a low hill nearby he laid out his cloak like a prayer rug and raised his hands. He said, "O my Lord, that which the sultan is praying for, I ask it of You also!"

When he had finished, Emir Hamid pulled himself onto his feet with his staff and leaned on it, but he found that it was sinking right into the ground. He scratched the soil with it and uncovered an opening—steps leading down into a vaulted room. Inside the room stood seven clay jars, each filled to the top with gold coins. What did he do? He moved his goat-hair tent and pitched it over the entrance to the underground treasure.

Now Emir Hamid was able to buy animals of every kind, camels and goats and horses and sheep, more than he had ever had before. He filled his tent with soft bedding and fine hangings, with knotted carpets and everything that he needed. His herds grazed in all four directions, and they were so numerous that the sun did not strike the ground where they stood.

And what of the sultan? One day many months afterwards, he said to his minister, "I wonder what happened to that man who butchered his only camel in our honor? He never came to claim his gold. Let us go and seek him out." When they went to the place where they had visited him before, they saw a spread of herds so dense that their shadow moved across the land in one piece, like the shadow of a cloud. "Who owns so many camels?" they asked the herdsmen in amazement. "Emir Hamid," they replied. "And the horses?" "Emir Hamid." And so on for every kind of animal in the herd. "When we met him before, he had nothing," said the sultan. "Where did such wealth come from? We must go and ask him."

When they entered the prince's tent this time, they were dazzled by its riches. The tent poles were covered with hammered silver and beaten gold, and the cushions were of yellow silk woven in Damascus. Among the embers which kept the shining coffeepots warm, pieces of incense smouldered so that the very air was rare and sweet. As before, Emir Hamid made them welcome. All that was rich and good he set before them, and they ate till the fat butter ran from their fingers.

Then the minister spoke: "O emir, last year when the sultan said, 'Come to the mosque on Friday and I shall give you the price of your she-camel,' you never obeyed. Why was that?" And the prince told them his story from beginning to end.

Now the minister leaned toward the sultan's ear and whispered, "Sire, you who are the ruler of our age do not possess seven jars filled with gold coins. Cut off this man's head, or tomorrow he will pay horsemen to rise up and fight against you." "The man has shown us kindness," said the sultan. "Can I repay him thus?" "O ruler of our day," the minister continued, "we must think of some ruse to be rid of him. Speak to him in the morning and say, 'As I slept last night I dreamed that I was saying *Au! Au! Au!* Can you interpret what this means?' Then he will tell you, 'Only a dog says *Au! Au! Au!*' That is insult enough, and good reason to cut off his head!"

Next morning when the sultan sat drinking coffee with Emir Hamid, he said, "O prince, a dream disturbed my sleep last night." When the prince invited him to tell his dream, he said, "I dreamed that I said *Au! Au! Au!* God grant that it is a good omen."

"O ruler of our time," said the prince, "the first *Au!* was the *Au* in *dhau*, which is 'light.' It stood for your sleeping thought, 'Praise be to Him Who dispersed the darkness and gave us light!' The second is the *Au!* in *djau*, which is 'air,' and it represents your thought, 'Praise be to Him Who launched the bird on her wing, lifting her into the air!' As for the last *Au!* it stands for *sau*, which is 'evil,' and your just wish, 'God's curse on him who plots evil!' "

When the emir had finished his explanation, the sultan frowned a terrible frown. With one blow of his sword he sent his minister's head flying from his neck. And from that time onwards he would not let Emir Hamid leave his side, but kept him as his minister and his counselor.

My tale I have told it.
In your bosom now hold it.

Atiyah,
the Gift of God

Syria

When a man wants to shoe his ox to plow rocky ground, first he taps him around the eyes, to distract him and keep him from getting up onto his hooves. God too, to Whom all praise and exaltation, distracts men to keep them from following their whims too freely in the world. Some He strikes with sickness, to some He brings poverty, and some He leaves childless.

There was a Beduin sheikh who had no children. Year followed year and his wife remained barren. More than once she begged him to take another wife who might bear him an heir, but he loved her so much that he had vowed not to marry again while she was still living. "Without a son, others will inherit our wealth," said his wife, "and what good will that do us? Let us use our riches now to feed the hungry and clothe the poor, since God loves him who cares for his neighbor."

From then on, every evening they would spread food and drink for all who were in need. Soon news of the sheikh's kindness to the poor was carried far and wide, and in time it reached his brothers. In their eyes these were black tidings. They sent a swift messenger to their brother to say, "Though you may be willing to forgo your wealth, do you dare to deprive us of our inheritance? Clothe or feed one man more after this day, and we shall kill you!"

"Wife," said the sheikh, "the time has come for us to move to a place where no one knows us." And he told her what had passed. So they took down their tent and loaded their camels and drove their herds eastwards for about ten days till they reached an unfrequented pasture far from all who knew them. But those who had tasted of the sheikh's generosity, not finding him at his usual site, followed him, one tent at a time or several tents together, and set up camp beside him. They still looked to him as their sheikh and moved their herds and stopped to camp at his bidding.

Then one day God sent him an angel, who said, "Your wife shall bear a son whose name shall be Atiyah, the Gift of God. Keep him out of the sight of men and sheltered from the sun till his fourteenth year, and you shall have joy in him." When the sheikh brought the news to his wife, she said, "I am too old! What scandal if I were to conceive!" But from here to there she became pregnant, and bore a son of such beauty that he well deserved his name.

With the passing of the years Atiyah's beauty grew. His face shone like moonlight on the smoothness of a trodden path, for his skin was the color of sesame when it is peeled. His eyes were like the dark anemone and his mouth neat as a gold ring set with pearls. Yet even beauty can be an affliction. When Atiyah entered his fourteenth year, he asked, "Am I a girl, that you protect me from the sight of men?" His mother repeated the angel's words to him. "But if I promise to go out only after the sun has set, and return before it rises again, and let none see me, will you let me go?" "God be with you, my son," said his mother.

That night when they had supped, Atiyah mounted one of his father's mares and rode out into the desert. He galloped after the grazing gazelles and in the light of the moon dropped one with his gun. Great was his mother's joy at Atiyah's first hunt. She dressed the game and cooked it for the sheikh's breakfast, and together they gave thanks to God for His blessings. Every night thereafter Atiyah would leave the tents as soon as darkness fell and return before dawn.

Now the women of the tribe noticed the pile of deerskins in Atiyah's mother's tent, and they asked her how she came to have so many. "My son goes hunting in the night," she proudly replied. When news of this reached the youths of the camp, they said, "Our sheikh's son has grown to be a huntsman and we have not yet set eyes on him. Let us join him tonight."

So they lay in wait and followed as he left for the evening's hunt. Then they rode abreast of him and greeted him and said, "O emir, son of our sheikh, will you not dismount and join us as we roast our game so that we may dine together?" "I have promised my father not to delay beyond sunrise," said Atiyah. "It is early yet," they replied. "We can return before it is even light." So they persuaded him, and together the young men built a fire and cut the meat. But by the time the food was cooked, it was the hour before sunrise when the girls go out to fill their water jars. Their path led them near the young huntsmen, and when the young women saw Atiyah, his forehead like a pearl and his mouth like the seal on Solomon's ring, they forgot their water jars and their errand as they gazed. Thus they stood as if bewitched until the youths rode back to the tents; then they hurried after, unwilling to let Atiyah escape from their sight.

The elders asked the girls how it happened that all their jars were empty. "On the way to the well," they answered, "we saw our sheikh's son Atiyah, and his beauty held us captive so that we forgot our purpose." This gave the elders cause for worry. "There will surely be scandal!" they murmured. "Our girls will lose their hearts to the sheikh's son. Then where shall we hide our beards when their first cousins come to claim them as their brides? Let us beg the sheikh to send away his son, or let us move elsewhere ourselves."

They gathered in their leader's tent to tell him. "Atiyah is your son," they said, "but there is no tie of blood between us. We ask you either to send away your son or give us leave to fold our tents and move our herds to other pastures." When the sheikh consulted Atiyah's mother in the women's quarter, she said, "O cousin, son of my father's brother, when a boy has grown to be a man, have no fear for him! It would be a thousand pities to disperse

our people, and yet so simple to send Atiyah on a journey." And she began to prepare the travel rations.

Next day Atiyah saddled his horse and bade his parents farewell. Heading eastward, he traveled by day and rested at night until after many days' journey he found himself at the door of a Beduin tent and sought guest-friendship. When the Beduin saw Atiyah lighting up his threshold as if he were the sun, he hastened to make him welcome and busied himself with the duties of a host. While he killed a suckling lamb for the guest, he sent his wife to borrow a cooking pot.

Now, this particular Beduin was known far and wide for his meanness, and word spread quickly that the miser who had never stewed meat for a guest was borrowing a cooking pot. Soon twenty curious tribesmen were gathered in the Beduin's tent to see what manner of guest had wrought this change. One and all were struck at the sight of Atiyah. "This is no man, but an angel come down to us from heaven," they whispered. The sheikh was told, "The miser has a guest, a sultan's heir or an angel fallen from the sky, or perhaps a houri's son escaped through the gates of paradise while the guardian slept." When the sheikh went to see with his own eyes, he too was dazzled and said, "While I am present, it is not meet that others should act as hosts—entertaining the guest is my privilege and my right."

Atiyah rose with the sheikh, and all the tribesmen too. As the company walked to the elder's tent, the girls of the tribe, noticing the stranger, followed him with their glances. Even when the men had entered the tent the girls pressed against the woven sidewalls and parted the seams to peer inside. "Do not blame us for lingering to admire your father's guest," one of them told the sheikh's daughter in the women's part. "Who is he?" she asked. "A stranger, but with a face like an angel's." The sheikh's daughter hurried to the cloth that divides the women's part from the guests, and as soon as her eye fell on Atiyah a great yearning pierced her heart.

When the men had eaten and and retired each to his tent, and darkness covered the camp, the sheikh's daughter waited till every footfall ceased. Then, like a thief, she crept from her bed and slunk into the guest quarters, where she settled herself in Atiyah's arms. What could Atiyah do but lie motionless lest he touch the girl? He awoke next day to the sound of the coffee pounders drumming the pestles against the wooden mortars. Yet he dared not stir from his bed. His host and the old men were already sitting in the door of the tent, and under the blankets the girl still hid at his side. "Wake up the guest and bring him coffee to drink," said each greybeard in turn. "No, let him lie and take his ease; he looks like a son of princes," the sheikh replied. So Atiyah feigned sleep until at last beneath his lashes he saw the girl's first cousin come into the tent. When the man turned his head and looked his way, Atiyah pulled out the girl's long braid, an arm's length and more, for him to see.

The cousin understood his meaning. "O uncle," he said, addressing the sheikh. "Speak, my brother's son," said the sheikh. "I was visited by a strange dream last night," the youth went on. "God grant a good omen," said the sheikh. "I thought I was on the back of my she-camel," said the youth, "and I rode into an oasis so lush that the grass at its top touched the animal's knee. Pleased to have happened on pasture so rich, I stopped to let her graze. But what follows happiness except sorrow? Sudden as a clap of thunder, a lion pushed his head from between the leaves. By your life, uncle, my only refuge lay in this sword here. Thus and thus I swung it . . ." At the words, the youth lifted his sword and brought it down against the main tent pole with such strength that it splintered and broke.

Down fell the roof, and the elders groping under the cloth were blinded for a time. Under cover of the noise and hubbub the sheikh's daughter was

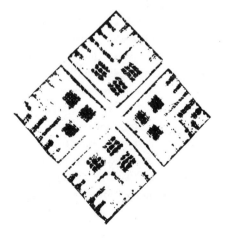

able to escape to the women's tent, and none was aware of her coming or going.

Evening is the time for banqueting, and when the men had taken their turns at the great dish laden with soft meat and fat-drenched bread, all to do honor to Atiyah, the girl's cousin spoke: "O my uncle, I shall not feel hunger for food until you have consented to the request that lies close to my heart." "Eat, O my brother's son," said the sheikh. "You have but to name it and I shall grant your wish." "Will you let me have your daughter?" asked the youth. "Is she not yours by right?" the sheikh replied, "your father's brother's daughter, betrothed to you since birth?" "If she is mine, then," said the cousin, "I wish to offer her to our guest Atiyah, to be his bride!" "By Allah," said the sheikh, "you shall not prove more generous than your elders. Hear us, O Arabs, and bear witness! Our daughter has been given to the guest Atiyah. And we ask from him nothing, neither bride-money nor compensation." The assembled tribesmen murmured their applause: "May God give you increase, O sheikh, both you and your nephew; may He shower His blessings on the generous givers."

So the prayer was read and the songs were sung and the guns were fired to celebrate the wedding of Atiyah and the daughter of the sheikh. While Atiyah withdrew to the festive marriage tent, the bride's cousin joined the bachelors' dance, keeping time to the goatskin drums with the kick of his boots.

When days and weeks had gone by, Atiyah said to his wife, "I hear the land calling home her children. Will you come with me or stay?" "My foot keeps pace with your foot wherever you go, O light of my eyes. Were you to fly through the air I should take flight to stay near you," said the sheikh's daughter. And they were ready to go. The sheikh made them a gift of one hundred purebred camels, and the tribe collected a purse of gold which could buy as many more. The bride's cousin, with thirty horsemen, accompanied them for the first part of the way, but when the time came for parting, Atiyah would not allow them to go. He said, "Let me take pride in my kinship with you, O my brother. How will my people know that I have ties to the best of the Arabs if you do not come with me to the camp?" And they continued together.

What joy there was, and what songs and dancing to welcome them! Kingly feasts heaped high in the copper trays and the sound of music and merriment made the night hours seem few. And when the new kinsman prepared to return, Atiyah's father chose the two most beautiful girls among his folk to be the brides of the guest amid yet more feasting and gladness. When at last the cousin rode homeward, he took with him, beside his thirty men, two wives, one thousand milch camels, one thousand purses of gold, and from Atiyah's father, four mares with their foals, the finest ever bred.

And from that day to this the two tribes have dwelt in peace and in friendship, for only he who is narrow-hearted and ungenerous is the enemy of God and man.

The Price of Pride

Saudi Arabia

A Beduin once had business in the cattle market of a town. He took his young son with him, but in the confusion of the place he lost track of his boy and the child was stolen.

The father hired a crier to shout through the streets that a reward of one thousand piasters was offered for the return of the child. Although the man who held the boy heard the crier, greed had opened his belly and he hoped to earn an even larger sum. So he waited and said nothing.

On the following day the crier was sent through the streets again. But this time the sum he offered was five hundred piasters, not a thousand. The kidnapper still held out. To his surprise, on the third day the crier offered a mere one hundred piasters. He hurried to return the boy and collect his reward. Curious, he asked the father why the sum of money had dwindled from day to day.

The father said, "On the first day my son was angry and refused to eat your food; is that not so?" "Yes," agreed the kidnapper. "On the second day he took a little, and on the last he asked for bread of his own accord," said the father. It had been so, the kidnapper agreed. "Well," said the father, "as I judge it, that first day my son was as unblemished as refined gold. Like a man of honor, he refused to break bread with his captor. To bring him back with his pride untarnished, I was ready to pay one thousand piasters. On the second day, when hunger made him forget the conduct of a nobleman, he accepted food at your table, and I offered five hundred piasters for him. But when he had been reduced to begging humbly for food, his return was worth but one hundred piasters to me."

The Foreign Wife

Morocco

There was a Beduin prince rich both in camels and in gold who had one daughter called Hamda. When the girl grew old enough to be eyed as a woman, her father pitched a tent for her apart, to hide her from the sight of men. This was the custom among the tribes. He also built a closed litter with windows in its sides so that Hamda could travel unseen whenever the camp was moved.

One day the settlement was preparing for a journey, and the people were busy pulling up the tent pegs and lowering the goat-hair cloths. Hamda climbed into her litter, which was strapped to the back of a camel resting on its knees. The wait was long, and the girl fell asleep. In the clamor and confusion of loading and packing, no one looked up when Hamda's camel rose of its own accord and walked away to the south. And when the string of burdened animals slowly began to move north, Hamda's father did not trouble about her, supposing that she rode with the van.

The sleeping girl was carried far from her people and away from those whom she loved into the lands of strangers. Her camel came to the grazing grounds of Prince Mohammad and the Beni Lahab, enemies with whom her father had fought. Their prince, who rode well and loved the chase, was out with his hawks hunting for birds when he saw Hamda's litter in the distance, rocking as her camel approached. While he watched it, the tired beast came to a halt, lowering itself to its knees. Curious to know what this might be, the prince spurred his mount and hurried up. He unfastened one slatted window and looked inside. What did he see but a girl deep in sleep, with skin fair as peeled almonds and a mouth like a grape, neat as the seal on Solomon's ring. He pushed the shutter to and hastened home to his tents. There he roused his two sisters and sent them to lead the lost camel with its strange load to the camp.

Hamda awoke and heard two girls talking as they rode, each on a white camel, one to her left and one to her right. She supposed they were her own people, for she lived screened in her tent and her father's clan was large. But soon she was in the midst of an unknown camp and knew that she had come among strangers. "Tell me, O girls," she said, "among those who rule the desert, whose guest am I?" They told her, "Your host is a great man and his kindness is known widely; you have no reason to feel fear or alarm."

A tent was raised for Hamda's use and filled with soft bedding and fine stuffs. Two slave girls lived with her to do her bidding. And so the days came and the days went, and Hamda stayed in Prince Mohammad's camp in comfort and peace. Not so the prince, whose head was filled with the memory of Hamda, sweet as the honeycomb, sleeping in her litter. "Ya Yimma!" he called to his mother, "does the stranger wish to return to her own people, or is she willing to be wed and become kin with our tribe?" When the mother put the question to Hamda, she said, "O my aunt, marriage is lawful and fitting for a maid. And what better husband can a girl hope for than your son? But I fear that my bride-price is too high. My father would not nod or consent until I am offered so many milch camels as the branding iron will mark in three days and one-third."

The prince's heart was full and his thoughts grew wings when he heard the news. "A daughter of princes!" he cried. "I shall have her even if all our cattle, to the last camel, should go to pay her dower." "Such beauty is worth this much and more," said his mother, "but where shall you find her price?" "God is bountiful," said the prince. "If a thing is worthy, He will grant it success. Let your mind be at peace while I visit our camps."

With a few horsemen for company the prince began to make his rounds. From every settlement, even from the outermost camps, he collected a few camels, for he was well loved and respected. Soon the herd that raised a cloud of white dust as it walked behind him was too numerous to count. The brander was called, and he was promised new clothes for himself and his wife, as well as coffee to brew and tobacco to smoke, if he did not lift his eyes from the job until three days and one-third had passed. The man was willing and heated his iron in the fire.

So Hamda was made the wife of Prince Mohammad, and the prayer was spoken and the nights of gladness were kept according to custom. When the prince entered the marriage tent, he found a pearl without price. In Hamda beauty reached perfection and modesty was its match. If love had seized the prince before, now he could not endure an hour away from Hamda's side. He forgot the two kinswomen he had married before and sent them away with their sons. And when Hamda's belly swelled and at the sum of her months she gave birth to a boy, his love for her was doubled by love for her son. He called the child Faris, for he was strong and well made like a hero of the tales. When other children were walking, Faris was running, following his father wherever he went, even into the guest tent to sit with the men.

Now, the prince had a servant whose work was to boil coffee to his master's taste. All through the years he had gone to the prince's old wives for the beans he roasted for each brew. When he asked for the ration of coffee as always, they wailed and complained, "Don't you know that now east has become west, and we who used to preside over provisions for household and guests are abandoned and neglected and have nothing to give you, for we hold not a thing in our hands!" The man was sharp-witted and quick to think of filling his own sack, and he said, "What if someone were to trip the foreigner who sits in your place, and make her fall in the sight of the prince? Would you have something for that one then?" "Anything you wish for, you have but to name it. On that day it shall be yours," said the women.

From that time it was Hamda who passed the coffee and the roaster to the servant when his master called for a brew. One morning when the man had filled one cup for the prince and a second, he took a sip himself and sighed a loud sigh, muttering, "A shame! The truth is that it is a shame!" "What have you seen among the tents that brings the word 'shame' into your mouth?" cried the prince. "Tell me at once, or you have only yourself to blame." "If I tell, do I speak in safety?" asked the man. "Say what you have to say and no harm shall touch you," said the prince, and the man began. "Before I could stop it, O my master, the thought entered my head that tomorrow Faris will be one of the young sports who race each other on horseback and test their strength with mock fights. I thought that when he is old enough to join those who make their swords ring, striking blade against blade, he alone among his well-born companions will not know the name of his grandsire or his uncles on his mother's side." The words struck the prince like a dagger, and the truth of this hint was like salt in a wound. For love of his honor and pride in his line, he closed his eyes to the virtues of Hamda, the bride he had found, and brought back his old wives, women from his own people, daughters of men of far renown.

Showing neither sorrow nor anger, Hamda withdrew with young Faris, her servants, and her herds, and set up her tents a distance away. But one thing she did without fail: to every guest whom Prince Mohammad received, she sent her servant to offer him a feast from the purse of Faris. Banquet for banquet she matched the father's bounty with that of the son. Young camels in herds were slaughtered to feed the best men of the quarter in the name of Faris, while the youth sat with them conversing like a sheikh. His mother had brought him a preacher to teach him the words of the holy book and a seasoned rider to train him in the tricks of the hunt and the fight. He was not fifteen years old, yet his name was repeated far and wide as a gallant rider and a princelike host.

Only the coffee maker heard the name Faris and frowned. He trembled when he saw how men leaned toward the youth and gave him their loyalty and their love. "The boy's name is on every man's lip," he cried. "Tomorrow he will be our leader and kill me for what I have done." He went to the two earlier wives of Prince Mohammad and warned them:

> The ruler of the roost is easy to know:
> While still inside the egg, he begins to crow.

"When the time comes, it will be the child of the foreigner—God knows of what stock or what land—who will stand in the place of our prince. Do nothing and be content to watch your own sons become servants, going when he beckons and coming at his call; or listen to me and help me with a plan to hush the name of Faris once and for all."

The very next day the sons of the two wives of Prince Mohammad, attended by the coffee maker, rode east to Hamda's tents. Faris ran to meet them, saying, "Welcome, brothers! What sweeter guest is there than a brother? Twice welcome and may God keep you, for you are dearer to me than my own neck." He killed camels in their honor, and they feasted and drank coffee and talked. Then one of the young men, repeating the lesson the coffee maker had taught him, said, "O Faris, how long must we continue to live in the shadow of our father's sword? We are grown men—is it not time to win respect for ourselves? What do you say to setting out on a raid? Let us ride against the camps to the east to plunder their riches and strike fear into their hearts! A strong sword and nothing less will catch the eye of our neighbors and make bright our names." There had been no keener horseman than Faris since Prince Mohammad was a youth, and a raid was an adventure suited to his taste. He promised provisions for their journey and was ready to start with the first light.

For ten days the three youths and their servant rode eastwards till they came to a land where nothing lived and no shadow moved. On a desolate plain they reined in their horses to rest. No sooner did Faris lay down his head than he dozed. But the others stayed watching, for their plan was to kill him in his sleep. Then the younger of the two sons said, "Why burden our necks with the weight of his death? Rather let us leave him as he is. If he dies of hunger, that is God's will and written in his fate." And they returned the way that they had come, leading Faris's horse behind them.

To those who asked, "Where is Faris?" they said, "We raided a brave tribe, which fought fiercely and retrieved their cattle. In the struggle our brother was killed, and we buried him where he fell, God have mercy on his soul!" And Hamda tore the cloth of her gown in grief and threw fistfuls of earth on her head. She cried like the she-camel who has lost her newborn calf. She sat by her fire never stirring, but wept without ceasing for the child of her body, Faris, her only son.

Yet that same Faris was alive and breathing. He awoke in the wilderness alone. Not even a bird flew above him, and the breeze scattered the marks of his brothers in the dust. Without waterskin or food bag to stay him, he knew that to retrace a ride of ten days was to walk toward death. So, swinging one hand before him and one hand behind, he continued walking forward until weakness from hunger and thirst bent and folded him. But just when he thought that his soul must depart from his body, he came to a large guest tent with poles like strong columns and the finest carpets and cushions. Inside was a young maiden, slim as the date palm and wide-eyed as a gazelle. "O daughter of nobles, I am dying of hunger," he said, and sank to the ground. She brought him dates and butter, and little by little she fed him until his strength revived. When the sheikh her father came in, Faris was able to sit up beside him and say, "O sheikh, I beg for your protection. Misfortune has caught me, and I am willing to serve you in return for your favor." "You are welcome to live with us, but how shall we call you when we need you?" asked the sheikh. "Call me Jalal—Splendor—and I will do whatever you ask," said the youth. When they heard this, the rest of the men began to laugh. They said, "He bears the splendid name of Jalal, but to look at him you would say he is closer to Abu Jallah—Father of Dung." And in this way Faris became dung gatherer for the fires of the camp.

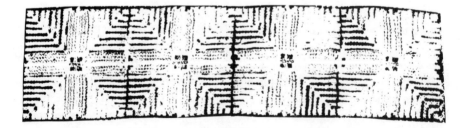

The weeks passed, and one day the sheikh left with his men for a distant place. Only Abu Jallah and one black slave remained to guard the camp. The horsemen were hardly out of sight when a shout went up from the pasture. A hundred raiders were making off with the tribe's cattle and the shepherd boys didn't know how to stop them. The sheikh's daughter ran out of her tent calling, "Where are you, O son of the Arabs, come help your brothers!" She saddled two horses, and Abu Jallah galloped off with the slave. They made for the haze of dust raised by the stolen herd. The slave was pushed from his horse before the fighting began, but Faris, like a falcon among sparrows, let no one stand in his path. When forty lay dead beside their fine horses, the rest turned their backs and fled.

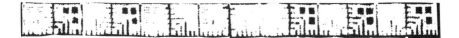

Bursting with pride, the slave drove the she-camels home; not one was missing or lost. Abu Jallah followed with the horses. He cut the left stirrup off each saddle and slipped the bridle off the neck of each horse. Then he hid them under a rock before returning to the camp with his spoils. How the slave was boasting to the daughter of the sheikh! Had she not seen with her own eyes that it was he who brought back the herd? But for him they would all be beggars with not a mouthful to eat. "Good health and rest for the fearless and the brave!" said the girl. Abu Jallah stood silent and said not a word.

The sheikh and his riders returned as night fell. "Whose army has tethered its horses at our door?" he asked. And the slave spoke first, telling of the raid and how he had saved his master's herd. "You have restored to me all that I own; may God bless you with His gifts. If you wish for anything of mine, ask and I shall not withhold it," said the sheikh. "I wish for one thing only, and that is your daughter," said the slave. The sheikh's mouth grew dry, but he could not unsay his own words. "Tomorrow we will send for

the preacher," he said in a low voice. "And now call Abu Jallah to boil us some coffee."

The men who were resting in the sheikh's tent looked up when Faris began to pound the beans. "I last heard that beat when I was guest of the Beni Lahab," said one. And when the youth poured the steaming drink into the cups and its fragrance filled the tent, another man said, "By Allah. no one makes coffee to equal this but Prince Mohammad!" Now Faris, sitting by the brass coffeepots, could not restrain himself. "O windbag with a loud mouth," he said to the slave, "since you fought hand to hand with the raiders, can you explain how they rode with one stirrup and no bridle?" The slave had nothing to say. "O windbag," Faris went on, "if you killed forty men and won a bride with your strength, will you test your might against mine with your bride for the prize?" The slave was dumb, nor could he refuse, with all the men of the tribe looking on.

When it was day Faris led the slave and the sheikh with his men to a great rock on the crest of a hill. "Whoever lifts this rock the highest shall be the winner. Let the tribesmen stand as judges," he cried. The slave pressed and pushed but could not shift it. "Did he move it, O tribesmen?" shouted Faris. And they all answered, "No." Then Faris slowly raised the great rock, uncovering the forty stirrups and bridles for all to see.

Now everyone was astonished and saw that this was no Abu Jallah but a true Beduin, strong and brave. The sheikh gave him his daughter and Faris told them his tale. Then he departed to find his own people, taking with him not only a bride but camels and horses in plenty.

First he sought out Hamda's tent. He found her crouched by the fire among the soot and the ashes. "O mother of Faris," he said, "I bring good news; your Faris is home at last!" She wept and said, "O cursed are your parents! Why mock me in my grief?" "Your son is not dead, I say he has returned," said Faris. But she scolded anew, "O wretch that you are, may you be destroyed for making light of my mourning!" Then Faris kissed his mother, and she breathed his smell and knew him. She asked, "Am I awake or do I dream?" And she fainted, so great was her joy.

Messengers rode off to Prince Mohammad, and each was rewarded with two camels for bearing the good news. The camp began to resound with the shrill trills of the women and the music and singing of the men. Faris kissed the hands of his father and made peace with his brothers. But the coffee maker he burned in a great fire, and his house and family with him.

Then Faris went to his mother and said, "Pack me food for a journey; I want to find out the name of my mother's father and my uncles." She told him, "Your grandfather is ruler over fifty tribes of which each tribe boasts five hundred horsemen. But he was the enemy of Prince Mohammad and the Beni Lahab."

Well, Faris found his mother's tribe, and they knew from the cut of his features that he was Hamda's son. They gave him his oldest uncle's daughter as a bride and sent him home with gold and cattle and serving girls to show they held him dear. As for his own people, they rode out on their horses to meet him, throwing their spears in the air to greet him. And Prince Mohammad said, "I have grown old and wish to spend my days at Hamda's side. It is time for you to lead our people."

So Faris became sheikh over the Beni Lahab, and his fame flew as if on wings among all the Arabs of that time.

Two Mothers
Mourning

Algeria

Emir Hasan, one of the princes of the desert, was traveling among his tribe when he came upon a woman weeping. When he asked her the cause of her grief, she replied, "I mourn for my son who has died." "What did your son do when he was alive?" asked the prince. "He worked for me. I am a poor widow and he kept me alive. Now I have no one to earn me a living," she said. "Cry no more," said the emir. "I'll make you a gift of a young mule. He shall work for you instead of your son, and you shall be as comfortable as you were before."

The prince rode on and met a second woman weeping over the grave of her son. "What did your son do when he was alive?" he asked her. "Aah! He used to gather the men of good repute and the nobles of high standing at his feasts. When they left he would ride with them, not parting from them until they were out of sight of his tent." "Weep on, O mother of a greathearted son," said the prince. "Weep and shed more tears, for we cannot comfort you or make good such a loss."

∵ ∴ ∵ ∴ ∵ · ∵ ∴ ∵ ∴ ∵ ∴ ∵

Successor to
the Sheikh

∴ ∴ ∴ ∴ ∴ ∴ ∴ ∴ ∴ ∴ ∴ ∴

Morocco

There was a sheikh of the Arabs called Ghanim who was respected above all
other men in his tribe. His sons were many, and the youngest was called
Diyab. One day, seeing that the sheikh was growing old in years, his people
said to him, "O Ghanim, choose one of your sons to be leader over us when,
after a long life, you are gone." He replied, "The best of my sons shall rule
the Hilalis; I give you Diyab." "O Ghanim," they said, "you have knowledge
and you have wisdom and your word is a command, yet Diyab is young."
"We shall see," he said.

One day the sheikh was with his wife, speaking of lineage and ancestry.
"Your tribe differs from us Hilalis," he began, but she said, "We too are
of the Beni Hilal!" "Oho, that is an easy thing to test," said the sheikh.
"With but three words one can always tell a true Hilali." "What are the
words?" "Ask your brothers this riddle: what of all things in the world is
the lightest, what the hottest, and what the sweetest? If they give you the
right answers, I shall add one hundred gold pieces to the sum of your bridal
dower."

The woman left for her brothers' tents, and when she challenged them to
solve the sheikh's riddle, they laughed and said, "That is simple. Has there
ever been anything lighter than a feather, or hotter than pepper, or sweeter
than raisins and honey? Go tell Sheikh Ghanim that your brothers were not
puzzled by his words." But along the path back to her own settlement, the
sheikh's wife met her youngest son Diyab. "Ya Yimma, O Mother, where
have you been?" he asked her. And she told him about the three words with
which his father had tested her brothers. Diyab was curious now to learn
their answers, and when he heard them he said, "Lah! Lah! They guessed
wrong, for this is the true answer:

There is nothing lighter than gunpowder in the barrel of a gun,
Nothing burns hotter than the lover's heart at the deathbed of the loved one,
Nothing is sweeter than a bed full of laughing daughters and sons!

"God send you health and happiness, my child," said his mother, "but do not mention that you have met me."

Sheikh Ghanim was waiting for her when she reached the tents. "What happened? What did they say?" he asked, and she told him what Diyab had said. "Ah! let me think awhile!" he said, and strolled between the tents. When he reached the edge of the settlement, he suddenly began to shout in alarm, "They have killed Diyab! They have killed Diyab!" His wife ran out of her quarters, saying, "It cannot be! He was here with me a short time ago!" And her husband said, "I was certain that the three words of the riddle can only be explained by a true Hilali."

Another time when the men were gathered round a large wood fire, Sheikh Ghanim said to Diyab, "What if I were to throw you into this fire?" "You would be throwing me into the arms of a fierce adversary, but one that is not unconquerable," answered Diyab. "What are you saying?" asked the sheikh. "Fire will overpower a man, but it must bow before water," said Diyab. "And what does water bow before?" "Water bows before a rise in the land." "And what overcomes a rise?" "A horse!" "And what does a horse yield to?" "His rider!" "And what does the rider yield to?" "To his children, for he loves them as he loves his sight." "You are right, my son," said Ghanim, "go rest now, for tomorrow you must pasture the camels."

Next day Diyab led out sixty-six she-camels. He was sitting and watching his herd when a man rode by on a mare with a pale grey filly following her. How that animal pleased Diyab! As soon as he saw her, he wanted to own her. He asked the man if he would sell the horse. "Yes, you may buy her off me," said the man. "I'll give you sixty camels for her," said Diyab. "You must be lying or making mock of me," said the man. "Count them and take them with you," said Diyab. And when the remaining she-camels began to follow the others, he called the man back and said, "Take the rest; then you will have them all."

When Diyab returned to the encampment with only a grey filly, the tribesmen laughed at him and said, "How foolish is our Ghanim's youngest son!" In the evening his father said, "I hear you have bought a filly. What is she like?" "Oh, she can see a little, and her back can carry a little, and her leg is bent a little," said Diyab. His father laughed. "She will bring you one hundred and a little," he said.

Not long afterwards the young horsemen in the tribe met and decided to have a race. "Let each man wager ten camels," they said. "We'll take them six hours' distance from the camp and hobble them. Then on the following day let's ride to the place together, each man on his horse. Whoever un-hobbles the camels first shall own them." Now Diyab had no camels left to wager. But he went crying to his aunt, his father's sister, that he could not take his place with the men, and she gave him ten camels of her own.

When the men led out their horses for the race, they said, "Where is your horse, Diyab?" "Ride on without me; I'll follow you soon," he answered. And they shook their heads and said, "Truly our sheikh's youngest son is witless."

When they had spurred their horses and galloped off, Diyab began to saddle his light-colored filly. The slave who was helping mounted her to test the saddle, but before he could seat himself, the horse reared high and threw him to the ground. Now Diyab leaped onto her back, and when he slapped her side she took off with the speed of an ostrich.

Meanwhile the other horses had tired and dropped out except for two. The two horsemen were riding side by side, their well-matched mounts foaming. "Why race any farther?" they asked one another. "Our horses have proved themselves equals. Let us rest, and when we reach the camels we can divide them between us." But when they had almost arrived at their goal, they saw a man riding toward them with the wagered animals, one hundred and twenty she-camels, following behind him. "Is that you, O Diyab?" they called. "Aywah!" he shouted. And now their tongues were knotted in wonder and they had nothing to say.

Sheikh Ghanim went to meet his son, and his heart was glad. "I told you your filly would bring you one hundred and a little!" he said. And from that day he made Diyab the sheikh of the Arabs, and the tribesmen were proud to ride behind him.

The Good
Neighbors

Iraq

Long ago there lived a sheikh of the Aneza who was so hospitable that they called him Essaffah, or the Welcomer. One day a stranger raised his tent pole not far from the camp of Essaffah, near enough to become his neighbor. The man was poor, but since it was the sheikh's custom to provide for all who lived in his vicinity food and drink and clothing from his own stores, the stranger lacked nothing.

For seven years the two men lived as neighbors, and to mark each year of their friendship the sheikh gave him a present of a pure-blooded mare. Whenever a raid was successful, the sheikh would give the neighbor and his sons a share of the spoils. In short, under Essaffah's protection the humble wanderer increased his possessions until he owned three herds of one hundred camels each. He was now a man of wealth.

Essaffah had one small daughter, and during these seven years she had grown to womanhood. Slim as a poplar, graceful as the deer which leads the herd, she caught the eye of one of the neighbor's sons. How eagerly he courted her, stalking her on the way to the wellhead and passing the nights outside her tent! But the girl refused him. The boy was stubborn, however, and at last the girl went to her father, asking what she should do. "One night more and I shall find a way to rescue you and save your name," he told her.

That night when the neighbor's son whispered to her outside her tent, the girl said, "Wait but one night more." Before the next day's dawn, Essaffah had given the shout to break camp, and by sunrise the animals were laden and men and cattle on the move.

Now, whenever Essaffah pitched his tent in a new camp, the neighbor had always set his own quarters a short distance to the left. Over the years the spot had come to be accepted as the neighbor's tent site. On this occasion when suitable pasture was found and the new camp site chosen, Essaffah paced the ground until he spotted a swarming anthill. Then he pitched his tent a short distance to the right of it. The neighbor prepared to spread his tentcloths in the usual place, but before raising the center poles he noticed the ants. "O sheikh," he said, "there is an anthill on my site." "So there is, brother," said the sheikh, "and God's earth is wide."

The neighbor said no further word. He packed his household and left the place, traveling far with his family and his camels to find new grazing grounds. But all the while he could not rest. Again and again he asked himself what lay behind the words of his friend. For seven years they had lived like brothers and uttered not a word that was out of place. His heart was troubled and he found no peace.

At last a thought came to him that he hoped might solve the riddle. While hunting with his oldest son one day, he said, "What a shame about Essaffah's bright-eyed daughter. We are but inferiors under his protection

and cannot look for his kinship or for marriage ties between us. Still, she was a fine-grained creature; what a shame to let her go!" "Are you not ashamed, Father?" cried the son. "Why? Were I not an old man with white hair in my beard, I would have found a way!" the father said. The boy replied, "Was she not our sister? Did we not eat from the same store for seven years? Only bastards and sons of shame can speak as you do." The father said, "I thought you had grown to be men, but I find that your hearts are soft like women's. Let us go home."

Next he spoke to his middle son, who answered as his brother had. But when he took his youngest child aside, the boy cried out, "One night more, Father, and she would have been mine!" "Bravo, my son," said the father. And as he spoke the words, he drew his sword and cut the boy's head from his shoulders.

Then he took from his wife's stores her new-spun wool and wound it round and round the dead boy's head so that it looked like a spool of homespun yarn. He waited until a traveler passed who was going toward Essaffah's camp, and he said, "Will you carry this present to my friend?"

Essaffah was sitting among his guests when the traveler set the spool of wool before him. "Who sends this?" he asked. "A man who says he was your friend and brother," said the traveler. "It is to weave new bridles for your horses." There and then the sheikh called some of his slaves to begin the work. While the sheikh and his guests conversed, the servants slowly unwound the wool. When the boy's head was uncovered, the sheikh gave a shout of lament. He struck hand against hand in remorse, understanding that his friend of seven years was truer than a brother and as jealous of his name. He turned to the guests, who stood in amazement demanding his

tale. When he had told it, they said with one voice, "Make him your brother by sending your daughter for one of his sons."

So it was that two men, one a sheikh and protector, the other a poor subject and neighbor, but equals in honor and pride, were tied by bonds of marriage and lived to take pleasure in the children of their children.

The Guest Who Ran Away

Tunisia

A weary traveler stopped at a Beduin's tent and asked for shelter for the night. Without delay the man killed a couple of chickens and handed them to his wife to stew for their guest's supper.

As the woman stirred the meat in her copper cooking pot, she smelled the rich steam and could not resist tasting a piece to see if it was soft. But mouthful followed mouthful, and soon nothing was left of the two birds but one neck. This she gave to her little son to nibble. The boy found it so savory that he whined, "Give me some, Mother, give me some!" The woman slapped the little boy and scolded him: "It's a shameful habit your father taught you; enough of it, I tell you!"

On the other side of the woven hanging which screened the women's part of the tent from the rest, the traveler overheard this exchange. "What habit has his father taught your child?" he asked curiously. "Oh," said the woman, "whenever a guest arrives at our tent, he cuts off his ears and roasts them over the fire for my son to eat." Making not a sound, the traveler picked up his shoes and fled.

"What ails our guest? Why has he left in such a hurry?" asked the Beduin, entering the tent soon after. "A fine guest indeed!" exclaimed his wife. "He snatched the chickens out of my pot and ran away!" Hitching up his robes, the Beduin gave chase, shouting, "Let me have one, at least; you may keep the other!" But his guest only ran faster.

·· ·· ·· ·· ·· ·· ·· ·· ·· ·· ·· ··

The Boy in
Girl's Dress

·· ·· ·· ·· ·· ·· ·· ·· ·· ·· ·· ··

S y r i a

There was a sheikh of the Beni Khalids who had only one child, a son called Husam, yet in other respects God had given him freely of His bounty. He was blessed with understanding and his words were like milk—pure of any fault, so that in the councils men looked to him for guidance. Good fortune blew his way with the ease of the quickening west wind, and he succeeded in whatever he undertook. Wherever he pointed his lance his aim was true, and the horsemen flocked to ride behind him in the raids.

But then God—may His mercy be upon us—willed that the sheikh's star should set. Another man rose in his place before whom the world danced as a bride dances for her groom, and whose triumphs blinded men's eyes like jewels in the sun. His was the word now, and his the counsel. It was at his side that the Beduins rode, and near him that they pitched their tents. The first man was regarded as no more than a common herdsman. Of his former wealth there remained but twenty milking camels, his mare and her two-year-old foal, and two swords and a lance. Feeling that his honor was diminished among his people, he said to his wife, "Woman, I can no longer endure life among the tribesmen and their tents. I must move to a place where none can see me and I can see no one." And he asked her to prepare rations for the road. He himself soaked a waterskin and filled it at the well, tightened the girths on his riding camel, stocked his saddlebags, and then, putting himself in God's hands, rode off to the east.

Riding by day and resting by night, he traveled for eight days until he came to an oasis thick and green with clover, oats, and other wild herbs. Happily he dismounted and hobbled his camel so that she might wander and feed. So rich was this pasture, however, that she could graze her fill without moving from where she stood.

Suddenly among the high grasses he caught the glint of sunlight on metal. Another man was in the oasis, a man carrying a gun. "Who are you?" called the Khalidi. "I am the man you see before you," said the stranger, who, like most, was unwilling to betray his name to a traveler he did not know.

"But you—what has brought you to this place?" "A swordsman must yield to one who carries a gun," said the Khalidi, "so I shall tell you what drove me here: my fortune and my misfortune." Hearing this, the other man lowered his gun, for he too had suffered a change of luck.

"What is your tribe?" the stranger asked. "O companion of a well-omened hour, for good or evil I am one of the Beni Khalids." "And I a Shammari, by God," said the stranger, "which makes us foes. Yet the desert is a haven and brings truce to noble men." So they sat together and told each other their histories. The Shammari, like the Khalidi, was seeking a sequestered corner in which to live. They swore friendship and resolved to live as neighbors in this well-watered spot, and since the sun was sinking by that time, they both slept in the oasis that night.

They parted the next day to fetch their herds and families, and the Khalidi asked the Shammari, "Do you have any children?" "Yes, by Allah, a girl called Halima. And you?" "I too have a daughter," said the Khalidi, though the truth was that he had just the one son, Husam. Yet he thought that if he told the Shammari he had a son, the man might be afraid for his daughter and change his mind about living so close.

When he returned to his camp, the Khalidi called Husam aside. "I have found excellent pasture for us to live on, my son," he said, "and a neighbor to share it with us. He is a Shammari, one of our enemies, but we have sworn friendship. When I asked him if he had any family, he told me that he had only a girl. And when he became curious about my children, I told him that I had a daughter too, else he might not have come to live as our neighbor. For this reason, my son, I want you to dress in girl's clothes and pass for my daughter. We will call you Halima, as the Shammari's daughter is named. But do I have to tell you that you must behave with modesty toward our neighbor's girl, must not kiss her even if she kisses you, and must not insult her with a careless word?" "Father," said Husam, "I swear by the life you gave me that I shall be a worthy son."

So his father bought him everything a girl might need: a silken sash and a fringed scarf, a cotton headcloth and a woman's robe that falls free to the ankles. Trinkets too he brought: a belt with bright embroidery, two pairs of bracelets, some rings, and shoes of yellow leather. His mother cut Husam's front hair level with his brow and braided black silk into his plaits so that they appeared as long as a girl's.

As soon as all was ready, the family loaded their camels and traveled eastward for seven days. When the eighth day dawned, they sighted the oasis before them like the shadow of a cloud on the bleakness of the desert. When they drew near and saw that it was like a pleasure garden, Husam hastened to help his father unload the camels that they might browse. He slipped into his woman's robes and was pulling at the ropes to raise the goat-hair tent when the Shammari's heavily laden pack animals came into sight in the distance.

As soon as the Shammari's daughter saw her new friend, she slid off her riding camel and ran to kiss her. From that moment the two were inseparable. Leaving their parents in the tents to their coffee brew, tobacco, and talk, they took charge of the camel herd. In the freshness of the morning they both would run out to stroke the milch camels' udders and prepare them for milking. Then, tying some bread and some dates into a cloth, each would swing herself onto the back of a favorite camel. Together they would sing the gentle melody which keeps the lead camels moving until the herd has reached its pasture. There the young people would dismount and play and chatter and weave garlands of wild grasses while the cattle grazed nearby.

At night in the camp the two slept alongside each other as any two girl friends might, except for one thing: the Shammari girl lay naked between her covers in Beduin fashion, while the Khalidi would say, "I am not used to taking off my clothes at night and cannot sleep without them." And when the Shammari girl kisssed her friend, the Khalidi would not kiss her back. "Is my breath so stale that the Khalidi Halima cannot bear to kiss me?" the Shammari girl complained to her father. "And why does she never take off her clothes at night?" "She may be timid, my child," her father said to comfort her, "or used to different ways. These things are matters of custom."

One day the two went out to hunt for desert truffles. By the time they had collected enough to take back for the evening meal, they had strayed far from their herd and the sun was beating fiercely on their backs. "Let's refresh ourselves in the pool we passed on our way," said the Shammari Halima. After a pause, the Khalidi agreed but added, "Only let us race and see who reaches the water first." Of course he knew he was the fleeter, and he was bathed and dressed again before the other panted up to the water's edge. Though he protected his secret in this way, he almost betrayed himself when he saw the Shammari Halima's graceful form. It so troubled him that he

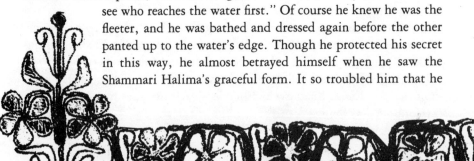

fainted clean away and, only revived when the Shammari girl, thinking that the heat had harmed him, shook the water from her wet locks onto his face.

The two friends were gone from camp a long time, and when they returned, they saw a band of raiders driving off the camels. "The cattle are stolen! Horsemen to the rescue!" the two shouted with one voice. Their fathers heard the shrill calls, and throwing themselves onto their horses, galloped after the raiders while the two young people looked on. In their old men's voices they croaked, "What about the *uqla*, O horsemen?" This was the portion of cattle left by raiders for their victims to feed on in that forbidding land. The foremost raider shouted to his men, "Let them have ten she-camels!" "Ten are far too few," the old men protested. The raider said, "For the sake of your daughters we shall let you keep six more." But the old men continued to argue: "We have no livelihood except through the grace of God and our camels. The times have wronged us, our people have shunned us, and we are alone in the wilderness, two white-haired men and their aged wives and tender daughters. Must we beg for their survival? Will you not relent?" "What are we to say to our women who ground the wheat for our travel ration?" retorted the leader of the raid. "Shall we tell them that we won a herd of camels but that two greybeards came after us begging for their *uqla* and we cut them loose again? This cannot be. Your lances must convince us. If you have any pride, fight for the cattle, or we shall add the girls to our spoils and leave you to the wild beasts."

Then the old men said, "The outcome is in the hands of Allah. You attacked us sure of your strength and numbers, but we shall put our faith in God." And so they rode into the fight.

Seeing and hearing all that was said, Husam headed for the tents, pulling off his women's clothes as he ran. His mother hurried out to meet him with his sword and red cloak. She began to saddle the foal, and the Shammari girl asked her, "Why are you saddling? Where is the rider?" "He is coming; you will see him very soon," said the boy's mother. And when Husam came out of the tent strapping on his sword belt, she raised her voice in the lululey of joy. Swinging into the saddle, he rode toward Halima and paraded before her, saying, "I am riding into the fight for the love of your bright eyes, O Halima. Will you not shout lululey for Husam?" "Who is Husam, brother?"

asked Halima. "Your former playmate, who is a man," he said, and Halima raised the joyful cry as loud as a mare's whinny. Then love of combat filled Husam's heart and he kicked his horse's side, while Halima let fall her night-black hair, trilling for him as Beduin girls have always done for the men who go to battle.

Like a hawk when it scatters a flight of pigeons, Husam rode straight into the cluster of raiders, calling Halima's name and swinging his sword till one of the robbers fell. How proudly then, O Husam, you led the horse you captured to Halima, throwing the reins into her hands! Again into the thick of the raiders he galloped, pushing three men from their mares. The rest did not linger but rode away in flight. And the two old men helped Husam lead the frightened camels and the four prize horses back to the tents in triumph.

Yet the Shammari stood with his head bowed to the ground, and pain overcast his heart as he took thought for his daughter. "What led you to deceive us so, neighbor?" he said. And his wife brought her sorrow to the boy's mother. "May God afflict you with sorrow as you have afflicted us," she wept. "How could you allow your son to call himself Halima and let him sleep in the same tent as our daughter for a season?" "May God plague us with the deadly curse that cuts off all offspring if Husam has done any harm to your daughter," said the Khalidis. "O neighbors under God, our only thought was your peace of mind when our children went to the pasture." Husam brought two of the horses he had captured that day as a gift for Halima's father. But the dish was already cooked in the pot: Halima had lost her heart to Husam, as he had his to her.

In the silence of that night when all were sleeping, the Shammari shook his daughter, whispering, "I'll give your head to the dogs to gnaw if you say a word." He did not want her to warn Husam. And in the darkness of that hour, he loaded his tent cloths onto his mounts and left with his family and his herd. By the time day dawned, he had crossed the grazing grounds of many tribes and was far away.

When Husam awoke and saw the abandoned site of his neighbor's tent, he told his father, "I cannot live where Halima has been, now that my eye cannot see her." His father said, "May Allah protect and shield our path! Bring round the pack camels and let us set out while the day is young, so we may find pasture for the herd by dark." And soon they and their cattle were heading back toward the territory of the Beni Khalids, their people.

For seven days they traveled, and on the eighth they caught up with their tribe. But how different was their state now from the day they left! Their camels had multiplied tenfold, and their horses were of the finest. For the price of one mare Husam bought five lengths of tent cloth woven of black goat hair. With this he widened their house by five poles and restored it to what it had been in the days of their happiness. He bought copper cooking pots and griddles for baking dough, and a tray of hammered brass which could hold a whole sheep and round which ten men could sit at one time. He bought beaked coffeepots and measures of coffee too. And he butchered young camels and lambs—enough to offer a banquet to every man in the tribe. Now once again the men gathered to become his guests as they had done in his father's tent long ago.

But Husam could think only of Halima. He neither ate nor drank in his distraction and soon was too weak to leave his bed. Neither the herbs of the healer nor the care of his people could soothe him, and his only solace was in sighing and weeping. Then one day a youth called Hussein with whom he had exchanged vows of brotherhood sent out all the men in the tent and said, "I have a cure for his ailment." He grasped Husam's hand and laughed. "You have brought your white-haired father and your aged mother to the brink of the grave," he said. "They think you burn with an unknown fever, but it is only love that consumes you. Tell me your tale and I promise to find the girl you pine for." Instantly Husam kicked back the bed-clothes and asked for a brew of coffee. Then he opened his heart to his brother.

The tribesmen assembled in Husam's tent to praise God that his health was restored, and a feast of goat's meat was set before them. Meanwhile Hussein instructed his sister to pack provisions for a journey. She filled leather bags with dates and flour and fat while he tied the waterskins onto the riding camels' backs. Then he rode to Husam's tent and said, "Let us go out into the desert and hunt for game." As they rode side by side, Hussein began to ask the name of the woman whom his friend so loved. He asked the where-abouts of her tribe and the direction in which their pastures lay. Then he said, "And how will you reward the man who brings you Halima?" "Life is precious, but I would give you my life if you asked for it!" said Husam. "God grant that your life be long and no harm touch it, but if it is Allah's will for you to have her, then I shall be the one to bring her to you!"

Night and day they pushed forward, stopping

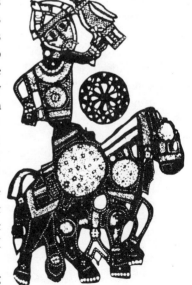

only when they had to sleep. At the close of the eighth day, they had reached the grazing grounds of the Shammari tribe and began to ask for the tents of Halima's people. Their Shammari host welcomed them with fine speeches and brought them meat and coffee. The tribesmen from the tents nearby arrived to keep the strangers company, and they sat in lively talk. Suddenly from far away the sounds of singing and the beating of drums reached their ears. Hussein asked, "What is this gladness? Is there a circumcision feast nearby?" "No, it is the men dancing for our kinsman Ali, who is to marry his cousin Halima." At the words Husam's head sank. He looked at the ground while fear entered his heart. Hussein told him, "Call on the name of the Compassionate. Have faith in God. If she is fated to be yours, no one shall have her but you." "O brother who holds up my head, do with me what you wish, but if I do not see Halima with this eye I must die." "Sleep," said Hussein. "Tomorrow you shall see her."

Next day they rose with the first light, and when they had received coffee from their host's hands, they started out walking toward the tent of Halima's father. They entered the guest quarters but found them empty. No one was in the place.

Now, all this time Halima had been crying to her cousin, who was the sister of Ali her betrothed. She told her all that had happened between her and Husam from the day they first met to the day that they were parted. Loneliness enfolded her heart, and her longing made her wail like a she-camel that has lost its calf. How many times had she spoken of Husam, saying such is his height, and such is his grace, and these are the signs of his beauty!

As Hussein and Husam sat alone in the Shammari's tent, this cousin of Halima chanced to come by. She looked at the two youths and recognized Husam from Halima's words. She brought the men coffee and fire, and when Hussein asked after the masters of the house, she laughed and said, "Those whom you wish to see have all but destroyed themselves with longing for you!" "You are mistaken," said Hussein, "we are but God's guest at your door." "God keep you, brother, wherever you come from," she said and hurried out to bring the news to Halima.

Halima's cheeks paled like wax from Mecca, and she said, "May Allah send you nothing but glad tidings if what you say is true! But O despair of my heart, where am I, and where is Husam? Twelve days of weary travel lie between us; can he have flown to me?" Dragging herself unwillingly, she followed her cousin. But on parting the felted curtain a crack, her eye fell on that of Husam! She turned away her face, and tears coursed across her cheeks. She whispered to her cousin, "Before my father returns, let them eat our food and become guests at our table."

The two girls set to work side by side, two heads with one mind. One measured flour from the bin while the other set the griddle over the charcoal embers. No sooner was the dough kneaded than the baking tray was hot and ready to receive it. One girl rolled out the dough and threw it onto the hot metal, while the other lifted the baked cakes and spread them with date butter. Halima took in the food, and Husam, whose strength melted into water when she was near, raised his eye as far as the dimple in her cheek and dared not look farther. "Eat, and may it do you good!" said the girl. And the youth replied, "Nothing but good comes from a well-omened face." She answered, "I bid you welcome: as many welcomes as your riding camels took steps to bring you. This hour is a blessing from the Compassionate." And she returned to the women's apartment while they ate.

When he saw who the guests were under his roof, Halima's white-haired father stood in the door of his tent and cursed the devil. "Had you not broken bread, I swear I should have parted your head from your shoulders," he told Husam. To calm him, Hussein said, "Praise God, uncle, that nothing but good has happened until now. They say a path does not always end where it points."

But in the evening when the young men were dancing, each resting his arm on his neighbor's shoulder, and all eyes were on the stamp of their feet as, faster and faster, they followed the beat of the drum, then Husam sought Halima. He found her in the wedding tent, for this was to be the night of the bridegroom's entering. And it was there the bridegroom Ali came upon them, their arms about each other's necks as they wept for joy. Without a sound he stepped away and returned to the noise and the singing, taking his place in the dance. One of the young men called out, "Are you not sleepy, ya Ali? Don't you want to rest in the lap of your gazelle?" And Ali replied, "I have seen a sign that says tonight is a night of ill omen. May God grant us a luckier day tomorrow."

Next day Ali went to Halima. "O daughter of my uncle," he said, "I renounce my right to you without anger. Your sins are upon your own neck. But if you want anything, ask, and it shall be between you and me, with only God as a witness." How she fell upon him and kissed him and said, "O Ali, I want nothing but the guest of our neighbors, Husam. May God deprive you of life on this earth if you deprive me of him!" And she told him everything from the beginning to the end. He said, "I shall kill a young camel and invite the whole tribe. When everyone is assembled, come to me and kiss me in sight of all. I shall say, 'What is this kiss for?' And you must say, 'It is for a thing I want from you.' And I shall ask, 'Ask, and by my life I shall give it to you.' Then you may ask what you wish and call on the people to bear witness to my promise." "May God reward you for this," she said, and each went home.

When the feast was steaming in the trays and the men had all gathered to eat, then did you, O Halima, walk up to Ali in the midst of the throng and kiss him while all looked on! "O Halima, what is the reason for this kiss?" he asked and she said what he had told her to say. "Ask, and I promise to bring it to you, O daughter of my uncle," said Ali. "By what do you swear?" she asked. "I have promised and there is no need for more," said Ali. "O kinsmen," said Halima, "will you be witnesses on my behalf? I ask only that Ali allows me my heart's choice, the guest Husam. May God grant his every wish if he grants mine." Now the word was yours, O Ali, and what did you say? "Be glad in Husam, O Halima, but where is he? Let me see him." "He is a man to fill the eye, O Ali, and a better man than he looks," said Husam's host. "Your cousin has fallen on a twig that will bear her."

So they brought the preacher to bind Halima to Husam, and that night they became man and wife. For eight days there was joy and celebration; then Hussein said, "The land is calling its people." Ali pressed them to stay ten days more, but they said, "Our people think we are hunting, and now twenty days have passed."

So they saddled the camels and set a women's traveling litter on the back of a shapely brown riding camel for Halima. Ali rode out with them to send them on their way, but when he stopped to take leave of them, they said, "We cannot let you go! Come be our guest!" They continued on the journey together, and before ten days had passed they were in the land of the Beni Khalids. A herdsman saw them from afar and went running to Husam's parents with the good news. Soon there was gladness and singing and women shouting lululey as the travelers arrived among the tents. There was killing of sheep and banquets and feasts, all that custom requires and more, in honor of Ali, who had done a great deed the like of which had not been heard of before.

Husam and Hussein each took thought on how best to reward their noble guest for his favor. And Husam's father said: "Our house and our property is yours to choose from; give Ali what you wish." Husam chose his finest horse and knotted its reins to the peg outside the tent where Ali was sleeping. And Hussein raised his voice and called his sister Hasna, who was more beautiful even than her name. He told her, "This guest of ours has done such a thing as was never done before. I wish to reward him, and what greater prize have I to offer than you? I give you leave to win him in what way you can." And he went to Husam's tent, leaving Ali alone.

Then you, O Hasna, whose heart had taken flight and aimed straight for Ali as soon as you heard of his deeds, went out to where he was sitting and kept him company, now drawing near him and now standing farther off, asking him about his country and sighing, "If only you had never left it!" Ali said, "Why, O my hostess, by favor of the Merciful?" And Hasna answered, "Then we should never have known you and never learned to long for you." "Then come and take your place by my side," said Ali. "Shame!" said Hasna. "But even without thinking of the scandal among the people, I have not the strength to stand on my feet for love of you. When it crosses my mind that you must return to your people and I must remain here, that your pitching grounds are so far that neither our men nor our cattle shall meet, then it seems as if I must die." After three or four days of this, with Hasna washing his hair and combing it and delousing it, Ali was finished. He ceased to eat or drink, and whenever the tribesmen invited him to a meal he said, "By Allah, O Arabs, my heart feels aversion to food and I cannot eat." And as soon as they left him he would retire with Hasna, for they were happiest when no one joined them and no creature saw them.

One day Ali spoke to Hussein, saying, "Take me home to my parents' tent, for you see me at death's door!" "Brother," said Hussein, "you have not stayed out your days with us." "Take me to my people, O you whose honor is bright as the white headcloth of our sheikh." So Hussein prepared a great feast in his honor, and Husam brought him gifts of the costliest: sharp lances and fine saddles besides the pedigreed horse. And the tribesmen who were seated around them said, "It is God's truth that Ali deserves all this and more!" Then Hussein said, "This is nothing; his reward is mine to give him. For his noble help to my brother Husam, I give him my sister Hasna!" Then up sprang Ali and kissed his beard, and up sprang Husam and also kissed Hussein's beard, while the tribesmen said, "It is God's truth that he deserves her!" And they bound them to each other as man and wife; Ali and Hasna were married that night.

When two days had passed, Ali asked leave to return to his own people. The camels were saddled and Husam and Hussein rode with him and Hasna until they reached safe territory. Then they took leave of each other, and each went to his own people.

When Ali returned to his tribe, the Arabs gathered about him and greeted him and killed camels and held a feast. Then Ali told them all that he had lived through as the guest of the Beni Khalids—how they had welcomed him and how respectfully and hospitably they had received him. He told of the presents he had received, the priceless mare, and the wife who was Hussein's sister and more beautiful by far than Halima. And the men said "By Allah, that is just, and you deserve it all!" And they drank coffee and each went to his tent.

> There we left them enjoying a life of bliss and delight.
> May God ease the lot of every man in sight.

The Beduin's
Gazelle

Saudi Arabia

A Beduin set out one day with his young son to graze his she-camel and look for wild herbs and roots to take back for his wife to cook. When they had loaded the camel and were heading toward home, a herd of magnificent gazelles suddenly appeared across their path. Silently and quickly the father made the camel lower herself onto her knees, and he slid from her back. Warning the boy not to stray until he returned, he hurried after the gazelles. The wild things leaped into the air and streaked off as soon as he stepped toward them, but the Beduin was a keen hunter and loved nothing better than the chase. Eagerly he followed on their trail.

Meanwhile the tender child waited alone. From destiny there is no escape. It was his fate that a She-Ghoul, that monster of the wilderness who loves to feed on human flesh, should spy him as he stood unprotected. With one leap she sprang upon him and greedily devoured him.

The father hunted long and far but could not catch a single deer. At last he resigned himself and returned without the game. Though the camel was kneeling where he had left it, he could not see his son. He looked on every side, but the boy was gone. Then on the ground he found dark drops of blood. "My son! My son is killed! My son is dead!" he shrieked. Yet what could he do but lead his camel home?

On the way he rode past a cave, and there he saw the She-Ghoul dancing, fresh from her feast, her hanging breasts swinging from side to side like the empty sleeves of the women's cloaks when they rock in mourning over the dead. The Beduin took careful aim and shot the She-Ghoul dead. He slashed open her belly, and in it he found his son. He laid the boy upon his cloak, pulled the woolen cloth around him tight, and so carried him home.

When he reached his tent the Beduin called his wife and said, "I have brought you back a gazelle, dear wife, but as God is my witness, it can be cooked only in a cauldron that has never been used for a meal of sorrow."

The woman went from tent to tent for the loan of such a pot. But one neighbor said, "Sister, we used the large cauldron to cook the rice for the people who came to weep with us when my husband died." And another told her, "We last heated our big cooking pot on the day of my son's funeral." She knocked at every door but did not find what she sought. So she returned to her husband empty-handed.

"Haven't you found the right kind of cauldron?" asked the Beduin. "There is no household but has seen misfortune," she answered. "There is no cauldron but has cooked a meal of mourning." Only then did the Beduin fold back his woolen cloak and say to her, "They have all tasted their share of sorrow. Today the turn is ours. This is my gazelle."

Of such things and the like is the world made, but lucky is the soul that God loves and calls to Himself.

⠒⠒ ⠒⠒ ⠒⠒ ⠒⠒ ⠒⠒ ⠒⠒ ⠒⠒ ⠒⠒ ⠒⠒ ⠒⠒ ⠒⠒

The Prince

in the Pit

⠒⠒ ⠒⠒ ⠒⠒ ⠒⠒ ⠒⠒ ⠒⠒ ⠒⠒ ⠒⠒ ⠒⠒ ⠒⠒ ⠒⠒

Syria

God spoke, and He spoke blessings.

Neither here nor there lived a Beduin prince who had no children. One day he stood under the open sky, uncovered his head, and prayed, "O Lord, bless me with a son and I vow never to ride out with the men on a raid again." A few months went by and the prince's wife found she was with child—sooner count the eggs you break into the pan than the months a woman carries her child. When her time came, she lifted one leg and pushed down the other and brought forth a son as strong and as sturdy as a young ram. From that hour the prince no longer joined the horsemen when they went out riding after loot or vengeance. Instead he stayed among the goat-hair tents and raised his son. The days passed and the boy grew.

One day when the boy was twenty, the chief among the tribesmen came to the prince and said, "O emir of the faithful, you are bound by your vow and cannot take part in our expeditions. But you know that the name of our tribe will be destroyed unless we take up the challenge of our enemies and raid them for every plundering raid they make against us." "You have my leave to go out and plunder as you wish," said the prince. "But what of your renown and your name?" the man went on. "If we cannot be led by our emir, we must at least take his son with us when we go!" At these words the emir paled. "The boy is my only child. I have no other. How can I let him go with you?" he said. "There is nothing to fear," said the man, "we take him only to uphold the honor and the fame of the tribe. He shall do no fighting; I give you my word, and you may have my head if I break it." What could the emir say? He was forced to consent.

Next morning the men set off on their horses and the boy went with them. One hoof lifting them and one hoof setting them down, they did not stop riding until they were three days' journey from their domain. As the men were preparing to set up camp, the emir's man took the boy aside and said, "O my son, do you understand that the foremost man in the tribe is he who serves it?" "Yes, uncle," said the boy, "in what way do you wish me to show my duty to the men?" "Do not ask to ride with us when we go in search of plunder," said the man. "Be content to remain in camp and cook bread for the riders to eat when they return." To this the boy agreed.

When the men left at dawn, the boy stayed alone. He mixed flour with water, enough to feed a whole band that is hungry and worn. He buried the flat dough in hot ashes and covered it with sand. Then he waited. But youth cannot sit still with hands hanging on either side. The boy was eager to follow the raid. At last he sprang into his saddle and took the path they had gone. He rode seven hours before he rested, and he saw neither men nor the dust of their horses. Emptying flour from his saddlebag and water from the waterskin, he set fresh loaves to cook in hot ashes and sand, then continued in pursuit of the men.

He was bent over his baking for the third time when he saw the riders returning, their horses panting beneath the weight of the spoils. "Why so far from the camp?" they asked him. "I wanted a share of the glory," he said, "but my fate is to serve as I promised to serve." He scratched in the sand, and when the men saw the steam rise off the warm loaves, they raised a shout for their prince's son and called on God to make him prosper, for they were broken with weariness and ailing with hunger.

Refreshed, they turned their horses' heads toward home and rode hard over the bare earth, till after seven hours they faltered and stopped. Again the boy dug in the ground and brought out food for his father's men. Well pleased with him, away they flew for seven hours more. But when they neared the place where the youth had first set his dough, they saw the black tents of another tribe pitched over the spot.

"Ride on," said the boy; "I shall follow with our bread." It was dusk, and he waited till darkness to slip in among the tents. But O calamity! where he had buried the dough in the ashes there now was raised a fine pavilion of a tent. Crawling on his belly, he entered it under the sidewall. What did he find? A prince's daughter asleep on her bed with a candle at her feet and a candle at her head. Her brow was of the whiteness of pearl, her cheeks were as smooth as polished silver, and her hair was like braided night smelling of amber. As he looked she opened her eyes, bright as two mirrors. Seeing the boy, she threw back her head to give the alarm.

"My purpose is pure; I come for no mischief," said the boy, "I am looking for the food I baked for my men. It lies buried just where you have laid your bed." "If this is the truth, you may go in peace and God's protection," said the girl. "But if you lie, I have only to shout and the prince my father will cut off your head."

Pulling aside the bedding, the boy uncovered his hoard of bread. When the girl saw that his word was true and that he stood like a hero and the son of a prince, she placed a pouch of boiled butter on top of the loaves and said, "Take this as a gift to eat with your bread, and may Allah smooth your path." But then she stopped him, holding him back by the arm. "To one side of our camp is a deep pit," she said. "Let me lead you through the dark."

Though they picked their way carefully hand in hand through the night, by some mischance the boy stumbled and fell over the edge of the hole. He dropped to the bottom. There was no way to climb out, for the sides were too high and steep. Fetching a tent rope, the girl started to pull him up, but the earth crumbled beneath her feet and she too slid and fell into the trap.

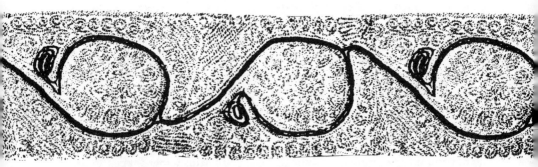

With the first showing of dawn's face, the girl's father, prince of his tribe, walked out of his tent with a pitcher in hand to perform the ablutions that precede the first prayer of the day. Hearing voices, he peered over the rim of the pit and was stricken to discover his own daughter with a stranger, a man not of his tribe.

His prayers forgotten, thinking only of protecting his name, the prince held his palm to the side of his mouth and called, "Up, O Arabs! Break up camp with no delay!" The men murmured, "What is wrong? We arrived but yesterday; must we move again today?" The emir gave them no answer but pulled up the pegs and folded the dark cloth of his tent, then quickly loaded his camel and led it away. Seeing their prince departing, each man packed his own household and followed.

They had traveled half a day when the prince called his black slave. "I left something at our last campsite," he said. "Ride back and look into the great pit. Whatever you find at the bottom, bring me its blood. If you speak but a whisper of what you see, there will be scandal, and you know that it is a lighter thing for me to kill you than to bear the shame."

Murjan, the black slave, mounted a horse of his master's, took up his master's great sword, and did not stop riding until he stood at the rim of the pit. When he saw his own emir's fair daughter with a man, a stranger at that, he bit his finger and cursed her: "Have you not kin enough, well-born and well-formed, that you seek out the company of a Gypsy?" Seeing her father's sword in his hand, the girl wept. "Have you forgotten that I am my father's daughter? Have you known me to do what is forbidden? What will the prince give you for my death? Help me, and we can flee together and seek refuge with another tribe."

The slave was persuaded. He let down a rope and lifted her out. "We must stop the mouth of this man from telling the tale," she said. "Bring firewood, O Murjan, and let us burn him to death." As fast as the slave carried brush and kindling, she threw it to the boy, saying, "Make a pile of it under your feet to help you climb out." To the slave she sighed and said, "This is hot and weary work. Take off your sword belt, Murjan, and lighten your task."

At last the boy was able to clamber out, and seizing the sword that Murjan had discarded, he hid behind the prince's horse. When the slave next hauled up a bundle of wood, he sprang out and severed the man's head from his trunk. Then onto the horse's back he leaped, lifting the girl into the saddle behind him. And chastely placing his sword between them, he dug his heel into the ribs of the horse and shouted, "Open up before me, O path!"

He did not stop riding until he was back at the tents of his tribe. The prince had been waiting for news, good or bad, like one sitting on embers. He kissed his dear son between the eyes and bent his knees twice in a prayer of thanks for his safe return. The men crowded round to embrace him and to hear what had happened since they left him on their ride back from the raid. And when they saw the girl he had brought, they said, "There is no fitter bride for the son of our prince." "If God wills it, it shall be so," said the emir and he sent to the women's quarters to put to the girl the son's wish. "I am willing," she said, "for there is no shame in a thing that is permitted according to the law of the Koran. But will your son be able to pay my price?" "What do you ask for your bride money?" asked the emir. And as she began to list the number of horses and number of camels and the slaves to serve her, all to be branded with her mark, his spirits rose and his heart lifted as if about to take wing with joy. For who else but one who was well-born and a fair match for his son would set so high a bride-price for herself?

Messengers were sent to her father's camp. Then a wedding was held, marked with loud joy and much feasting, for two tribes were thus joined by marriage. And the bride's father, thanking God that she was safe and praying for forgiveness that he had doubted her, departed with gifts of cattle and gold.

> So they lived in peace and in plenty year
>   after year.
> May God send such good fortune to you who sit
>   and hear.

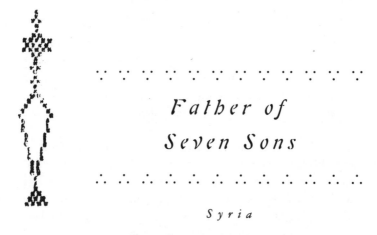

Father of
Seven Sons

Syria

If you love the prophet Mohammad, pray for him!

Neither here nor there lived a prince who—through the bounty of God—had seven sons like fresh dates. Whenever he rode out with them, they sat straight in their saddles and shot where they aimed, even at a gallop, as if they were men, as if they were his brothers.

The boys grew to want wives, and their father swore that he would marry them only to seven sisters, fruit of one back and one belly, like themselves. Now, when a man wants to marry so many sons, he has to travel far to find brides for them—and this prince was searching for a man with seven daughters from the same mother. After many months he was told at last of a Beduin with little wealth who had seven such daughters. So the prince filled his sons' saddlebags with silver and gold and, calling on God's name, set out with them to find the campsite of this Beduin's tribe.

For many days they traveled across the wilderness, one place receiving them and one place sending them on, until they reached the settlement of the Beduin's tribe. He lived in a modest tent on the outskirts of the camp, but he greeted them with all the attentions that custom requires. Though the man spread straw matting on the ground as they entered, the prince remained standing and grasped the central tent post with his hand. He said to his host, "I shall not sit down, by Allah, until I have asked what I have come to ask." The man replied, "Speak your wish, and may nothing but evil be denied you!" So he said, "I am a prince of the Beni Such-and-Such, and I come seeking kinship with you. I want your seven daughters for my seven sons." And the Beduin replied, "It costs nothing to ask for what is dear, but the girls are yours. I ask for no bride-money, neither lump sum nor interest, for it is wealth enough to have ties with one of your standing." For their part, the prince's sons unfastened their saddlebags and tossed them at the Beduin's feet to indicate that they deemed their gift unworthy of his daughters.

Now the tribesmen assembled to begin the celebrations, and music sounded through the nights of jubilation. The words were written which bound the prince's seven sons to the Beduin's daughters, and seven tents were raised—for each couple a tent apart. When the time came, the bridegrooms went in to their brides—may the same come true for all who stand in need—and the people withdrew into the tents to sleep.

With the dawning of the day there was movement and business among the tents. The beasts were butchered for that day's feast. The coffee pounders were beating their rhythms, now together, now each alone, like drummers who are famed far and wide. But the sun rose and the bridegrooms did not appear. The people waited, and the prince's sons did not come out. "Now they'll come. Soon they'll come," the people said. But no one came.

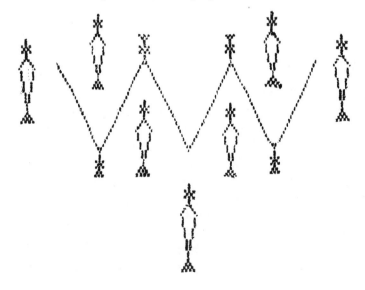

Finally their father went to look for them in the wedding tents. A slave girl met him, her eyes red with weeping and swollen to the size of dumplings. "Lord protect us from bad news! What has happened, girl?" he asked. "May a long life be yours! May God keep you from all sorrow after what has struck your sons!" she said. The prince ran to the tent of his oldest son and found him lying dead, stretched out on his wedding bed with his wife shedding tears as she combed the braids of his hair on her lap. He rushed to the next tent and found the same scene, and in the next. His sons, all seven, were dead, and their brides were wailing and weeping over their heads. When he saw this sight, God help him! May no living man see such a thing, neither friend nor foe! The father wrung his hands and took a seat near the sheikh of the tribe, and the men came in turn to condole. When the poor Beduin, so newly related to him through marriage, stood before him, the prince said, "O uncle, what you had to give, you gave, and I am grateful! But I, what can I say to you now that you are father of seven widows, except 'Whatever comes from God is sweet!' " And he kissed him on each shoulder and bade him farewell.

"Where shall I go? Where shall I turn, O my Lord?" said the prince to himself as he rode. "By God, I cannot return to my own people. They will pity me and say, 'He went with plenty and came back empty.' No, I shall travel about until I meet someone who has suffered as much as I. Only then will I go home." And so he went, following the road before him.

The years went by, and one day the prince came to a big city. He stabled his horse and sat in the coffeehouse filling one pipe and emptying another, spending what he had until his money was all gone. Then he was forced to sell his horse and next its trappings. His gold-threaded headband he exchanged for a length of rope, his silk headcloth for a rag of cotton. How did he look now? No different from a beggar.

Neither crying nor complaining, he who once had been a prince now lived the life of the poor. One day a woman took pity on him, seeing him walking

with the gait of one who commands, yet with rags on his back and nothing
in his hands. She sent her servant to bring him to her house and gave orders
that everything be set before him that a man likes to eat and drink. After
three days of hospitality, the period when a guest must be entertained and
no questions asked, the lady of the house came down to greet the prince
and find out who he was, of what city or what tribe. And slowly as they
talked, he told her his tale from beginning to end.

When she had heard it, the lady said, "My own misfortune is as great,
if not greater. Listen and judge for yourself. My father and his brother were
rich men; their wealth was in gold and such things that fire cannot consume.
Yet neither had a child to sit on his knee. So they went to Mecca in the
month of the Hajj and prayed to Him to Whom all praise and glory. The
Lord is bountiful and His mercy without bound. On their return the two
brothers found that their wives had conceived. On the same day my uncle's
wife gave birth to a son and my mother to me. As they were cutting the
cords, they spoke our names, promising us to each other for husband and
wife.

"When we were both grown, our parents died, and my uncle's son came
to me and said, 'Cousin, you are in my name and I in yours. Let us get
married and keep our parents' pledge.' 'What you say is just and right,' I
told him, and became his wife. For four months only was I a wife; then he
died and left me with child. Though the gold and the houses of my father
and uncle remained to me as a blessing from God, I had no one to call my
own but the poor creature in my belly.

"One day when my time was near, I saw a sand reader in the street. I sent
for him and promised him a fee if he could tell me what my child would
be: boy or girl. He smoothed out his cloth and sprinkled it with sand;
he drew lines and poked holes. Then he lifted his hands in amazement, saying
not a word. 'What do you see?' I asked him. But he just brushed out the
sand and started afresh with new lines and new dots. 'Tell me what you
see,' I said. But he frowned a black frown and shook out the cloth, taking
fresh sand for a third attempt. 'God grant your news is good news!' I prayed,

and at last he spoke. 'This is the last time, and all three times were alike. You shall give birth to a boy, but he shall grow up to be your husband.' 'Change your words; tell me something other than this!' I cried. But he said, 'What God sends is fated and cannot be changed!'

"Go day, come day—the time was due and I gave birth. As the sand reader had said, it was a boy. Now I was afraid. Without pausing to think, I stabbed the child in his belly and bundled it into a cloth and threw it into the ditch by the side of the road.

"Now, unknown to me a peasant woman passing that way home from the market heard the baby crying. She put him into her basket and carried him home and cared for him until he was well. He grew to be like a hero of the tales. His fame spread wide, and his name was counted with the best of men. In time the peasant woman began to think of marrying the youth. 'My son,' she said, 'I should like to eat sweets at your wedding feast before I die. Let me ask for the hand of the rich widow who lives by herself in the house on the way into the city.' The youth agreed, and when all that had to be done was accomplished, we were married—for I was the widow she had meant.

"A few months passed, and then one evening when I was rubbing the youth's back in the bath, his loincloth slipped and I saw a scar where his belly had been sewn. I asked him the history of his wound and he told me what he knew. 'Do you know who you are?' I shrieked. 'They call me the peasant woman's son,' he said. 'But what are your roots? I tell you, you are my son!' And I related to him his history on the day he was born. He went to his mother to ask her again, and when he was certain that what I spoke was the truth, he snatched up a knife and cut short his own life, unable to exist in such shame. And here I remain, with neither father nor uncle nor husband nor son. What a pair we two bereft souls make, abandoned as we are and left hanging in the air!"

When he had heard this story, even worse than his own, the prince was ready to make his way home. Eventually he found the settlement of his tribe. He walked to his own tent and called to his wife, "O mistress of this house, let me in!" "Who are you?" she asked from inside. "A guest at your door," he said. "Guests go to the hall of the sheikh," she told him. "I thought this was the tent of the prince of your tribe," said the prince. And his wife replied, "The prince who was sheikh of the tribe once lived here, but fate willed that he should ride out one day with his seven sons beside him and never return. That was long ago; do not remind us of the sorrows that are behind us."

So the prince went to the guest tent of the new sheikh. It was full and well attended: a company of well-formed and proud-looking youths had entered before him. He greeted the assembled men and quietly took his place, pulling his headcloth across his mouth lest any should know him in his present poverty and want. But when the coffee bearer made his round and the prince let the cover drop as he lifted the cup to drink, the new sheikh knew who he was. He kissed him on the head and welcomed him, saying, "It is a blessed hour when God brings our prince safely home! Rejoice, for the men you see around you are your grandsons—the sons of your sons who died on their wedding night!"

And the prince resumed his place as sheikh and elder of his tribe, and he lived to see his grandchildren wed.

> Well is it with him who submits to the ordinance of God; praises
> be to Him, and exaltation!

A Trip to
Paradise

Saudi Arabia

An Arab of the tribes who live in the desert fell sick and lay in his tent knowing nothing, for his soul had left him and flown away to join the dead. After seven days or eight, God willed that he should be cured and the man regained his senses.

His fellow tribesmen crowded into his tent. "What did you see?" they asked. "God grant that the news you bring is good!" He said, "I saw things of wonder and great beauty, brothers. I found myself at the gates of heaven, and I saw Sayyidna Mohammad sitting on a throne with a sword dancing in his hand. When he looked toward me where I stood, he said, 'This way, welcome, O Beduin; come this way!' And he seated me by his side.

"In a while some city dwellers approached, wanting to enter heaven. To them he said, 'Be off with you! You shopkeepers who tinker with the scale and give false weight cannot enter here!' After they had gone, governors and preachers appeared. 'For you there will never be admittance here,' said the Prophet, and he drove them away. Nor could they find any other gate into paradise. After a little time had passed, the *fellahin,* who till the soil, came up and pressed themselves against the gate like a herd of cattle, impatient to come in. 'You who put a price on your daughters and sell them into wedlock as you sell your young asses shall have no access to this place,' he told them.

"Well, brothers, not long after this, who should come riding up at a gallop astride full-blooded horses but some Beduins, brandishing their spears and waving their inlay swords and wearing such boots, such fine boots— praise be to Allah! Sayyidna Mohammad sprang up and greeted them: 'Welcome, O slayers of souls!' Just as he was leading them into paradise, I slipped away and returned here." "Is there no pasture for camels in paradise?" asked one of the listeners. "Plenty: the grass grows high as my cartridge belt."

Full-Moon-of-the-Night

Egypt

Prince Hasan was out walking one day, his headcloth snapping like a banner on his head and his sword swinging by the side of his leg. He met a young maiden, tall as the sugarcane and as sweet, a water jar on her head and her tread as free and as balanced as that of a young foal. Her grace made him stop in his path. Then he swung his sword with a wide sweep and passed it cleanly between the jar and her head, hurting neither the vessel nor her hair.

The girl laughed, and he saw that her teeth were like hailstones that fall from the sky. She said, "Away with you, Prince Hasan, may the Lord God plague you with the love of Badr-al-Dujja, the daughter of the sultan of Wadi Adan. Her face is the full moon [*badr*] and her camels as black as the night [*dujja*]." The prince turned homeward, his thoughts in a whirl with one wish only in his head, to find Badr-al-Dujja, this Full-Moon-of-the-Night, and see her with his own eye.

He led out his horse and tightened the girth. He packed what he needed to eat and drink in a bag. Then he set off through the mountains and across the world until he had covered great distances, and still he had a way to go.

He met an old shepherd and asked him which was the road, and the man told him, "Ride on and may God make your path even and smooth, for such camels as Badr-al-Dujja milks are not to be found anywhere else on this earth." He rode onward until he saw a stone house shining white like a dove in the distance. When he asked at the door where to find Wadi Adan, the maidservant said, "Ride on and may God cast the mantle of His protection across your path, for the sultan's daughter is such that none has seen her equal in all the lands of the world."

At last the prince reached the desert where live the people of the tents, and he rested in the guest hall of a sheikh. When he inquired about Badr-al-Dujja, none knew her name or how to reach Wadi Adan. But next morning as he prepared to move on, he noticed an old woman spinning in the door of her tent, and the wool on her spindle was camel's hair as black as a night with no moon. "Where do you get such fine wool, O my aunt? I have seen none like it before," said the prince. She pointed to a bird's nest in a thorn tree and said, "I pull it out of that nest. A crow carries it in his beak from behind the steep hills to the south." Now Prince Hasan felt that he held one end of the string. He watched for the bird and waited, and on the third day when it flew to the hills, he followed without letting it out of his sight.

Over rocks and through gullies where the hillside was steep as a city wall Prince Hasan rode. When he had climbed halfway to the sky, he came to a clearing where an old Beduin was watching a herd of camels whose hair was blue-black like the night. Each camel, hobbled and secured to a stake, grazed the rich clover that grew all around. The old man moved the cattle one beast at a time, pulling up each stake and planting it afresh where the

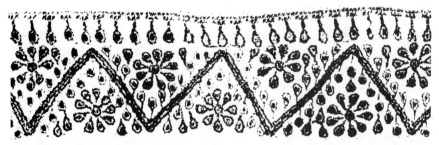

pasture was lush. The herd was so great that when he had moved the last camel, the first had browsed the ground clean and was ready to be moved once more. Up and down the herd the man went, pulling up one stake and pounding in the next, coming and going, pulling and pounding without a rest.

Prince Hasan asked him, "What are you doing, uncle?" And the old man said, "I work for the sultan of Adan. I stake his black camels in his pastures from one year's end to the next." "How much does he give you in wages for your work?" asked Prince Hasan. "By Allah," he said, "my wage, for which I work the whole of the year, is the right to go into the presence of Badr-al-Dujja the sultan's daughter and say, 'Good morning to you O Badr-al-Dujja!' And she says, 'Good morning, O uncle Mohammad.' Then I say, 'May every year bring nothing but good, O Badr-al-Dujja!' And she says, 'And to you also, with peace and good health, O uncle Mohammad!' That is my wage all the year long!" And Prince Hasan said, "Indeed she must be a wonder to behold! Is there much farther to travel before I reach her, brother?" "Wadi Adan lies straight before you," said the shepherd.

So with a beating heart the prince rode down into the city. He bowed in the sultan's presence and wished him peace. Then he told him his tale from the moment he had met the girl with the water jar and how he would know no rest until he had seen the princess Full-Moon-of-the-Night. The sultan said, "But for the old herder who tends the black camels, no man may see her except the bridegroom who unveils her face on her wedding night." "I am here to ask for your kinship. You have but to name the bride-wealth— though nothing of course is equal to her true worth," said the prince. The sultan frowned and replied, "I have sworn that my daughter shall be the bride only of the brave fighter who can bring me victory over the enemies who surround my city. Many are the young horsemen who have ridden out into the fight and their bodies lie buried outside the city wall." "I am willing to offer my life as bride-wealth for the princess Full-Moon-of-the-Night if Allah so wills it," said the prince and nothing that the sultan said could dissuade him.

The next day he tied his red and white headcloth to his lance like a banner and led the sultan's men into battle. The fighting was heated and the men were pressed hard but wherever the prince rode with his sword lashing and flashing like lightning in a storm, the line of the enemy buckled before him. Neither that day nor the next was the battle resolved. But after much bloodshed and many wounds, fighting through many days and many moons, at last Prince Hasan routed the foes of the father of Badr-al-Dujja. If any were left living they fled behind the hills and never turned their faces in the direction of Wadi Adan again.

Then at last were the arms of the sultan used for reasons of joy rather than sorrow. The horsemen rode in formation, tossing their lances into the air, and the guns were fired to celebrate the wedding of Prince Hasan and the Princess Full-Moon-of-the Night.

> They lived together in happiness and joy
> And were blessed with many a girl and boy.

The Jewel in
the Sand

Iraq

Sheikh Hamid, the elder of his tribe, and Ali his sister's son, were riding home together once. To while away the long hours on horseback Sheikh Hamid began to tell a tale. Ali was glad to listen, for his uncle was famed for the sweetness of his tongue, but his mind strayed for a moment when he saw something golden winking in the sand. He was curious, but of course he would be shamed if he interrupted the sheikh's narrative for a trinket of gold. So he let his lance slip through his hand till its point scratched the ground. As the two men rode on, it traced their path all the way to the camp.

As soon as they arrived and were welcomed, the sheikh retired to his tent

to rest. But Ali paused only to instruct his wife to tell all who might ask
for him that he was asleep, and without getting off his horse, he wheeled
about and retraced his steps. The mark of the spearhead led him straight to
the trinket, a finely worked pendant with scrolls and gold beading surrounding the words of God. It was a jewel that would grace no neck but that of
a prince's daughter.

When he returned, Ali's wife said, "Sheikh Hamid has come twice to ask
for you, and I told him you were sleeping within." So Ali hurried to the
sheikh's guest tent, where he found him in the midst of his folk. When Ali
had greeted all the men present, he tossed the gold ornament into his uncle's
lap and sat down. "This is the work of a master of the trade," said the
sheikh, turning it over in his hand. "Tell me its history, son." And Ali
told him all that he knew. "The mistress of so fine a treasure must herself
be rare," the sheikh went on, "and I say that we must find her!"

He summoned the old woman who was midwife to the tribe and said,
"Take this jewel and visit the tribes all around. Find out for us who lost it.
Discover her name, the details of her descent, and the place where her people
pitch their tents."

The old woman went off on her mission. From campsite to campsite she
traveled, stopping wherever people lived. At last she reached a great spread
of black tents and entered the women's quarters of a house that was eight
poles long. She was welcomed by a young woman whose face shone like
white marble, so that she might with justice tell the full moon: "Set, for I
can light the world in your place!" "Welcome, grandmother, and may your
coming be well-omened," said the girl.

When the old woman had sat awhile and rested, she untied the knot at
the corner of her sash and carefully shook out the jewel that Ali had found
in the sand. She explained that she was looking for the owner. The girl
dived into her wooden chest and brought out a gold pendant, the twin of
the first. She shook the two jewels in her clasped hands and invited her
guest to say which was which. The old woman looked carefully but they
were a pair, the work of one man, a great craftsman at that. The midwife
said, "Now that I have found you, take your lost jewel, but tell me your
name and your tribe, my child." The girl replied, "Grandmother, I want
you to keep the jewel you brought me for all the trouble it caused you, and
accept the other because they are a pair."

When the old woman took back the good news and showed the two
pendants as proof of her find, how much more keenly Sheikh Hamid burned
with longing for their owner—a girl with the jewels of a prince's daughter
and the generosity of a prince. In less time than it takes to tell, he had

fitted out a party of his horsemen. Swiftly he set off with Ali his nephew for the girl's camp to ask for her hand.

At the camp with the many black tents, the men came running in welcome, bearing fodder for the horses, while the women spread out the mats on the guest tent floor. Whole sheep and young camels were butchered in plenty. When three days had been spent in feasts and banquets, the prince who was the girl's father asked the sheikh the purpose of his coming. Sheikh Hamid told the story of the jewel, ending with these words: "Then I began to feel a longing for its owner. And discovering that she is your child, I have ridden here to ask for her of you."

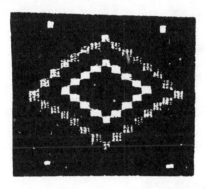

The father sighed. To ask is cheap and a daughter is dear. Yet how could he refuse a guest, one of such standing and send him away empty-handed? He said, "My daughter and my neck bow to you. Take her." The girl was made ready, and seventy camels laden with bedding and carpets, knotted rugs, and plump pillows were led out. A manservant and a slave girl came with her to serve her in her new home. When all was set for travel, the girl's father kissed Sheikh Hamid and said, "God grant that you are blessed in your bride."

So Sheikh Hamid returned to his people with a bride and a sumptuous camel train. A wedding tent was erected on the edge of the camp. The drums began to beat and the music to sound.

Then the sheikh called his nephew and said, "Ali, your bride is in the wedding tent, her eyes rimmed with *kohl* and waiting for her groom." "She is yours, uncle," said Ali. "You were the one to find her and ask for her from her father." But Sheikh Hamid threw the fine wedding cloak over Ali's back and said, "The jewel was your find; none but you shall have her. Hurry to the tent."

Yet as Ali walked toward the wedding tent, a man threw himself on the ground and began to kiss Ali's feet. "Grant me the rights of a guest, Sheikh Hamid," he said, mistaking Ali for his uncle because of the wedding cloak. "Do not deny me, and may God brighten your destiny and good fortune bless your days." "Speak without fear," said Ali. "Then know that this girl is my cousin," said the youth. "We were promised for each other but her father, who is my uncle, could not shame you by a refusal you when you came as a guest to his tent." "You ask for what is yours by right," said Ali. He pulled the wedding cloak off his own shoulders and threw it onto those of the youth, saying, "May you find joy in your bride."

Next morning as Sheikh Hamid was stirring the slaves to prepare a wedding meal, he saw Ali in his old clothes. "Is the feasting done? Are you not a young bridegroom today, son?" he asked, and Ali told him what had happened the night before. Then Sheikh Hamid called for seventy of his best camels to be harnessed and laden with gifts. Adding these to the girl's own train, he sent her and her bridegroom thus enriched back to her own people.

So it is when men are noble!

∴ ∴ ∴

Djinn,
G·h·o·u·l·s,
a·n·d
A·f·r·e·e·t·s

Tales of Magic
and the
Supernatural

.·.

hile the Beduin stories celebrating ideal conduct of noble men and describing adventures of love and war pass the night hours in the men's guest tent, tales of magic peopled with Ghouls and Afreets are distinctly the entertainment of women. These are the household tales proper. Men know the stories well, of course, having heard them as children. But a grown man's world is outside the house, while many great storytellers dwell within it. Where a household is extended to include single daughters and the families of married sons all living under the same roof with a father and his wife or wives, there is almost always someone with a fund of history or magic whose gifts will hold the restless children and draw the adults too. Often it is a grandmother, or maybe a servant grown old in the house but born in another village whose stock of stories, therefore, is not the usual and familiar.

In the winter evenings when the men are out with the men, and the whole female household gathers round a tray of charcoal embers, the women may make a party of it, either telling their own stories or calling in a popular storyteller, some matron known for her "sweet" tongue. Though not a professional like the itinerant reciters of epics, who depend on their art for a living, she may be a working woman like a seamstress or midwife, or a widow with no kin to support her who is happy to share a tasty treat in return for her talk.

Sweet tea heavily scented with mint or rosemary clears the teller's throat, and salt melon seeds, roast chick-peas, and dried figs occupy the listeners. Woe betide the child or thoughtless adult who whispers or moves about once the opening rhyme is spoken:

> *Kan ma kan*
> *Fi qadim azzaman*
>
> There was, there was not,
> In the oldness of time.

A European story usually takes place "once upon a time." In Arabic there is some variety to the opening formula:

> *Kan ma kan*
> *La han wa la han*
>
> There was, there was not,
> Not here, not there.

or

> *Kan ma kan*
> *Ya su'ad ya kiram*
>
> There was, there was not,
> O you who are fortunate, O you who are generous.

The last suggests that the teller is poorer than the listeners and expects to
have reason to be grateful to them at the end of the tale. In the days of the
Ottoman Empire, tales often began:

> *Kan ma kan*
> *Allah yunsur assultan*
>
> There was, there was not,
> Allah send victory to the Sultan.

What never changes is the suggestion of vagueness—there was or there
was not, neither here nor elsewhere. This shrouds the narrative that follows
in a veil of doubt and uncertainty. The teller avoids the judgment that what
she is saying is a chain of lies, for after all, maybe such things did happen—
or maybe not. But more important, this kind of jingle may act as a charm
protecting the teller and her listeners from any harm.

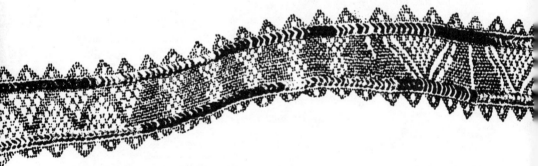

The power of the spoken word is magic, strong enough to attract unknown
forces of evil. It is not only the princesses in the tales who have to remain
silent until the right invocation is uttered. In everyday conversation there
is no mention of death, sickness, or accident without the immediate addition
of "May Allah keep such and all hateful things from you," or more briefly,
"[May it stay] Far from you!" Fearing the evil eye, women will hastily cover
the face of an infant if it is admired without the protective words *mashallah*
or *'smallah* ("It is what Allah wills," or "May Allah's name be upon him").

How much more threatening, then, to embark on a story in which the names of the Ghouls, the Djinn, and the Afreets are bandied about and their deeds described. With the spirits so close at hand, invisible but within earshot just beyond the spot where the house light falls on the threshold, it is as well to place a safety curtain between their mysterious world and ours. It would not do to stir them up.

At the beginning of a story the teller often calls on the audience to pronounce the name of Allah. "No talk is sweet which does not mention God!" the speaker may say. This is the cue for listeners to proclaim that there is no God but God. Or she might say, "O you who love the prophet, pray for him," eliciting a chorus of "A thousand prayers and peace be on you, O prophet of God!" Christians will say, "Pray for the Virgin Mary." Even stories told as factual anecdotes may begin, "There was a one—God alone is unique— . . ." or "There was a wealthy man—what riches compare with God's . . ." As a man walking out into the dark will murmur a protective *bismillah* "in the name of Allah," so it is auspicious at the beginning of a tale to speak the name of God.

There is in the Koran a whole *sura*, or chapter, named for the Djinn. Indeed, just as God created man from potter's clay, so he formed the Djinn from a smokeless fire. He sent the prophet to enlighten both worlds of sentient beings, that of the Ins, or humans, and that of the Djinn, or spirits. Much of the excitement in the tales of magic lies in the removal of the boundary between the two worlds. Whether they are potential helpers to be wooed or dangerous enemies to be overcome, the spirits are as much a part of the landscape as the heroes. When a merchant watering his camels pulls a handsome youth up from the bottom of the well with his rope, or when a prince hunting in the wilderness comes upon a girl whose hair shines like threads of gold, the question "Are you Ins or are you Djinn?" is asked as a matter of course.

To the ranks of the Djinn belong the Ghoul, the She-Ghoul, and the terrible Afreet, snatcher of women. It is an Afreet who, in the Koran, offers to carry the throne of the Queen of Sheba from her kingdom in Yemen to Solomon in Jerusalem. For God had made the Djinn subject to King Solomon for the duration of his life, placing their great strength and skills at his service. Often a magic formula will begin, "In the name of Suleyman (i.e., Solomon) the prophet. . . ."

In the popular imagination the Djinn are also master craftsmen, especially in metal. No human is able to copy their work. Knowing this, the fair maiden in "The Bird of the Golden Feather" agrees to be married, but only to him who can duplicate her earring. The guild of goldsmiths is in despair:

it is beyond their combined ability. The heroine would be worried indeed if it were otherwise: having given the earring's mate to the man she loves, she expects no one else to match it. A similar device is important to the plot of "The Ring of the King of the Djinn."

In appearance and power the Djinn are frightening; three sisters in one story faint outright on seeing them. Their strength is overwhelming: they enter a house by cracking the wall open from ceiling to floor. To face them is like facing a storm, and the earth itself trembles at their tread. Yet their wits are rarely equal to their might. Legend has it that Solomon died leaning on his stick and continued standing upright long after his death. The Djinn, deceived, went on fearing him until a worm riddled the wood and the stick crumbled under the weight of his body, and at last he fell.

Mere men can easily outwit the Djinn. In "A Tale Within a Tale" the hero escapes from a white-haired spirit who is about to behead him by begging to be allowed to say one last prayer. It does not occur to the spirit that the rug on which the man stands is no prayer mat but a magic carpet, and that it is not the name of Allah but a magic formula that he is reciting. Later in the same tale two young Djinn are cheated of their inheritance by the simple device of being made to race for a distant stone while the hero makes off with their property.

Wildest and most repulsive-looking of the spirits are the Ghouls. Hairy and unkempt, their teeth are long and sometimes made of brass. They love to eat men and can scent human flesh acutely. Their set entrance speech to the human hero who has stammered his *salaam* or "Peace be with you" is something like—

> *Lawla salaamak*
> *Sabaq kalaamak*
>
> Had not your greeting
> Come first before your speaking,
> I would have torn your muscles each from each
> And used your bones to pick my teeth.

And yet they often prove surprisingly sentimental and good natured, particularly when humored. Not only do they respond to good manners, but in return for a little grooming or a taste of mastic gum, they seem ready to carry the hero wherever he wishes. Make no mistake; their diet is carrion and preferably human flesh, but the wise hero knows how to disarm them.

In the case of the *ghouleh*, the monstrous sister or mother of the Ghouls, the trick is to establish a foster relationship. The She-Ghoul is most often met squatting at her hand mill busily working, her pendulous breasts flung over her shoulders out of the way. If the hero manages to creep up and suck from her breast, she will treat him as a child of her bosom and protect him even from her own Ghoul children. The "milk relationship" is a real one in Islam. If they were nursed from the same breast as infants, two otherwise betrothable people are "milk brother and sister" and therefore unable to marry.

The Djinn are never far away. They inhabit a world just beyond the world of men, beneath the seventh layer of the earth. It is an easy enough place to stray into if one is a hero or a fool. Any abandoned well or cistern, any lonely cave or ruin may have an Afreet or a giant Marid waiting in it. The ghoulish presence may be visible or unseen, or it may take the shape of a human or an animal (most often a black cat or a dog). Luckily the spirit world is so different from our own that there is no mistaking it. In it a lighted candle will make its bearer invisible. A resting demon's eyes will fall open when his sleep is deepest. One blow of a sword will kill, but two will bring to life; and so on. With guidance from a friendly inhabitant, a hero may travel through it unscathed.

Also fortunate is the fact that even terrible monsters are vulnerable to him who knows their weakness or the secret to undoing their chains. A sprinkle of water can break a spell, for example. In "The Camel Husband" the spirit banquet becomes visible after a shower of rain. And the strongest demon depends for his life on three white hairs that grow between his eyes, or a fragile flask, tied to a deer's hind leg in which he hides his soul. Once the rules are set and the obstacles identified, the listener can happily settle down and follow the hero as he picks his way to the triumphant finish.

To add to the drama of the journey (and the tale) there is the sumptuousness of the supernatural world. Banquets are always laid for forty—since Noah's flood, a number meaning more than plenty. Diners sit on thrones of gold. Dishes come and go of their own accord, and even speak. Birds have golden plumage, and palaces of the Djinn are built with bricks of silver and of gold. Spirit women are more beautiful and their horses fleeter than their earthly counterparts.

And yet despite the props, the Djinn go about their lives (through the air, to be sure) with the same trials and bothers as humans. The king of the Djinn in "One-Tooth and Two-Teeth" is suffering from a boil in the back of his throat. In "The Ring of the King of the Djinn" the Ghoul, like any Arab host, is unable to refuse his guest's request. The spirits suffer the pains of jealousy. They fall in love, even with humans, and marry them, as in "The Camel Husband." Like men, they can be good and bad: there is the benign Ghoul who hounds Sit Lahab for her own good, and the evil ogre of "The Woodcutter's Wealthy Sister."

However unearthly their nature, the Djinns' existence was disturbingly real for most people who listened to the stories about them. Many a personal tale is told of actual meetings with the spirits. Quoted as fact is the adventure of the woman who agreed to go out early with her neighbor so that they could fill their jars without being crowded at the well. In the middle of the night, when the moon shone as if it were first light, she was awakened by what she thought was her friend. Only when she saw sparks flying from hooves beneath the dress of the creature walking in front of her did she understand that it was long before dawn and she was alone with a *djinniyeh* of the night.

And many and many is the time that a person has wasted away for no explicable reason—like the sister in "The Girl Who Banished Seven Youths"—and a religious sheikh or a dervish of the wandering brotherhood of mystics has had to be called in to save the sufferer. The inscription of an amulet, or perhaps a flogging with twigs of pomegranate (the tree that grows in paradise), has been known to drive off whatever harmful spirit was "riding" the invalid. Similarly, in the stories when the hero is on the brink of entering the dubious world of the Djinn, he meets a man in a white turban, like a sheikh or in some parts, a hermit, who gives him a talisman to see him through.

Like the opening formulas, the ending of the stories is frequently in rhyme. A popular couplet goes—

Tuteh tuteh
Khilsat al hadduteh

Mulberry, mulberry,
Here ends my story.

There are several of these couplets scattered among the stories in the text. Where the storyteller is hoping for something for herself, she might drop a hint such as,

My story I have told to you.
One-half of it is far from true.
But if you thought it a good try,
Give me a taste of yeast-dough fry.

or

> Now, if my house were on this street,
> I'd fetch three pomegranates to eat.
> One would be for me,
> One for Imm Ali [name of teller]
> And one for the teller of the story!

In a more subtle style, the storyteller who describes the marriage of a prince and princess then reminds the listeners that some are not so fortunate:

> We were with the happy pair
> But returned just as we were.

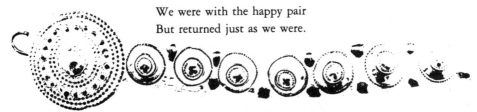

Some say that by disassociating himself from the splendors listed in the story, the teller is warding off the evil eye. He is making clear that he has gained nothing for himself and is in no way to be envied. A quaint verse formula recorded in Morocco a century ago seems to bear this out:

> I traveled up this road, and I traveled down that.
> What have I to show for it? Nothing flat.
> All I brought were slippers made of straw
> Which I took off and left by the door.
> A silly calf ate them, soles and all.

The Arabic equivalent of "and they lived happily ever after" would be a rhyme like:

> God sent them children, both girls and boys,
> And they lived in great bliss and great joy
> Until He parted them, Who everything destroys.

Or

> We left them happy, and back we came.
> May Allah make your life the same!

This last is employing word magic to attract good luck. For again, it is polite when mentioning a success or stroke of good fortune—say, the graduation of a son, or marriage of a daughter—to add, "May God bring the same to you and all who stand in need."

∴ *A Curtain Raiser* ∴

Sometimes in order to hush the audience and warm up her voice, the story-teller recited not just the short rhyming couplet of the opening formula but an extensive passage in rough verse. In Syria this is called the *bisat*, literally "carpet," in the sense of presentation, of smoothing the way for bringing a topic onto the carpet. In Egypt the word is *dahliz*, or entrance lobby, leading to the main subject of the evening.

Totally unconnected with the tale, this is a passage in a peculiarly Arabic form, rhyming prose, in which sentences of unequal length and unpredictable meter end in an identical or echoing sound. The subject matter can range from praises of our lady Fatima, the daughter of the prophet, to meaningless nonsense like

> *Untaq turuntaq*
> Roast lamb and *waraq* [grape leaves]:
> Pull it by the ear,
> Out runs butter clear . . .

To prepare the way for us as we enter the strange world of the tales of magic and the supernatural, here is a *bisat* from Iraq.

THE OLD WOMAN OF KARAMAN
There was—or was there?
Not here, not elsewhere,
An old woman from Karaman.
Who loved her? No man.
With a comb of wood inside her purse
Upon her grey locks a curse!
She walked to the town
In a pistachio gown
And a veil the color of aubergine.
Into the spice market she went,
Over the grocer she leant,
And she said,
"Do you have peppers both black and red,
And the root that burns like a flame?"
He asked, "For whom do you want the same?"
She answered with disdain:

"For her whom they call the Beauty of Our Time,
Whose brow is as graceful of line
As the moon's crescent in the month of Sha'ban.
Her cheeks are two apples from the gardens of Sham.
Her lashes a flourish of the calligrapher's quill,
Her eyes as wide as those of the gazelle.
Her lips are soft as the cotton boll,
Her teeth, pearls set in coral.
Her nose is curved as a sultan's scimitar,
Her neck long and slim as a candelabra.
The parting of her breasts is wide as the road,
Her belly as soft as the risen dough,
And her navel as deep as a coffee cup . . ."
"Where can I find her?"
Shouted the grocer.
"Don a wide turban of lavender,
Fill your pockets with gold and silver,
Ride a horse full-blooded and dapper,
Go down into the passageway
Hung with silk bright and gay.
Sound the bell—
You'll hear its knell.
When you see a slave girl the color of slate,
Bearing on her head a round silver plate,
Hurry and run and go after her!"
How that poor grocer man
After the servant ran!
He entered a palace yard
Paved with marble shards.
He stood beside the pool
Where golden fish swam in water cool.
A feast was brought on a polished tray,
But he could not eat; it was borne away.
He saw a threaded needle and it cried,
"I weep because the needy wield me; by the hands of the poor I am plied,
Yet here poverty is banished and want kept at bay."
He walked beneath full orange trees
And heard the fruit speak words like these:
"I weep because my peel is bitter as the truth,
Yet here all words are sweet."

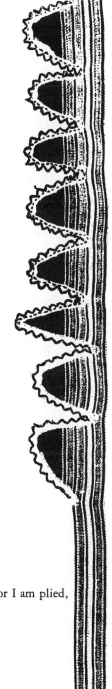

He passed a blooming jasmine
And the blossom said to him,
"I am the flower that scents the breeze.
Here, the hearts of parted lovers even feel at ease."
And a rosebush rustled and whispered,
"I am the rose of Damascus, queen among flowers.
I weep that my tears become an essence in your long-necked bottles.
Though I visit for a month and hide for a year,
My perfume sweetens the generations year after year."
He pushed a door in a white stone wall
And found himself in a long marble hall.
In its center a brazier with red embers gleamed;
On the hot charcoal two coffeepots steamed.
A tray stood nearby with two cups.
One of them spoke when he picked it up.
"O coffee brewer, so handsome of face,
Pour coffee for the guests,
That their hearts may bless you."
He lifted his eyes and saw on a couch reclined
Her whom they call the Beauty of Our Time.
She leaned toward him and touched him with a wand
And in a second his soul returned.
Once more he was a grocer man,
Standing before the witch of Karaman,
Grinding pepper both black and red,
And the root that burns like a flame.

The Girl Who Spoke Jasmines and Lilies

Iraq

Neither here nor elsewhere lived a merchant whose years were many and whose riches were countless. His home was a palace like that of a king, and men bowed to him when he came and when he went.

One morning he called the eldest of his three daughters and said, "Can you explain how I came to be so wealthy and so respected?" The girl had been schooled and tutored by the wisest and most learned teachers, and she pursed her dainty mouth no larger than a lady's ring and said, "All that is yours you have won through your efforts." The merchant was pleased with this answer, and he stroked her hair and sent her for her middle sister. This second daughter was able to satisfy him as well as the first. But when his youngest daughter came to sit next to him and be questioned, she said, "These and all other blessings are from Allah." Angered, her father said, "Since you place so little value on what I can do for you, go and discover how many are the blessings of Allah!"

The girl tied a few clothes into a kerchief and, trusting herself to God's protection, stepped out of her father's house. She had no idea where to turn, so she walked in the direction that her face was pointing until she came to some ramshackle sheds. Mule drivers were using them for stabling their animals, and here she felt safe for the night. Next morning one of the men told her that he was looking for a wife, though he had little to spend on bride-money. She said, "You have nothing to give and I have nowhere to live. 'The cooking pot has found its lid.' With God's will we are a well-matched pair." And she married him.

When the months had passed, the mule driver's wife gave birth to a baby daughter so faultlessly fair that the midwives could not help but say, "All praise to her Creator!" And when they dipped her in the metal basin to give her a bath, they found that every drop of water that rolled off her limbs turned into a spangle of gold. And whenever the child spoke, jasmines and lilies fell from her lips. Nothing is impossible with the Almighty.

Thus where there had been poverty, now there was prosperity, and distress became success. On the land where the mule sheds had stood, a fine mansion rose every bit as tall and costly as the merchant's house. Marvels do not remain hidden long. The news was carried from tongue to tongue and the merchant's older daughters came running to see with their own eyes whether their little sister who had married the mule driver was indeed living like a queen. They went home biting their fingers with envy.

When it is time for the marriage of a handsome girl whose lips let fall jasmines and lilies every time she speaks, who but a prince deserves her? Soon enough, from a distant city across the desert came a king's son riding his camel to ask for the far-famed maiden. The *qadi* was brought to write the writing that bound the son of King So-and-So to the daughter of Such-and-Such a mule driver. Then the prince returned to his own country to prepare the welcome for the train of camels that would transport his bride when all her gowns had been stitched with blue threads and red and she was equipped to go to her husband's house to be wed.

How it twisted the older daughters' faces to look on while their niece prepared to take her place by a prince's side! "Sister," said the eldest to the bride's mother, "the child is far too fine and years too young to travel without companions. And who is there more fitting than her own aunt and her aunt's daughter to protect her and entertain her on the way?" The mule driver's wife agreed. The camel girths were tightened. The bride climbed into the curtained bridal litter and the camel drivers turned their beasts' heads toward the desert.

They journeyed for many days until they were far from any town or village. The girl grew thirsty and asked for water. But her aunt said, "If you drink, there will not be enough for us." The girl's throat became dry and her mouth as hard as wood. She begged for water, if only a drop. Her aunt said, "I am saving the water for your cousin. If you die, she must be able to sit in your place." The girl wept and asked again, and at last the woman said,

> I'll give you water by and by,
> But first I'll have your right eye.

What could the maiden do? For a few sips she let her aunt cut out her right eye.

One day passed and another, and then the girl felt thirsty again. She pleaded with her aunt for water and her aunt said,

> I'll give you water by and by,
> But first I'll have your left eye.

The maiden surrendered to the inevitable and her aunt cut out the other eye. Her aunt said, "Now that you're blind, you are no bride for a prince! My daughter must ride the litter." Then she threw the girl off her camel and rode on, abandoning her in that wilderness.

Having no eyes to see where she was or where she should go, the poor mule driver's daughter began to walk, step after step until she stumbled for weariness and fell asleep. A poor man, old and white-haired, came riding by on his donkey. His heart was moved to pity by the beautiful girl all alone and unprotected. Setting her on his donkey's back, he led her to his home. But when his people saw what he had brought into the house—a girl, and a girl who could not see—they fell upon him, saying, "Have we not calamities enough that you bring us a new one: one that will need feeding and care?"

Now the maiden spoke and said, "Grant me a stranger's favor and bring me water to wash in." The women of the house, seeing the sweet jasmines and lilies falling as she spoke, hurried to catch the blossoms. "What kind of wonder is this girl?" they said to themselves, and did not linger but did as they were bid. In less time than it takes to go from here to there, the bowl in which she had bathed her face was filled with coins of gold. How they kissed her then!

Meanwhile the aunt and her daughter were welcomed by the prince. Horsemen rode out of the city to meet them. Musicians accompanied them through the streets with great festivity. But when the prince was able to sit alone with his bride, he saw that she was different in shape from before. When they spoke together, no jasmines and no lilies fell from her lips. The prince asked her the reason, and  she said that every flower has its season. A doubt entered the prince's heart. He asked to see the ring that he had given her in her mother's house. She said, "I lost it." Now the prince was certain that this was not his bride. But what should he do? If he spoke, he would blacken his own face in the sight of his family and his people. So he kept silent.

Let us retrace our steps to the blind girl. One day she said to the old man with white hair, "Take this basketful of jasmines and lilies to the city where the prince has his palace. Peddle them in the streets and say this and this and this." The old man went. From house to house he called,

> I sell jasmines, I sell lilies!
> I don't want silver, I don't want money!
> The basketful for one eye, my lady!

Who heard him? The aunt. Her daughter had to have jasmines and lilies to show the prince, so she cut out the girl's right eye and exchanged it for the basket-load of flowers.

When the old man brought her cousin's eye to the blind girl, she prayed to God, bending her knees twice, and set it where her own eye had been. Praise be to Allah! She closed her eye and opened it and it was as if it had never been sightless! When the prince came home that evening, his bride sat with her neck turned so that only one side of her face showed. She said, "While you were hunting, look: a whole basketful of blossoms fell from my lips."

Next day the old man returned to the city with another basket of flowers. He offered them up and down the streets, calling,

> I sell jasmines and I sell lilies!
> I don't want silver, I don't want money!
> The basketful for one eye, my lady!

This time the aunt cut out her daughter's left eye to trade for the flowers. When the prince came home from hunting, he found his bride lying in her bed with her headcloth pulled over her face. She said, "I am sick; my head aches from much talking, but look how many jasmines and lilies fell from my lips today!"

And the blind girl? She wasn't blind any longer. When the old man brought her the cousin's left eye, she placed it where her other eye had been and said a prayer to Allah. Now she could see as well as before, and not a sign was there that her eyes had ever been sightless.

The mule driver's daughter bid the old man and his family goodbye. She gave them the rich robes she had worn as a bride and asked for the clothes of a boy in return. Then she set out for the prince's city.

When she reached the palace she spoke to the gardener. "Uncle, I am poor," she said. "Will you let me live near you and work for you? I can lead the mule that drives the millstone." The gardener, seeing the blossoms that fell from her lips, said, "Yes, my son." So every day the girl led the

mule round and round while it pulled the spoke that turned the heavy millstone and ground the wheat.

After noon, when everyone in the palace was resting, the girl would creep down to one of the pools in the palace garden. Taking the boy's clothes off her back and the rings off her fingers, she would bathe. The mule, catching sight of the fairness of her skin and the beauty of her unbound hair, would trot round and round to see it again and again. And the next day's flour would be ground and ready long before sundown.

The cooks in the kitchen were astonished. "The new boy who works for the gardener is slight as a bamboo cane," they said, "yet he can grind the flour by the time the call comes to afternoon prayer. It used to take till sundown!" The prince overheard them and decided to seek how this could be.

Next morning he hid in the garden near the mill. In the middle of the day he watched as the girl took the boy's clothes off her back and the rings off each of her fingers to bathe. He saw the mule breaking into a trot at the sight and the millstone turn, Drrn! Drrn! as fast as it could go. When the girl was not looking, the prince stole to where her ten rings were lying on the edge of the pool and took one. It was a brother to the ring he had given his bride when he went to ask her father for her hand.

Now the girl came out of the water to dress. She slipped on her rings and—eh!—something was not right. She spread out her fingers and counted: "This one has one, this one has one, this one has one . . ." Then she came to her little finger, she said, "This one has *none!*" She counted a second time, and still her little finger had none.

The girl was beginning to cry over her lost ring when the prince jumped out of his hiding place and said, "Here is your ring. But first tell me, who are you? I want to hear your story from beginning to end, forgetting nothing."

So the prince found his true bride. He sent the jealous aunt and her daughter back to their own city and held a new wedding feast that lasted forty days and forty nights without stopping.

> I left them happy, and home I came.
> May all your lives be the same!

⠒ ⠒ ⠒ ⠒ ⠒ ⠒ ⠒ ⠒ ⠒ ⠒ ⠒ ⠒

The Bird of
the Golden Feather

⠒ ⠒ ⠒ ⠒ ⠒ ⠒ ⠒ ⠒ ⠒ ⠒ ⠒ ⠒

Syria

There was or there was not a king who had three sons. One day as he was sitting in the hall of his palace, a bird flew in and plucked a hair off the king's chin. "What kind of bird is this, I wonder," said the king. On the next day at the same time the bird returned and, in one darting movement, made off with another hair from the king's beard. "Why is this bird plaguing me?" said the king, angry now. On the third day when the bird swooped in at the open window, the king stood up and tried to catch it, but all he could grasp was one feather from its tail. Look, and what did he see? A feather of pure gold!

The king called for his minister and said, "O *wazir*, tell me what I must do about a bird who comes every morning and steals a hair off my chin. A little more of this and I shall go beardless!" The *wazir* answered, "O king of our age, this is a wonder never seen or told of before. It is a puzzle for no one but your three sons to solve. They must catch the Bird of the Golden Feather."

So what did the king do? Early next morning he gave his blessing to the three princes, who departed on their journey saying, "May Allah will it that we do not return without the bird with the beautiful feather!"

From city to city they traveled, laying down their heads in one place and raising them in the next until they had gone a distance of forty days. On the following noon they came to a parting of the ways. Here they found a smooth slab of stone on which was carved,

> This way lies the Road of the Burning
> This way lies the Road of the Drowning
> This way lies the Road of No Returning

Wondering what they should do next, the princes stood in front of the stone and looked at the three paths before them. Then the youngest prince, Ala'i, spoke and said, "Brothers, let each of us choose a road to follow. But before we part, let us leave our rings beneath the stone until we have returned once

more to this place. Only so shall we know who has gone and who has come."
So they pulled off their rings and hid them under the stone. Then they
embraced each other and each headed off in a different direction.

Let the two older princes go their way, one along the Road of the Burning
and the other on the Road of the Drowning. We shall stay with the youngest,
Prince Ala'i.

Starting down the Road of No Returning, he walked swinging one hand
before him and one hand behind, day after day, until he came to a mountain.
One foot lifting him, one foot setting him down, he climbed step on step
until he came to the top. But what is this thing that is like another mountain
in the middle of the road? Why, a Ghoul, with hair as knotted as the nest
of a bird and teeth hanging down to his chin! Yammah! O my mother! But
Ala'i had brought some mastic gum to chew on when he felt like something
under his teeth, and he popped a lump of it into the monster's mouth and
sweetened his tongue. "May Allah sweeten your days!" said the Ghoul,
delighted. "Listen to me and let me carry you back, my son. The bird that
you seek is difficult to catch." "As surely as I wish you a long life, uncle
Ghoul," said Ala'i, "I cannot turn back—not if a hundred deaths await me."
"Then you must consult my brother, who is older than I am by one day
but wiser by an age," said the Ghoul, and showed Ala'i the way.

The second Ghoul was as horrible as the first. His hair was matted like
the wool of a mattress before the carder has come, and it had grown so long
that it covered his eyes. Ala'i trimmed it with his knife, and the Ghoul
said, "You have restored my sight! May Allah give you clear vision in all
that you do. Believe me when I say that the best help I can offer is to take
you to my brother, who is older than I am by one day but wiser by an age."
And without straying or turning either left or right, he took Ala'i to the
third Ghoul.

The prince kissed this monster's hands and trimmed his nails and shaved
his face until the third Ghoul was as pleased as his two brothers, and more.
"Listen to one who knows," he said, "and let me carry you home." "I can
only travel forwards; I do not know how to go back," said Ala'i, "and if
death finds me on the way, then I have only met my destiny." "It is in
Allah's hands, then," said the Ghoul. "Climb onto my back and I shall fly
with you to the Garden of the Birdcages."

When they stood at the gate of the garden, the Ghoul said, "This far and
no more can I come. You must enter alone. In the center of the orchard is
an arbor covered with vines. Inside it, in a golden cage, hangs the bird you
want. Take your bird in its cage, but touch nothing else inside the garden."

Fine. Ala'i made for the arbor in the middle of the orchard, as the Ghoul had told him. When he entered, it was not like passing from sunlight into shade, as in an ordinary grape arbor, but like walking from darkness into the heart of a lamp. For the whole place seemed to be lit by the bird's plumage, which was of shining gold. Ala'i took his bird in its cage and started back. But the eye is greedy. When the young prince saw the hundreds upon hundreds of birdcages hanging like ripe figs from the branches of the trees in the garden, and when he saw the birds with feathers of blue and yellow and red—well, he wanted one for himself. "Do I come this far every day?" he said.

But no sooner had he laid his hand on the second cage than a deafening cry filled the garden. Every bird in every tree opened its beak and began to call, "A stranger! A stranger!" On the instant an army of men surrounded Ala'i, and though he unsheathed his sword to fight them, they were too many. Very quickly they tied his hands and marched him to their king.

"Is this the dog who dares to steal our treasures?" said the king. "Cut off his head." But Ala'i spoke and said, "Will you shed royal blood for the sake of a bird? For as you are king and a son of kings, so am I the son of a king." The king thought and then said, "Since you are no common thief but a prince, I shall let you go. I am willing even to make you a gift of the Bird of the Golden Feather. But first you must bring me the Horse Who Leaves All Others Behind." "You shall have that horse," promised Ala'i, and returned to the Ghoul.

While the prince was still some distance away, the Ghoul began to shout and upbraid him. "I would kill you now if, having carried you on my shoulder, I did not look upon you as a younger brother! Didn't I tell you to take only the bird of gold and nothing else? Your greed has nearly cost

you your life!" "What has happened is past," said Ala'i. "I shall have the bird as soon as I bring the king the Horse Who Leaves All Others Behind." But the Ghoul said, "Think neither of horse nor bird. Think only of returning home!"

Did Ala'i listen to the Ghoul? Of course not. Rather face death than the disgrace of returning empty-handed! There was nothing for the Ghoul to do but take Ala'i to the Horse Who Leaves All Others Behind. At the gate of the stable the Ghoul said, "This time do not forget my advice. Go into the stall where the horse is tethered and saddle him with the saddle that is hanging there. But be sure to ride back to me without touching any of the things you see. Remember!" "I'll remember," said Ala'i and opened the gate.

He found the horse and did all that the Ghoul had told him. But just as he was riding away, his eye was caught by a row of swords and daggers hanging on the wall. They shone with the colors of precious gems, for their hilts were studded with jewels, and Ala'i longed to own a weapon so finely worked. "Who would know among so many if I took only one?" he said, and reached for a saber that pleased him. But he had hardly touched it when the whole building seemed to shout, "A stranger! A stranger!" In a minute a thousand men surrounded him and took him to the king.

"Kill the dog who tried to steal from us," said the king. And Ala'i said, "Tell me the price of your horse and I will give you more, for as you are a king, so am I the son of a king." The king then said, "Since you are a prince and wish for my horse, you may take it as a gift. But first you must bring me the One Who Excels All Maidens for Beauty, Badiat-ul-Jamal." "You shall have her," said Ala'i and left the king's presence.

The Ghoul was waiting for him with impatience. "How much longer, O Allah, is this youth destined to trouble me?" he said. And Ala'i told him, "I have but one wish more: I want to find the city of Badiat-ul-Jamal." "And I will take you to your own city, and to no other!" replied the Ghoul. Then Ala'i kissed the Ghoul's hands and said, "You have been like a father to me. Is it not ignoble to come this far and fail?" Well, when Ala'i begged in this way, could the Ghoul help but give in? No. He picked him up and flew with him to the land of Badiat-ul-Jamal.

Soon they stood at the outskirts of her city. The Ghoul lit a candle and said, "As long as you hold this in your hand, no one can see you. Walk through the city until you reach the palace. Enter the palace and look for the princess's chamber. You will find her lying on her bed. If her eyes are yellow—O misery and wretchedness! turn your back on her and return to me. But if her eyes are red, then yours is joy and happiness. Wrap the braids of her hair about your wrist and bring her with you."

When Ala'i stood at the princess's bedside, her eyes were red as blood. He twisted her hair in his hand and said, "Come, O Badiat!" Out of the palace gates, through the city streets, and beyond the city wall he led her without stopping once until he rejoined the Ghoul. The Ghoul lifted each of them onto one of his shoulders and flew straight to the land of the king who owned the Horse Who Leaves All Others Behind.

The Ghoul said, "Now take the girl to the king and he will give you the horse." "Aywah!" said Ala'i. "Let him keep the horse as long as he lives, for I shall never give up the princess. Allah bears witness to what I say!" "This cannot be!" said the Ghoul. "It shall!" said Ala'i. At last the Ghoul said, "Listen to me, Ala'i. I shall take the place of Badiat-ul-Jamal, and you can give me to the king. Tell him that the princess is weak from her journey, not only hungry but thirsty. Tell them to give her what food they have, but to be sure to offer her only rose water for her thirst; she must not drink anything else."

With a shake of his body, the Ghoul changed shape. What did he become? A sister to Badiat-ul-Jamal. How happy was the king when he caught sight of the Ghoul in this form! "Quickly take her to the palace," he said, and commanded his grooms to lead out the Horse Who Leaves All Others Behind for Ala'i. Before mounting, the prince explained to the king that Badiat-ul-Jamal was hungry and thirsty and that she could drink only rose water.

The palace slaves brought dishes filled with the daintiest foods for the Ghoul to dine on, as well as a pitcher of rose water. The Ghoul drank and asked for more. They brought him a larger jug, and what did he do? He jumped feet first into its mouth and plunged into the rose water and disappeared from sight.

The Ghoul caught up with Ala'i, who was riding the horse with the princess behind him. On and on they traveled till they came to the land of the Bird of the Golden Feather. Here the Ghoul stopped and said, "Now Ala'i, give the horse to the king and let us take the bird for your father." But Ala'i said, "This shall never be! I cannot give up a horse as strong and fast as this one." "If Allah wills a thing, it comes about," said the Ghoul. And he gave a violent shudder and transformed himself into a horse. "Ala'i," he said, "keep your horse and take me to the king. But remember to tell him that I feed on shelled almonds and drink only rose water."

The king was very pleased to receive so fine a horse and gladly handed Ala'i the cage with the Bird of the Golden Feather. "This is a horse like no other," said Ala'i. "He will accept only peeled almonds to eat and rose water to drink." Then he left. The grooms of the royal stable filled the Ghoul's trough with rose water, and the Ghoul bent his sleek horse's neck, curving like the moon's crescent, and dipped his nose into the rose water. Then, diving headfirst, he vanished, leaving not a trace.

Walk, walk, Ala'i and the Ghoul traveled with the princess and the bird and the horse till they came upon the second Ghoul. The second Ghoul accompanied them to the mountain where the first Ghoul lived, and from there Ala'i rode on alone, seating the princess behind him on the horse and holding the golden birdcage in his hand. At the parting of the ways, he looked under the stone slab and found one ring: his own. He knew then

that his brothers had returned and retrieved their rings, and he began the journey back to his father's kingdom.

In the evening he came to a city. He rented a room in the *khan*, then walked through the crowded streets to take the air. Stopping at a food vendor's, what did he see? His oldest brother working in the kitchen, his face sooty from blowing on the smoky fire. Ala'i bought a dish of grilled meat and asked the shopkeeper if the hireling (meaning his brother) could carry it to the *khan*. So out they stepped together, Ala'i walking in front and his brother, who did not know it was he, a few steps behind carrying the food like a servant.

As soon as they were inside the *khan*, Ala'i threw his arms about his brother's shoulders and kissed him, saying, "I am Ala'i! Where is our third brother?" "He is working as an errand boy in a baker's shop," said the eldest prince and began to weep. Ala'i said, "There is no cause for sadness, O my brother, this is a day of joy. Take these twenty dinars and go to the baths with our brother. Buy fine clothes, the best you can find in the *suq*, and bring him to me."

Ala'i's oldest brother took the money and went running. He called for his brother at the baker's, and they both went to the bath and washed themselves and rested. After buying suits of striped silk and robes of camel's hair edged with threads of gold, they returned to the *khan*. Ala'i welcomed them and set a rich meal before them. "Praises and thanks be to Allah that I have found you," he said, "and that we have nothing but good news to tell our father who waits for us with his hand on his heart." And he entertained them with an account of all that had happened from the time he left them at the parting of the ways until he held them in his arms again. "You saved us from misery; we are yours to command, brother," said the older princes. And they all set out for their father's kingdom the next morning.

In the heat of the day they came to a well. Ala'i's brothers whispered to each other: "How can we free ourselves of this hero? It is far better that we older sons present the Bird of the Golden Feather to the king." They turned to Ala'i and said, "You are the slightest of us. Let us lower you into the well to bring up water to drink." Badiat-ul-Jamal, hearing them speak, warned Ala'i against his brothers, but he did not believe her. "How can they betray me? They are my brothers," he said, and began to tie the rope

around his waist. Badiat-ul-Jamal said, "Wait. Do as you wish, but first take these three walnuts. In one there is a golden earring, in the second a golden bracelet, and in the third a folded gown made of the finest cloth of gold."

Then Ala'i was lowered into the well, where he filled the water bags for his brothers. When they had drunk and watered their animals, he said, "Pull me up." And they answered, "No. Die where you are, and may no one know that you have lived."

They left Ala'i in the well and resumed their journey home. But on the way the looks of the One Who Excels All Maidens for Beauty faded until she was changed into a black slave woman. The Bird of the Golden Feather lost his color and became plain as any other bird. And the Horse Who Leaves All Others Behind shrank and shriveled into a worn-down pack animal. Thus the two princes arrived at their father's palace. They kissed their father's hand, touched it to their foreheads, and said, "We have brought what you asked of us." The king was happy that they had returned safe and whole, but he asked, "Where is your brother?" They said, "May you live long: our brother died. We washed him and shrouded him and buried him by the wayside." The king said, "There is no power or strength except in God."

So much for the two princes. Now for their youngest brother. As he sat at the bottom of the well, he heard a sound above him and saw a rope swinging down from its mouth. He caught it and shouted to the men who were holding the other end, "Pull me out!" The men were terrified to hear a voice in such a place and replied, "Who are you? Djinn or Ins?" "By Allah, I am a man," said Ala'i, and they lifted him out. Indeed they found he was a youth as pleasing to the eye as the sight of the full moon in the dark night. They heard his tale and gave him a horse and said, "May Allah make the road before you a smooth one."

When Ala'i neared the city of his father, he met a shepherd. "Uncle, will you give me your clothes in return for mine?" the prince said. The shepherd agreed, of course, counting it a blessing from Allah to be made richer without effort. As for Ala'i, he dressed himself in the shepherd's rags and looked as bedraggled as any urchin in the bazaar. He wandered into the goldsmiths' *suq* and entered the workshop of the master of their guild. He said, "Will you let me work for you?" The goldsmith asked, "Can you fetch and carry? Will you buy coal for my workshop and meat for my cookpot?" "Whatever you wish," said Ala'i.

Now, as soon as Ala'i had reached his father's city, the plain brown bird became golden again, and the drab workhorse became sleek and swift again, and the serving girl became the fair princess again, causing the hearts of the two princes to burn with love for her. They said to their father, "How long must we wait? We want to get married!" But when the king climbed up to the princess's quarters, she said, "I shall not marry any man until you bring me the mate of this earring."

So the king sent for the master of the goldsmiths' guild. He said, "I want you to make me an earring, a twin of one I have. It is not big or heavy but will fit into a walnut shell." "On my head and eye be it," said the master goldsmith. But when he saw the earring, he said, "No jeweler can make such a thing, it is not the work of men!" The king replied, "Bring me the mate tomorrow at this time, or I shall put out your eyes and cut off your head."

The master goldsmith gathered all the jewelers of the city into his shop and told them of the king's command. But when he showed them the earring, all turned their heads away and each returned to his work. So the master goldsmith sat in his shop and began to weep. When Ala'i found him thus, he asked him why he grieved. The goldsmith said, "I am mourning my own life, which will be cut off at noon tomorrow." And he told Ala'i all that had happened between him and the king. "Show me the trinket that is causing you so much sorrow," said Ala'i. As soon as he saw Badiat-ul-Jamal's earring, he began to laugh. He said, "When I was a small boy playing with knucklebones I could cast earrings like this, and better. Lock up the shop and leave me here; you shall have the earring's mate in the morning." The goldsmith said, "Do not make a joke of my troubles. If all the jewelers in the city have not the skill for the work, will you be able to do it?" "If I can't," said Ala'i, "I shall offer my own head to the executioner's sword instead of yours." So his master left him.

Next morning Ala'i took the second earring out of the walnut the princess had given him and presented the pair to the master goldsmith. When he looked and could not tell which was old and which was new, the master was overjoyed. He ran to the king with the earrings and received a rich reward.

The king took the jewelry to the princess and said, "Now will you choose one of my sons for a husband?" When the princess saw the second earring, she knew that Ala'i was near. She said, "First let the man who brought this earring make me a bracelet to match the one on my arm." And she gave the king her bracelet.

The master goldsmith had hardly begun to enjoy his good fortune when he was summoned to the palace again. He returned to his shop with the bracelet in his hand and his head bowed in despair. Ala'i asked him why he was still sad now that he had grown rich from the king's reward. Unable to lift his sorrowing eyes from the ground, the goldsmith showed him the bracelet. "Is this all that is clouding your happiness?" asked Ala'i. "This is my work, not yours. Leave the bracelet with me overnight, and you shall have its twin in the morning."

Well, the next day the goldsmith received an even greater purse of gold from the king. But the princess still refused to choose a husband until the king had matched her *kaftan* made of cloth of gold. The goldsmith said, "O king of our time, is not this rather work for the tailors?" The king replied, "Take it to the ironmongers if you wish, but bring me another like it by tomorrow."

The goldsmith begged Ala'i to help him, and Ala'i matched the princess's gown with the dress of gold gossamer so fine it fitted into the walnut. When the king took it to Badiat-ul-Jamal, she said, "Now I am ready to choose one of the princes to be my bridegroom. But which one? Let them ride and show their skill on horseback, and I shall marry the winner."

The city was decorated with flags and banners, and the criers walked the streets announcing a royal wedding after three days and a display of horsemanship in which all the young men of the city could take part. The sons of ministers and the sons of pashas flocked on their horses to the open ground before the palace. Ala'i bought a horse for himself and joined them.

There was racing, shooting at targets from a galloping horse, and jousting. And in every sport Ala'i beat all the young men, including the two princes. Word reached the king that a youth of the people had unhorsed his sons and beaten all contenders. He called for his horse and rode out to meet the hero and challenge him. But when he came near, he saw that it was his youngest son Ala'i. He kissed the youth between the eyes and said, "Are you alive, O my loved one?" And Ala'i described to him all that he had done from the day that he left his father's palace. The king said, "You shall sit on my throne and rule over me and your brothers, O Ala'i. Take your revenge! Kill them if you wish!" But Ala'i said, "No. Today I shall marry Badiat-ul-Jamal. A wedding cannot be stained with blood." And he ordered the celebrations to begin.

So Ala'i married the princess and ruled justly over the people to the end of his days.

 Mulberry, mulberry,
That makes two.
I've told my story,
So must you.

The Nightingale
That Shrieked

Egypt

This happened, or maybe it did not.
The time is long past, and much is forgot.

A king once sent his crier through the kingdom to inform the people that for three successive nights they must light neither lamp nor fire—that their houses must show no spark or glimmer of light or they would suffer terrible punishment. Then the king said to his minister, "Now we shall judge for ourselves who obeys the sultan's word and who is careless of his command."

Night fell, and the king and his minister disguised themselves to look like two wandering dervishes. Together they roamed the streets of the city, from which every straying foot had withdrawn, since the night was black as blindness. There was not a light to be seen. But on turning a corner, the two noticed a faint glow coming from a hut that stood by itself. They peeped through the window and saw three girls busily spinning wool in the light of a lamp which they had dimmed with an upturned sieve.

One girl was saying to the others, "How I wish I were married to the sultan's baker! Then I should have bread to eat as often as I wanted." Another said, "If only I were the wife of the sultan's cook! Then I should dine off meat every day of my life." But the youngest said, "I would never consent to marry any lesser man than the sultan himself. If he made me his queen, within the year I should bear him twins—a boy with locks of silver and gold, and a girl for whom the sun shines when she smiles and the rain falls when she weeps."

In the morning a messenger came from the palace to summon the three girls to the king's presence. The first two sisters sank on the doorstone and trembled, saying, "Allah protect us as we stand between two fires. If we obey the king's command and do not work at night we die of hunger, and if we disobey we die of punishment." But the youngest sister told the messenger, "Let the king send us fine robes to wear, for we are poor and have no clothes in which to enter a royal court." And when the three girls stood before the king they wore gowns of velvet striped red and black.

They say, "the talk of the evening is covered with butter and melts in the morning," but the king married the eldest girl to his baker as she had wished and the next to his cook. The youngest girl who had said, "I shall bear the sultan twins before the year is out, a boy with locks of silver and gold, and a girl for whom the sun shines when she smiles and the rain falls when she cries"—this girl he kept for himself. As soon as the necessary preparations were made, he married her according to the tradition of the prophet.

Who grew jealous of her? The king's old wife. As one before our time has said, "When have women loved a fair-skinned girl or men loved a hero?" What did the old queen do? For a long time she did nothing, biding her time. She saw the new queen's belly rising, and she waited. She heard the midwife sitting at the new queen's pillow, chanting,

> O great father Noah,
> Who saved our souls,
> Save this child in her hour of woe!

and she waited. But when the new queen gave birth to a pair of twins—as golden and as radiant as she had promised—the old queen said to the midwife, "Take the newborn infants from their mother's side, and in their place put this little dog and this clay jar."

Does not gold achieve all things? The midwife did the old queen's bidding and threw the two princelings into the palace garden.

Now the women began to wail and beat their cheeks. "A calamity and a scandal! The king's new queen has given birth to a puppy dog and a water jug!" The king, ashamed, sent his queen away to live the life of a discarded wife.

What of the twins? Our God is praiseworthy indeed, for they were found by the king's gardener, whose wife was barren and had grown old childless. She pressed the babies to her breast, resting one on her right shoulder and one on her left, and nurtured them as if they had been the fruit of her own body.

The child in a tale grows fast. So it was with these two. In time the gardener built them a little house to live in. The fair brother with the locks of silver and gold, and his sister for whose smile the sun shone and for whose tears the rain fell, were such as fill the eye and set the tongue wagging. News of them reached the old queen, and once again she sent for the midwife to instruct her what to do.

The midwife waited until the brother had gone hunting and the girl was sitting in the house by herself. Then she knocked at the door and paid a visit. "How perfect is this house!" she said. "You lack nothing but the Tree of Apples that Dance and Apricots that Sing growing before your door. Then it would be complete."

When the brother returned, he found his sister weeping. "Why such tears?" he asked. And she told him of the midwife's visit, confessing that now she could not be truly happy until she had the magic fruit tree growing by her door. "Gather up provisions for a journey; I shall set out tomorrow morning in search of your tree," said her brother.

Next day the boy began to walk, trusting his fate to the All-Merciful. From place to place he traveled asking where he should seek the magic tree, but none knew how to advise him. At last he reached the foot of a high mountain. He climbed to its top, and there stood a Ghoul with one foot pointing to the east and one foot pointing to the west. The hair of his head was matted and covered his brow. The hair of his brow was thick and covered his eyes. "Peace, O father Ghoul," said the boy.

> Had not your greeting
> Preceded your speaking,
> I should have torn you limb from limb
> And snapped your bones and picked them clean!

the monster replied. The boy went up to the Ghoul and cut the knotted hair on his head and shaved the bushy hair of his brows. The monster sighed with pleasure and said, "You have brought back the light into my face, so may Allah light up your path before you. Tell me: what are you seeking and what have you come for?" The boy explained his search, and the Ghoul said, "If you follow this road you will come to the land of Ghouls. The tree that you seek grows in the garden of the king. Its leaves are so broad that you could swaddle two infants in each. But first go to my brother. He is older than I am by one day and wiser by one year. Ask him to help you."

The boy journeyed onward until ahead he saw the Ghoul's brother sitting in the middle of the path with his legs stretched out before him. "Peace, O father Ghoul," said the boy, and the monster replied as his brother had done,

> Had not your greeting
> Preceded your speaking,
> I should have torn you limb from limb
> And snapped your bones and picked them clean!

The boy did as he had done with the first Ghoul, snipping the hair that covered his forehead and trimming his eyebrows. Then the Ghoul asked, "What has brought you from the land of men to the land of spirits and Djinn?" "Allah brought me and I came," the boy said. And he told the Ghoul how he was looking for the Tree of Apples that Dance and Apricots that Sing to give to his sister. The Ghoul said, "Continue along this road, and you will see my sister sitting at her handmill grinding salt or fine white sugar. If you find her grinding salt, stop where you stand and do not let her see you. But if she should be grinding sugar, run to her as quickly as you can and nurse at each of her breasts. For once you have tasted her milk, she will do you no harm but help you as a mother helps her son."

The boy did as the Ghoul had told him. Finding the Ghoul's sister milling sugar, he pounced on her right breast before she could look up and see who was coming. She said,

> Whoever suckles the breast on my right
> Is dear to my heart and a son in my sight.

When he turned to the other breast, she said,

> Whoever suckles the breast on my left
> Is dear as the son whom I love the best.

"What is the cause of your coming?" she asked the boy, "and for what reason will you be going?" When he had told her about the Tree of Apples that Dance and Apricots that Sing, she said, "Wait till my seven sons come home in the evening; they will help you. But for your protection I must hide you." And she turned him into an onion like the other onions in her basket.

When it was dark the seven young Ghouls came home, saying, "Mother, Mother, there is about you a smell of men!" She said, "How can that be, when I have been sitting in this place all day long. It is you who have gone abroad and mingled with the humans in their towns, and their smell has clung to the tails of your gowns." Despite her words, the young Ghouls said, "If you are hiding a woman we shall guard her like a sister, and if you are hiding a man we shall help him like a brother. May God protect him and visit a traitor's punishment on his betrayer." At that, their mother returned the boy to his own shape and told her sons how he was searching for the Tree of Apples that Dance and Apricots that Sing. "I know the place, and I can take him there in a month," said

the oldest son. "I can lead him to it in a week," said another. And the youngest said, "Climb onto my back, and I shall carry you there in the twinkling of an eye."

So the boy flew on the youngest Ghoul's back to the garden of the king of Ghouls. With a monster's strength the young spirit uprooted the Tree of Apples that Dance and Apricots that Sing. And the boy took it to his sister to plant by the door of their house.

What did the king's old wife say when she saw that the boy with the locks of silver and gold had returned from his journey, whole and unharmed? She sent the midwife to visit his sister again. "How cool it is in the shade of your tree, and how merry to see the apples dancing and hear the apricots sing!" the midwife said. "Now indeed you own everything there is to own . . . except Bulbul Assiah, the Nightingale who Shrieks." "How can I find Bulbul Assiah?" the girl asked. "He who brought you the tree of of dancing apples and singing apricots will surely bring you Bulbul Assiah," the old woman said.

The sister told her brother about the nightingale and admitted that she could not live happily until she possessed it. The boy loved his sister, and to make her content, he set out once more. This time he took the shortest road to the home of the Ghouls, his adopted brothers. And the youngest flew with him to the aviary of the king of the Ghouls and showed him the cage that held Bulbul Assiah. The boy lifted it from its hook and brought it home to his sister.

Now the gardener, seeing the wonders that his children had collected— the tree with the dancing and singing fruits and the golden cage of Bulbul

Assiah—went to the king and said, "For forty years I have worked in your garden, yet you have never visited my house. Now I wish you to come and eat my food." "If Allah wills it, I shall come tomorrow," said the king. Next day when the king entered the gardener's yard, the apples danced and the apricots sang on the tree in front of his children's house. And Bulbul Assiah began to shriek from his perch,

> Who but a she-dog
> Born of a she-dog
> Knows how to whelp pups?
> A queen can only bear
> Noble lords and ladies fair.
> Our sultan's wife bore no pup or jug of water
> But a golden son and a comely daughter,
> A boy with shining locks of gold and silver
> A girl—why, the sun shines at her laughter.

So the king discovered that the brother and sister were his own twin son and daughter. He called their mother back from her seclusion and ordered a feast to last forty days and forty nights to celebrate her return.

> As for the wicked old midwife,
> May torments hound her all her life!

A Tale
Within a Tale

Iraq

There was or there was not (is anything sure or certain but that God's mercies are many, more numerous than all the pebbles on the land or the sum of the sea's sand?) a rich man and his wife who had one son. An only child is the child of indulgence. And everything that gold could procure, the boy,

Hasan, was given to enjoy. When in time Hasan reached the age for marriage, his parents wished to complete their duty toward their much-loved son and pair him with a bride fairer by far than all the other young women in those parts. Indeed, they found such a girl, with a face as broad and luminous as a tray of polished silver and eyes as wide as my finger is long, one who equaled in beauty the moon when it is full. Happily did Hasan's father count out the bridal portion in gold coin, and the whole city rejoiced with him for seven days and seven nights. Then the bride was led in festive procession from her father's house to her husband's chamber.

But though the girl fell asleep at her groom's side on the wedding night, when she awoke in the morning—Allah protect us!—he was gone. When Hasan's mother brought in the sweetmeats with which a new couple first breaks its fast, she found the bride alone. Then how quickly was joy turned to sorrow and elation to despair! At such times is there any cure except the patience to endure?

The days passed and the weeks, and the fate of Hasan remained locked beyond the seven heavens and beneath the seven levels of the earth. Then Hasan's wife spoke to her husband's father: "O my uncle, will you give me leave to act for your son in his absence and do what he would do himself if he were here? Perhaps I shall find a way to bring you back your only son and myself regain the husband I knew a few short hours." The poor man, bowed with grief, nodded his assent.

That very day Hasan's wife flung open the doors to the guest hall in her husband's house. One and all she welcomed with such attentions and such generous fare that though Hasan himself had vanished, his fame was spread throughout the land. For Hasan's wife had brought slaves and servants in their dozens to her kitchens and her stables. Should a lone guest appear, one servingman would greet him, bring him everything he desired, and lead away his horse. If ten visitors came together, ten men stepped out and waited on them like slaves. If a hundred strangers chanced to approach at one time, one hundred servants received them and heaped before them feasts of food.

It was not long before Hasan's guest hall became a byword for hospitality. And soon its renown reached the ears of the celebrated father of generosity himself, Sheikh Hatim at-Tai, whose name was spoken as though it were another word for the Beduin virtue, hospitality. How could the sheikh remain unmoved? With his own eyes he had to see whether it was true that the guest-friendship which he himself offered with open hands, for which his name was sweet as musk in men's regard, could be matched under another's roof. With a hundred of his horsemen he rode to Hasan's hall. One hundred and one servants welcomed them, each bearing in his hand a long-beaked coffee pitcher of yellow brass. And for the traditional three days and one-third of a day, Hatim and his company were entertained as if they had all been kings. Though his men were impatient to return to their own country, Hatim lingered on to address the mistress of the feast whose liberality had exceeded all descriptions. Who better than such a hostess could suit him as a wife? She said, "I have heard your name spoken, and always with high praise. I must consent to be your wife. But on one condition: that first you bring me news of the fate of my lost husband."

To win such a bride Hatim set out next day, placing his life in the hands of Allah and following where his horse's hooves pleased to lead him. He rode so far and so long, making no distinctions between the night and the day, that the leather on his saddle was worn away and he could not continue without buying a new one.

In the next city he came to, there worked a saddler called Hasan as-Sarraj. This craftsman measured Hatim's old saddle and promised to sew him a new one to replace it, in the shortest time. When Hatim returned to collect his new saddle he was pleased: he found that it was closely stitched and far finer than the one he owned before. But hardly had he tightened the girth and begun to ride away when the saddler called him back. "Here is your money; give me back the saddle," said Hasan as-Sarraj. And while Hatim looked on amazed, the man slashed at the leather with his knife, shredding it into so many pieces that Allah alone knows their number. "Tell me the reason for this thing that you have done," said Hatim. But the man would not speak. At last, after much urging, he said, "I shall reveal my secret, but on one condition only: that first you tell me the story of Yusuf al-Iskafi, the shoemaker, in all its details."

So now Hatim was forced to travel on a further quest, to seek not only news of the vanished Hasan but of this shoemaker too. After wandering far and wide, he stopped to rest in a certain village. And here he came upon a cobbler working in the shadow of the mosque. With his tools spread on the ground around him, this worker hammered at his last. Then all at once up he sprang and darted up the steps of the minaret, looking eagerly to right

and left when he reached the top. Descending again, he hunched himself over the unfinished shoe—and as suddenly dropped his tools and ran up the winding stairs. Hatim observed him repeat this several times. Then he said, "What is your name, and why do you conduct yourself in this unusual way?" "My name is Yusuf al-Iskafi," said the cobbler, "and I will disclose my secret, but on this condition only: that first you tell me the story of Yakub al-Haddad, the blacksmith, leaving out nothing."

Hatim departed, cursing the fate that had led him into these strange and far-flung adventures. He traveled when it was light and he traveled when it was night, laying his head down in one city and rousing himself up in the next, until he came to a place distinguished in one thing only. In it he saw a blacksmith who would look up from his anvil, and instead of bringing the hammer down on the iron, would strike it on his own brow. Then he would look to the right and swing the hammer against his temple, then look to the left and strike his head.

When at last the man had sunk under these self-inflicted blows, his friends lifted him and carried him to his house. Hatim followed in their wake, and as soon as the blacksmith began to stir, asked him, "Who are you, and what is the purpose of your actions?" "I am Yakub al-Haddad," said the blacksmith. "I can relate to you the secret of this matter, but on one condition only: that first you tell me the story of Dawud as-Sammak, the fisherman, as it happened, without omissions."

Now Hatim sighed, resigning himself to a venture without ending, for it seemed that the longer he chased the answers, the more numerous grew the riddles. At least his path was clear in the case of this fisherman: no doubt he would find him in the vicinity of the great rivers. And Hatim was right, for after some straying he arrived in a region previously unknown to him in which he saw a crowd of men on a riverbank. They were casting fistfuls of lentils and wheat and barley into the water while a man who stood apart directed them. Hatim walked up to this man and asked, "What kind of being are you, to waste good food in such quantities?" "I am Dawud as-Sammak, the fisherman," said the man. "What I do is my concern, for which I do not have to give explanations." Hatim pressed him and he relented. "I shall share my secret, but on one condition: that first you tell me what it is that causes the winds to rise and the rains to fall."

Hatim grasped his horse's reins and called on Allah to protect him while he unraveled the web of this mystery to the last thread. Across deserts and wildernesses he rode, neither pausing nor resting until he could not advance another step for weariness. In the place where he dismounted lay a carpet, and beside it were two men wrestling so fiercely with each other that the dust rose into the air about them. But on seeing Hatim they desisted and cried, "Here comes a Moslem; let him judge between us!" And they explained to Hatim that they were brothers and that their father, one of the Djinn, had given them the flying carpet now spread on the ground. A man had but to step on it and say, "Fly, O carpet, in the name of Suleyman the prophet," and it would carry him even to the farthest ends of the earth. "But tell us how can we divide it between us," said the sons of the Djinn. Hatim said, "I shall throw a stone as far as I can reach, and whichever of you picks it up first shall be owner of the carpet." He threw the stone and the young Djinns raced after it. As soon as their backs were turned, Hatim stepped onto the magic carpet and said, "Carry me, O carpet, in the name of Suleyman the prophet, to the place where I may discover how the winds are made to rise and the rains to fall."

In the glancing of an eye, the carpet rose off the ground and carried Hatim through the air till the earth beneath him sank and seemed no larger than a copper coffee tray. Crossing the seven seas to a place where no mortal had ever dared to go, it came to rest at last upon the roof terrace of a marble palace. In the courtyard of the palace sat an aged man from whom the years had taken all that they had taken until the hair on his head shone white like carded cotton. He looked up and said to Hatim, "Do you come from the spirit world or from the world of men? Are you Ins, or are you Djinn? Whichever you are, how did you find your way to me?" Hatim said, "Allah the All-Powerful led me to this place." So the old man welcomed him and bid him descend from the roof and sit by his side.

In a corner of the courtyard where the sun fell hot on the stones, a sorry-looking dog was tied, a black female, who could not reach the shelter of the shade. Hatim asked, "Does not the prophet instruct us to show kindness to the beasts? Why do you torment that bitch in the sun?" "My child, this regards me and me alone. Do not question further," said the old man. But Hatim pleaded eloquently and in the end the old man said, "My tale is one of scandal and disgrace that must not travel beyond these walls. I'll tell you its secrets on this condition only: that you are willing to forfeit your life at my hands when I have done." Since there was no other way to learn the truth of the affair, Hatim agreed.

"Know then, my son," the old man began, "that I am one of the Djinn, a servant of the prophet Suleyman. He it was who entrusted into my care two supernatural mares. Ride the one, and the skies will unlock their fountains and let fall streams of rain abundantly; ride the other, and stormy winds begin to blow which cannot be scattered or abated. This wand he also gave me, which at a stroke will transform a man into any form I wish. You

asked me to tell you the history of that black bitch. She is my wife, my father's brother's daughter. My uncle died when she was young, and I was left to raise her until she grew to womanhood. Then I married her, and counted myself among the fortunate whose life is bliss, until one night I awoke and found that my wife had left my side. I searched the house but she was gone, and the rain-mare was missing from her stall. So I lay down again, pretending sleep, and waited for her return."

While the servant of Suleyman the prophet spoke these words, the dog before him wept human tears that fell onto its black fur and wet it thoroughly. The old man continued, "Next night I cut my arm and rubbed the wound with salt. Though I lay down as if in deepest slumber, the pain chased sleep from my eyes. I saw my wife softly rise, and I followed her. Bestriding the rain-mare, she vanished into the night. But I mounted the wind-mare and spurred it in pursuit. What a storm there was that night! What lightnings and thundering! And a raging tempest blew winds from every side.

"The wind-mare being the fleeter of the two, I was able overtake my wife and see her dismount by a vast cave. A monster too terrible to describe, an Afreet, stood at its mouth, calling, 'What delayed you, O woman? Your children weep and ask for you with never a pause.' Now I knew the truth. But holding in my rage, I waited until the eastern sky began to lighten and she took leave of her unlawful mate. Neither she nor the Afreet noticed me where I lay hidden. As soon as the monster stretched his hideous length in sleep, I cut off his head and, throwing it into a sack, raced the rain-mare home. The winds my speeding mount had raised beat in the other's face and slowed her. I was in bed with eyelids weighted as if in sleep when my wife crept stealthily to my side.

"Next day I told her that I wished to break my fast on fruit. Since it was winter, she laughed and said, 'This is no time of year for fruit.' 'Look in my sack,' I said. She turned it upside down and stood in terror when the monster's head rolled out. Then she threw herself upon the ground and kissed my hands and, weeping, begged forgiveness for her erring ways. But how could I countenance so dark a stain upon my honor? With Suleyman's wand I struck her and changed her into the black dog you see tied there, where the sun beats hottest. Her food is dry bread, her drink warm water, and I punish her with a whip." As the man concluded his tale, the black-haired beast could not contain herself but sobbed so loudly that it was painful to hear.

"Now you have heard my story," said the old man to Hatim. "You know of the shame that has blackened my honor and destroyed my name, and you must not live to speak it. Bid your life farewell, my child, and prepare to give up your soul." "I ask one final favor, uncle," said Hatim. "Let me pray to Allah but two genuflections; I wish to ask forgiveness for my sins before I face my Maker." "It is granted," he said, and Hatim climbed to the roof terrace and spread the magic carpet like a prayer rug, pointing in the direction of the holy city of Mecca. Standing upon it, he raised his hands in the attitude of prayer and said, "By Suleyman the prophet, O carpet, carry me away." Before the old man could touch him, Hatim had disappeared over the first of the seven seas.

The two sons of the Djinn were still fighting when Hatim returned to them. He gave them their father's carpet and mounted his own horse and rode to the great rivers where he had left Dawud as-Sammak. "Have you brought me the history of the wind and the rain?" asked the fisherman when he saw Hatim. "I have," said Hatim and repeated to him everything that the Djinn had related, from beginning to end. "Now tell me your story," said Hatim. "I shall hide nothing of what you ask to know," said the fisherman, "but I beg a kindness in return. When I have spoken, put an end to my sufferings; with your sword cut off my life." When Hatim assented, the fisherman began.

"I used to be a simple fisherman, owning nothing beyond the modest earnings of my catch. Then one day as I stood on the river bank hauling in my net, I felt it to be unusually heavy. With all my strength I pulled as hard as I was able and landed a giant fish, larger than any I or my father before me had ever caught. As it thrashed on the dry sand at my feet, it suddenly coughed and spat out a jewel, a diamond larger and more full of light than any ever seen. In the time it took me to bend down and pick up the stone, the fish had leaped into the water and disappeared.

"I was excited, of course, and took my find to the jewelers' market, where I sold it for thousands of gold dinars. But ever since that day, I have spent every daylight moment and every penny that I possess in trying once more to find that strange large fish. My strength and my riches have gone the ways of the wind and have left not a trace. There is no sweetness in my days and I have no peace. I beg you now to give me rest and strike off my head with your sword." But Hatim replied, "The thousands of dinars that the magic diamond brought to you could have kept you and fed your children and grandchildren to the seventh generation. It was Allah's will to punish you with the urge to find the fish once more. Who am I, then, to kill you? Live on in suffering, for it is the decree of the Almighty."

Having unlocked the first link in the chain of puzzles that had held him so long, Hatim rode on, full of hope, in the direction of the city of Yakub al-Haddad, the blacksmith. As before, he followed him to his house and waited for him to recover from his faint. Then Hatim imparted the narrative of the fisherman from its *aleph* to its *ya*, saying finally, "I have brought you the fisherman's story; now it is your turn to tell me why you inflict such violence on yourself and make your life loathsome." The blacksmith answered, "I will hold back nothing, but when I have spoken, I ask you as a favor to release me from this wretched existence with the sharp edge of your sword."

Hatim agreed and the blacksmith began, "I used to be a leading merchant in this city. One day I set out on a journey to further my trade. I had stocked the house with plenty and was leaving my pregnant wife in the care of my mother. Chance willed that the caravan was delayed many years, one decade and more. But my trading had been profitable, and our procession of richly laden camels enchanted the eye and dazzled the imagination. We made our return to the outskirts of this city at dusk. I requested of our company that we camp by the wayside overnight so that we might enter the city when it was day, both in order to show our goods to best advantage and gain fame for our success, and in order not to disturb my relatives asleep in their beds.

"Yet I was like a man lying on hot embers, so inflamed was I with a longing to be reunited with my beloved family. I found myself running toward the city in the greatest agitation. When I reached the courtyard of my house, a light shone in the window. I looked inside. There sat my wife with her hair loose around her face, fair as the full moon at its brightest, and next to her a youth handsome of feature and proud of carriage. At the sight, my powers of reasoning deserted me. I resolved to wash this scandal from my honor, first with the blood of my mother, who had permitted such things, and then with that of the sinners. When I had taken my revenge, I returned to the camp under cover of darkness, my heart full of sorrow at this homecoming.

"Next day when I entered my house, I found it full of weeping neighbors lamenting the tragedy that had cut off three generations in one night. In fact I had mistaken for an adulterer my own son, whom I had left in his mother's belly! Do not ask, you who are wise, the degree of unhappiness that overwhelmed me then. My heart was torn, and in my mind everything seemed as nothing. But from the decree of Allah there is no escape.

With the passage of time my riches disappeared and I took up the black-smith's trade. Now whenever I lift my hammer to strike the iron, my mother appears to me and asks, 'What did I do, child, to make you want to dye the white hair on my head with my own blood?' Then my wife stands at my side and says, 'Husband, did I wrong you or take your gold, that you have made my name one to set every tongue wagging?' Lastly my son takes shape before my eyes, saying, 'Fifteen years I awaited your return, saddened by your absence, and when you came at last, you were my murderer. Can you tell me why, Father?' So I cannot help but turn upon myself and stun my brain so that I might escape the truth. Now I pray you, stranger, hasten and deliver me from the torments of remorse. Put an end to my life!" But Hatim said, "Continue as you are, and may Allah increase your sorrow. Your own right hand has brought it upon yourself."

So saying, Hatim pulled his horse's reins toward the town where Yusuf al-Iskafi plied his trade. He repeated to the shoemaker the events that had led to the blacksmith's woe and said, "Now for your own tale, and the reasons for your strange ways." "You shall hear my adventures, every one," replied the shoemaker, "but when I have told them, I beg you to save me and bring to a finish this luckless life of mine."

Hatim consenting, the shoemaker began: "One day I was sitting here in the shade of the mosque in my usual place, when a giant many-colored bird flew overhead, so large it seemed to fill the sky. It came to rest upon the minaret. 'If I could only catch this one . . .' I thought, and tiptoed up the steps. Without a noise I reached the top and even grasped the bird by one leg. The next moment it had taken flight, and I with it. I clung to its talons expecting to fall to a terrible death, but when I next felt firm ground beneath my foot, it was in a princely courtyard closed in by shady trees and orchards richly laden with fragrant blossoms and ripening fruits. Before me was a banquet: forty dishes of finest ware heaped high with steaming food. I was hungry and began to eat. I took one mouthful from each plate until I reached the last but one. Then I could eat no more and left the fortieth bowl untouched.

"Just then I heard a rushing of powerful wings and voices talking. I hid myself and saw forty colored birds, each a twin of the one that brought me, glide to the ground and begin to feed. Then one after another, as they noticed the missing mouthful, they joyfully chirped,

   He who ate
Off my plate
Shall be my mate.

Only the fortieth bird, which was the creature I had first encountered, was silent. Its dish was the one I had not touched. Then the bird said in a mournful voice,

   Now you must be my brother,
Like one born to my mother,
Never to become my lover!

For these were the forty daughters of the Djinn, who had been bewitched and imprisoned in the likeness of feathered birds. Now I found myself the cherished husband of thirty-nine wives, and after one year, the father of thirty-nine sons. But in the midst of such luxury, though lapped in love, a devil spoke in my ear, asking, "Why not make the fortieth one your wife also?" I yielded to the evil one's prompting and approached the last bird. But she gave her wings one shake and I found myself sitting here under the wall of the mosque again. Ever since, I have been watching for the bird's return, bitten with regret for the life of bliss I lost. My existence is hateful to me, my only comfort the thought of death. Have pity, and with your sword bring me rest at last."

But Hatim replied, "He spoke well who said, 'Allah, exalted be His might, gives walnuts to the toothless.' When you held good fortune in both hands, greed turned your eyes away from it. I shall not pollute my sword with the blood of one who is careless of God's blessings."

Leaving the shoemaker, Hatim hastened to find Hasan as-Sarraj and tell him this tale in all its particulars. Then Hatim said, "I have uncovered the truth about Yusuf al-Iskafi, as you wished. Now it is for you to explain why you tear apart a new saddle which you have fashioned with so much skill and care." "I shall tell you everything, if only you promise when I have done to relieve me of my troubles with one quick thrust of your sword."

Hatim agreed, and the saddler said, "I was the only son of rich parents. As soon as I attained manhood, my mother began to think of marriage, for she longed to decorate her eyes with *kohl* for my wedding. The bride was found, the contract written, and the wedding portion paid. On my wedding night I fell asleep next to the most beautiful woman I had ever seen or imagined, and when I awoke I found myself alone in this city. To feed myself I learned the saddler's trade. But whenever I begin to make a saddle, I cannot prevent my fingers from stitching into it the portrait of my fair bride, such is my longing for her. As soon as I sell the saddle, I regret parting with the picture of my beloved's face and tear it rather than have it in another's hands. This is the calamity that has befallen me. Now kill me, brother, and give me peace."

When Hatim heard these words, he knew that at last he had found Hasan, in whose name his wife had opened the most renowned guest hall in the land. He said, "No, brother, I must take you home to your bride and people. Prepare yourself for travel."

Together the two men rode until they came to Hasan's house. After many years of mourning, great was the rejoicing in his hall. The groom was reunited with his bride, the son with his parents.

As for Hatim at-Tai, he was indeed well named the most generous of Arabs. For, yielding his claim to Hasan's wife, he mounted his horse and returned to his own lands.

Flowers That Vanished in the Night

Syria

There was or there was not—for we live in ignorance and Allah is the All-Knowing—a mighty king. He had three sons whom he prized above the light of his eyes. Around his palace the king had built a garden in which grew every flower the mind might call forth or the heart desire. There were cultivated plants carefully arranged in beds, and wild flowers growing randomly as they do in nature. There were lilies and jasmines to scent the air and bright anemones and irises to delight the eye. And there was one plant, the most precious in all the garden, whose perfume could revive the weariest soul and whose grace would enchant the most jaded beholder. It grew here and nowhere else in the world.

One morning as the king was taking the air in his garden, he noticed that one of the blooms of this rarest plant had been plucked. On the next day a second flower was gone. Only this plant seemed to entice the robber in the night; no other tree or shrub in the garden was touched.

The king called his three sons and charged them to catch the flower thief. So the eldest youth commanded the servants to pitch a tent in the garden and furnish it with mattresses and soft cushions. There, as soon as the screen of darkness hid the world from sight, the prince took up his position, holding a naked saber in his right hand. But long before the night had reached its midpoint, sleep sealed the prince's eyes and stopped his ears, and the crashing of thunder would not have stirred him. When the light dawned, the king found his son asleep and a flower gone.

On the next night the second prince took his turn as sentry in the tent. He too lost the struggle with sleep long before he could confront the intruder.

But time lies in ever-watchful ambush and permits no wrongdoer to escape without penalty or crime to go without punishment. When the sun set on the third night, the youngest prince was ready, sitting on the bare stones near the flowering plant with his unsheathed sword by his side. He had cut his arm and rubbed salt into the wound so that whenever his head began to droop in sleep, the sting of the salt would keep him awake.

Hour after hour went by. Then at last there was a rustling of leaves as before an approaching storm and a trembling in the ground like an earthquake, and suddenly a giant monster appeared—a Marid with eyes like two braziers showering sparks. Fear loosened the prince's limbs and his chest shrank about his beating heart, but he gripped his sword in both his hands and sank the blade into the Marid's bulk, wounding him and driving him back the way he had come.

Next day the Marid's trail of blood led the princes out of the royal garden and beyond the city wall. It stopped at the opening of a deep well, once the watering hole for camels and mules but long since dry and abandoned. Is it not well known that Marids and Afreets, giants and spirits, linger near cisterns and wells? What are such places if not gateways from their subterranean world to ours?

At the brink of the well, the oldest prince claimed his right to be the first to destroy the Marid in his lair. He knotted a rope around his waist and lowered himself into the blackness of the hole. But he had hardly disappeared from sight when his shouts came out of the well: "Pull me out! For the love of Allah, pull me out!" For he had seen the flicker of his own shadow on the wall of the shaft and thought the giant was upon him. The second prince did no better. Halfway down the well his sword struck a projecting rock, and the clash of metal against stone sounded to him like the giant baring his weapon. He cried out, "Save me! By the life of the prophet, I say save me!"

Now it was the turn of the youngest prince. As he prepared to descend, he said to his brothers, "Remember, whatever you might hear me shout, it is a signal to pay out more rope." And down he went without stopping until his heels touched the bottom. The well was dry and empty, but in its wall the prince saw the entrance to a passageway. He walked into it to see where it would take him and found himself on the threshold of a palace built of shining marble. From within the palace came a fearsome noise like the roar of a waterfall, but the prince pushed open the door of ebony and silver and stepped inside.

In the center of the lofty hall was seated a maiden whose beauty would make the light of day seem dim. On her breast, like stars paled by the halo of a full moon, hung the flowers stolen from the king's garden. And in her lap lay the hideous head of the sleeping Marid. The loud noise, which made every hair on the prince's body stand by itself, was the snoring in the giant's detestable cave-like nostrils.

The maiden said nothing but pointed to the giant's sword where it lay upon the ground, both of its edges black with blood. The prince understood her meaning, but first he shook the monstrous creature awake, for he was no coward who killed his enemies while they slept. As soon as he saw the giant's eyes glow like embers, he struck with all his strength. The Marid's severed head rolled on the ground and made the earth shake with its weight, and slabs of marble and blocks of masonry fell from the palace walls.

Now the girl took courage to speak and tell the prince her tale. The Marid had stolen her from her father's house to keep her in his underground hall, and she begged the prince to return her to the light of the sun. How could that be? The way to the well was now a wall of tumbled stones. Just then, in the garden behind the Marid's marble palace, there appeared an old man with a long white beard and the turban of a scholar. The prince asked him how to escape from this underground place and return to the light and air of day. The old man said, "Two rams butting each other, one black and one white. Ride one of them and it will carry you up to the face of the earth."

The old man went out, and out of the ground where he had stood two

rams appeared, one black as night and the other whiter than snow. They locked their horns and fought, pushing one another first this way, then that. The prince caught the white ram and held it while the king's daughter climbed onto its back. In less time than it takes to blink, the ram had lifted the girl to the mouth of the well outside the king's city, where the two princes were waiting for their youngest brother.

As soon as they saw the princess, her beauty brighter than the moon at the full, her brow luminous like the Pleiades among the stars, the two princes immediately thought of marriage. They took her to the palace to show their father. But the king asked, "Where is your brother?" "He vanished into the watering hole outside the city wall, and there has been no sign or sound from him since we let him down on the rope," they reported. The king began to weep for his son. He put the palace into mourning and commanded the city to show its grief, forbidding all festivals or weddings or celebrations until one year had passed.

What of the youngest prince? He shut his eye and opened it and found the princess gone. The black ram was left, so he mounted it. Down they sank through the seven levels of the earth until they reached a region of shadows inhabited by ghosts. The prince dismounted and wandered in this strange world. When he could walk no more, he threw himself down beneath a tree with spreading branches and fell asleep.

He had not rested long when the sound of screaming birds awoke him. In the leaves above him was a griffin's nest filled with frightened fledglings. Poised over them, its tongue playing and its breath blowing with a hiss, a serpent was preparing to strike. The prince pulled out his sword, climbed up the trunk without a sound, and sliced off the serpent's head with one firm blow. He cut its flesh in pieces to give the helpless birds to eat, and laid himself down to sleep again.

Soon the mother bird returned. She spotted the sleeping man beneath her nest and, fearing danger to her young, lifted a rock in her talons to drop and crush his head. But the baby griffins, fluttering on their tiny wings, shielded their savior from the mother's wrath. The griffin was astonished. Then she saw the serpent's flesh inside her nest, and astonishment became shame and remorse. How nearly she had repaid good with evil! Waiting for the prince to wake, she fanned her wings to cool his brow. And when he sat up at last she addressed him thus: "You who have saved my sons from death, ask and it shall be done for you!" "I have one wish only," said the prince. "Again to see my people, whom I love."

"Easier to bear the destruction of my brood than contemplate such a task!" sighed the griffin. "But I must help you as you saved them." The distance between one level of the earth and the next is such that a griffin needs the fat and flesh of one whole sheep to sustain her through the crossing. The prince went to round up seven sheep: one for every level. When he had lifted the provisions onto the griffin's back, he himself climbed behind her neck. At every level of the earth, the prince fed one sheep into the bird's beak. They had left the sixth level and were nearing the surface of the earth when the last sheep slipped from the prince's grasp and fell into the emptiness below. "My strength is failing!" said the bird. What was there left for the prince to do? He took out his sword and fed the bird his own right leg.

The smell of human blood filled the bird's nostrils, and she understood what he had done. Holding the prince's limb, she wrung out the last of her powers to reach daylight and the youth's own country. "I have kept my word and carried you home," said the griffin. And she licked his wound and told him that he had only to press his leg in place and it would knit as though it had never been parted.

The bird flew off, and the prince walked and leaped and ran to his father's palace. He was welcomed like one returning from the dead. His father kissed his brow and wept for gladness, but his brothers were shamed when they saw his face, and they fled the kingdom.

As for the fair princess, before the week was out she became his bride.

I was at their wedding, and then home I came.
There was butter-cooked chicken and honey pastry,
But I left in a hurry to bring you the tale
And ate not a thing that was tasty.

The Maiden of the Tree of Raranj and Taranj

Iraq

There was or there was not—is anything sure or certain but the greatness of Allah?—a king so powerful that man and Djinn bowed before him. In battle he had no equal, and his court was more splendid than any of his time. Yet fate withheld one thing from him: year after year his queen remained childless. In vain the king traveled to far places to consult the wise sages. In vain he besought Heaven with unceasing prayer that his longing might be fulfilled and the palace made glad with the birth of a prince. Then in her prayers the queen made a secret vow. She swore that if she were blessed with a son, she would cause the streets of the city to flow with fat and honey when he reached manhood.

Heaven is bountiful. Hardly nine months passed before the queen gave birth to a well-formed boy in whose face shone the light of understanding. From day to day he grew in strength and grace until he came to be the ornament of the kingdom and the very crown on his father's head.

But with the passing of the years the queen forgot her promise, and a sorrow more grievous by far than childlessness would have shrouded the palace had not fate kindly intervened. For it sent a dream to the prince in his sleep, a warning shadow that said, "Let the queen fulfill her promise, or I shall snatch you from her arms and hide you where all the king's armies will not know how to find you." In the light of the following day the prince forgot the dream, and when it appeared to him a second time, he forgot again. But on the third night the shadow seemed to shake him, so that he cried out in his sleep. King and queen ran to their son's bedside, and he told them what he had seen.

The queen struck her own fair cheeks in remorse at her forgotten vow. And in that very hour she roused the masons and the stonecutters and commanded them to build two troughs the length of the city. One she filled with honey the color of copper, and into the other she poured boiled butter that ran like liquid gold. The twin scents of so much goodness and sweetness were like a crier's call. From every house and hovel the people came to fill their silver pots and jars of clay with the royal bounty. By evening the troughs were dry. Only one withered old woman remained, carefully scraping the stones with her fingers to catch a few licks in her earthenware bowl.

Just at that moment the prince chanced to look out of the palace window. With the thoughtlessness of youth he fitted an arrow to his bow and aimed at the woman's bowl. Tach! The dish broke in two, spilling butter and honey onto the ground. The old woman turned round and shrieked in anger, "As you broke my bowl, so may your heart break for love of the Maiden of the Tree of Raranj and Taranj."

That very instant the prince felt his heart choke in his breast. He was stricken with a restlessness that he knew would not be stilled until he had found this tree and the maiden who was named for it. Neither the tears of his mother nor the entreaties of his father could change his purpose. That same night they prepared for his travels, and before the sun rose next day he had set out on his search.

Across the lands of the earth he wandered, picking his way over rugged mountains and speeding through smooth plains, setting his course by the Maiden of the Tree of Raranj and Taranj as others are guided by the stars. Long and far he roamed, until he came to a place where three ways parted. To one side lay the Path of Security and to the other the Path of Obscurity, and the third was the way that he had come. The prince stopped, not knowing in which direction to turn his face. As he stood in hesitation, an old man grizzled with years came up to him and spoke: "Retrace your steps, my son. Go back, and spare your people the sorrows of mourning."

But since hearing the old woman's curse, the prince had held his life worth less than an onion peel. He related to the old man all that had befallen him. The old man said, "You are resolved to take the road that leads to certain death, for you must travel on the Path of Obscurity. Listen carefully to what you must do. Ride for seven days without stopping until you see a grove of palm trees. Tether your horse to the outermost tree, and rub this ring. A horse from the stable of the Djinn will appear to carry you to your journey's end. Jackals will howl and wild beasts roar as you ride between the trees, but though the bravest heart must tremble at the sound, look neither before you nor behind. No harm can come to you as long as you are astride the horse.

"In the center of the grove stands the tree you seek. Its leaves are so full you'd say it was a cloud hanging in the sky. Its branches are so outspread that an army could rest in its shade. But beware. To the right of the tree are ravening lions with eyes that glow red as burning coals, and to the left are wild rams, their horns as sharp as spears. In front of the lions lie grass and hay, and by the rams, raw flesh. Dismount and, as quickly as you can, bring the fodder to the rams, the meat to the lions. While the starving beasts are feeding, climb the tree. This will be your only chance to pick the fruit.

"Here is my ring. Take it for protection, since I cannot dissuade you from this foolish quest. Go, and may God smooth your way."

The prince listened to the old man's words and thanked him for his ring. He turned his horse's head along the Path of Obscurity and rode for seven days without rest or pause. Then in the far distance, like a dark stain on the earth, he saw an oasis. When he had reached the first of its trees, he tied his horse and rubbed the magic ring. Instantly there appeared a white pure-blooded mare more graceful than any he had seen before, with a neck arched like a sickle moon and wide nostrils the size of coffee cups. Who can wait to mount such a horse? Without a touch of his spur, she plunged among the palms, folding the earth beneath her hooves. The prince was near to fainting from the horror of the sounds and sights about him. But he remembered what the old man said and looked neither to the front nor to the back until the magic horse stopped before a giant tree. Three fruits, bright as lamps, hung from its branches. On the ground below, a row of lions and a row of rams stood guard.

In the greatness of his desire the prince forgot all fear and leaped from the magic horse. As the old man had told him, he threw the grass from the lions to the rams and the meat from the rams to the lions. Scrambling up the broad trunk of the magic tree, in three heartbeats he had pulled the three fruits from their stems and thrust them into the bosom of his robe to rest against his belt. By the time the wild creatures lifted their heads from their food, the prince was out of reach, streaking away on the back of the white mare with the speed of a bolt of lightning.

Carrying the fruits of the Tree of Raranj and Taranj safely in his bosom, the prince was able to think of home. He mounted his own horse and started on the journey back. But soon curiosity began to overtake prudence. What was inside the fruit? He stopped his horse, unsheathed his knife, and cut open one of the golden fruits of the Tree of Raranj and Taranj. There is no God but Allah! Out of the fruit emerged a maiden like a houri, so radiant that she put the sun itself to shame. She opened her lips to speak and said,

> I am thirsty. I am dry,
> Give me water, or I die!

The prince ran for his waterskin. But in the short time it took to fetch it, the girl had sunk to the ground without breath or life.

The young man rode on a little longer. "If the first of the magic fruits contained a living girl of such surpassing beauty," he thought, "what can there be in the second, I wonder?" He could not wait. As if by itself, his hand sliced into the second fruit. Allah! Like a vision in a dream a second maiden appeared, sister to the first in beauty and as blinding to the eye as a diamond shining in the light. She also said,

> I am thirsty. I am dry,
> Give me water, or I die!

But now the prince was ready. He held the waterskin to her lips and she drank and drank and called for more. He had no more to give her, so he could do nothing but watch as before his eyes she too reached the sum of her years, sinking lifeless to the ground.

To lose two such maidens fair as the light of day only troubled the prince's heart the more. He was maddened with a wish to open the last of the golden fruits of the Tree of Raranj and Taranj, but he did not dare. He could not live if he were to return from the magic tree with nothing to show. Only when he reached the borders of his father's kingdom, only when he stood on the edge of the great river which flows through its lands and makes them fruitful, did he bring out the remaining fruit.

Nothing could prepare him for the perfection of this maiden's face. To look at her made every thought fly clean out of his head. Then she bent to the river to drink, and her beauty doubled as she revived. The prince could not restrain himself. Thanking fate which had sent him such good fortune, he swore that the Maiden of Raranj and Taranj would be his wife.

But a prince's wife would have to ride to the royal palace in proper fashion: in a bridal litter on a she-camel's back, with the drums and music of a festive procession. So he begged the beautiful maiden to wait for him on the riverbank until he came for her with his horsemen and his courtiers and brought her the jewels and robes that the bride of a king's son wears.

The girl, suddenly afraid to be left alone, clambered into the branches of a nearby tree to hide from danger. Soon she heard heavy footsteps. Peering through the leaves, she saw a slave woman the color of the carob fruit coming down the path with a huge water jar swaying on her head. The woman leaned down to fill her jar, when what did she see but the fair face of the Maiden of Raranj and Taranj reflected in the water at her feet. She looked

to her right and looked to her left. There was no one near. Whose reflection could it be, then, but her own? The poor thing began to dance for joy, singing,

> My mistress calls me black,
> But oh, what do I care!
> My mistress beauty lacks,
> And Allah made me fair!
> Nothing will take me back,
> Nevermore shall I serve her!

Watching the woman's antics from where she sat, the magic maiden cried out, "Mind your jar! Be careful or it will break!" Looking up at the voice and seeing the very face that had been in the water, the poor slave woman understood the truth, and bitterness filled her heart. "Why are you sitting in the tree if you are not a bird?" she asked. "I am waiting for the king's son to take me to his palace and make me his bride," said the maiden. "A prince's wife should dress her hair in better fashion! Come, let me comb it smooth," said the slave woman. So the girl slid down from the tree and bent her head for the servant to comb. But instead of a comb, the jealous woman pulled a magic pin from the seam of her gown and stuck it into the girl's head. One sharp cry, and she was transformed into a white dove fluttering round and round the tree.

When the prince and his train arrived with a curtained litter and slave women carrying silk and velvet for the Maiden of Raranj and Taranj—lah! what a blow—instead of a houri there sat a woman the color of the carob fruit, with hanging lips so broad and thick they swept the pebbles at her feet! "Where is my bride?" demanded the prince. "She stands before you," said the slave woman. "An evil Djinn flew by and an ill-starred fate put me in his path." And she began to weep. The prince, also shedding tears, nevertheless took his changed bride home to the king's palace as he had promised.

After that day, every morning a white dove would fly into the royal kitchen and say to the cook, "Is your master sleeping still, or has he risen?" And the cook would reply,

> My master's sleeping; he has not risen.
> He lies abed with the most ugly of women.

Then the white dove would shake with sobs, and she would say,

> Shed, O eyes, tear upon tear
> Of bright pearl and coral rare.

And from her cheeks priceless gems would fall onto the kitchen floor. The cook would fling himself on the ground, chasing after the precious stones and leaving the royal dinner to burn on the fire.

When the prince's dinner was charred three times in three days, he summoned the cook to explain. "Every morning," said the cook, "a white dove flies in through the kitchen window and asks me a question, always the same question, and when I give her the answer, she begins to weep, saying,

> Shed, O eyes, tear upon tear
> Of bright pearl and coral rare.

The cook continued, "And instead of tears she lets fall jewels. A man is a son of Adam, and I cannot stop my hand from reaching for treasure, and I forget the dinner." "What you describe is a wonder," said the prince. "Let me hide in your kitchen and see this thing."

Next day the white dove flew in at the window, and everything happened as the cook had said. But while the cook stooped to pick up the coral and pearls, the prince cornered the strange bird and caught her in his hands. How her little heart beat under her white breast feathers! So the prince began to stroke her with his fingers. Suddenly he felt the head of the pin. He pulled it out, and as he did so, the dove began to grow. She rose taller and taller until her head reached the prince's shoulder. Then she shook her feathers once, and there before him stood his own bride, the real Maiden of Raranj and Taranj.

The crier was sent out through the streets to call,

> All who love the son of our king,
> Hitch your belts and come running!
> Bring with you firewood and kindling.

So the false slave woman was burned to death until nothing was left of her, and the prince was married to the Maiden of Raranj and Taranj.

> Now trim your nails, if they are long;
> Wear fine robes and costly gowns.
> For seven days and seven nights
> All food and drink and gay delights
> Will cost us nothing—not you, not me—
> But all will come from the king's treasury!

Seven Magic Hairs

Palestine

A sultan had two wives. The first had one son, the other two. When the first wife died, the other said to herself, "I must free my sons of my rival's child."

It so happened that this boy burned with a love of horses. He had raised a colt from the stables of the Djinn which raced faster than lightning. One day when he came home, what did he find but his favored colt shedding tears like a man. "What is the trouble?" he asked. And the colt said, "Your father's wife has stewed three geese, two for her own sons and a third, a poisoned one, for you."

When it was time to eat, they all sat down, the sultan's three sons each with a savory goose in front of him. The orphaned boy waited until his father's wife was busy and looking another way, and then he switched his goose for one of the others. They began to eat. One minute they were biting into the food, and the next the son with the poisoned goose was toppling over backwards—dead before a tear could mist his eye.

It was the midwife who had told the boy's stepmother what to do. Now she said, "Dig a deep pit just inside the doorstep. He will tumble into it and break his neck, and that will be the end of him." Fine. The stepmother prepared the hole and set a flimsy cover over it. When the boy came home, he found his horse weeping again, its whole face wet. "What is the matter?" he asked. And the horse said, "That accursed woman, your father's wife, has dug a pit just inside the door for you to fall into and die. Beware of her." Well, when the boy went off to the house he ran up to the door and leaped so far into the room that he landed in the middle of the rolled-up bedding. But his half-brother, who was just behind him, fell headlong into his mother's trap and was killed.

When she had buried her second son, the sultan's wife said, "But for my stepson's horse, none of this would have happened. I wonder how I can kill it." The midwife told her, "Make a brew of barley chaff and bathe in it." The woman washed herself in the boiled water and turned as yellow as saffron. Next the midwife brought flat cakes of toasted bread and spread them under the woman's mattress.

The king looked in on her and said, "What ails you, O queen of our time?" She told him that she felt feeble and asked him to send for a healer. Of course the doctor and the midwife were in on the plot. In less time than it takes to smoke a cigarette, the doctor appeared. He bent over the patient to examine her, and she began to toss from side to side so that the dry bread underneath her cracked every time she moved. "This woman's ribs are broken; can't you hear?" said the doctor. "The only thing that can cure her is the flesh of a young horse. Kill your horse for her." The king called his son and told him. And the boy said, "Yaba, I do not hold my horse dearer than the queen. Yet give me leave to ride him for one last time in parting." "Fine," said the king.

The boy saddled his horse and pulled the girth so tight that its belly stuck into its back. Next he paraded back and forth till the horse warmed up, and then he pulled on the reins and turned the animal away from the palace. "Clear before me, O path!" he said, and in the blink of an eye he had left the palace and the city and his father's kingdom far behind. They reached a seashore, where the horse said, "I have to leave you, but here are seven of my hairs. If ever you need me, burn one and I shall come saddled and ready to go."

After the horse had galloped away, the boy found work to earn his living as a watchman in an orange orchard. To disguise himself he had bought off a butcher the stomach of a sheep and had fitted it over his hair. Since he appeared hairless, he went by the name of Qureyoon, or Baldhead. But whenever he longed for of his horse, he set alight one of the hairs the colt had given him, and like a spirit it appeared all saddled and ready. Then the prince jumped onto its back and galloped up and down the beach to his heart's content.

Now, the king of this country had a palace by the seashore, and every evening the king's daughters would step down to the water and bathe. One day the king's youngest daughter caught sight of Qureyoon flying by on his

horse. "That is the man I want," she said. She called her sisters and told them, "Come, let us ask our father to give us in marriage." Her sisters agreed, and when the king next came to visit them, they said, "Yaba, the woman who was free to wish for whatever she wanted asked for a mate. Won't you marry us?" "That I will," said the king, and he sent his crier to announce through the town: "Every unmarried youth is commanded to pass under the windows of the royal palace." Up came the young men, dressed in their best, and walked past. As for the princesses, they sat in the windows and each let fall her headcloth to the man she loved. One chose the son of a pasha and one the son of a minister, a third the son of a nobleman, and so on till each had singled out a husband. Whom did the youngest princess choose? Why, Qureyoon.

The celebrations were begun and the brides led to their husbands' houses. But the king went home to his palace with a heavy heart. He loved his youngest daughter, and he sorrowed over her choice of a bald gardener's boy. He mourned her fate till he fell sick.

The doctors and astrologers who were brought to the king's bedside said that nothing could save the king but the milk of a white gazelle. So the king's sons-in-law rode here and there looking for such a deer, but they found not a single common one, so how much less a white? Then Qureyoon went into the wilderness and burned one of his magic hairs. He asked the Djinn horse to find him a white gazelle, and—Yamm!—there came a herd like a field of cotton and knelt down to rest in the open. Now the king's sons-in-law rode up, and when they saw a whole herd of white gazelles they asked Qureyoon to give them one. "You may have it, but at a price," said Qureyoon. "Name the sum," they answered. "I'll give you a gazelle, but only after I have branded each of you on his buttocks with my iron." The men conferred and said, "Who will ever know?" So Qureyoon branded them, and they took the gazelle and milked it and offered the milk to the king. The king sipped one sip and pushed aside the bowl, saying, "It tastes bitter;

I cannot drink it." Yet when Qureyoon brought him a bowl of gazelle's milk, the king drank it all, perked up, and recovered.

When some time had passed after the king's illness, a second misfortune struck. A neighboring army invaded his land. All the king's sons-in-law mounted their horses and rode into battle at his side. "What about me?" said Qureyoon. They brought him a lame nag and set him on it backwards, and the boys chased after him with stones.

As soon as he was out of sight, Qureyoon burned a magic hair. Suddenly his horse, equipped with sword and armor, blew in like the wind. Tall as a tower, Qureyoon rode into the battle, scattering the enemy as a wolf scatters sheep. Cutting and slashing and throwing and pulling, he put the enemy to flight. Then in the time it takes to clap one's hands, he rode away and disappeared.

Now, during the battle Qureyoon had received a wound in the hand that the king had bound up with his own kerchief. So when the bald gardener rode into the town sitting backwards on the lame horse, the king recognized  the kerchief tied round his hand and knew which of his sons-in-law had saved him. He went to his youngest daughter's house, saying, "So this is the man the youngest princess chose to marry! Come and sit by my side at the feast in the palace tonight." And he asked Qureyoon to tell his story. "I am a sultan's son," began the youth and listed the events of his life till the day he was married.

Back in his house Qureyoon took the sheep's stomach off his hair and dressed in the fine clothes of a prince. He walked out of the youngest princess's doorway with the bearing and splendor of a king. Seeing him, the other princesses ran to their father, crying, "Our sister has a lover! Our sister has a lover!" "That is Qureyoon," said the king, "and his story is thus and thus and thus." And it silenced them.

In the king's guest hall were assembled all the foremost men of the kingdom. The princes and the pashas and the ministers and the judges had been seated each according to his rank. And in the frontmost row of all in the heart of the great room sat the king's sons-in-law, the husbands of his daughters. None thought of the bald gardener's boy when Qureyoon took his place beside the king. The slaves bore in the trays of food and the king and his guests fell to, all except the husband of the youngest princess. "Why don't you eat, O Qureyoon!" said the king. At the sound of the name every hand paused on its way to the dish. "Is this Qureyoon?" the men asked of each other in their beards. Then the king explained his whole history and said a second time "Why don't you eat, Qureyoon?" "A sultan's son may not sit to a meal with his slaves, O my uncle," said the youth. "What slaves?" asked the king. "This and this and this," said Qureyoon pointing to each of the king's sons-in-law. "Since when are the king's sons-in-law your slaves?" demanded their fathers. "Since the day I branded them on their buttocks with my mark," said Qureyoon. "It is an easy thing to discover. Lift up the back of their robes and cut off my head if I lie!"

But of course it was so. The king sent his shamed sons-in-law away to work at Qureyoon's beck and call, and he set Qureyoon upon the throne to rule in his place.

How often it comes about that fortune turns man's fate around!

The Girl Who
Banished Seven
Youths

Morocco

There was a woman who had seven sons. Whenever she felt her labor pains begin, she said, "This time I shall bear a daughter." But it always was a boy.

Say that she carried again and her month came round. Her husband's sister came to help as her time drew near. Her seven sons went out to hunt, but before they left they told their aunt: "If our mother gives birth to a girl, hang the spindle over the door. When we see it, we shall spin around and come home. If she gives birth to another boy, hang up the sickle. When we see it, we shall cut loose and go." The woman hated her nephews, so although the child was indeed a girl, she hung the sickle over the door. When they saw it, the seven went off into the desert.

The child was given the name Wudei'a Who Sent Away Subei'a, or The Girl Who Banished Seven. She grew and began to play with the other girls. One day she quarreled with her friends, and they said to her, "If there was any good in you, would your seven brothers have left for the desert on the day you were born?"

Wudei'a ran home to her mother. "Is it true that I have seven brothers?" she asked. "Seven brothers you have," her mother said, "but on the day you were born, they went out hunting, and—O sadness and affliction—we have heard nothing of them since." "Then I shall go out and find them," said the girl. "How can you do so, when we have not seen them these fifteen years?" asked her mother. "I'll search the world from its beginning to its end until I find them," said Wudei'a.

So her mother gave her a camel to ride and sent with her a manservant and a maid. A while after they had set out, the manservant said, "Get off the camel and let the maid ride." "Ya Ummi, O my mother," called Wudei'a. And her mother replied, "Why do you call?" "The servant wants me to get off the camel," said Wudei'a. Her mother told the servant to let Wudei'a ride, and they traveled on a little further. Again the servant tried to make Wudei'a dismount, and again she called "Ya Ummi!" for her mother to help. The third time, however, her mother did not reply to her call, for they were too far away to be heard. So now the servant forced her off the camel and let the maid ride. Wudei'a walked on the ground with the blood pouring from her bare feet, for she was not used to walking so far.

Three days they traveled in this way, the maidservant riding high on the camel's back while Wudei'a walked below, weeping and tying cloths around her feet. On the third day they met a merchant's caravan. The servant said, "O lords of this caravan, have you seen seven men hunting in the wilderness?" "You will reach them before noon; their castle is on the road," they answered.

Now the manservant heated pitch in the sun, and with it he rubbed the girl Wudei'a until all her skin was dark. Leading the camel to the castle gate, he called out, "Good news, masters! I have brought your sister to you." The seven brothers ran to greet their father's servant, but they said, "We have no sister; our mother gave birth to a son!" The servant made the camel kneel and pointed to the maid. "Your mother gave birth to a girl, and here she has come." The brothers had never seen their sister; how could they know? They believed their father's servant when he told them that the maid was their sister and that Wudei'a was their sister's slave girl.

Next day the brothers said, "Today we shall sit with our sister; we shall not go to hunt." The oldest brother said to the black slave girl, "Come and look through my hair for lice." So Wudei'a laid her brother's head on her knee and wept as she combed his hair. A tear fell onto her arm. Her brother rubbed the spot, and the white flesh beneath the pitch appeared. "Tell me your story," said her eldest brother. Sobbing and talking Wudei'a told her tale. Her brother took his sword in his hand, went into the castle and cut off the heads of the servant and the maid. He heated water and brought out soap and Wudei'a washed herself until her skin was white again. Her brothers said, "Now she looks like our true sister." And they kissed her and stayed with her that day and the next. But on the third day they said, "Sister, lock the castle gate, for we are going hunting and will not come back till seven days have passed. Lock the cat in with you and take care of her. Do not eat anything without giving a share to her."

Seven days Wudei'a waited in the castle with the cat. On the eighth her brothers returned with game. They asked, "Were you afraid?" "What should I fear?" said Wudei'a. "My room has seven doors, six of wood and the seventh made of iron." After a time the brothers went away to hunt again. "No one dares to approach our castle," they told her. "Be careful only of the cat; whatever you eat, give her half of it. And should anything happen, she knows our hunting grounds—she and the dove on the windowsill."

Cleaning the rooms while she waited for her brothers to return, Wudei'a found a broad bean on the ground and picked it up. "What are you eating?" asked the cat. "Nothing. I found a broad bean among the sweepings," said Wudei'a. "Why didn't you give me half?" asked the cat. "I forgot," said Wudei'a. "Watch and see how I'll repay you," said the cat. "All for half a bean?" asked Wudei'a. But the cat ran to the kitchen, pissed on the fire, and put it out.

There was no fire now to cook the food. Wudei'a stood on the castle wall, looking till she saw a light far off. She set out in that direction, and when she reached the place she found a Ghoul sitting at his fire. His hair was so long that one whisker was a pallet beneath him and the other a blanket above. "Greetings, father Ghoul," said Wudei'a. And the Ghoul replied,

> By Allah, had not your greeting
> Come first before your speaking,
> By now the hills around would hear
> Your young bones crack and your flesh tear!

"I need a fire," said Wudei'a. The Ghoul answered,

> If you want a large ember, you must give a strip of skin
> From your tallest finger to just below your chin.
> Or if the ember you want is a small one,
> From your ear down to your thumb.

Wudei'a took the large ember and began to walk back, the blood flowing from her wound. A raven followed behind her throwing earth on each bloodstain to bury it. When she reached her gate, the bird flew up to the top of the wall. Wudei'a was startled and she scolded, "May God give you cause to feel fear as you have frightened me." "Is this how kindness is rewarded?" said the raven. Down from the wall he dropped and ran along the ground, baring the blood he had covered all the way from her doorstep to the Ghoul's camp.

In the middle of the night the Ghoul woke up and followed the trail of blood until he came to the brothers' castle. He charged through the gate but he found the girl's room shut with seven doors—six made of wooden panels and the seventh a door of iron. He said,

> Wudei'a Who Sent Away Subei'a,
> What was your old father doing when you came?

She answered,

> Lying on a gold bed frame,
> Of fine silk his counterpane
> And his mattress of the same.

The Ghoul laughed and smashed down one of the wooden doors. Then he went away. But the next night and the next, the same thing happened until he had broken all six doors of wood. Only the seventh door was left, the door of iron.

Now Wudei'a was afraid. She wrote a message on a piece of paper and tied the paper around the neck of her brothers' dove with a thread. "O dove, whom my brothers love," she said, "carry my words to them through the air above." The tame bird flew off and did not alight until it sat in the lap of the oldest of the brothers. He read from his sister's paper,

> Six doors are broken down; only the seventh remains.
> Come quickly if you want to see your sister again.

The seven youths jumped into their saddles, and before the middle of the afternoon they had returned home. The castle gate was broken, the six wooden doors of their sister's room were splintered. Through the seventh door of iron they shouted, "Sister, sister, we are your brothers; unlock your door and tell us how it happened."

When she had repeated her tale, they said, "May Allah grant you wisdom, did we not tell you never to eat without giving the cat its share? How could you forget?" Then they prepared themselves for the visit of the Ghoul. They dug a deep pit and filled it with firewood. They lit a fire and fed it until the pit was heaped with glowing coals. Then they laid a mat carefully to cover the opening of their trap and waited.

The Ghoul arrived and said,

> Wudei'a Who Sent Away Subei'a,
> What was your old father doing when you came?

She answered through her door,

> He was flaying mules and donkeys,
> Drinking blood and sucking entrails.
> Matted hair so wild and long
> It was his bed to lie upon.
> O pray he may fall into the fire
> To toast and burn till he expire.

The Ghoul boiled with rage. With a roar he broke down the seventh door and burst in. Wudei'a's brothers met him and said, "Come neighbor, sit with us a while." But when the Ghoul folded his legs to squat on the straw mat, he tumbled into the pit of embers. The brothers threw wood on top of him, heaping more and more until he was all burned up, even his bones. Nothing remained of him except the nail of his little finger, which had jumped into the middle of the room. It lay on the floor until later, when Wudei'a bent down to wipe the tiles with a cloth. Then it pricked her finger and slipped under the skin of her hand. That same moment the girl fell to the ground without life or movement.

Her brothers found her lying dead. They wept and wailed and made her a bier and tied it onto their father's camel's back and said,

> Carry her, O camel of our father,
> Carry her back to her mother.
> Stop not to rest on the way thither
> Stop not for man, or woman either.
> Kneel only for him who says "Shoo!"

The camel lifted itself up to do as they bid. Neither halting nor running, it walked along the road it had traveled before. When half the distance had been crossed, three men spied what looked like a riderless camel lost in the wild. "Let us catch it for ourselves!" they said and shouted to make it stop. But the camel continued on.

Suddenly one of the men called to his friends, "Wait while I tie on my shoe!" As soon as the camel heard the word "shoe" it began to lower itself onto its knees. Joyfully the men ran to seize its halter. But what did they find? A wooden bier and lying on it a lifeless girl! "Her people are wealthy," said one, "look at the ring on her finger!" And swiftly as the thought entered his head he began to pull off the shining jewel for himself. But in moving the ring the robber dislodged the nail from the Ghoul's little finger which had pierced Wudei'a's skin as she swept. The girl sat up alive and breathing. "Long life to him who brought me back from death," she said. Then she turned the camel's head towards her brothers' castle.

Weeping and falling upon Wudei'a's neck, the youths welcomed their lost sister back. "Let us go and kiss the hands of our father and mother before they die," said the eldest. "You have been a father to us," said the others, "and your word like a father's." Mounting their horses, all seven, with their sister on her camel making the eighth, set out for home.

"O sons, what made you leave the world I live in?" said their father when he had kissed and welcomed them. "What made you leave me and your mother weeping night and day in grief over you?" On the first day and the second and the third, the youths rested and said nothing. But on the fourth when they had eaten, the oldest brother told the story from the time when their aunt had so falsely sent them into the wilderness until they had all found each other again. And from that day, they all lived together and were happy.

So ends the story of Wudei'a Who Sent Away Subei'a.

The Bald Man at the Funeral

Morocco

If you wish to hear my story,
Say: God is One
Equal has He none
To Him all praise and glory!

There was or there was not a merchant with one son. As you well know, an only child is a spoiled child. Wherever the merchant walked, the little boy would trot between his legs; whatever the child asked for, his father would give him. Out of love the man was ready to ruin his son.

One day they happened to pass the Gypsies dancing on a tightrope to the tune of a flute, while a trained monkey now jumped up, now lay down in time to their clapping. Delighted, the boy stopped to watch, and what pleased him most was the monkey. Is not every child a child inside his gown, even if he grows to rule the town? The boy begged for the monkey, and he cried, and he would not let his father be until he had asked its price. "Were I to sell that beast, I should lose my living," said the owner. "I possess no field to plow, I have no cattle to pasture. My only income is from the bare bottom of that munificent son of shame!" But gold is a strong argument, and in the end the boy led the monkey home as his pet. Next morning he tied him to the doorpost of his father's store.

Now, the men of the town liked to sit in the entranceway of the merchant's warehouse, some to buy but most to pass the time in talk. When they saw a monkey in their accustomed spot, they curled back their lips in disgust and went elsewhere. The merchant's trade fell off, and his standing. At last he begged his son to take his pet and tie it in the house before it destroyed their livelihood and made them beggars.

With frequent meals and much lazing, little work and much grazing, the monkey grew fat and sleek as a calf. And the boy did nothing but pamper his pet and play. Then one day the merchant came home to find his wife in tears, her face red with scratches from the monkey's claws. In a minute he reached for his gun and shot the monkey dead. When the boy began to weep loud and long over his lost pet, his father suddenly cried, "Are you mourning an unclean creature that nearly destroyed my business and tried to kill my wife! I have been lenient to blindness. Now everything must change."

From that day onwards the boy went down to his father's store to learn the work of buying and selling. Up early and home late, he spent his hours fetching and carrying and adding and subtracting, and woe to him if he ever made a mistake! Go day, come day, in time the spoiled child grew to be a fine youth, able in his work and generous in his ways.

One day as he made his way through the town to the store, the merchant's son saw a crowd of men surrounding a shrouded corpse. "O Protector! What has happened?" he asked. They told him that when the man was alive he had owed money, and now his creditor would not permit the sons to bury their father until the amount had been paid. They, poor things, being penniless as tinkers, did not know what to do. The merchant's son felt for his purse and shook its contents into his lap. By some wonder it contained the very sum of the dead man's debt—not a penny more and not a penny less. So he dropped the coins into the dead man'a hand and made them ring. And his sons were able to take up the bier and carry him to his grave.

"This and this and this is how it happened," said the merchant's son to his father. And the merchant said, "What you did is good; may God reward you. But now complete the favor and buy a funeral meal according to the custom. Let your mother cook a sheep with rice and also a simple stew of lentils. When the mourners leave, I wish to speak to the man who helps himself from the humbler dish."

The funeral guests arrived and pulled back their sleeves to reach into the tray of rice and meat. Then God—let Him be praised and exalted Who has power over all His creations—brought the dead man back to life and sent him to the merchant's house in the shape of a baldheaded man. The merchant's son did not know him when he slipped off his shoes at the door, but he did see that of all the guests at the house, the latecomer alone ate of the meatless dish. "Why look at lentils when there is meat?" said the youth. "It was the food of my father and my grandfather before him," the bald man said.

When the guests began to rise and call for water to wash their hands, the merchant's son told the lentil-eater, "Do not go with the rest; my father wishes to say a word to you." The merchant said, "My son is young and still untried; will you work for a wage and be his guide and mentor?" And the bald man said, "In God's eyes this boy and I are brothers. May God fail all who fail their brothers!"

From one day to the next the merchant's house increased in trade and riches. Where ten dinars had been a profit before, one hundred now piled up. The merchant's son grew bold. He spoke to his father and said, "The caravan is loading in the *suq*. I wish to try my fortune with the rest and take a place beside the traders of renown." His father agreed to give him a load of wares, but only if he traveled with the bald man as his companion.

Next day they led out the mules and set off. For seven days they journeyed until they came to a desolate country, wild and waterless, where even an Afreet might suffer thirst, and a hero feel the prick of fear.

"Let us rest here tonight and tomorrow move elsewhere," said the bald man, and he hobbled the animals and watched while the boy slept in the tent. The night dimmed into darkness and the stars began to show. Suddenly the bald man noticed a light. First it shone then it disappeared.

"Ya Allah, what is this which goes on and off? Let's go and see," he said to himself and took his dagger with him.

When he reached the place he bent low and hid. What he saw was forty thieves busy around their fire. He heard one say, "Make sure that all is quiet in the tent so we can rob it." Another went to look, and when he had walked beyond the light of the fire, the bald man cut off his head. They sent a second and he suffered the same. And so it went until all forty were dead. The bald man listened for anyone left in the camp, but there was no sound. Then he picked over the robbers' treasure, choosing from it all that was of little weight and great value and returned with it to the boy, letting him sleep till morning.

When it was light, they saddled the mules and traveled seven days farther. They arrived at a great city. "Why does no man enter and none come out of its gate?" wondered the bald-headed man. Leaving the boy with the mules he went to discover the reason.

From house to house he wandered and each was like the one before, empty and without the sound of people. At last he came to a palace with high walls and went inside. Sitting by herself was a girl like the morning sun. "Can you tell me the story of this silent city?" he asked her. "O sir," she said, "a Ghoul lives here who has emptied our town so that not even the light of day brings life to it." "Why did he not eat you with the rest?" asked the bald-headed man. "For the beauty of my face," said the girl. "He hunts in the desert round about, feasting on all that moves. Then he comes home and has me clean his teeth while he sits and admires my beauty. Be warned by me and leave this place! Go far away before the Ghoul devours you too." "If Allah wills it, I may kill him instead," said the man. "You know your own wishes," said the girl, and they sat together and waited.

Soon there was a sound of footsteps that shook the ground like an earthquake. It was the Ghoul coming home with his head towering to the sky. He slammed back both leaves of the door and said, "What brings this human?" "Allah brought me," said the bald man. "And I shall eat you," answered the Ghoul. "Only if you catch me," said the man, unsheathing his sword.

They began to fight and God gave the bald-headed man the upper hand so that he struck the Ghoul a deadly blow. "Strike again," cried the Ghoul, hoping to have his life restored. But the bald man said, "My mother taught me not to do the same thing twice!" Then the Ghoul kicked the wall with his foot, turned over and died.

Trilling for joy, the girl said, "Now you shall be my husband and I no man's wife but yours." "Let us first find my brother," said the bald man. And they filled their cloaks with gold from the riches of the palace and left.

"We have wealth ten times beyond the price of our wares," the bald man said to the boy. "It is time to turn homewards." They loaded one mule with the robbers' treasure and a second with the treasure of the silent city and taking the Ghoul's fair-faced prisoner with them, they started on the journey back.

When they came in sight of the boy's home town, they halted. The bald man said, "We have been good partners; let our parting be as good. Divide the riches between us." Then gold and silver and pearl and coral were heaped into equal shares. "And now the girl," said the bald man. "Take her, brother, she is yours," the boy told him. "No," said the bald man. "We have lived like brothers and, as brothers do, must take one half each." And he seized the girl by one foot and gave the other to his brother and lifted his sword into the air to cut her in two pieces. The girl trembled and shook and let fall one egg and then two more, which the bald man crushed with his heel to kill the half-formed Ghouls inside.

"As you once saved me, now I have made you safe," he said. "Take the girl and God send you happiness. My time is up." And he walked away and did not turn his head.

"Where is your brother, child?" said the merchant when he had welcomed his son back. "He took leave of us near the burial ground," said the youth. "Let us bring him back," said his father. The two men hurried to that place and saw the bald man huddled over a grave. "Come back!" they shouted; he did not reply. They went to him and touched his shoulder, but he crumbled and turned to dust between their fingers.

God is good; so is the end He metes out for men!

The Good
Apprentice and
the Bad

Syria

Once there were two poor boys who worked for a baker. Their job was to stoke the hot oven. Though it was wintertime and still raining in their city in the hills, the harvest had already begun in the plains far to the south. One of the boys said, "Come brother, we can earn better money working in the fields than in this bakery!" So they packed two goatskin bags full of rations for the journey and set off.

One of the young men was called Abu-Sharr, or Father of Evil—and the other Abu-Kheir, or Father of Good. As they were walking away from the city, Abu-Sharr said, "Let us begin by eating the bread in your bag, and later when that is finished, we can eat mine." "Why not?" said his friend. But when Abu-Kheir's bag was empty and he asked for a bite to eat, Abu-Sharr refused to share the food in his own bag. For three days they continued along the road, and Abu-Kheir did not taste a crumb of bread or wet his tongue with a sip of water. At last he stopped and said to his companion, "Since we are not of one heart let us part." The other agreed and said, "I am comfortable on this level road. Why don't you take the rocky path up there?"

Too weak with hunger to argue, Abu-Kheir stumbled up the steep track that wound through the hills. All of a sudden he came to a huge fig orchard planted on the side of a slope. Now, as we said before, it was still the middle of winter, but in this orchard the trees were laden with ripe fruit, both green and black! The starving boy fell on those figs and ate and ate until he could eat no more. Then he dipped his hand into a well that was brimming with water, and after drinking his fill he threw himself under a tree to rest.

Just then three white doves flew down into the branches of the tree. One of them was saying, "That blind cobbler just outside the city hammers away all day and cannot save a penny. Yet three pots of gold lie hidden under his last. What if someone were to tell him?" And another replied, "What about the people in Damascus who pay for every cup of water they drink? If they only knew to dig under their gate, they would have water welling out in floods!" And the third dove said, "Then there is the sultan who has beheaded all the doctors because they cannot cure his daughter. If he would but feed her a mouthful of his hunting dog's flesh, she would recover at once."

All this while Abu-Kheir was listening. When the birds flew off into the sky again, he picked himself up and washed and said, "The first thing I'll do, by Allah, is go to the blind man and see if any of this is true or not!" And he tightened his belt about his hips and swung down the slope.

When he reached the cobbler's shop, he gave him a shoe and asked, "How much do you want for patching it?" "One penny," said the cobbler, and sewed it up. Abu-Kheir paid him and left. But when he had walked a little way, he took off the shoe and tore out the stitches. He waited till the sun was low; then he returned to the shoe mender and said, "Here, brother, I'll give you two pennies instead of one, but work more carefully this time." The blind man worked away until the sun had set. When it was dark, Abu-Kheir said, "I am a stranger in this town, O my brother, and have no place to sleep. Will you let me spend the night in your shop? Don't worry; I shall not gnaw at your leather!"

Well, the cobbler locked Abu-Kheir into his workshop and went home. As soon as he found himself alone, Abu-Kheir began digging under the last. He found one, two, three pots, each filled with gold coins. On the lid of the third was an inscription which said, "Cursed child of a cursed father is he who enriches himself off the money of the poor!" He returned the treasure to the earth where he had found it, keeping only a few gold pieces, which he tied into his headcloth.

Early in the morning when the shoemaker came to open the shop, Abu-Kheir said, "Brother, I am dying of hunger. Take this gold coin and bring me a trayful of cheese and honey cake, since your city is famous for it." The blind man did as he was told. When Abu-Kheir had eaten a share of the sweetmeat, he said to the cobbler, "Carry the rest to your family." The cobbler's wife, who had tasted only want and humiliation till then, began to sing. She fed her children and gave thanks to God.

After a while Abu-Kheir said to the cobbler, "Here is more money; buy me a suckling lamb roasted brown and crisp!" When he had eaten what he wanted of it, he sent the rest to the cobbler's house. The poor woman said, "Where do all these blessings come from that have fallen upon us today?" And she laughed with joy.

When the shoemaker returned to his shop, Abu-Kheir said, "Come, let me show you what is yours." And he dug out the three pots full of gold from under the last and put them into the blind man's hands. But the cobbler said, "No, brother, when two men go hunting together, they split their catch share and share alike. Let us divide this treasure between you and me." "Let God alone be between you and me," said Abu-Kheir. "I'll only accept a kerchief full to see me to Damascus." And he took leave of the shoemaker.

When Abu-Kheir arrived in the great city of Damascus, he went to the covered bazaar, sat in one of the stores, and said, "I am thirsty! Give me a drink of water, if you love God." The men around him said, "How can we give you water just like that, when every glassful costs us money?" "Just give me a drink," said Abu-Kheir, "and I'll find you enough water to flood your valley." The people rushed to inform the sultan, and Abu-Kheir was summoned to the palace.

"I'll give you all my kingdom if you find me water," said the sultan to Abu-Kheir. "I need only ten or fifteen men with tools to dig," said Abu-Kheir. The men were sent for and began to break the ground where Abu-Kheir showed them by the city gate. The trench they had made was hardly as deep as their belts when the water began to flow in torrents. All Damascus was filled with joy. "Whatever you wish for, we shall grant it," said the sultan. But Abu-Kheir asked only for money enough to see him to the land of the king with the ailing daughter.

When he came to a city with a row of human heads on the wall, Abu-Kheir knew that here was the city of which the doves had spoken. He went into the king's presence and boldly said, "Sire, I am the one who shall cure your daughter!" The king warned him, "Do not undertake what is beyond your power. Take a look at all those heads. Yours will join them if you fail. But should you heal her, my daughter is yours to wed." Abu-Kheir accepted the king's conditions. He called for the royal hunting hound, killed it, cooked its flesh, and fed the princess one mouthful and then another. She sat up in bed and opened her eyes. "Where have I been?" she said.

"My daughter is yours for one cup of coffee! I ask no other bride-wealth," said the king. After dressing the princess in a long silk gown, they brought the sheikh to recite the words that would bind them to each other as man and wife. The king said, "You saved the princess and she is yours by right. What do you wish from me?" And Abu-Kheir said, "More than anything else, I want a bakery to be built in my name, a bakery where whoever comes to eat bread may eat free." So the king had a fine bake oven built. And from all around, the hungry and the wretched crowded into it to eat good bread without paying.

Meanwhile Abu-Sharr had worked in the harvest and finished, but he spent all the money he had earned and was forced to wander about begging for every mouthful he ate. One day someone said to him, "Why do you come whining to me! There is a man who has opened a bakeshop in which the bread is free. Go there and fill your belly and sleep." "I'm off," said Abu-Sharr. When he came to the place, he looked in at the window, and who should be sitting there but his old partner Abu-Kheir with his wife. "So it is that starveling who owns this bakery!" said Abu-Sharr. "How did it happen?" Then he shouted up to Abu-Kheir, "Come down, brother, and show me what road led you to such good fortune, for if you don't I'll kill you." "All blessings are from Allah! I'm ready to go," said Abu-Kheir, and from here to there he set Abu-Sharr under the fig tree in the magic orchard and left him.

That fig tree had dried up in the meantime, and the spring of water had shrunk to a puddle. Three Afreets rose and said, "Someone must have been listening when we were talking. Don't you see how the cobbler has found his pots of gold, and a river has begun to flow in Damascus, and the king's daughter has been healed?" Abu-Sharr heard their words. He said, "Of course someone was here and overheard, or do you suppose there's no one in the world but you with your big mouths? Abu-Kheir heard you!" "What do they call you, then?" asked the spirits. "Abu-Sharr," he replied. "Then let each of you be rewarded according to his name," said the Afreets. And they caught Abu-Sharr and tore him to pieces and threw him into the empty well.

A Lost Shoe
of Gold

Saudi Arabia

Here you have One, the Unique God in his high heaven, and there you have a girl, a sultan's daughter. Her beauty was so bright and her heart so warm that her mother likened her to a flame of fire and called her Sit Lahab.

Every day Sit Lahab went to the sheikh's house to be tutored in the Koran with the other children. One day her teacher said, "Whoever brings me a stuffed goose for my lunch tomorrow will receive the prize!" The children scattered, each vowing to bring what the teacher wanted, but they all forgot. All, that is, except Sit Lahab, who went home and told her mother.

"Why not?" said her mother. And she roasted a goose this fat, and stuffed it with rice, and stuffed it with nuts, and browned it in gravy till it was just right—fit to delight the sweet-faced listener sitting before me. Early in the morning Sit Lahab's mother packed the food in a pot and said, "Go, child, or the others will get there before you!" So the girl put on her slippers— one of silver and one of gold—and set out.

When she reached the sheikh's house and opened the schoolroom door, what did she see? A dead horse hanging from the ceiling, and the sheikh tearing at the raw meat with his teeth. O Lord! O Protector! So this was no ordinary teacher but a Ghoul. Sit Lahab fled. But as she stooped to snatch up the slippers left by the door, in her hurry she picked up only one.

That night when she lay sleeping on her bed, the Ghoul came and stood by her pillow and said,

> O Sit Lahab, Sit Lahab, when you came, what did you behold
> That made you take the shoe of silver and leave the shoe of gold?

She answered,

> There was nothing; nothing odd.
> I saw my teacher fasting,
> Praying to the Everlasting,
> The true and living God.

"Tell me what you saw, or I'll eat up all your father's camels," said the Ghoul. "Eat them, then!" said Sit Lahab. And he did.

The next night at the same time, the Ghoul returned and asked,

> O Sit Lahab, Sit Lahab, walking in so bold,
> What made you take the silver and leave the gold?

And she said,

> I saw the Koran open on my teacher's knees
> And in my teacher's eyes a look of peace.

"Tell me what you saw, or I'll devour your father's sheep!" said the Ghoul. "Do it, then!" said Sit Lahab. And when the day dawned, the sheep were gone.

Night after night the Ghoul visited the poor girl, and night after night her answer was the same. At last he said, "Tell me what you saw, or I'll take away your father and mother!" But still she replied as she had done before. So now she was fatherless and motherless, an orphan to be pitied.

Sit Lahab sat all alone. Of her father's palace and his possessions, nothing was left but a heap of dust blown by the wind. What was the girl to do? She waited until it was evening. Then she placed the hem of her gown between her teeth, so it would not trip her when she ran. She put the setting sun in her face, for in the other direction lay desert and sand, and she said, "Save me, O You Whose wide gate is ever open, O You from Whose door no one is turned away!" After which, she hurried on her way. She walked and she walked until she came across a party of potters camping in the dark. So she flung herself down beside their load of earthenware to rest. She was almost dead for weariness. What sultan's daughter had come or gone this far?

Well, Sit Lahab's eye had hardly sunk in sleep when who should come after her but the Ghoul!

> O Sit Lahab, Sit Lahab, when you came, what did you behold
> That made you take the shoe of silver and leave the shoe of gold?

And she said,

> I saw my teacher fasting,
> Praying to the Everlasting.

"Tell me what you saw, or I shall overturn this load of earthenware and smash every pot and jar!" said the Ghoul. "You turned my father's palace into an empty ruin; shall I stop you from breaking these pots?" she said. So the Ghoul broke all the potters' wares, and Sit Lahab continued on her journey.

All through the night and the following day she traveled without stopping. Then at sundown she came across some olive growers on their way to market. They had tethered their donkeys and were lying asleep next to their goods— precious olive oil sealed into leather bottles, each made of a whole sheepskin. Sit Lahab settled down nearby to sleep. It was not long before the Ghoul came to ask his question. She said,

> I saw the Koran open on my teacher's knees
> And in my teacher's eyes a look of peace.

"Tell me what you saw, or I'll spill out the farmers' oil and gobble up their donkeys!" said the Ghoul. And she said, "Are they dearer to me than my father and my mother?" So the Ghoul burst all the sheepskins full of oil and made away with the tethered donkeys.

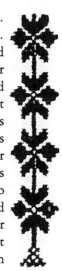

As for Sit Lahab, she did not know where to take herself next. She knew only that she must avoid the places where people lived. So, putting the east before her, she started to walk. She walked away from the cities and houses of men into the wilderness. For three days she wandered, thanking God whenever she found a wild herb to eat or a pool of water to drink from. Then fate willed that a prince of that region, son of a sultan, should go snaring birds with his companions in that same wilderness. How great was his astonishment to find a girl alone so far from the protection of her family! Lifting her onto his horse, he carried her to his father's palace. He handed her over to his sister's care, and when Sit Lahab had been bathed and dressed and restored to her former bloom and beauty, the prince's sister said, "We must gain her as a bride for my brother." But the sultan said, "We know nothing of her. What is her tribe, what is her clan? One day my son will sit where I am sitting; what if she is not well-born?"

Next morning the prince's sister tied sticks together and wrapped them in colored rags to make two dolls. "Will you play?" she asked Sit Lahab, and they sat together, each speaking for her doll. "I am seeking a bride for my son," said the princess's doll. "Do not ask and risk refusal," said Sit Lahab, "for the bridal portion I demand is greater than the contents of your coffers." But the princess's doll pressed her suit. At last Sit Lahab said, "My bride-price equals all the camels that a man can brand in one day, starting with sunrise and stopping at sunset."

The prince's sister went running with the happy news. "Who but one of noble line would ask for a bridal portion worth so many camels?" So with feasting and dancing, with much singing of songs and ringing of gongs, Sit Lahab was married to the sultan's son according to the law of the prophet.

What next? Sit Lahab became pregnant. Her months went by and her days, and Allah lightened her burden and opened the ways. She lay down in childbed and gave birth to a boy fair as the moon and fat as a lamb, the

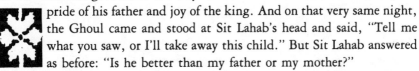

pride of his father and joy of the king. And on that very same night, the Ghoul came and stood at Sit Lahab's head and said, "Tell me what you saw, or I'll take away this child." But Sit Lahab answered as before: "Is he better than my father or my mother?"

Next morning—look!—there was no child. How the gossip broke out then. "The prince's wife is a monster. The prince's wife is a Ghoul. She has stuffed into her stomach the child she had carried under her heart." But the prince said, "She is my wife; she will bear me another son." So the women locked their fingers round their lips and muffled the story in silence.

Well, on one day Sit Lahab took the bath of the forty days and was cleansed, and on the next she was pregnant again. All that had happened before was repeated. In the morning she was delivered of a strong and handsome child, and in the evening the Ghoul was at her bedside.

> O Sit Lahab, Sit Lahab, when you came, what did you behold
> That made you take the shoe of silver and leave the shoe of gold?

She said,

> I saw my master fasting,
> Praying to the Everlasting,
> The Koran open on his knees,
> In his eyes the light of peace.

The Ghoul threatened to take her second child and she said, "Is this son dearer to me than my father and my mother?"

Next morning when the women wailed over the missing child, the prince spoke to them as he had spoken before. But when Sit Lahab gave birth to a third son, and this child could not be found in the morning any more than the others, the prince's father, the sultan, stood by no longer. First he bound the prince with ropes to keep him quiet. Then he sent a crier to call through the city,

> Whoever loves the king,
> A living ember bring,
> And sticks and kindling.

And all the people came to the palace and built a bonfire as big as a house. Then the sultan, dragging Sit Lahab, prepared to throw her into the fire and burn her to death.

But look! Four horses in the distance, galloping hard toward them. The sunlight was flashing off stirrups of the purest gold, and the bridles were jingling with jewels of coral and pearl. On the first horse sat an old man with a white beard that hung to his belt and a turban as wide as a banqueting tray. Behind him rode three small children so fair they seemed like pieces of the moon.

As the sultan and his people watched, the old man dismounted and went to Sit Lahab. He kissed her between the eyes, saying, "I look upon this woman as my daughter, and whoever harms her with a drop of water will pay for it with blood. Her name is Sit Lahab, and I was her teacher." And he told her story from "There was, and there was not" to "peace be with you." Then he said, "I threatened her with horrors and hounded her with punishments, but she endured in silence. I destroyed her house and scattered her tribe, yet she did not speak. He who submits himself to Allah's will with patience is rewarded." And he lifted the three children off their horses and said to Sit Lahab, "Here are your sons whom I stole from your arms. Everything has returned to what it was. Your father and your mother wait for you in their house." Then, stamping his foot on the ground, the old man was transformed into a terrible Ghoul and vanished.

And what of Sit Lahab? With the prince by her side and her sons to fill her eyes, she lived a life of happiness to the end of her days.

> So we left them, and back we came,
> And never saw them again.

The Woodcutter's
Wealthy Sister

Syria

> Believe him who tells his story first,
> And bring him grapes to quench his thirst.

There was a man with ten children who lived at the foot of a hill. Every day he climbed to the hilltop and collected firewood to sell in town. At sunset his hungry family would wait, watching for his return, and he would bring them a loaf of bread with perhaps an onion or an olive for flavoring. He was a poor man—but what was worse, he lacked not only gold but brains.

One day when the dead wood on the hilltop was almost gone, he decided to try another hill farther off which was covered with trees. As he was walking home in the evening, his load on his back, he met a finely dressed woman jingling with gold bangles and rustling with rich stuffs. "Don't you recognize your own sister, O my brother?" she asked. "I wait and wait in vain for you to visit me, but there, not every heart is tender." "I have no sister," said the man. "What! Will you deny me altogether now? But tell me, brother, what you are doing here?" "I am heading home after my day's work," sighed the woodcutter. "You should give yourself a rest from drudgery and let me care for you," said the woman. "Why not come and share my good fortune? Bring your children and your wife to live with me in my big house. I have plenty of good things: enough to suit your every mood!" "Is that so?" replied the man, not knowing what to say. "Would I deceive my own brother?" said the woman. "Come with me now and see for yourself; then you will know the way tomorrow." And she pulled him by the hand.

And what a house she had! Sack upon sack of wheat and lentils and dried broad beans! Row upon row of jars filled with olive oil and butterfat! The woman invited the woodcutter to eat, and cooked a suckling lamb just for him. "Now, doesn't that remind you of our days of long ago?" she asked him. The poor man pounced on the food like a beggar, because it had been many months since he had tasted meat. "I have never seen her before, but who can she be except my sister?" he wondered. "Who else would make me so welcome, who else show me such hospitality?" And he hurried back to tell his wife, running so fast that it's a wonder he didn't hurt himself.

But the woodcutter's wife was not convinced. "Wouldn't I have heard of it if I had a sister-in-law?" she asked. "And if she is not my sister-in-law, for what good purpose does she want us all to live with her?" She tried to reason with her husband; she tried persuasion; but in the end she had to gather her ten children and, leading their scrawny cow by a rope, follow him to his sister's house.

Feast upon feast awaited them. For a month they did nothing but eat and drink and lie in the shade to rest. The children's faces, which had been thin as knife blades, began to fill out. The woodcutter laughed and said, "A curse on all toilsome work! May Allah never bring back those weary times, but let us live forever like this—fresh as the cool of the day."

Then one night while the woodcutter's family slept in the lower room of the house, the sister crept down from her loft and tried the door, muttering,

> All my fat and my flour eaten and gone,
> But now they are plump; I need not wait long.

For this was a She-Ghoul of the kind that feeds on human flesh. Then the cow who was tethered to the doorpost turned on the monster and said,

> My eyes can burn you like a flame,
> My tail can whip you till you're lame,
> My horns can tear and gore and maim.

And the She-Ghoul had to go back the way she had come.

The next night the monster crept down again, and the cow kept her out as before. But on the third night the cow, moving to fend off the Ghoul, kicked the wooden door with her hoof and woke the woodcutter's wife. So the woman heard her husband's sister when she said,

> All my fat and my flour eaten and gone,
> But now they are plump; I need not wait long.

And she heard the cow's reply:

> My eyes can burn you like a flame,
> My tail can whip you till you're lame,
> My horns can tear and gore and maim.

She shook her husband to wake him, but he was sunk in sleep from too much eating and would not stir.

In the morning when the woodcutter's wife told him all she had heard in the night, he said that it must have been a bad dream. Yet at noon his wealthy sister came to him and said, "O my brother, I have a craving for cow's meat today. Surely you will not begrudge me that bony beast of yours." How could a man refuse his sister? So he killed his cow and made his wife cook the meat. She set the tastiest portion on a plate, and send her oldest daughter to take it to her aunt. When the girl looked into the sister's room, she saw not her aunt but a demon. Its hair was wild and its eyes blazed red, and from the rafters men and women were hanging dead. Without a sound she tiptoed back, but in her hurry she stumbled on the stair, and all the food slipped off the dish and onto the floor. Her mother came to scold her, and the girl reported what she had seen. The mother repeated the tale to the father, but still the woodcutter said, "That is childish talk. How can you want to kick away such comfort, when you should be thanking God and saying prayers for our blessings!"

That night there was no cow to stop the She-Ghoul from entering. The woodcutter's wife watched as the demon, feeling each of the children in their beds, repeated to herself:

> All my fat and my flour eaten and gone,
> But now they are plump; I need not wait long.

"Sister-in-law, what do you want?" called the woodcutter's wife, who had not closed an eye. "I was just covering my nieces and nephews to keep them from the cold," said the She-Ghoul and climbed back up the stairs to her own bed.

Next day the woodcutter's wife boiled a ground lentil soup to feed her children and watched them splatter and stain their clothes without a word. Then she went to her sister-in-law and said, "I want to go to the stream to wash my children's clothes. Lend me your copper pot so that I can heat water and bathe the children too." And down she went to the *wadi* and lit a fire and heaped green wood on it to give off smoke. She hung a couple of rags where the wind would catch them and called her children to her. Then she prayed, "Open for us, O spacious gate of Allah's protection!" And holding the hem of her long gown between her teeth and pulling her children along by the hands, she ran and ran away from the She-Ghoul's home back to her own home at the foot of the hill.

From time to time the She-Ghoul stepped out of her house to cast a glance down into the valley. She saw the thick smoke rising and the cloth playing in the wind and she said, "There she is, still busy at her washing!" But when the day waned and the sun began to set and still her guests had not returned, she hastened down to see what could delay them. There she found the place abandoned and mother and children gone. She howled so loud that the hills around her rang. And she cried,

> Why did I fatten and fatten them
> When by now I might have eaten them!

The woodcutter, who was dozing under the grape arbor outside the door, heard her howl. Now he began to be alarmed. He looked around for a place to hide. He could hear the She-Ghoul coming and he knew that her knife was hot and sharpened for him and no one else. In his fright he dived into a rubbish heap and buried himself completely. The She-Ghoul entered the yard like a storm, biting her fingers and snorting when she breathed. Inside and out, from the pigeon houses on the roof to the hen coop under the stairs, she searched for him.

At last the She-Ghoul climbed onto the hill of rubbish to gain a better view. As she shifted her weight to the place where the woodcutter was hiding, out of his mouth popped a loud belch. "Was that you sighing, O my headcloth?" shouted the demon. And she pulled it off. She stood on her toes to look as far as she could, and the woodcutter's stomach rumbled again. "Was that you complaining, O my robe?" she said. And she threw it off. And now she stood in her own hairy skin, a monstrous She-Ghoul for all to see and run from. She heard the woodcutter beneath her once again, and she said, "It is the rubbish making a noise! Let me see why." And she flung one half of the heap to the right and the other to the left and pulled the poor woodcutter out.

"Now," she said, "tell me, O my brother, where shall I sink my teeth in first?"

> Start with my two ears,
> So deaf to my wife's fears!

he wept. "And then?" said the demon.

> Then go on to both my arms
> Which dragged her into such harm.

"And then?"

> Then go on to my two legs
> Which did not go where she begged.

And so on, until she had eaten him all and nothing of him was left to question or to give an answer. But so it is with lazy men: using their own hands they dig the hole into which they fall.

> My story I have told it the best I can.
> Now it is for you to tell one in return.

.. ..

The Ring of the
King of the Djinn

.. ..

Egypt

Neither here nor there lived a poor fellow like me. He could find no work to do, so he just sat home idle. His wife said, "May Allah ruin your house, man, have you no gumption? Can't you go ferreting here and there a little and bring home something for your children to eat?" "What can I do?" said the man. "I have no money to spend, and whom do I know to borrow from?" "Has friendship cut you off, then?" said his wife. "Ah!" sighed the man.

Well, like other married women, this wife wore a headdress with a row of forty coins sewn across it to adorn her brow. These she cut off and gave to her husband, saying, "Here are a couple of pennies to last you till you find some work." So the man went off to see what lay in store for him at God's gate.

Now, there was another man who had leased a fig tree. That is, he had promised its owner a sum of money in return for the harvest. And what a tree it was! Every fig on it the size of a meat dumpling! But as soon as ever a fruit began to ripen, a bird flew down and gobbled it up. The man complained, "What does that leave me but the price of the lease?" And he hid and lay in wait for the bird. Sure enough there it came, thrashing its wings in its hurry to get at the figs. As soon as it perched in the tree, the man sprang out of his hiding place and grabbed it. "Did I catch you at it, you thieving wretch, or was it the wind that blew you this way, hah?" he said. And he tied the bird's feet together and began to beat it with a stick. Who should be passing that way just then but our hero, the poor fellow! "Stop!" he said. "Have some pity, and let the bird go!" "Is this your business to meddle in?" replied the man, "I won't let it go unless you pay me twenty piasters." "I can only spare you ten," said the poor man. "I'll take them," said the man, and handed over the bird.

The poor man cut the string and was about to free the bird, when it ruffled its feathers so that a couple of them dropped to the ground. "If you find yourself in a tight place," it said, "burn one of my feathers and I shall come to you."

The owner of the figs, wishing to taunt our compassionate friend some more, began to kick a stray dog. He would not stop until the poor man gave him another ten piasters. Next he began to torment a kitten that had hardly opened its eyes, and in this way he earned ten more. At last he caught a mouse and would not set it free until the poor man gave him his last ten piasters.

Now the man had nothing left, not even the price of a bite of bread or a sip of milk. He said to himself, "What does it matter now what I do or leave undone?" And he set fire to one of the bird's feathers. What happened? A huge winged creature, the size of this straw mat we are sitting on, dropped from the sky and alighted on the ground beside him. "Tell me your trouble," said the bird. And the man told him the story. "Climb onto my back and come with me," said the bird. "I am a son of the king of the Djinn. I shall take you to my father's court, but remember, though he offers you the richest gifts, accept nothing and ask only for the ring he wears on his little finger."

They came to the court, and the king of the Djinn said, "This and this is yours to take." But the poor man answered, "Sire, I wish for something dearer still!" In the end the king said, "Tell me, what is the thing you wish for?" And the poor man confessed that it was the ring on the king's little finger. "Take it; it is yours to keep," said the king.

The poor man immediately tried out the ring. Straight away an Afreet reared himself before him, saying, "Subbek Lubbek at your beck and call to do your will and wish." "Carry me to such and such a city!" said the man. And there he was in that city, as pleased as pleased could be. Whatever wish he made was fulfilled. So he began to wish for gardens filled with trees, and streams running with water, and all that follows from there. He said, "O give me a house like the sultan's palace, but finer." And a house appeared just as he wished, built with bricks: one of silver for every one of gold, with shady arbors to sit in and pools for fish. The man invited the sultan and his minister for a visit, and they pulled their shoestraps tight and gladly followed him.

When the sultan saw the man's palace and his possessions, he said to himself, "I don't have anything to equal this!" Then he told the poor man, "I want to give you my daughter as your wife, O my uncle." And the man answered, "That may well be, sire."

Toward sunset they brewed coffee and called the girl. "Will you take this man?" they asked her. She said, "I am no different from other women. I think of marriage." So they brought the *qadi* to pronounce the man's right to the girl, and he took her to his palace where it stood in the middle of its gardens. There they lived all by themselves for one day and two days and more.

The girl admired the pretty ring on her husband's little finger. Why not? It was the work of the Djinn. She asked him to give it to her, but he refused. This did not please her. When the man saw that his bride was unhappy, he sent for the goldsmith and he sent for some gold, and he engaged the man to make another such ring for his wife. In the morning the goldsmith brought her a ring as like the ring of the king of the Djinn as he could fashion. But she was not satisfied, and day after day she sent him away to try again. At last the goldsmith's soul was choked out of his body with his sighing. "I need to earn my fee," he said. "If I were to have your husband's ring for just one night, I could copy it."

That evening the sultan's daughter sat by her husband and, in such a way that he could not refuse her, begged and begged to have the loan of the ring for one night. It chanced that on the very next day the sultan expected all the notables of the land to attend him in his *diwan*. The poor man, now without his ring, went with the rest. In his absence the sultan's daughter sent for the jeweler and happily gave him the ring to copy in his workshop overnight. By now the man was weary to the point of death with this ring. Turning it over in his hand, he said, "O Lord, how I wish that this whole palace with its garden were in the middle of the seven seas!" On the instant the ground heaved and lifted itself up. The people looked and looked, but where the palace had been they found nothing.

Word reached the sultan very soon that his daughter and the palace she lived in were gone. He turned on her husband, and the poor man said, "You see what has happened. I know no more than you do." "Where is my daughter?" demanded the sultan. "Bring her to me or I shall cut off your head." "Give me three days' grace, and if God wills it I'll find her," said the poor man.

Having neither palace nor ring, the man was at a loss where to begin. Then he remembered the bird's second feather. When he set it on fire, the huge fowl immediately appeared and listened to his story. Summoning the dog and the cat and the mouse, the bird described to them what had happened to the ring of the king of the Djinn. The dog hunched his back and the cat jumped onto it. Then the cat spread its lap and the mouse sat in it. Thus they ran through the streets, the mouse in the cat's arms as if he were its

infant, while the people marveled at the sight of three such enemies in sweet
agreement.

They reached the shore of the sea, and the dog began to swim. One day
passed and a little more; then they came to an island and dragged themselves
ashore, worn thin with hunger, washed out with sea water—in short, in a
state to be pitied. But look! There was the palace and everything in it safe,
every stone upon the other, and the princess and the goldsmith not missing
a hair from their heads.

The cat jumped up to the window, and the mouse slipped in under the
door. There sat the goldsmith with the sultan's daughter, side by side on a
soft cushion, feeding each other supper. The animals hid till they saw them
both fall back asleep, and then they began their search. From the top of the
cupboard to the floor under the rug they hunted, leaving not a palm's breadth
untouched; but they could not find the ring. The mouse said, "There is no
place left. I say it must be under the tongue of that misbegotten sinner."
And he stuck his tail up the goldsmith's nose. Of course the man sneezed,
and the ring popped out of his mouth. Now they could begin the journey
back.

The dog bent down and the cat climbed onto his back. The cat leaned
back and the mouse rode on his knees with the ring in his paws. And they
plunged into the waves. When they had crossed six seas and the seventh
was still before them, the dog said, "It is not just, when I have borne the
heaviest burden, carrying you all the way, that you should give the man his
ring and receive the praise and the favor. Let me have it, or I'll toss you
into the sea." What could they do in such a place and time but obey? And
the dog, who was made to hold quails and partridges in his jaws and nothing
smaller, had hardly swum a few strokes when he dropped the ring and it
sank out of sight. But he said nothing until they reached the land and all
fell down exhausted, finished.

At break of day a fisherman came to the water's edge where the animals
were sleeping. When he saw a dog and a cat and a mouse lying side by side,
he said, "Praise be to Allah, a miracle! This cast of my net shall be in the
name of Mohammad the prophet." He cast his net, and when he pulled it
in, he fed some of the fish to the animals on the shore. The poor creatures,
starving from their journey, fell upon the gift of food. And—praise be!—
what did the cat feel under his tooth but the ring, the very ring they had
lost! This time they hung it for safekeeping on the mouse's tail, where they
could see it as they walked, and off they hurried.

Where did they find the poor man? In prison, with the king's swordsman
coming to cut off his head. The three days' grace was spent, and the poor

man was preparing himself for his end, the name of his Maker upon his tongue. But at the very door and doorstone of death, he was able to turn around and come away. On the brink of execution the mouse brought his salvation. The man rubbed the ring, made his wish, and returned everything to what it had been before—except that the goldsmith was fast asleep and snoring with his head against the belly of our princess, by Allah!

Now the poor man put on a fine robe and hurried into the presence of the sultan. "Allow me one last question," he said. "Why do you want to cut off my head?" "Answer my question first," said the sultan. "What have you done with my daughter?" "Why, nothing! Come and see her sitting in her house," said the man. And they went together and found that it was so.

Now the sultan did not know where to hide his head, for had he not been unjust to this poor man? So he set him by his side and made him first minister of the land and promised him forty gold coins . . .

When he heard the words "forty coins," the man jumped up, remembering his wife, the mother of his children. Down through the *suq* he hastened, buying robes of silk and shoes of leather for his sons and gowns of velvet for his wife. Tying the presents into his saddlebags, he went off to find them.

When the children put on the shoes of leather, they became as fine as ministers' sons. The people said, "Who are they?" and, "Can this fine lady with the velvet dress and drawers to match be the poor fellow's wife? Why, only yesterday she was picking weeds and wild herbs to feed her children and gathering dry cow dung for her fire!" But the poor man only said, "Come with me, wife." And he took them home with him to his palace.

The bird has flown away;
God send a sweet end to your day.

What God Wrote
Cannot
Be Unwritten

Iraq

All you who love the prophet, say:
May God pray for our lord Mohammad and grant him salvation!

Once two sisters married two brothers, one of them rich and the other poor. For a space of years both wives remained without seed. One day a man entered the room where the women were sitting and looked into their faces. He took out a handful of dates and divided it, giving half to this one and half to the other. To the wife of the rich brother he said, "You, sister, will carry a daughter before the month is out." And to the poor man's wife he said, "You, sister, will have a son. The children will be born in the same month and they will marry each other."

The rich man's wife began to scold: "That will be the day, when my child, a rich man's daughter, takes a poor man's son as her husband! Indeed, even if the stranger speaks the truth and Allah has written it, I shall rub it out!"

Come day, go day, and rise O you poor man, and lay your head down and die—leaving a pregnant wife to be her sister's servant.

One day the poor man's wife did not come to her sister's house as she was accustomed to. So the rich man's wife said to the maid, "Run and find out whether my sister has given birth to a girl or a boy!" The maid went and returned with the news that a nephew had been born. Her mistress then said, "Run back to her and let her come with her child. For whether she has given birth or not given birth, the clothes still need to be washed."

The poor man's wife left her bed, went to her sister's house, and took the laundry out to the river to wash. While she was gone her sister put the baby boy into a chest that had been tarred like a boat. Next to him she placed a sack of coins, gold anklets and bracelets, and a bundle of clothes. Then she dropped the chest into the river. Into the baby's bedclothes that remained in the house she put some meat—a sheep's heart—and soon the dog smelled the meat and ate it up.

When the baby's mother finished her work and came to check her child, she lifted the covers in the cradle and found the bedding all smeared with blood. "Where is my little son?" she cried. They told her, "The dog ate him!" Back to her hut the poor woman went to mourn her baby. She tore her clothes and scratched her cheeks and wept so long and so hard that eventually she became blind. And because she could no longer see, people gave her the leftovers, the bones, from what they had eaten, and their old clothes.

Now to go back to the child. A peasant was turning his waterwheel, raising water from the river to water his crops, when something blocked the stream. What was it? A chest. He saw some young boys nearby and called out, "Fetch it for me! You can have the outside and I'll take the inside!" He looked and what did he find? A newborn child. "Praise and thanks be to Allah!" he said, and kissed the back of his hand and touched it to his forehead to show his gratitude. "Children, this blessing is meant for me. Had it been anything but a child, I would have let you have it," he said, and taking the chest as well as the child, he went dancing home to his wife, who was childless. "O wife, now is the time to spout your prayers! God has given us a son!" The woman pulled off her headcloth and bared her head before her Maker, giving praise and thanks to Allah. She had a goat that she milked to feed the child. Eventually she weaned him. Then he was old enough to go to the sheikh to learn the Koran.

All this time, through some wonder, every morning the man found a gold piece where the boy had slept. He spent the money on seed and planted more land, and still there was more gold. Soon they were rich, very rich. The chest they put away, with all the things that had been inside it.

Years passed. The father's soul bid farewell, and he died. The mother remained, the boy's dear little mother. More years passed and then she fell ill. She said, "My child, send for the clerks and the notaries." And in front of witnesses she wrote down all her property: so many warehouses, so many stretches of land, so many houses, so many estates, all in the boy's name. Then when the men had left she said, "Bring over that chest and open it." The boy looked inside and found baby clothes, a bonnet, and swaddling bands and blankets. His mother said, "My son, you were bundled up in these clothes when we found you in the chest with a sack of coins and the baby jewels. We took you from the chest and raised you as our son." Then she laid down her head and died.

The boy sold all that he owned, packed the money that came to him into wooden boxes, and loaded them into boats. He filled four boats and set sail for Baghdad. When he reached that city, a man said to him, "Welcome to you; may God keep you! Are you a stranger, my son?" "Yes, a stranger, father," said the boy. "Then come with me and let us dine together," said the man. "No, uncle," replied the boy. "I cannot, I have to watch my property. What I need is an inn or an empty courtyard." "I have a storehouse," said the man. So they hired porters and moved the boxes full of gold from the boats to the storehouse. The man's wife saw them crossing the yard time and time again and said, "Where is this youth from?" "He is a stranger," said the man. "He brought four boatloads of stuff with him and he is storing them in our warehouse." "Go bring the sheikh. We'll marry the young man to our daughter," said the woman. "My daughter is destined for you," she told the boy.

Well, the boy went to the cloth merchant and bought seven arm's lengths of cloth. He sewed them into seven sacks and filled them with wedding presents for the bride. Meanwhile her mother had everything made ready for the wedded pair, the washbowl and the ewer, the quilt and the pillow. And on every one of the things she scratched or embroidered the words, "God wrote it and I rubbed it out!"

They were married. When the boy lay down to sleep, he placed a sword between himself and his wife. One day, two days, three days, and four went by. The woman kept after her daughter, asking, "Child, tell me: does he talk to you? Does he pay you attentions?" And the daughter said, "Not a word." "He is a stranger," said her mother. "Maybe that is their custom." So it continued, and in the end she could not remain silent. "My son, this is your wife; does she not please you? Why do you pay her no mind and say no word to her?" "My wife, I place her above my head! She is an ornament and a source of pride!" said the boy. "It is the words, 'God wrote it and I rubbed it out,' that stop me. How can God's word be erased? What is it that you rubbed out?" And she told him the whole story.

He asked, "Is the mother of the child who was eaten by the dog still alive?" "Yes, my son, she is alive, but she is blind and lives off what the people give her." "Take me to her," said the boy. So his wife's mother sent him to a little hut, where he poked his head in at the door and saw an old woman hunched up in a corner. "Mother!" he called to her. "I have no son. The dog ate up my child, sir!" she said. "No, I am your son, whom the dog did not eat," said the boy, and fell on her neck. She breathed in his smell and was so filled with joy that the sight returned to her eyes.

With God everything is possible. Say, "Let God pray for the prophet and grant him salvation."

The boy returned to his wife's mother and showed her the tarred chest. "I am the child whom the dog ate up," he said. And he commanded her and his wife to serve his mother, to wash her clothes and bathe her feet, and every morning to kiss her hands.

So they all lived a happy and comfortable life.
May it be so for every husband and wife!

The Green Bird

Egypt

There was a man whose pride it was to offer hospitality to those traveling through his town. At the first news of a visitor he would begin to think what to feed him and how to entertain him. For this he was known, and people came gladly to his house.

He had a wife and two children: a girl and a small boy. His wife fell ill and died and, feeling sorry for his motherless children, he married a second time. But the new bride, who had no children of her own, very soon became jealous of her husband's love for his son and daughter.

One day some merchants were passing, and as usual the man bade them rest in his house and offered them a meal. He butchered one of his young lambs, cut it into pieces, and handed it to his wife to prepare. Then he returned to sit with his guests.

The woman dressed the meat and began to cook it, every now and then pulling out a mouthful to taste. Fine. An hour passed in this way, and when she next dipped into her cooking pot, the woman found there was no meat left to taste. "What have I done?" she cried in panic. "What will I place before my husband's guests? His face will be blackened if the strangers go hungry from his house!"

Then with a toss of her head, she called her husband's daughter: "Run, child, and tell your brother to come home." The girl did as she was told, hurrying to the place where the boys of the town were playing with a ball sewn from rags of cloth. But instead of fetching her brother home, this is what she did. She called out softly, "Do not," and then, so her stepmother could hear her: "COME HOME! Brother, whatever you do, do not COME HOME!" So the boy went on playing.

A child, however, remains a child. When he was chasing the ball, he followed it unthinkingly even when it rolled right up to the door of his father's house. His stepmother pulled him inside, saying, "You have been scratching your head. Come, I want to delouse your hair." She laid his head upon her lap and, with one swift slash of her kitchen knife, cut it off. Quickly she tore his flesh apart and tossed it into the cooking pot. Then she called her stepdaughter and said, "Watch the fire while I go to the well for water. And do not uncover the pot."

But no sooner was her stepmother outside than the girl lifted the lid off the cooking pot. Inside she saw a small finger with her brother's ring on it, and she began to weep and could not stop. When the woman returned with the water jar, she saw that the girl's eyes were red. She asked, "Did you touch my cooking pot?" The girl was sobbing so hard that she could only shake her head. "Why are you crying, then?" "It is the wood smoke burning my eyes," said the girl.

The food was ready. The woman set it before her husband and his guests, and they began to eat. When the men had satisfied their first hunger, the husband turned to his daughter and said, "Have some supper, child." But she told him she had eaten earlier. Yet all the time that the men were dining, she watched them carefully. And whenever they threw a bone to the ground, she picked it up and saved it in the fold of her robe. And when she had gathered every one of her dear brother's bones, she carried them outside and buried them near the hen house.

The guests meanwhile had finished their meal, and the father said to his wife, "Call my son; let him have a bite to eat." "He is at his mother's sister's house," she said carelessly. "He will be home after a little."

But of course the boy never came.

When it was dusk the man asked for his son again, but this time a bird, a great rooster whose every feather was green as a palm leaf, opened his beak and began to sing,

> My father's wife, she took my life.
> My father ate me for his dinner.
> My loving sister gathered up my bones
> And hid them from those sinners.

"Listen to that bird," said the father. "I have never heard one like it. What is it saying?" "It is a rooster crowing like any other," said his wife. "Be still and eat."

Then the green bird flew over the marketplace and sang,

> My father's wife, she took my life.
> My father ate me for his dinner.
> My loving sister gathered up my bones
> And hid them from those sinners.

A street vendor heard him and called, "Will you sing your song once more?" "What will you give me for it?" asked the bird. "I have sweetmeats made of ground sesame and honey," said the vendor. And the bird repeated his song. When the man gave him his sweetmeat, the rooster flew with it in his claws to his sister where she lay sleeping and dropped it in her mouth.

Again he flew to the marketplace and sang,

> My father's wife, she took my life.
> My father ate me for his dinner.
> My loving sister gathered up my bones
> And hid them from those sinners.

This time the blacksmith heard him. "Will you sing your song a second time?" he asked, and gave him a fistful of nails for it. With the nails in his claws the green bird flew to his stepmother where she was lying on her back asleep. He dropped some into her mouth so that she died, and the rest he put into his father's mouth because he had eaten his own son's flesh.

When the stepmother and the father were both dead, the bones of the little boy jumped together. And there he stood, his very own self from head to toe, nothing in him different and nothing missing. And he and his sister lived in the house together happily and long until they had lived the sum of their days.

God keep your head safe!

∴ ∴ ∴

Magical, Marriages and Mismatches

More Tales of the Supernatural

..

At the birth of a boy, Arab women trill joyously, sheep are killed, and meat is distributed among the poor. If he is the firstborn son, his happy parents will from then on be identified by his name. For example, if they named him after the prophet: Abu Mohammad and Umm Mohammad, Father-of- or Mother-of-Mohammad. In contrast a daughter's birth goes unmarked and it still happens that a man, when asked the number of his children, will count only the sons.

Friends and relatives are invited to celebrate again when a boy is circumcised. Though not yet ten the young male child will see grown men shooting their guns in the air, women dancing and everyone feasting on his account. Where a comparable female rite survives, the operation takes place furtively within the women's quarters.

The one occasion when a girl is the center of attention and she sees her existence celebrated by kin and neighbors is the marriage feast, the event which brings so many household tales to a happy ending. This is the Arab family's showiest entertainment, and the festivities usually include the whole community.

As a child a girl plays with her friends at pretend weddings, and when she is a little older she may spend many hours stitching carefully at what will be her wedding gown. But at fifteen she is at last a real bride, and all the women crowd and push to see how she looks and try to guess from the row of gold coins on her headdress how much bride-wealth the groom's family has settled on her.

As a girl goes from her father's house to that of her future husband, she hears her praises sung by the crowd of well-wishers walking in procession with her. Her beauty and her grace and the excellence of her descent will be boasted of in traditional chants. Young and old clap the rhythms, the palms of their hands dyed a merry red with henna. Mothers and aunts sound the joyful, trilling lululey until their voices are worn to a hoarse whisper. This is a girl's greatest day and a popular topic among women whether in gossip or in story. No wonder that in the household tales, the women's repertoire, there is much talk of weddings.

The listeners would find little strange in a prince falling in love at the sight of an anklet, as in "Sheikh of the Lamps," or the glimpse of a clog, as in "The Little Red Fish and the Clog of Gold," or the smell of perfumed water with which the heroine washes her face in "One-Tooth and Two-Teeth." Men and women are so carefully segregated that no decent girl is seen by her bridegroom until the "night of the entering" (unless he hides in a tree to catch a glance of her face, like the prince in "The Fair Foster Child of the Ghoul"). Thus a token of the girl can well be the inspiration to love, where seeing the girl herself is forbidden. Just as the queen in "The Princess in the Suit of Leather" fires her son with a description of the unknown girl at the wazir's entertainment, a modern young man will be moved to begin negotiations for a bride on the strength of his mother's or his sisters' recommendation, having no occasion to meet such a girl himself.

Weddings and the parties stemming from the ceremony are also opportunities to display nubile girls to prospective mothers-in-law. A favorite setting in the stories is the "night of the bride's henna," when the women help to decorate the bride's arms and legs with patterns of henna dye and stain their own palms a lucky wedding red. The fisherman's daughter in "The Little Red Fish and the Clog of Gold" draws attention at such a gathering while her unkind stepmother sits neglected near the door. Village girls still love to go together to a wedding just as the girls do in "Jubeinah and the Slave," though now they might do so in a rented bus. And if they sight a likely bride for son or brother, they still report back, "We saw a girl just like the moon!"

When the prince in a tale is aching with love, it is only right and proper that he should turn to his mother for help. The queens and sultan's wives are ready to search with golden clog or anklet through every house in the kingdom for their son's bride. This is woman's work, for a girl worth having would not be exposed to the sight of men outside her household and her family. In such circumstances the Cinderella story seems entirely realistic, and it is told in countless versions in the Arab world. Indeed, a modern mother questing for a daughter-in-law without the benefit of the golden anklet will sometimes burst in on a young prospect uninvited and unannounced, in order to catch her unprepared and see her as she really is.

When the dancing and the feasting is over and the wedding gown has been folded in the chest, the young bride finds herself the most junior of the women in her in-laws' household. Often this is an uncle's home, since she is likely to have married a first cousin. She has to be deferential to her husband's mother and respectful of the wives of his older brothers. But she will gain status and confidence when she has produced a son. However much her husband may love her, his reason for marrying was to have children.

For the forty days of childbed the young mother is indulged and fussed over and her food is fancy, traditionally chicken and white bread. But after the cleansing "bath of the fortieth day," she is expected to return to her post. How natural, then, that the jealous older wives and less successful sisters of the stories should plot their revenge around the moment the fair princess gives birth. How well the listeners would understand the precariousness of the mother's position in "The Nightingale That Shrieked" when her fine twins are replaced by a puppy and a clay pot. At the same time, they would readily accept the possibility of such hate as that of the envious co-wives. For does not each of them tremble a little when her husband's riches increase, lest he be tempted to pay bride-wealth for a second wife?

Sit Lahab, in "A Lost Shoe of Gold" of the previous section, is made to endure a mother's worst nightmare when the Ghoul steals all three of her infant children. Yet she accepts her lot without flinching, and for this she is rewarded at the story's happy end. Capacity for endurance and patience—sabr—is one of the Islamic virtues. Stemming from the theological debates over predestination in the middle ages, it became a doctrine well suited to a society in which individuals have few opportunities to change their lives. The strange motif of the Sit Lahab story is found across the Arab world. A "doll of sabr" is a prop in a series of related stories. When the oppressed and uncomplaining heroine finally unburdens her heart to the doll, she is overheard by the hero, who sees that justice is done.

As frequent as the stories extolling sabr and endurance are those demonstrating the uselessness of trying to evade the fate written in the book of destiny for each soul at birth. "What Is Inscribed on the Brow the Eye Will See" and "What God Wrote Cannot Be Unwritten" prove that it is clearly not just blasphemous but ineffective to resist. These being household tales, the fate unsuccessfully defied is marriage. Inevitably the match takes place as it must, having been foretold magically in the opening of the story; it often proves to be, after all, the ideal happy ending.

"He walked, walked, walked," is how a journey of a hundred miles is described. "One foot lifting him and one foot setting him down" a hero will travel from Baghdad to Damascus. "From here to there" the good apprentice and the bad find themselves at the scene of their parting. Such tricks of economy with words suggest a crisp pace, and the frequent expression "not to spin out a tale," as if the teller is impatient to be done, is counterbalanced by equally conventional devices of plot to prolong the experience. In "A Tale Within a Tale" the construction of the episodes, arranged like Chinese boxes, one subplot contained in the next, contributes to the pleasure of the entertainment. More frequent is the tripling of each element, as in "The Bird of the Golden Feather" where there are three brothers at the parting of three ways and three Ghouls and three tasks.

But when the light is gone and there is little to do except pass the evening hours, it does not matter how intricate and unlikely the tale. And if, into the plainness of a peasant room, it brings wonders like a tree of apples that dance and apricots that sing, a lamp that is able to speak with a human voice or a fish whose scales are coins of gold, then the longer the better. And when at last the storyteller is done, the more eagerly are the date cakes brought out to sweeten her mouth.

The Iron Pestle
and the Girl with
the Donkey's Head

Libya

There was a youth called Jamil and his uncle's daughter was Jamila. Their two fathers had named them for each other at birth and betrothed them. When the time came for them to be wed, Jamil set out on a three days' journey to town to buy the bridal clothes, while Jamila remained in the village.

One day when the girls of the village went to collect kindling in a nearby wood, Jamila went with them. As she was stooped over the ground picking up dry twigs and thorns, Jamila found an iron pestle lying in her path. She added it to her bundle, but when the girls were ready to go home and Jamila lifted her load to carry on her head, the pestle would not stay with the wood. As often as she raised her bundle the pestle fell to the ground. All the while the girls were waiting. At last they said, "Ya Jamila, it is getting dark. If you want to come, let's start. If not, you can follow by yourself." "Go," said Jamila, "for I cannot give up this iron pestle even if it keeps me here till midnight." So the other girls went off and left her.

When the night grew black and thick, all of a sudden the iron pestle changed into a man who threw Jamila across one shoulder and hurried away. He walked and walked into the desert until they were one month's distance from her home. There he locked her into a castle with the words, "Live here under God's protection for I shall do you no harm." But Jamila wept bitterly, crying, "What have I brought upon myself with my own two hands!"

As the other girls were returning home, Jamila's mother saw them. "Where is my daughter?" she asked. "We left your daughter in the wood outside the village," they told her. "We warned her, 'Come with us now or we'll go without you!' And she said 'Go then! I've found an iron pestle and I cannot leave it even if I have to stay till midnight.' " Dark as it was, Jamila's mother made for the wood at a run, sobbing and screaming for her daughter.

The men of the village went after her saying, "Go home to your house! We'll bring her back for you. A woman may not wander into the night! We men will search for Jamila." But the mother cried, "I am coming with you. What if we find her killed by an adder's bite or eaten by the beasts?" So the men set out with the mother and took with them one of the girls also to show them where they had left Jamila.

They found the firewood sitting where she had dropped it, but the girl was missing. They shouted and called her name but no one answered. They lit a fire and searched till dawn then they told the mother, who was crying still, "Your daughter has been stolen by a son of Adam. If the wild beasts have eaten her, where is the blood? If a snake has bitten her, where is the body?" And they all returned to their homes.

On the fourth day Jamila's father and mother said to each other, "What shall we do? That poor boy has gone to buy her bridal clothes. What shall we tell him when he comes?" At last they decided. "We'll kill a goat and bury its head, with a tomb to cover the grave. When he comes we'll show him the stone and say she died."

Well, the cousin arrived bringing with him all the finery he had purchased. When he walked into the village Jamila's father went out to meet him. "May blessings and good fortune be yours in future—Jamila is dead." The youth broke into tears, crying loudly in his grief. He would not go another step until they showed him where she was buried. "Come," they said and he followed, carrying the bridal clothes under his arm. Throwing the wedding things onto the grave, he sat weeping and striking the tombstone in his sorrow. All day he stayed thus, till nightfall. And the next day he returned again to sit and weep and beat on the stone marker while the bridal clothes lay on the grave. For six months he continued in this way.

About that time a man was traveling in the desert. One day he found himself before a tall castle that stood by itself with no house near it. "I'll rest in its shade," he said and sat down at the foot of the wall. A little while and a girl looked out asking, "Are you Ins or Djinn?" "I am of the race of Adam," he said, "and a better man than your father and your grandfather!" "What brought you here? What are you looking for in this land of Ghouls and Afreets?" she asked, then advised him, "If you are wise, my friend, you will go before the monster finds you here or he will make an end of you and eat you for his supper. But before you leave tell me first: in what direction are you heading?" "Why should you care about me and where I am going?" he said. "I wish to ask a favor. If you should go as far as my home village, take this message to the man they call Jamil:

> From the top of a castle tall
> Jamila sends you greeting.
> From within her thick prison wall
> Jamila heard the bleating
> Of the goat they buried in her grave
> To deceive a mourner young and brave.
> While all alone she weeps
> Where the desert wind sweeps.

"But for this girl," said the man to himself, "I should have been dead before the morning. A service can only be repaid with another, so I must do her bidding."

One day, two days—the poor man had to walk a whole month before God led him to the gate of the young man's yard. As he stood there looking about him, a youth stepped out with uncombed hair falling over his eyes and unshaved beard hanging over his breast. "Peace, stranger," said the young man. "Where are you from?" "I come from the west and I am walking east," said the traveler. "Then come inside and sup with us," said the youth and the man followed him into the house where the food was spread and the household sat together eating. All except the youth, that is, for he sat on the doorstone by himself. "Why do you not eat?" asked the traveler. "Huss!" said the others. "You are a stranger to his story but he has no heart for food." The traveler held his peace until he heard someone say, "Pour us some water, ya Jamil!" Then the stranger cried, "The word 'Jamil' reminds me of something, O you people! As I came through the desert I saw a great fortress and in its window a girl who—" "Huss!" interrupted the others,

"Mention no girls before Jamil." But the youth had caught the words and said "Speak on, stranger!" "If an untruth can save a man, will not the truth make him safer still?" said the traveler and he told his whole story concluding with the message:

> From the top of a castle tall
> Jamila sends you greeting.
> From within her thick prison wall
> Jamila heard the bleating
> Of the goat they buried in her grave
> To deceive a mourner young and brave.
> While all alone she weeps
> Where the desert wind sweeps.

"Ho!" said Jamil. "So she ran away and you told me she died!"

A lie hangs by a short rope. Soon the youth had sped off with his pick-ax and uncovered the goat skull. And the villagers could say only, "It happened thus and thus and thus and now be led by your own judgment." "Pack me rations and lend me arms," said Jamil. "I am starting now with the stranger to guide me!" But the traveler said, "I cannot walk a second month; it is too far." "God will repay you for a kindness and I shall give you a wage, if you but show me the road to take," pleaded the youth. So the two set off together and when they gone a two days' journey the stranger said, "This path will take you straight and bring the castle right before you. Let safety be your companion!" Then he turned back the way that he had come.

Jamil traveled on alone for days and weeks until finally, before a month had passed, he saw the castle shining white as a dove in the distance. In his joy he began to run and did not stop until he stood at the foot of its wall.

"What shall I do now, O my Lord?" he said. "This fortress had neither gate nor door. Its smooth walls are far too steep for climbing." He was sitting in thought when his cousin looked out the window and called "O Jamil!" He lifted his head and their glances met and the sobs burst from his breast and the tears flowed from his eyes. "What brought you this far O my cousin?" said Jamila. "Love of you drove me and I came," he answered. "If you love me run back before the Ghoul comes to eat your flesh and suck your bones," cried Jamila. "By Allah and your own dear head, I cannot leave your side even if I am to die." "O what shall I do to save you, cousin?" said Jamila. "Will you climb a rope if I let it down?" No sooner had she dropped the rope than he had clambered to her side. How they clung to each other, heart against heart! And how they wept! "O where shall I find a place to hide you, cousin?" said Jamila. "Will you lie still without a word if I cover you with the cooking pot?" Hardly had she upturned the cauldron over the boy when the Ghoul came home with human flesh for himself in one hand and a dead sheep for her in the other. He sniffed the air and said:

> A smell of men
> Inside my den!

"O father, what can reach this high and lonely fortress but the desert winds and breezes?" said Jamila and began to cry. "Do not weep," said the Ghoul. "I'll burn incense to ease my breathing." And he stretched himself out to rest.

But as the girl began to cook, the human flesh jumped in the pot and spoke:

> A man! A man!
> Beneath a pan!

And the mutton joined in:

> Her own first cousin
> God make her barren!

"What are they saying, O Jamila?" asked the Ghoul sleepily. "They say 'We need salt! Add more salt!' And I have done so." In a little while the flesh jumped a second time and said:

> A man! A man!
> Beneath a pan!

And the mutton repeated:

> Her own first cousin
> God make her barren!

"What was that, O Jamila?" asked the Ghoul. "They say 'We need pepper! Add more pepper!' Which I have done."

A third time the human flesh jumped and called out:

> A man! A man!
> Beneath a pan!

And the mutton:

> Her own first cousin
> God make her barren!

When the Ghoul asked "What do they say?" Jamila said, "They are telling me 'We are cooked and ready, take us off the fire!' " "Let us eat our supper then!" the Ghoul replied. And when he had done so and washed his hands he said, "Roll out my bedding, O Jamila, I want to sleep."

The girl spread the mattress and smoothed the pillow and to distract the Ghoul's attention until he fell asleep she sat by his head combing his hair and talking. "You are no tailor, father, yet you have a needle, tell me why." "This is no ordinary needle," said the Ghoul. "When I throw it on the ground it grows into a thicket of sharp thorns that no path can probe." "You are no cobbler, father, yet you have an awl, tell me why," said the girl. "This is like no cobbler's awl," said the Ghoul. "When I throw it on the ground it swells into a hill of iron too hard to tunnel." "You are no farmer, father and yet you have a hoe, tell me why," said the girl. "This is no peasant's hoe," said the Ghoul. "When I throw it on the ground it digs a sea so wide no man can cross it. But these are secrets which you must not betray, my child."

When he had spoken, the Ghoul fell back and went to sleep, his eyes shining so yellow that the whole room was lit with an amber glow. From beneath the metal cauldron the youth called out, "O Jamila, let us flee!" "Not yet, O cousin. Though he is asleep he still can see," said the girl. They waited in silence until the Ghoul's eyes turned red filling the room with scarlet light. "Now!" said Jamila. She tied the magic needle, awl, and hoe in her cousin's cloak and took the rope into her hand. Out of the window and down the rope they slid and set off for their village as fast as they could go.

All this time the Ghoul was snoring away on his bed. Now his hunting dog tried to wake him:

> O sleeping sleeper, I warn you,
> Jamila's gone and will harm you!

But the Ghoul only raised himself enough to beat the dog and fell back again and slept till morning. He woke up and called, "O Jamila! O Jamila!" But there was no sign of Jamila to be seen, no sound of her to be heard. Now the Ghoul began to hurry. He took his arms and he took his dog and how he ran to chase after her!

Jamila turned her head and cried, "O my cousin, the Ghoul is coming for us!" "Where is he? I can't see him," said Jamil. "He is so far he seems no larger than a needle," she said and they began to run, but the Ghoul and his dog ran faster. They had almost caught the fleeing pair when Jamila threw down the magic needle, and a forest of thorns appeared to block the way. It stopped the Ghoul at first but he cut and his dog cut until they had cut a trail through the spines and were able to continue.

Jamila looked over her shoulder and cried, "O my cousin, the Ghoul is coming after us!" "Show me, I can't see him," said Jamil. "There he is with his dog no bigger than an awl," said Jamila and they ran a little faster. But the Ghoul and his dog were quicker and soon they were almost touching the two cousins. Jamila threw down the magic awl and an iron mountain rose and barred the path. The Ghoul paused but then he dug and his dog dug until they had dug a passage through the iron and resumed the race.

Jamila glanced behind her and shouted, "O my cousin, the Ghoul and his dog are here!" She threw down the magic hoe and a great ocean spread between them. The Ghoul began to drink and his dog began to drink to make a dry road across it, but the dog's belly was filled with salt water so that it burst and he died. Then the Ghoul sat where he was and cursed Jamila saying, "O Jamila, may Allah make your head a donkey's head and your hair yellow twine!" And in that instant Jamila was transformed. Her face became long as a female donkey's and her hair hung coarse as sacking. When Jamil looked round and saw her he said, "Have I come all this way for a bride or a donkey?" And he ran home and left her. But halfway there he stopped and said, "She is my cousin, how can I leave her for the beasts? Maybe Allah, who changed her, will changed her back one day." He retraced his steps and said, "Come, O Jamila! But what will the people say? They will laugh at me for marrying a monster with human hands and human feet but—O shame and horror! a donkey's face and hair like twine!" "Take me to my mother's house when it is dark and do not say a word. No man need know," she wept.

So they waited for the sun to set and only then knocked on Jamila's mother's door. "It is I, Jamil. I have brought home my cousin." The poor woman came out running in her joy. "Where is my daughter, let me see her!" But when she saw Jamila she said, "Allah protect us, is my daughter now a donkey? Or are you laughing at me?" "Do not speak so loud or the people will hear you," said Jamil. And Jamila said, "O my mother, I can show you that I am your own daughter." She bared her thigh and said, "That is where the dog once bit me." She bared her breast and said, "Here is where the lamp-oil burnt me." Then her mother took her in her arms and wept while Jamila told her what had happened. "Hide me now," she said "And, O my cousin, if the people ask you, tell them you did not find me. May God have pity on us!"

So Jamila lived like a prisoner in her mother's house, daring to go out only in the night. And when the people asked Jamil he said, "I did not find her." "We will get you another bride, better than Jamila," said the people. "No, I shall not marry. She has set my heart aflame, and I cannot rest as long as I know that she is not dead," replied Jamil. "What of the bridal finery?" they asked. "Why, let it lie in the chest until the worms eat their fill of it!" he said. "O Jamil, you are a madman," said his friends. "I ask no one to come with me," said Jamil and he went to live in his cousin's mother's house.

Three months passed. In the desert a peddler stopped by the tall castle. The Ghoul caught him and said, "If you do an errand for me, I'll not harm you." "I am ready," said the peddler, almost dead with fear. "Go along this road until you find a village where a youth called Jamil and a girl called Jamila live. Say, 'Here is a present from the Ghoul your father, a mirror to see yourself in and a comb for your hair.' " And the Ghoul put the things with the peddler's wares.

By the time the peddler reached Jamila's house he was worn with hunger and heat and travel. Jamil found him lying in the sun and said, "You will fall ill if you stay outside." The peddler replied, "I am finished already. I have come a month's journey on the desert road." "Did you see a castle?" asked Jamil. "I did, O my master," said the peddler and he told him the words of the Ghoul and handed him the presents for the girl.

When Jamila looked into the Ghoul's mirror her face returned to what it had been before. When she pulled the comb through her coarse twine, it became her own hair once more. Her mother sounded the trill of joy and the people came running and crowded into the house. When all the questions had been asked and all the answers given the wedding preparations were made. Jamila became the bride of Jamil and together they raised many daughters and many sons.

> And so they lived happily and flourished
> Till at last she died and he perished.

The Boy Magician

Morocco

God was here and in every place,
No land or country but felt His grace,
And the prophet, on whom prayer and salvation,
Sat with a lap full of mint and carnation!

There was a merchant who had no children. Early and late, at dusk and in the dawn, he prayed to God and he begged for a son. The Compassionate One heard his prayer and gave him his wish. After a stretch of time the merchant died, leaving the little boy in his mother's lap. The days passed and the years, and the boy grew. Coming and going he brushed away all traces of his father's skirts in the dust; in other words, the money that his father left he spent here and there until he had nothing to comfort him but the mercy of God.

Now he had to learn a trade. His mother said to herself, "Nearby there lives a magician. That's a trade my son can master." She chose a present and, clutching the boy by the hand, went to find the magician's house. The neighbors pointed it out to her, and she knocked on the door. When he stepped out, she said, "God's guest at your door!" He welcomed her, and she handed him her gift, saying, "In the name of Allah, I beg you to teach my child." Fine. She left the boy and went home.

Then what did the magician do but push the boy into a large room, close the door, and lock him in. The master went his own way. From time to time a servant took bread in to the boy, and after eight days had passed the magician returned with a whip in his hand. "What have you learned?" he asked. The boy replied, "What should I learn? You teach me nothing, and that is what I learn." And the magician gave him a hard thrashing, locked him in again, and set off on his own business.

What was the boy to do? He wandered through the room and found a pile of books. He began to busy himself studying, reading as much of the books as he could understand, until he had learned all the master's magic. He returned the books to their places and sat down to wait. When eight days were over, the magician appeared and asked the same question as before. "You teach me nothing, and that is what I learn from you!" said the boy. The magician gave him another beating and left him locked up.

Now, there was a young girl who worked as a maid in the magician's house. Feeling sorry for the boy, she said one day, "What are you waiting for, all this time? Why don't you run away? Don't you know that as soon as he thinks you've learned his tricks, he will kill you?" She unlocked the door and said, "Go, and go far away!"

The boy returned to his mother's house. He found her so needy that she had no food to eat in the evening and fell asleep hungry. When night came he told her before he retired to his room, "In the morning there will be a pair of saluki hounds in my bedchamber. Take them to the *wazir*; he will pay you their price. But be careful not to give him their leash. Remember, whatever should happen keep the leash!"

Morning dawned and the woman found the two dogs as her son had promised. Quickly, quickly she led them to the house of the *wazir*. She knocked. Out stepped the servants to ask, "What has brought you to our doorstep, woman?" "I have come with this present for the *wazir* of the emir," she said, and they ushered her in. On and on they went before her, down one hall and up the next, until she was standing in the presence of the *wazir* himself. She bowed to him, and he asked, "What is your wish, woman?" "As truly as God has mercy on us all, I have brought you a present!" she said, and showed him the pair of hounds. Now, the *wazir* was enamored of the saluki breed, and he could not contain his joy when he saw the two dogs. "What do you ask for them, woman?" "Whatever my master gives me is more than enough." The *wazir* slapped his leather purse, shook out a handkerchief in which were tied one thousand gold pieces, and placed it in her hands. She unfastened the leash that bound the hounds and retraced her steps to the house.

She threw the leash into her son's room and closed the door. A little and another little, and there was her son coming out of his room. "What fortune?"

he asked. She told him, "I did your wish and what you told me, and this is what the *wazir* gave me."

For a long time they lived by spending this treasure, feeding their two heads until the money was almost gone. At last the boy said to his mother, "If God wills, tomorrow you will find a mule at the door of my chamber. Take it to the *suq* and sell it, but remember not to sell its bridle!"

The following day the woman found at her son's door a white mule that had no equal. Driving it down to the *suq*, she handed it to a crier, who mounted the beast and advertised its virtues. The first bidder offered one hundred, but another and another soon raised the price.

Meanwhile what of the magician? After eight days he returned to the room in which he had imprisoned the boy, and it was empty. "This good-for-nothing had discovered some magic," he said to himself. And he stumbled out of the house to search for him. He had no success until he was walking through the *suq* and saw the white mule. He knew by the pureness of its color that it was the work of the boy he was looking for, so he stood with the other men and bid until he had outbid them all. Now the mule was his. When the woman came up to settle the sale, he paid her. She reached for the mule's bridle to slip it off, but he pushed aside her hand, saying, "It was for the bridle that I bought the mule." In that moment she did not know how to refuse him and so let it pass, forgetting the earnestness of her son's warning not to sell the bridle.

When the woman reached home her son was not there, and she sat in the house and waited for him. One day, two days, three days, and he did not return. Where was the boy? Well, he was no other than the white mule, for he had transformed himself with the magic he learned. Now his master rented him to a mason, and all day long the white mule was forced to carry heavy rocks from the quarry to the stonecutter's yard. If ever he slacked or took a rest, he was beaten with the goad.

At last after a stretch of days, it was God's will to release him. The sultan sent his crier to announce a royal open-air banquet: "Listen, O people of the land, everyone, the young and the old, the humble and the great, must come to the sultan's picnic. No one can remain at home. all must go out and enjoy themselves." Even the magician went to the feast, leaving the mule in the charge of his own son.

When the sun began to wane, the magician's son went to water the mule at the well. But the mule would not drink. Thinking that the bridle was hindering it, the son pulled the bridle off. Just then, who should be coming at a run? The magician. So the boy who had been a mule jumped in the well and changed himself into a fish. The magician, looking in the well and seeing the fish, dived in after it and changed himself into a net. The fish turned into a razor and cut the net, and the boy escaped from the well in the shape of a dove. The net changed into a falcon and chased the dove. Quickly, quickly the dove flew away and into the sultan's palace.

The sultan was sitting in the women's quarters when the dove entered through the window and changed into a pomegranate. Now the falcon swooped in after it, startling the sultan with its speed. The pomegranate burst; every seed rolled into a corner. Changing to a rooster, the magician began to peck at the scattered seeds. One of them, the very seed in which the magic lurked, turned itself into a jagged rock, and when the rooster bent his neck to pick up another seed, the stone lifted itself into the air, dropped onto his head, and killed him.

In the moment when the chicken died, the magician's dead body fell to the ground and the boy returned to what he had been in the beginning. The sultan, who had been watching all this movement in great amazement, asked, "For the love of God, tell me: are you Djinn or are you Ins?" And the boy told him the story from beginning to end.

Seeing that the boy was handsome and strong, as well as being a clever magician, the sultan gave him his daughter for a wife.

> We have traveled from mountain to mountain,
> We have traveled from wood to wood,
> We have heard this story from good men,
> And have told it to men who are good.

One-Tooth and
Two-Teeth

Syria

There was an old woman who lived with her sister. Neither had tasted the joys of marriage, and now they were so old that one sister had lost all the

teeth in her head but one. She was nicknamed One-Tooth, while the other had fared little better and was known as Two-Teeth.

One day—it was a Friday—Two-Teeth said to her sister, "Today the king's son walks under our window on his way to the mosque to pray. And today I shall spill a little water on his head. As I do so, I want you to scream, 'Sister, how could you wet our prince's head with the water you used to wash your face and hands! If he should discover who we are, God save us from his punishment!' " Then this crafty Two-Teeth went bustling through the house and yard, mixing rose water with essence of jasmine and a handful of orange-tree buds just beginning to bloom.

At noon, as the prince with all his men was passing down below, she sprinkled the scented water onto his head. And One-Tooth shrieked as she was told, "Sister, sister, what have you done? You have poured the water you used to wash your face and hands onto the royal prince's head! Tomorrow when he finds us, God save us from his punishment!" But all the prince said in fact was, "How graceful and dainty must she be who uses such perfume to wash her face and hands!"

As soon as he returned to the palace, the prince went to his mother and said, "Mother—may Allah keep you from all harm—will you go to the house whose window overhangs the street by the mosque, and ask for the hand of the beauty who sat behind the shutters at noon today?" The queen laughed. "My son, there are no girls in the house you describe!" But the prince insisted: "I know it holds one girl of surpassing grace and beauty." So the queen went to the house of the two old maids to see for herself.

She stepped into the room, and there was One-Tooth sitting all alone. "Where is your sister?" asked the queen. "Oh, no one may look at her until her marriage day!" said One-Tooth. "Not even her little finger?" asked the queen. "Sister," called One-Tooth, "uncover your little finger for the prince's mother to see." Now, Two-Teeth had hidden herself inside the wardrobe, and she quickly held out a white candle onto which she had slipped her rings. "If her fingers are as slim and lily-white as this," said the queen mother to herself, "what a graceful beauty she must be indeed!" And she hurried joyfully to her son and said, "I shall begin the wedding preparations today."

The marriage day was named. The bride was brought to the palace, preceded in the streets by the sound of drums and song. The prince entered the bridal chamber to lift the veil that covered his love's face. And Two-Teeth was revealed. "This is not my bride!" said the prince, and threw her out of the window so that she fell into the palace garden and landed upside down.

At that time the son of the sultan of the Djinn was suffering from a swelling in his throat. When he saw the old woman with her head in the ground and her feet in the air, he laughed and went on laughing until the swelling burst and he was relieved of pain. So he called his seven sisters, seven wonders of beauty, and said, "Reward her for what she has done!"

The first Djinn sister said, "May her hair resemble mine." And straightway Two-Teeth's hair grew in night-black locks till it touched her heels and became hair that had no equal. The second Djinn sister said, "Let her face be a twin of mine." And Two-Teeth's brow shone smooth as the flat of the blade of a sword—a face that had no rival. The third Djinn sister spoke, "Let her eyes be like my eyes." And Two-Teeth's eyes widened like the rim of a coffee cup so that there were none like them. The fourth, fifth, sixth, and seventh Djinn sisters also made their wishes and when they left her Two-Teeth was a beauty without compare.

Next morning, when the prince woke up he looked out and saw his bride sitting in the garden. He looked at her and went mad, hurrying down at a run. "Are you my bride?" he said "It is I. I have not come or gone," said Two-Teeth. And brimming with delight, the prince set her at his side. Then her sister came and said, "If I am One-Tooth, are you not Two-Teeth? Then why are you so beautiful and I remain the same?" Two-Teeth told her, "I went to the cotton carder and asked him to card me for five dinars; and this is what I became!" So One-Tooth paid the cotton carder and said, "Will you card me for five dinars?" He put her under the carding tool, and soon her bones were scattered and her flesh ground fine, while her sister lived with her husband the sultan's son in happiness as pure as twenty-four-carat gold.

> Mulberry, mulberry,
> Here ends my story.

.: .: .: .: . .: .: . .: .: . .:

What Is Inscribed
on the Brow
the Eye Will See

.: .: .: .: .: .: .: .: .: .: .: .:

I r a q

There was a merchant who had a wife and daughter and no one else besides. When death knocked at his door, the child remained alone with her mother. Now, this woman knew the art of divination from a bed of sand.

She could cast a handful of sand and read the future from the pits and mounds it formed. One day she unrolled her prayer mat and asked God to guide her hand. But when she scattered the sand, she saw that her black slave was destined to marry her only daughter. She called for Allah's protection against the devil and tried again. What was revealed to her was no different. It was written that her servingman would be husband to her daughter. "How can my fair child be paired with one like him?" she said.

Soon she began to plan a way to be rid of him. She called him and said, "I wish to send you on a mission. I want you to go to Eye of the Sun, Ain Ash-Shams, and ask her, 'Whose good fortune will my mistress's daughter be?' " "I go gladly," said the man. So she prepared what he needed for his journey and sent him off.

The servingman had no experience. He did not know cities from countries and had no inkling where to turn or how to go. But as he walked he came upon a man with a crook in his hand, herding sheep, both white and black. "Peace!" said the slave. And the man answered, *"Salaam!"* So the slave asked him, "Tell me, what are these roads and where do they lead?" The man said "Which of them do you wish to enter? What place are you seeking?" The slave said, "I am looking for Ain Ash-Shams to ask her, 'Whose good fortune will my mistress's daughter be?' " "Ho ho!" said the man. "If you reach Ain Ash-Shams will you ask her for me, 'How much longer must the herdsman look after the flock?' "

The slave agreed. Then he walked on and on. He came to a man who was harvesting, cutting both the green plants and those that were dry and throwing them all into the river. *"Salaam!"* said the slave. The man replied,

"On you be peace! Where are you heading, brother?" "I am going to Ain Ash-Shams to ask her, 'Whose good fortune will my mistress's daughter be?'" And the man said, "When you get there will you say only this thing more to Ain Ash-Shams: 'How much longer must the man throw all his harvest into the water, making no difference between the unripe and the yellow?'"

The slave agreed and went on, walking and walking and walking, until he came to a sea which had neither source nor bottom. On its surface a fish was floating. "Where are you going?" it asked. "To Ain Ash-Shams to ask her, 'Whose good fortune will my mistress's daughter be?'" "How will you find her?" asked the fish. And when the man said he did not know, it said, "I shall take you. I shall carry you across the sea on my back, but when you are there you must say to Ain Ash-Shams, 'Why does the fish float on top of the water?'" The slave agreed, and the fish carried him to the other shore and promised to wait for him till he returned.

The man walked and walked and walked until he saw Ain Ash-Shams. The first thing he asked her was, "O Ain Ash-Shams, whose good fortune will my mistress's daughter be?" And she said, "Your good fortune. Yours. Yours." Then he said, "The shepherd wanted my to ask how much longer he must herd the flock." And she answered, "He is the one who herds the days and the nights. This must be his work to the end of time." And he said, "Good. But what about the harvester who cuts both the green and the ripe and throws them into the water, making no distinction? How much longer must he work?" She answered, "He is the one who brings death to old and young, and his work has no ending. The green crops are the young and ignorant, the ripe are the white-haired among men."

"I have one more question," said the man. "Speak," invited Ain Ash-Shams. "This fish, why does it float on the top of the water, unable to dive or sink?" "Let the fish first carry you across the sea," replied Ain Ash-Shams. "When you are safely on land, tap it on its back. It will spit out a pearl as large as a hazelnut and then be able to join its fellows beneath the waves. The pearl is your reward. On either side of the road that leads you home, you will find a stone basin. In one is treasure, in the other water. Bathe in one and it will turn you white as silver. The treasure is yours to keep."

What she told him the black slave did. He turned white as silver and went home with all his riches tied onto the backs of a string of mules.

In this grand state he arrived at his mistress's door, with all the people of the town following behind him in amazement. He entered, and his mistress did not know him. Wondering, she said to herself, "This must be my husband's brother's son who lives in another city. He must have heard of his uncle's death and come to claim his cousin. Who has more right to her than her first cousin?"

And so the slave lived in the house like an honored guest. All the while he asked no questions and she asked him nothing. Then she said, "Would you like this girl to be your wife?" "If you wish it," he said.

So they made the preparations. They set the sum for the bride-money. What had to be sewn was sewn, and what had to be stitched was stitched. The girl was taken to the bathhouse and the guests were invited.

Now it was the wedding night. The girl sat in the bridal chamber. The groom was dressed in fine robes, and his beard had the smell of incense. He stood as tall as a hero of the tales, his arms folded over his chest and his beauty glowing like moonlight. The girl blushed to look at him. Though she waited for him to speak, he said nothing. She hoped that he would sit by her side, but he continued to stand. At last she said, "Why not rest yourself?" And he replied, "O daughter of my master, O child of my mistress, how can I come or go without your leave or your command?" "What odd things to say! Why do you speak thus?" asked the girl. "Because I am he who was your servingman," he said. "Your mother sent me on a journey to Ain Ash-Shams, and this is what I have become!" "What you have revealed to me must not be repeated to another soul!" she said. And laughing in his fair face, she said to herself, "Praise God for my fate! Praise God for my fortune!"

The Fair Foster Child of the Ghoul

Tunisia

A man who had seven daughters decided to go on a journey to a distant land with his wife. Filling his storerooms and bins with provisions for three years, he locked the seven girls into the house by themselves. Before he went, he warned them not to cross the threshold of the street gate until he and their mother came back again. "Yes, Father," said the girls; and they followed his advice for one year and a second.

Then one day they washed all their clothes and hung them out to dry on the flat rooftop. They stood by the wall, looking down into the street and watching the people coming and going to market with round baskets full of vegetables and fruits and whole sheep hanging from the butcher's hook. One of the girls said, "Just look at all the good food piled up in stacks down there! Let's go and get some; we need it!" But the youngest of the sisters said, "Our father told us not to cross the step of the outside door until he was back again." For that the oldest slapped her on the face, the next girl spat in her direction, and third rained curses on her head, the fourth pushed her to the ground, the fifth kicked her as she lay, and the last lifted her robe and pissed on her.

Taking no notice of their youngest sister's warning, they marched out of the house with a large bag and walked down to the market to fill it with all that the belly craves and the tongue delights in. Back they hurried and set to work cooking and basting till everything was just right. In their haste, however, they forgot to lock the outside door. While the six sisters settled down to enjoy their meal, the youngest sister hid in the courtyard under the broken half of a storage jar and wept.

In the middle of their feast, who should steal in on the sisters but the She-Ghoul. In through the open door she sped and pounced on the eldest girl, saying,

> Tell me, child, where shall I begin—
> With your fleshy neck, or your chubby chin?

And the girl said, "Begin with my hand, for hitting my dear little sister!" And the Ghoul gobbled her up, and turned to the next girl.

> Tell me, child, where shall I begin—
> With your fleshy neck, or your chubby chin?

And the girl said, "Begin with my mouth, for spitting at my sweet little sister!" And the Ghoul swallowed her down and turned to the third girl.

> Tell me, child, where shall I begin—
> With your fleshy neck, or your chubby chin?

And this girl said, "Begin with my arm, for hurting my wise little sister!" The one after her said, "Begin with my leg, for kicking our good little sister!" And the last one said, "Begin with my belly, for soiling our poor

little sister!" So the Ghoul devoured the six girls one by one, until she had eaten them all up.

But the littlest sister fled through the open courtyard gate and went running without stopping, running without looking back, for she was maddened with fright. At last she came to an open door. She ran inside into a yard, and it was empty. She stepped into the house, and no one was there. So she crept into a dark corner to rest, and fell fast asleep.

In the evening the owner of the house returned from the hunt, and he was a Ghoul. He sniffed here and he sniffed there, and he said,

> A smell of men
> Inside my den!
> Who brought them in?

He looked and he searched, but he did not find the girl where she was crouching. So he called out in a loud voice,

> Step out, whoever you may be:
> I promise you health and safety!
>
> If an aged man or crone,
> I shall greet you like a son.
>
> If a gentle youth or maiden,
> I shall make this house your haven.
>
> If a little girl or boy,
> I shall try and bring you joy.
>
> God above protects you;
> I shall not molest you.

Now the girl found the courage to show herself. "Don't be afraid!" said the Ghoul. And she lived in his house, staying there every day while he went hunting. For her he brought back venison or hares or partridges to cook, and for himself the flesh of men to devour. So they lived, she calling him "Father," he calling her "Daughter" and never harming her or pronouncing a word of impurity in her presence.

In the Ghoul's house there was an upper story of seven rooms. The Ghoul had given the keys of six rooms to the girl, but the key of the seventh he had kept. One day she said, "Father, why don't you let me have the key to the seventh room?" And he replied, "There is nothing there for you to see, O little daughter." And he did not give up the key. But the girl thought to herself, "Tonight I shall lie down in the courtyard and make myself look asleep. But I shall keep watch and see where he hides the key." When she and the Ghoul had eaten their meal, she stretched out in the yard and closed her eyes. But through her lashes she took note of where the Ghoul buried the key in the ground. As soon as he had gone to his sleeping place indoors, she dug the key up.

Next day the Ghoul rose early and found the key gone. But rather than wake the girl, he said to himself, "Let her have it today; no harm will come." As soon as she awoke, the girl climbed quickly to the seventh room and unlocked its door. What did she find? Nothing; it was empty. But there was a window that was shuttered and latched. She pushed it open to look outside and saw below her the garden of the sultan's son. No one was in it except an ox, yoked to a waterwheel, walking round and round to water the trees. The ox looked up and saw the girl at her window. He said,

> Good morning, O monster's fair daughter.
> Don't you know what your father is after?
> Today he's feeding you and filling you;
> Tomorrow he'll be chasing you and killing you.

The girl ran downstairs sobbing so hard that she could not cook or clean the house. When the Ghoul returned from the hunt, he found her with her head drooped over her arms. "Why are you weeping?" he asked. "Did you unlock the room?" "I did," she said. "And what did the ox in the garden say?" "He said:

> Good morning, O monster's fair daughter.
> Don't you know what your father is after?
> Today he's feeding you and filling you;
> Tomorrow he'll be chasing you and killing you!

But the Ghoul told her, "If he says that to you again, here is your reply:

> My father will harm no hair of my head,
> He'll let no grain of dirt fall on my bread!
> But I shall be queen of all the land,
> And have a prince for my husband.
> Then if the sultan's son gives me your eye,
> I'll make it a mirror to see me by.
> In your eye so large and black,
> I'll see my front and I'll see my back.
> May you be blind in both your eyes
> For seven nights and seven days.
> For seven days and seven nights,
> Lie useless, though your girth's pulled tight.

Next day she opened the window in the seventh room and the ox said what he had said before. She replied in her father's words, and as soon as she had finished speaking the ox fell to the ground and did not move for seven days and seven nights. The waterwheel stopped turning, the stream stopped running through the water channels, and the garden wilted and dried up. The sultan's son saw that all the trees and plants were withered and hard, and he saw the ox lying motionless on the ground. So he beat the ox and said, "Bring another to work in its place."

In the morning when the girl looked out, there was a different ox turning the waterwheel. But the new ox spoke the old words, and she replied as the Ghoul had instructed her. Tubb! down fell the ox in its tracks and did not stir for seven days and seven nights. On the eighth morning he heaved himself up and resumed his tasks. And on that day the prince visited his garden, saying, "Let me see the new ox and what it does." He saw the animal plodding round and round and the wheel turning and the water rushing—but every leaf and twig was dry. He drew his sword and went to the ox to kill it, but the animal said, "O my master, promise me my safety while I tell you about the girl who looks out of that window. She speaks words to make me fall useless to the ground for seven days and seven nights. Yet in all the world there is no second girl with such beauty." "You lie!" said the prince. "That's the Ghoul's house. Since when do monsters raise daughters that are fair?" "O my master, if you think I lie, come tomorrow and see her with your own eye," said the beast.

Next morning early, the sultan's son came to the garden. The ox told him, "Climb into the nearest tree; she'll soon appear." The window opened and the girl looked out. The ox said,

> Good morning, O monster's fair daughter.
> Don't you know what your father is after?
> Today he's feeding you and filling you;
> Tomorrow he'll be chasing you and killing you!

And she said,

> My father will harm no hair of my head,
> He'll let no grain of dirt fall on my bread!
> But I shall be queen of all the land
> And have a prince for my husband.
> Then if the sultan's son gives me your eye,
> I'll make it a mirror to see me by.
> In your eye so large and black,
> I'll see my front and I'll see my back.
> May you be blind in both your eyes
> For seven nights and seven days.
> For seven days and seven nights,
> Lie useless, though your girth's pulled tight!

The ox sank to the ground, and the girl stepped inside the room again and closed the window. As for the prince he slid down from the tree with his back in forty pieces like prayerbeads when the string is broken. For the beauty that was in the girl had no like or equal in the world.

The sultan's son wanted the Ghoul's daughter for his wife. He filled a large cistern with meat and another with spiced couscous as a supper for the

Ghoul. He cut down a young date palm as a toothpick for the Ghoul's teeth and spread a bolt of cotton as a napkin on which the Ghoul could wipe his hands. Then he sat with his men in the doorway to the Ghoul's courtyard and awaited the monster's return.

"Welcome to my neighbors," said the Ghoul when he arrived home from hunting. "Why have you not come to visit me before?" The prince said, "We have come tonight and we wish to share a meal with you." "Welcome to my house. I have brought much game, and we shall feast together," said the Ghoul. "Let the honor be ours tonight, O Ghoul. The food is cooked and ready, since we prepared for your coming before you yourself knew of it." So the Ghoul went with them and supped in their company. Then the prince said, "I stand before you as a suitor for the daughter of good people and a girl of high standing." "I have no daughter," said the Ghoul, but the prince replied, "Suppose I tell you that I saw her at the window with my own eye this morning." "Then she is yours, by Allah," said the Ghoul.

Early next morning the prince brought the wedding clothes and came to take his bride. Before she left, the Ghoul told her: "Be warned by me and do not say one word to the sultan's son. If he speaks to you, be dumb. Not until he begs you with the words, 'by the head of the Ghoul your father,' may you talk to him." The girl promised and swore that it would be so. The first night and the second, the prince tried to make her answer when he spoke, but she did not. On the third night he said, "Since you refuse to say a word, I shall take another wife." The girl remained silent.

The new bride was brought to the sultan's house and a crowd of women accompanied her. Up jumped the Ghoul's daughter and said to the women, "Rest, and I shall bring you food to eat." The women sat and the girl began to give out orders: "Come, O firewood." And a bundle of sticks appeared by itself. "Come, O fire and come, O pan!" Until everything was ready and the oil was hissing in the pot. As the women watched, the girl dipped her ten fingers into the oil, and they turned into ten fried fishes. Then in all her clothes, with her silks and jewelry still on, she jumped into the oven and turned into a loaf of bread baked red as coral. As though nothing had happened, she appeared again and said, "Eat, O ladies; you are strangers and have come a long way."

The women began to raise their voices in cries of wonder. The new bride said, "Why are you so astonished; is this such a big thing? Why, I can do the same." And she bent over and stepped into the oven, and the fire burned her up. The women went running to the sultan's son, crying, "Come, your bride is dead!" "Let her be buried," said the prince; "nothing else can be done for her. We didn't tell her to throw herself into the fire."

The bride was buried. The prince did not go to the funeral, because his heart still sorrowed over the wife who would not speak to him, and he did not want to see her. But next day the prince climbed over the wall to a place where he could watch the Ghoul's daughter unseen. She called to the water pitcher and jar and said, "Bring me a drink of cool water from the well!" And off went the two pots without anyone carrying them. But as they were descending into the well, the water jar knocked into the pitcher and broke off its beak. "O mistress, break the water jar!" said the pitcher. "He has chipped off my beak." But the water jar said, "I beg you, mistress, by the head of the Ghoul your father, do not break me." And the girl said, "If only your master would say those words! He will marry another wife and another as long as I do not speak to him, and I would have spoken from the first if he had known to ask me by the head of the Ghoul my father."

The prince was listening, and in no times at all he jumped down and begged her to speak "by the head of the Ghoul your father." And she spoke to him, and they lived happily together as man and wife.

The Little Red
Fish and the
Clog of Gold

Iraq

Neither here nor there lived a man, a fisherman. His wife had drowned in the great river and left him a pretty little girl not more than two years old. In a house nearby lived a widow and her daughter. The women began to come to the fisherman's house to care for the girl and comb her hair, and every time she said to the child, "Am I not like a mother to you?" She tried to please the fisherman, but he always said, "I shall never marry. Stepmothers hate their husband's children even though their rivals are dead and buried." When his daughter grew old enough to pity him when she saw him washing his own clothes, she began to say, "Why don't you marry our neighbor, Father? There is no evil in her, and she loves me as much as her own daughter."

They say water will wear away stone. In the end the fisherman married the widow, and she came to live in his house. The wedding week was not yet over when sure enough, she began to feel jealous of her husband's daughter. She saw how much her father loved the child and indulged her. And she could not help but see that the child was fair, and quick, while her own daughter was thin and sallow, and so clumsy she did not know how to sew the seam of her gown.

No sooner did the woman feel that she was mistress of the house than she began to leave all the work for the girl to do. She would not give her stepchild soap to wash her hair and feet, and she fed her nothing but crusts and crumbs. All this the girl bore patiently, saying not a word. For she did not wish to grieve her father, and she thought, "I picked up the scorpion with my own hand; I'll save myself with my own mind."

Besides her other errands, the fisherman's daughter had to go down to the river each day to bring home her father's catch, the fish they ate and sold. One day from beneath a basket load of three catfish, suddenly one little red fish spoke to her:

> Child with such patience to endure,
> I beg you now, my life secure.
> Throw me back into the water,
> And now and always be my daughter.

The girl stopped to listen, half in wonder and half in fear. Then retracing her steps, she flung the fish into the river and said, "Go! People say, 'Do a good deed for, even if it is like throwing gold into the sea, in God's sight it is not lost.' " And lifting itself on the face of the water, the little fish replied:

> Your kindness is not in vain—
> A new mother do you gain.
> Come to me when you are sad,
> And I shall help to make you glad.

The girl went back to the house and gave the three catfish to her stepmother. When the fisherman returned and asked about the fourth, she told him, "Father, the red fish dropped from my basket. It may have fallen into the river, for I couldn't find it again." "Never mind," he said, "it was a very small fish." But her stepmother began to scold. "You never told me there were four fishes. You never said that you lost one. Go now and look for it, before I curse you!"

It was past sunset and the girl had to walk back to the river in the dark. Her eyes swollen with tears, she stood on the water's edge and called out,

> Red fish, my mother and nurse,
> Come quickly, and ward off a curse.

And there at her feet appeared the little red fish to comfort her and say, "Though patience is bitter, its fruit is very sweet. Now bend down and take this gold piece from my mouth. Give it to your stepmother, and she will say nothing to you." Which is exactly what happened.

The years came and the years went, and in the fisherman's house life continued as before. Nothing changed except that the two little girls were now young women.

One day a great man, the master of the merchants' guild, announced that his daughter was to be married. It was the custom for the women to gather at the bride's house on the "day of the bride's henna" to celebrate and sing as they watched the girl's feet, palms, and arms being decorated for the wedding with red henna stain. Then every mother brought her unwed daughters to be seen by the mothers of sons. Many a girl's destiny was decided on such a day.

The fisherman's wife rubbed and scrubbed her daughter and dressed her in her finest gown and hurried her off to the master merchant's house with the rest. The fisherman's daughter was left at home to fill the water jar and sweep the floor while they were gone.

But as soon as the two women were out of sight, the fisherman's daughter gathered up her gown and ran down to the river to tell the little red fish her sorrow. "You shall go to the bride's henna and sit on the cushions in the center of the hall," said the little red fish. She gave the girl a small bundle and said, "Here is everything you need to wear, with a comb of pearl for your hair and clogs of gold for your feet. But one thing you must remember: be sure to leave before your stepmother rises to go."

When the girl loosened the cloth that was knotted round the clothes, out fell a gown of silk as green as clover. It was stitched with threads and sequins of gold, and from its folds rose a sweet smell like the essence of roses. Quickly she washed herself and decked herself and tucked the comb of pearl behind her braid and slipped the golden clogs onto her feet and went tripping off to the feast.

The women from every house in the town were there. They paused in their talk to admire her face and her grace, and they thought, "This must be the governor's daughter!" They brought her sherbet and cakes made with almonds and honey and they sat her in the place of honor in the middle of them all. She looked for her stepmother with her daughter and saw them far off, near the door where the peasants were sitting, and the wives of weavers and peddlers.

Her stepmother stared at her and said to herself, "O Allah Whom we praise, how much this lady resembles my husband's daughter! But then, don't they say, 'Every seven men were made from one clod of clay'?" And the stepmother never knew that it was her very own husband's daughter and none other!

Not to spin out our tale, before the rest of the women stood up, the fisherman's daughter went to the mother of the bride to say, "May it be with God's blessings and bounty, O my aunt!" and hurried out. The sun had set and darkness was falling. On her way the girl had to cross a bridge over the stream that flowed into the king's garden. And by fate and divine decree, it happened that as she ran over the bridge one of her golden clogs fell off her foot and into the river below. It was too far to climb down to the water and search in the dusk; what if her stepmother should return home before her? So the girl took off her other shoe, and pulling her cloak around her head, dashed on her way.

When she reached the house she shucked her fine clothes, rolled the pearly comb and golden clog inside them, and hid them under the woodpile. She rubbed her head and hands and feet with earth to make them dirty, and she was standing with her broom when her stepmother found her. The wife looked into her face and examined her hands and feet and said, "Still sweeping after sunset? Or are you hoping to sweep our lives away?"

What of the golden clog? Well, the current carried it into the king's garden and rolled it and rolled it until it came to rest in the pool where the king's son led his stallion to drink. Next day the prince was watering the horse. He saw that every time it lowered its head to drink, something made it shy and step back. What could there be at the bottom of the pool to frighten his stallion? He called the groom, and from the mud the man brought him the shining clog of gold.

When the prince held the beautiful little thing in his hand, he began to imagine the beautiful little foot that had worn it. He walked back to the palace with his heart busy and his mind full of the girl who owned so precious a shoe. The queen saw him lost in thought and said, "May Allah send us good news; why so careworn, my son?" "Yammah, Mother, I want you to find me a wife!" said the prince. "So much thought over one wife and no more?" said the queen. "I'll find you a thousand if you wish! I'll bring every girl in the kingdom to be your wife if you want! But tell me, my son, who is the girl who has stolen your reason?" "I want to marry the girl who owns this clog," replied the prince, and he told his mother how he had found it. "You shall have her, my son," said the queen. "I shall begin my search tomorrow as soon as it is light, and I shall not stop till I find her."

The very next day the prince's mother went to work, in at one house and out at the next with the golden clog tucked under her arm. Wherever she saw a young woman, she measured the shoe against the sole of the maiden's foot. Meanwhile the prince sat in the palace gate waiting for her return. "What news, Mother?" he asked. And she said, "Nothing yet, my son. Be patient, child, put snow on your breast and cool your passion. I'll find her yet."

And so the search continued. Entering at one gate and leaving at the next, the queen visited the houses of the nobles and the merchants and the goldsmiths. She saw the daughters of the craftsmen and the tradesmen. She went into the huts of the water carriers and the weavers, and stopped at each house until only the fishermen's hovels on the bank of the river were left. Every evening when the prince asked for news, she said, "I'll find her, I'll find her."

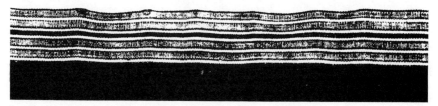

When the fisherfolk were told that the queen was coming to visit their houses, that wily fisherman's wife got busy. She bathed her daughter and dressed her in her best, she rinsed her hair with henna and rimmed her eyes with *kohl* and rubbed her cheeks till they glowed red. But still when the girl stood beside the fisherman's daughter, it was like a candle in the sun. Much as the stepchild had been ill-treated and starved, through the will of Allah and with the help of the little red fish, she had grown in beauty from day to day. Now her stepmother dragged her out of the house and into the yard. She pushed her into the bakehouse and covered its mouth with the round clay tray on which she spread her dough. This she held down with the stone of her handmill. "Don't dare move until I come for you!" said the stepmother. What could the poor girl do but crouch in the ashes and trust in Allah to save her?

When the queen arrived the stepmother pushed her daughter forward, saying, "Kiss the hands of the prince's mother, ignorant child!" As she had done in the other houses, the queen set the girl beside her and held up her foot and measured the golden clog against it. Just at that moment the neighbor's rooster flew into the yard and began to crow,

> Ki-ki-ki-kow!
> Let the king's wife know
> They put the ugly one on show
> And hid the beauty down below!
> Ki-ki-ki-kow!

He began again with his piercing cry, and the stepmother raced out and flapped her arms to chase him away. But the queen had heard the words, and she sent her servants to search both high and low. When they pushed aside the cover off the mouth of the oven, they found the girl—fair as the moon in the midst of the ashes. They brought her to the queen, and the golden clog fit as if it had been the mold from which her foot was cast.

The queen was satisfied. She said, "From this hour that daughter of yours is betrothed to my son. Make ready for the wedding. God willing, the procession shall come for her on Friday." And she gave the stepmother a purse filled with gold.

When the woman realized that her plans had failed, that her husband's daughter was to marry the prince while her own remained in the house, she was filled with anger and rage. "I'll see that he sends her back before the night is out," she said.

She took the purse of gold, ran to the perfumer's bazaar, and asked for a purge so strong that it would shred the bowels to tatters. At the sight of the gold the perfumer began to mix the powders in his tray. Then she asked for arsenic and lime, which weaken hair and make it fall, and an ointment that smelled like carrion.

Now the stepmother prepared the bride for her wedding. She washed her hair with henna mixed with arsenic and lime, and spread the foul ointment over her hair. Then she held the girl by her ear and poured the purge down her throat. Soon the wedding procession arrived, with horses and drums, fluttering bright clothes, and the sounds of jollity. They lifted the bride onto the litter and took her away. She came to the palace preceded by music and followed by singing and chanting and clapping of hands. She entered the chamber, the prince lifted the veil off her face, and she shone like a fourteen-day moon. A scent of amber and roses made the prince press his face to her hair. He ran his fingers over her locks, and it was like a man playing with cloth of gold. Now the bride began to feel a heaviness in her belly, but from under the hem of her gown there fell gold pieces in thousands till the carpet and the cushions were covered with gold.

Meanwhile the stepmother waited in her doorway, saying, "Now they'll bring her back in disgrace. Now she'll come home all filthy and bald." But though she stood in the doorway till dawn, from the palace no one came.

The news of the prince's fair wife began to fill the town, and the master merchant's son said to his mother, "They say that the prince's bride has a sister. I want her for my bride." Going to the fisherman's hut, his mother gave the fisherman's wife a purse full of gold and said, "Prepare the bride, for we shall come for her on Friday if God wills." And the fisherman's wife said to herself, "If what I did for my husband's daughter turned her hair to threads of gold and her belly to a fountain of coins, shall I not do the same for my own child?" She hastened to the perfumer and asked for the same powders and drugs, but stronger than before. Then she prepared her child, and the wedding procession came. When the merchant's son lifted her veil, it was like lifting the cover off a grave. The stink was so strong that it choked him, and her hair came away in his hands. So they wrapped the poor bride in her own filth and carried her back to her mother.

As for the prince, he lived with the fisherman's daughter in great happiness and joy, and God blessed them with seven children like seven golden birds.

Mulberry, mulberry,
So ends my story.
If my house were not so far
I'd bring you figs and raisins in a jar.

The Camel Husband

Palestine

Lord have mercy on his slave,
From all harm and evil save.

Once there was a poor woman. Not only was she poor, but she was barren. Summer and winter, winter and summer came and went, and still she did not bear a child. The brides of her year carried a son on one arm and a daughter on the other; she alone remained childless. When she walked to the well for water with the other women and saw a camel resting with a newborn calf in the crook of its haunch, the poor woman wept.

That night she stepped out of her house and stood under the open sky. Lifting her headcloth off her brow, she prayed to God to grant her the blessing of a child. "No matter if it be son or daughter, so long as it is a child. Man or beast, so let it only be mine to hold in my arms—a newborn camel would be a greater solace than no son at all!"

The Merciful One heard her prayer and granted her wish: the days passed and the woman knew that she was pregnant. When the months were counted out, she gave birth—and what she brought into the world was a baby camel. Her neighbors lifted their hands in disbelief. But the poor woman named her son Jumail, or Little Camel, and loved him with all the love of a mother's heart. Early in the morning she let him out to pasture with the sheep, and at nightfall she brought him into the courtyard of her house.

When Jumail was fully grown, he came to his mother's room and spoke: "Mother, I want a wife." From here to there the woman went searching for a bride for her son. At last she found a peasant girl whose father was content to receive one gold piece as bride-money. They bathed her and combed out her hair with rose water. They dressed her in striped velvet and brought her to Jumail's house. But Little Camel refused to look at her. "I want the sultan's youngest daughter to be my wife," he told his mother.

The poor woman knew that the sultan's youngest daughter, Princess Ward, was the fairest of all his daughters, and that her father loved her like the light of his eyes. "How can a wretched woman like me ask for Princess Ward?" she cried. "I shall have my head cut off!" But her beloved son Jumail replied, "I want the sultan's youngest daughter to be my wife."

Can a mother refuse her only son? The woman swallowed hard, for she was very frightened, and requested an audience with the king. She was brought into the royal presence. "Tell us your desires," commanded the sultan, for he was great of heart and gentle with all who asked his help. "I have come seeking kinship with my lord," the woman said. "I come to ask for Princess Ward as a bride for my only son." "Who is your son?" asked the king. "I named him Jumail," the woman said, "because he was born a baby camel." The sultan smiled into his beard but did not want to shame the poor woman in front of all his court. So he said, "Nothing forbids the union as long as your son can pay the princess's bride-money." "How much is that?" "Her weight in gold!"

When she returned home the woman began to chide her son. "Now you shall have no wife at all," she said. "You refused a peasant girl and wanted the sultan's daughter. Show us now how to collect a princess's bride-money!" "I will," replied Jumail. "Go to the palace again tomorrow and tell the sultan this and this and this."

Next day the soldiers rounded up every camel driver in the city. "God save the sultan's health, but his brain has flown or else he would not make us do the bidding of a beast," they grumbled. Jumail, who was waiting outside the city wall, led them to a hill of rocks. At his word the stones moved and an entrance opened to a dark cave. Inside lay heap upon heap of silver and gold and trays of precious stones: pearls and corals and jewels without price. The men loaded their animals and when they had done the rocks closed behind them like a wall.

The sultan paled to see before him a heap of gold and treasure many times the weight not of one but of all his daughters. How could he have guessed that a poor woman's son, and one who was a camel, would bring him what he asked for and more? But his word had been given and could not be recalled. So he sent for the *qadi* and went to explain the calamity to his daughter.

At first the princess wept and moaned and begged her father to release her. But at length reluctance allowed itself to be persuaded, and the crier was sent to clear the streets by calling, "Everyone into his house! Empty the streets of people, for Princess Ward will be passing on her way to her bridegroom's house tonight."

When the procession came into sight, it looked like a funeral not a wedding. The women peeping through the shutters shook their heads and whispered, "Lah! Lah! What a pity and a shame that a sultan should give his daughter to a camel in return for gold!"

Princess Ward sat bowed in grief waiting for Jumail. When she looked up she screamed with fear. For there before her stood a youth, and what a youth! All height and beauty, with such grace and bearing! "Don't be frightened," he said, "I am your husband Jumail. I am the son of the king of the Djinn but have been caught in a camel's form. I shall visit you each night if you promise not to tell my secret. Break this promise, however, and I shall disappear never to be seen again."

Grief was turned into joy. When the sultan came to greet the bride next day, he found her laughing and wanting nothing. "All I wish for is your well-being, Father," she said.

Come day, go day, the king of the neighboring country marched up to the sultan's city. His soldiers stood outside the wall, and their numbers filled the people with fear. The sultan prepared for war with a heavy heart. When Princess Ward told Jumail of her father's troubles, he said, "I shall fight in tomorrow's battle, wearing white robes and riding a white horse, but do not say that it is I."

Next morning the people climbed to the roofs of their houses to see how the fighting would go. With the women stood Princess Ward and her sisters. And one said, "Look at my husband! None stands taller than he!" Another claimed, "My husband's courage puts to shame all who boast and say nothing but 'I this and I that . . .' for next to him, what are they?" Just then a horseman in white robes spurring a white mare came galloping into the thick of the battle. Swinging his sword right and left, he cut off five heads with each blow. The sultan's soldiers rallied, and from the city came the trills of the women shouting for joy. "Where is Ward's husband, now that the sultan needs him?" mocked one of the princesses. The rest laughed and said, "Did you not know that Ward's husband is tethered in the courtyard of her house, eating the grass that grows between the stones?"

All the time that her sisters had been pointing out their husbands, Princess Ward turned away her head to stop herself from speaking. But her heart was full, and before she could hold in the words, they tumbled out: "The brave horseman in white who is saving the day is none other than my own dear husband Jumail!" She clapped her hand over her mouth, but it was too late. She had said what she must not say.

While the city feasted the sultan's victory through the night, the princess searched for her camel husband Jumail. He had vanished and was not to be found. She sent travelers to look for him in all the known and unknown corners of the world—to cities with fine buildings and to ruins of rubbled stone—but though they paced the far horizons, they found no trace of him. The princess grieved and wept until she fell sick and took to her bed. Neither doctor nor healer was able to help. But the sultan her father thought of a way to keep her mind from dwelling on her loss.

He built a fine bathhouse, a *hammam*, with basins of marble and pools of clear water, and called it the Hammam of Princess Ward. Any woman could come and bathe in it on condition that she tell the princess a story. Old and young, rich and poor flocked to the bath and told the princess a tale.

Now, there was a poor old widow who, not having the money to pay, had never wet her body in the hot water of a public bath. At last she pulled her courage together and said to herself, "I have no tale to tell, but still let me go to the Hammam of Princess Ward. Maybe I can think of something on the way." And she called her grandson to accompany her.

Halfway to the palace the moon sank and the woman was left in pitch darkness. So she and her grandson climbed into the branches of an olive tree to spend the rest of the night in safety. As they sat there, they heard a hen and a rooster light in the tree. The rooster crowed, "O rain, scatter!" and the hen clucked, "O wind, sweep!" At which a wind rose and a rainstorm raged. When it was over, the earth in front of the olive tree split open. Forty black slaves came out of it carrying thrones studded with gems and tables laden with delicate foods. Then forty white doves flew down and bathed in the pools of rainwater. They turned into forty beautiful maidens, and each sat at one of the tables set out by the slaves. But as soon as any of them stretched her hand toward the food, a voice would say:

> Hold back! Refrain till after
> I have been tasted by your master!

At length a youth appeared, handsome beyond the power of words to describe. He sat upon soft pillows of silk sipping tea in the midst of the banquet of maidens. Yet all the while he wept, and the tears coursed down his cheeks. He reached for an apple and cut it into four pieces, saying:

> One piece I cast to the east,
> One piece I cast to the west,
> One piece is mine on which to feast,
> And one for the woman I love best.

After which he kicked the ground with his foot so that it opened into a pit. And all the tables and chairs and food fell in and disappeared.

When the morning dawned, the old woman and her grandchild climbed down from the branches of the olive tree and continued their journey to the palace. There they found Princess Ward lying on seven mattresses and covered with seven quilts. The old woman said, "My lady, halfway here the moon set on me, so I was obliged to climb into an olive tree to spend the night in safety. As I lay on its branches a rooster and a hen came by, saying, 'O rain, scatter! O wind, sweep!' And a storm arose, with lashing wind and pelting rain. Then it blew away, and the earth opened and forty slaves set a feast with golden thrones and tables laden with dainty dishes. Forty white doves flew down and bathed in the pools of rainwater, turning into forty fair maidens. But none could touch a bite of food, for voices warned them:

> Hold back! Refrain till after
> I have been tasted by your master!

The princess lay still, listening. So the old woman continued, "At last a youth appeared, tall as a sugarcane." At this the princess kicked off one of the quilts. "With wide-set eyes." Here the princess threw off a second quilt. "And a princely bearing"—which made the princess push aside a third quilt. By the time the old woman had described how this youth divided the apple, and after she recited the rhyme—

> One piece I cast to the east,
> One piece I cast to the west,
> One piece is mine on which to feast,
> And one for the woman I love best.

—Princess Ward had tossed away all seven quilts and sat up on her seven mattresses. She said, "Take me to the olive tree you speak of."

The old woman led the princess to the tree in which she and her grandson had rested. For six nights the princess watched from its branches and saw nothing. But on the seventh she saw a rooster and a hen hurrying by, saying, "O rain scatter! O wind sweep!" and a storm of wind and rain came raging overhead. When it had subsided, all that the woman had described took place. The white doves flew down and changed into maidens, and in the midst of their feast her own husband Jumail reclined on soft pillows, weeping. When he kicked the ground with his foot and the pit opened into which the whole banquet disappeared, Princess Ward followed him underground and flung her arms about his neck and said, "Come back to your wife, who has been sick with grief over you!"

And Jumail said, "You have chased me into the land of the Djinn and crossed the boundary between the world above and the world beneath, you have opened the way for my return. From today I can live not as a camel but as a man."

> We left them happy, and back we came.
> May all your lives be the same.

The Princess in the Suit of Leather

Egypt

Neither here nor elsewhere lived a king who had a wife whom he loved with all his heart and a daughter who was the light of his eyes. The princess had hardly reached womanhood when the queen fell ill and died. For one whole year the king kept vigil, sitting with bowed head beside her tomb. Then he summoned the matchmakers, elderly women wise in the ways of living, and said, "I wish to marry again. Here is my poor queen's anklet. Find me the girl, rich or poor, humble or well-born, whose foot this anklet will fit. For I promised the queen as she lay dying that I would marry that girl and no other."

The matchmakers traveled up and down the kingdom looking for the king's new bride. But search and search as they would, they could not find a single girl around whose ankle the jewel would close. The queen had been such that there was no woman like her. Then one old woman said, "We have entered the house of every maiden in the land except the house of the king's own daughter. Let us go to the palace."

When they slipped the anklet onto the princess's foot, it suited as if it had been made to her measure. Out of the seraglio went the women at a run, straight into the king's presence, and said, "We have visited every maiden in your kingdom, but none was able to squeeze her foot into the late queen's anklet. None, that is, except the princess your daughter. She wears it as easily as if it were her own." A wrinkled matron spoke up. "Why not marry the princess? Why give her to a stranger and deprive yourself?" The words were hardly spoken when the king summoned the *qadi* to pen the papers for the marriage. To the princess he made no mention of his plan.

Now there was a bustle in the palace as the jewelers, the clothiers, and the furnishers came to outfit the bride. The princess was pleased to know that she was to be wed. But who her husband was she had no inkling. As late as the "night of the entering," when the groom first sees the bride, she remained in ignorance even though the servants with their whispers were busy around her, combing and pinning and making her beautiful. At last the minister's daughter, who had come to admire her in her finery, said, "Why are you frowning? Were not women created for marriage with men? And is there any man whose standing is higher than the king's?"

"What is the meaning of such talk?" cried the princess. "I won't tell you," said the girl, "unless you give me your golden bangle to keep." The princess pulled off the bracelet, and the girl explained how everything had come about so that the bridegroom was no other than the princess's own father.

The princess turned whiter than the cloth on her head and trembled like one who is sick with the forty-day fever. She rose to her feet and sent away all who were with her. Then, knowing only that she must escape, she ran onto the terrace and leaped over the palace wall, landing in a tanner's yard which lay below. She pressed a handful of gold into the tanner's palm and said, "Can you make me a suit of leather to hide me from head to heels, showing nothing but my eyes? I want it by tomorrow's dawn."

The poor man was overjoyed to earn the coins. He set to work with his wife and children. Cutting and stitching through the night they had the suit ready, before it was light enough to know a white thread from a dark. Wait a little! and here comes our lady, the princess. She put on the suit— such a strange spectacle that anyone looking at her would think he was seeing nothing but a pile of hides. In this disguise she left the tanner and lay down beside the city gate, waiting for the day.

Now to return to my lord the king. When he entered the bridal chamber and found the princess gone, he sent his army into the city to search for her. Time and again a soldier would stumble upon the princess lying at the gate and ask, "Have you seen the king's daughter?" And she would reply,

> My name is Juleidah for my coat of skins,
> My eyes are weak, my sight is dim,
> My ears are deaf, I cannot hear.
> I care for no one far or near.

When it was day and the city gate was unbarred, she shuffled out until she was beyond the walls. Then she turned her face away from her father's city and fled.

Walking and running, one foot lifting her and one foot setting her down, there was a day when, with the setting of the sun, the princess came to another city. Too weary to travel a step farther, she fell to the ground. Now her resting place was in the shadow of the wall of the women's quarters, the harem of the sultan's palace. A slave girl, leaning from the window to toss out the crumbs from the royal table, noticed the heap of skins on the ground and thought nothing of it. But when she saw two bright eyes staring out at her from the middle of the hides, she sprang back in terror and said to the queen, "My lady, there is something monstrous crouching under our window. I have seen it, and it looks like nothing less than an Afreet!" "Bring it up for me to see and judge," said the queen.

The slave girl went down shivering with fear, not knowing which was the easier thing to face, the monster outside or her mistress's rage should

she fail to do her bidding. But the princess in her suit made no sound when the slave girl tugged at a corner of the leather. The girl took courage and dragged her all the way into the presence of the sultan's wife.

Never had such an astonishing creature been seen in that country. Lifting both palms in amazement, the queen asked her servant, "What is it?" and then turned to the monster and asked, "Who are you?" When the heap of skins answered—

> My name is Juleidah for my coat of skins,
> My eyes are weak, my sight is dim,
> My ears are deaf, I cannot hear.
> I care for no one far or near.

—how the queen laughed at the quaint reply! "Go bring food and drink for our guest," she said, holding her side. "We shall keep her to amuse us." When Juleidah had eaten, the queen said, "Tell us what you can do, so that we may put you to work about the palace." "Anything you ask me to do, I am ready to try," said Juleidah. Then the queen called, "Mistress cook! Take this broken-winged soul into your kitchen. Maybe for her sake God will reward us with His blessings."

So now our fine princess was a kitchen skivvy, feeding the fires and raking out the ashes. And whenever the queen lacked company and felt bored, she called Juleidah and laughed at her prattle.

One day the *wazir* sent word that all the sultan's harem was invited to a night's entertainment in his house. All day long there was a stir of excitement in the women's quarters. As the queen prepared to set out in the evening, she stopped by Juleidah and said, "Won't you come with us tonight? All the servants and slaves are invited. Aren't you afraid to stay alone?" But Juleidah only repeated her refrain,

> My ears are deaf, I cannot hear.
> I care for no one far or near.

One of the serving girls sniffed and said, "What is there to make her afraid? She is blind and deaf and wouldn't notice an Afreet even if he were to jump on top of her in the dark!" So they left.

In the women's reception hall of the *wazir*'s house there was dining and feasting and music and much merriment. Suddenly at the height of the talk and enjoyment, such a one entered that they all stopped in the middle of the word they were speaking. Tall as a cypress, with a face like a rose and the silks and jewels of a king's bride, she seemed to fill the room with light. Who was it? Juleidah, who had shaken off her coat of leather as soon as the sultan's harem had gone. She had followed them to the *wazir*'s, and now the ladies who had been so merry began to quarrel, each wanting to sit beside the newcomer.

When dawn was near, Juleidah took a handful of gold sequins from the fold of her sash and scattered them on the floor. The ladies scrambled to pick up the bright treasure. And while they were occupied, Juleidah left the hall. Quickly, quickly she raced back to the palace kitchen and put on the coat of leather. Soon the others returned. Seeing the heap of hides on the kitchen floor, the queen poked it with the toe of her red slipper and said, "Truly, I wish you had been with us to admire the lady who was at the entertainment." But Juleidah only mumbled, "My eyes are weak, I cannot see . . ." and they all went to their own beds to sleep.

When the queen woke up next day, the sun was high in the sky. As was his habit, the sultan's son came in to kiss his mother's hands and bid her good morning. But she could talk only of the visitor at the *wazir*'s feast. "O my son," she sighed, "it was a woman with such a face and such a neck and such a form that all who saw her said, 'She is the daughter of neither a king nor a sultan, but of someone greater yet!' " On and on the queen poured out her praises of the woman, until the prince's heart was on fire. Finally his mother concluded, "I wish I had asked her father's name so that I could engage her to be your bride." And the sultan's son replied, "When you return tonight to continue your entertainment, I shall stand outside the *wazir*'s door and wait until she leaves. I'll ask her then about her father and her station."

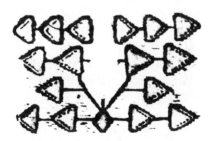

At sunset the women dressed themselves once more. With the folds of their robes smelling of orange blossom and incense and their bracelets chinking on their arms, they passed by Juleidah lying on the kitchen floor and said, "Will you come with us tonight?" But Juleidah only turned her back on them. Then as soon as they were safely gone, she threw off her suit of leather and hurried after them.

In the *wazir*'s hall the guests pressed close around Juleidah, wanting to see her and ask where she came from. But to all their questions she gave no answer, whether yes or no, although she sat with them until the dawning of the day. Then she threw a fistful of pearls on the marble tiles, and while the women pushed one another to catch them, she slipped away as easily as a hair is pulled out of the dough.

Now who was standing at the door? The prince, of course. He had been waiting for this moment. Blocking her path, he grasped her arm and asked who her father was and from what land she came. But the princess had to be back in her kitchen or her secret would be known. So she fought to get away, and in the scuffle, she pulled the prince's ring clean off his hand. "At least tell me where you come from!" he shouted after her as she ran. "By Allah, tell me where!" And she replied, "I live in a land of paddles and ladles." Then she fled into the palace and hid in her coat of hides.

In came the others, talking and laughing. The prince told his mother what had taken place and announced that he intended to make a journey. "I must go to the land of the paddles and ladles," he said. "Be patient, my son," said the queen. "Give me time to prepare your provisions." Eager as he was, the prince agreed to delay his departure for two days—"But not one hour more!"

Now the kitchen became the busiest corner of the palace. The grinding and the sieving, the kneading and the baking began and Juleidah stood watching. "Away with you," cried the cook, "this is no work for you!" "I want to serve the prince our master like the rest!" said Juleidah. Willing and not willing to let her help, the cook gave her a piece of dough to shape. Juleidah began to make a cake, and when no one was watching, she pushed the prince's ring inside it. And when the food was packed Juleidah placed her own little cake on top of the rest.

Early on the third morning the rations were strapped into the saddlebags, and the prince set off with his servants and his men. He rode without slackening until the sun grew hot. Then he said, "Let us rest the horses while we ourselves eat a mouthful." A servant, seeing Juleidah's tiny loaf lying on top of all the rest, flung it to one side. "Why did you throw that one away?" asked the prince. "It was the work of the creature Juleidah; I saw her make it," said the servant. "It is as misshapen as she is." The prince felt pity for the strange half-wit and asked the servant to bring back her cake. When he tore open the loaf, look, his own ring was inside! The ring he lost the night of the *wazir*'s entertainment. Understanding now where lay the land of ladles and paddles, the prince gave orders to turn back.

When the king and queen had greeted him, the prince said, "Mother, send me my supper with Juleidah." "She can barely see or even hear," said the queen. "How can she bring your supper to you?" "I shall not eat unless Juleidah brings the food," said the prince. So when the time came, the cooks arranged the dishes on a tray and helped Juleidah lift it onto her head. Up the stairs she went, but before she reached the prince's room she tipped the dishes and sent them crashing to the floor. "I told you she cannot see," the queen said to her son. "And I will only eat what Juleidah brings," said the prince.

The cooks prepared a second meal, and when they had balanced the loaded tray upon Juleidah's head, they sent two slave girls to hold her by either hand and guide her to the prince's door. "Go," said the prince to the two slaves, "and you, Juleidah, come." Juleidah began to say,

> My eyes are weak, my sight is dim,
> I'm called Juleidah for my coat of skins,
> My ears are deaf, I cannot hear.
> I care for no one far or near.

But the prince told her, "Come and fill my cup." As she approached, he drew the dagger that hung at his side and slashed her leather coat from collar to hem. It fell into a heap upon the floor—and there stood the maiden his mother had described, one who could say to the moon, "Set that I may shine in your stead."

Hiding Juleidah in a corner of the room, the prince sent for the queen. Our mistress cried out when she saw the pile of skins upon the floor. "Why, my son, did you bring her death upon your neck? The poor thing deserved your pity more than your punishment!" "Come in, Mother," said the prince, "Come and look at our Juleidah before you mourn her." And he led his mother to where our fine princess sat revealed, her fairness filling the room like a ray of light. The queen threw herself upon the girl and kissed her on this side and on that, and bade her sit with the prince and eat. Then she summoned the *qadi* to write the paper that would bind our lord the prince to the fair princess, after which they lived together in the sweetest bliss.

Now we make our way back to the king, Juleidah's father. When he entered the bridal chamber to unveil his own daughter's face and found her gone, and when he had searched the city in vain for her, he called his minister and his servants and dressed himself for travel. From country to country he journeyed, entering one city and leaving the next, taking with him in chains the old woman who had first suggested to him that he marry his own daughter. At last he reached the city where Juleidah was living with her husband the prince.

Now, the princess was sitting in her window when they entered the gate, and she knew them as soon as she saw them. Straightway she sent to her husband urging him to invite the strangers. Our lord went to meet them and succeeded in detaining them only after much pressing, for they were impatient to continue their quest. They dined in the prince's guest hall, then thanked their host and took leave with the words, "The proverb says: 'Have your fill to eat, but then up, onto your feet!' "—while he delayed them further with the proverb, "Where you break your bread, there spread out your bed!"

In the end the prince's kindness forced the tired strangers to lie in his house as guests for the night. "But why did you single out these strangers?" the prince asked Juleidah. "Lend me your robes and headcloth and let me go to them," she said. "Soon you will know my reasons."

Thus disguised, Juleidah sat with her guests. When the coffee cups had been filled and emptied, she said, "Let us tell stories to pass the time. Will you speak first, or shall I?" "Leave us to our sorrows, my son," said the king her father. "We have not the spirit to tell tales." "I'll entertain you, then, and distract your mind," said Juleidah. "There once was a king," she began, and went on to tell the history of her own adventures from the beginning to the end. Every now and then the old woman would interrupt and say, "Can you find no better story than this, my son?" But Juleidah kept right on, and when she had finished she said, "I am your daughter the princess, upon whom all these troubles fell through the words of this old sinner and daughter of shame!"

In the morning they flung the old woman over a tall cliff into the *wadi*. Then the king gave half his kingdom to his daughter and the prince, and they lived in happiness and contentment until death, the parter of the truest lovers, divided them.

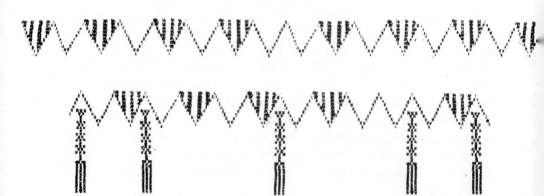

⠒ ⠒ ⠒ ⠒ ⠒ ⠒ ⠒ ⠒ ⠒ ⠒ ⠒ ⠒

Sheikh of
the Lamps

⠒ ⠒ ⠒ ⠒ ⠒ ⠒ ⠒ ⠒ ⠒ ⠒ ⠒ ⠒

Syria

Most is uncertain, but this is not:
Allah is One and metes out our lot.

There were or there were not three sisters who were very poor. Their father and mother had died, leaving them only the house they lived in. To earn their keep they spun wool into yarn, which the oldest girl took to the wool merchants' *suq* to sell.

One evening the sisters were working in their room when the call to sundown prayers began to sound over the city. "It will soon be dark," said the youngest, "It is time to light our lamp." The eldest looked about for matches but found there were none. "I'll go to the neighbors," she said. She unhooked the lamp from where it hung and climbed the steps up to the flat roof. It was the women's custom to visit by crossing from roof to roof into each other's terraces, and so avoid the public gaze in the crowded street.

The neighbor's house was dark, however. There was no answer to the eldest sister's knock. She tried the next house, with no better luck. Then she went further across the quarter, stepping from one rooftop to the next until she arrived at a terrace she had never noticed before. Its tiles were slabs of marble, and the lamps upon it as many as you'd find at a prince's wedding, turning night to day. She counted forty oil lamps and in the middle one lamp more, taller and brighter than the rest. She tipped her own lamp toward this strongest light, and as she did so she heard a voice deep as a cave, saying,

Since you kindled your wick at my flame,
You shall bear a child in my name.

She glanced around her fearfully, but no one was there. "Can a lamp speak like a man?" she said, and she steadied her light and bore it carefully home.

"Where were you this long while?" her sisters asked. "Here you left us sitting in the dark, our hands idle in our laps while you went visiting!" "A strange thing happened," said the girl, and she told them about the roof of marble, the forty lamps, and the voice's words. "Have you ever heard of a lamp that spoke?" she asked.

The sisters laughed, for were they not all maidens? But after six months has passed and they saw their eldest sister's belly rising beneath her gown, they leaned on each other's shoulders and wept for her shame and misfortune. The days went by in sadness and sighing until her time was counted out.

At the birthing the younger girls stood by their sister, calling on Him Whose Eye Never Shuts in Sleep but Watches All-Seeing, when suddenly the wall of the room cracked from floor to ceiling. Through the opening strode an Afreet. His greeting was gentle, but his voice like the rumble of thunder and his face was so fearsome that all three girls fell to the ground in a faint.

"I am your sister's husband," said the Afreet, splashing water on their heads to revive them. Then he cut into the eldest sister's side and lifted out an infant girl so fair that the room brightened as if a shaft of sunlight had flooded it. He said,

> Until she is of age to be a bride
> All this child's food and drink I shall provide.

And before the infant's mother could say, "Go in peace and with God's protection!" the Afreet had vanished and the two halves of the wall had become one again.

Children grow by night, but this child grew by night and day. In no time she had reached womanhood. One day when she was fifteen years old, she said, "Mother, the water is running full in the *wadi*; let us go down and enjoy it." They carried a lunch of thyme-seasoned bread to eat by the river's edge, and they trailed their feet in the stream. All at once the Afreet's daughter gave a cry. The current had pulled off one of her anklets, the handiwork of the Djinn and the gift of her father. Her eyes filled with tears to watch it sink beyond her reach, and all the way home she cried with her head on her mother's shoulder.

A little while and who should pass by but the king's son, riding on the same bank of the *wadi*. A shiny something in the water caught his eye, and he sent his servant for it. When the prince held the anklet in his palm, he said,

> Some men brave dangers and risk adventures bold,
> Seeking large fortunes and treasures of gold,
> But to me, dearest by far to have and to hold
> Is the maiden whose foot was this ring's mold.

He returned to the palace a stricken man. His face was pale as the crocus and his voice a feeble wail. He called,

> Mother, Mother, sweep away all signs of gladness,
> Shroud the house in cobweb sadness.
> Your son loves to the brink of madness
> And will die of his longing.

And he begged the queen to search the kingdom for the owner of the anklet, for he could neither eat nor sleep until he had made her his wife.

The queen set out without delay, fearing for her dear son's health. She swept through the streets and alleys, knocking at every door. But night after night she returned without success to watch at her son's sickbed. At last she reached the house where the three sisters lived. There she saw a girl fair as the morning sun, bending to her work just as a young palm tree bends in the wind. When she showed her the anklet, the girl lifted the hem of her gown and uncovered the jewel's twin. Now the queen's joy was so great that the whole world seemed too narrow to contain it.

To the girl's mother she said, "Give me your daughter to be the bride of my only son the prince." "How can I say 'yes' or 'no' without first telling her father?" the eldest sister replied. The queen had left to restore the prince with the news that the girl who owned the anklet was found, when the wall of the house gaped open with a roar like an earthquake, and the Afreet appeared.

"A prince is a fitting groom for my child," he said, "but for her to taste happiness, she must do as I say." And he took his daughter to one side and advised her with these words: "When you are wed, speak to your husband only if he asks you—

> By the life of the Sheikh of the Lamps that shed light,
> And by the seven bright stars that shine in the night.

The girl promised to do her father's bidding, and the Afreet vanished as quickly as he had appeared.

For seven days and their nights, there was feasting to mark the royal wedding. Food and drink for all the city was bought from the king's purse. There was gaiety in every courtyard, and the sound of lute and tambourine rang in every alley. As for the prince, the minute he caught sight of his bride and saw that she was as fair as he had guessed she must be, the blood began to race in his veins and his strength returned.

The Afreet's daughter was beautiful as the light of the sun, and to look at her made the prince's mind wander. But when he addressed her, his heart

felt smothered in his chest, for she uttered not a word. Still, beauty has its claims, and the prince was content to live by the side of his fair and silent wife for one whole year.

But when the year was out and the prince found himself with neither wife nor yet a child who might air their tongues with words of love, he began to look for a second wife. Even then, the Afreet's daughter said nothing. When the procession of people was bringing the new bride to the palace, the silent wife was sitting on the palace roof spinning the rays of the sun into threads of gold. As soon as the saw her rival, she jumped from the roof to the street and lightly ran to give her a sister's welcome. Those who saw her do it could speak of little else. Then the new bride, wanting to prove herself every bit as able, watched for her husband from the edge of the palace roof when next he went to the hunt with his men. On his return, she leaped down to greet him and was dashed to death on the stones below.

When the days of mourning were over, the prince took yet another wife. The Afreet's daughter sent word that she wished to hold a banquet in the new bride's honor. The guests who assembled in her quarters found a bare room with only a pot of oil simmering on the fire. They whispered to each other, "Can there be a feast with no food?" But the Afreet's daughter plunged her hand into the bubbling oil, and instantly the pot was filled with frying fish and meats of every kind. The prince was delighted by the trick, which made his new wife jealous. When a week had passed she determined to invite her husband's court to dine. Like the Afreet's daughter, she heated a cauldron of fat. But when she dipped her hand inside it, she was burned and died from the pain.

Again the palace mourned; again the prince searched for a bride. This one too was bidden to visit the Afreet's daughter in her reception hall. She sat on a pillow and watched in disbelief as the bowls and pitchers bustled to and fro, moving of their own accord to bring her sweetmeats and fragrant drinks. Then one of the bowls came speeding by, and knocked against the water pitcher, breaking off its spout. "What will our mistress say?" cried the pitcher. "She will never upbraid us as long as we entreat her by her father, the Sheikh of the Lamps that shed light and by the seven stars that shine in the night," said the bowl. Then the dishes fell silent. But the prince's new bride had heard them and the curious words stayed in her mind.

That night the young bride repeated to the prince all she had witnessed and heard in the rooms of the Afreet's daughter. She recited to him the odd words the bowl had spoken to the pitcher. On hearing them, the prince sprang up and hurried to find the Afreet's daughter. He begged her:

> By the life of the Sheikh of the Lamps that shed light,
> And by the seven bright stars that shine in the night,
> Will you not speak and give delight
> To him who loves you as his sight!

And at last the Afreet's daughter spoke, saying, "O king of my soul and ruler of my heart!"

> After which they lived in happiness and bliss,
> With plenty of sons and daughters to kiss.
> May God grant each of us joy such as this!

Jubeinah and the Slave

In a village there lived a man and his wife. They had one child, a daughter whose face was white and pure as a cake of boiled *jubnah* cheese so they called her Jubeinah. People would say, "as beautiful as Jubeinah," speaking her name like a proverb. For she was the measure of beauty in the countryside round about.

Why not? Her cheeks were round and rosy like the apples that come from Syria. Her hair, black as the carob, rested on her feet when it was loose—it was that long! Her arms were as smooth as bolts of silk, and altogether she was so shapely that she might have been turned on a carpenter's lathe.

Her fame reached far and her suitors were many, but her people refused to give her in marriage.

In a distant land a king's son heard of her and wanted her for his wife. But if her parents refused, what could he do? He went to one of the shrewd old women and bade her invent a trick to steal Jubeinah for him.

Tho old woman traveled to Jubeinah's village and called together all the girls. She told them that she needed a party of young women to fetch her son's bride from the next village and keep her company on the way. What unmarried girl dislikes a wedding party? The young women ran to tell Jubeinah. She said, "Ask my father." He was careful; he said, "Ask her mother." Her mother was careful; she said, "Ask her uncle." In the end, however, Jubeinah's relatives agreed to let her go.

But before she left, Jubeinah's mother gave her a bead of blue glass, warning her to guard it carefully and not to lose it. To keep it safe her mother threaded it onto a length of string and hung it around the girl's neck.

The village girls set out together. When they were some distance from home, a Nubian slave woman joined them. She led Jubeinah's horse along a different road away from the rest of the party. As soon as they were alone, she said,

> Jump down, Jubeinah of the fair face,
> Walk, and let me ride in your place!

But before Jubeinah could reply, the blue bead said,

> Trudge on,
> Dark one.

Whenever the slave woman tried to make Jubeinah dismount, the blue bead prevented her.

That is how they traveled until they came to a river. As Jubeinah bent down to drink, the bead slipped from her neck and fell into the water. And the next time the slave woman said,

> Jump down, Jubeinah of the fair face,
> Walk, and let me ride in your place.

—the bead's voice sounded faintly from the bottom of the river:

> Trudge on,
> Dark one.

Soon they were too far to hear it at all, and then the woman pulled Jubeinah off the horse and mounted in her place.

They were near a limestone quarry, next to which the charcoal burners had built their kiln. The slave woman rubbed her own face and skin with handfuls of powdered chalk and forced Jubeinah to darken her fair face with coal dust. So when they reached the king's palace, the prince married the chalk-covered black slave thinking that she was Jubeinah, whose face was white as ewe's-milk cheese.

Since the woman had threatened to kill her if she told the truth, poor Jubeinah did not dare to say a word. To earn her keep she was put to work herding the sheep. Every morning she led her flock to where the grass grew, and there she would sit in the shade of a tree, weeping and saying,

> O birds that fly high on the wind,
> O streams that flow low on the ground,
> Carry greetings to my father,
> Carry greetings to my mother,
> Tell them how their own dear daughter
> Now leads sheep to grass and water.

And all the sheep, and the goats as well, when they saw her tears and heard her crying, would weep with her and forget to graze.

The king's son was puzzled that the sheep went out to pasture every morning and came back looking as if they had stayed in the pen all day. No, instead of growing fat, they became thinner and thinner. "I must find out the reason for myself," he said, so he followed the shepherdess in secret. He heard the words she uttered as she wept, and he saw how the sheep mourned with her and did not eat. Now he understood the cause of the animals' weakness, and he guessed that this must be Jubeinah, his true bride.

When the prince returned to the palace, he lit a fire and asked his wife to pour the water for a bath. As soon as it was hot, he said, "Wash yourself first, O woman." But she refused and would not do it. So he put her into the bath and scrubbed her against her will. All the chalk dust melted off her skin, and there she was, a black slave woman. The prince picked her up in his arms and tossed her into the fire.

In the evening when Jubeinah returned with the flock, the prince sent her to the bathhouse. And when she came out, all the coal dust was gone, and everyone could see that this indeed was a maiden that a prince might woo.

What happened next?

> The king's son made her his wife,
> And they lived a happy life!

∴   ∴   ∴

Beasts
That Roam
the Earth
and Birds
That Fly
with Wings

Animal
Tales

*I*f you listen carefully in Jerusalem, you will hear the doves of that holy city say over and over as they bow their heads and lift them, *"I'bidoo Rabbakom! I'bidoo Rabbakom!* (Worship your God! Worship your God!)" And in Morocco, the rooster perched on the courtyard wall sometimes crows these words: *"Allah yihmeena min deif al ashaa!* (Allah protect us from the dinner guest!)" He knows that he risks being sacrificed on the altar of hospitality. The young chicks pecking on the ground, being in no danger, say, *"Yiji! Yiji! Yiji!* (Let him come! Let him come! Let him come!)" Wherever men have lived near birds and beasts they have explained the distinctive animal calls and markings with stories. Arab folklore is rife with picturesque reasons why the scorpion has no head or why the pigeon's feet are pink.

Hearing the myths and legends told in the Scriptures, the unlettered peasants have added fanciful webs of their own imagining. "Who Has The Sweetest Flesh on Earth?" in this collection is an elaborate accounting for the idiosyncrasies of a number of creatures. Close to it in spirit is a myth from *The Arabian Nights*—folk literature, after all. One of the kings of Egypt is said to have been told by a bird of the birds of paradise,

Know that when Allah, may His name be exalted, banished Adam from paradise, He banished him with nothing but the four leaves with which he was hiding his shame. The leaves fell to the ground. One was eaten by worms and they began to manufacture silk. Another was nibbled by the deer and it was transformed into musk. The third was eaten by the bees and they made honey, and the last fell in the land of Hind, and from it grew the trees which bear spice.

Moslems are enjoined to treat their animals with respect. In the *sura* called "The Cattle" in the Koran, "all the beasts that roam the earth and all the birds that fly with wings" are described as "nations like your own" who will be "gathered before their Lord" on the day of judgment. And in the *sura* called "The Ant," King Solomon on the march with all his armies overhears an ant tell her fellows, "Take shelter in your dwelling places lest Solomon and his soldiers destroy you, not knowing that you are there." And Solomon "smiled laughingly" and diverted his army to spare the insects.

Solomon the son of David, Suleyman bin Dawood, whose knowledge is deep as the valley of Jordan, understood the utterance of birds, the Koran tells us, being favored of God. The story "Suleyman and the Little Owl" in this collection begins exactly like a story in the Koran in which Solomon reviews the assembled birds. Finding that the *hudhud*, or hoopoe, is absent, he threatens punishment unless the bird has a good reason. The hoopoe in the Koran has been to Sheba and brings news of a woman ruling on a mighty throne whose people do not worship God. The folk story replaces the *hudhud* with an owl and goes on to present a puzzle that a "clever daughter" would relish.

But the favorite type of animal story in Arabic is a trickster tale in which two animals, or a human and an animal, try to outwit each other. It takes the form of a short dialogue ending with a punch line that is wise or witty, as in "The Cat Who Went to Mecca" and "Division of the Prey."

These stories may have been inspired by two "imported" collections of literary animal tales. *Kalila wa Dimna*, now read by every schoolchild, is an eighth-century translation of a Pahlevi version of the Sanskrit *Panchatantra*, or *Fables of Bidpai*. It is named for two jackals who discourse on the ways of governments and rulers through animal fables. In one of the early episodes of this work, for example, Kalila reminds Dimna that since they are both dependent on the lion, their king, they have to accept what he likes and reject what he dislikes. Kalila says, "Whoever meddles in word or deed with what does not concern him will suffer as the monkey suffered at the hands of the carpenter." "How was that?" asks Dimna, giving the cue for an animal story. Of course, he has one of his own in rejoinder, and so the debate goes on.

It is possible that without the classic *Kalila wa Dimna*, imported from a culture more sensitive to animals than their own, the Arabs might not spontaneously have created animal fables. Yet the form of *Kalila wa Dimna*— that is, anecdotes demonstrating instances of wit, courage, and wisdom, or presenting moral dilemmas in the wider implications of the events narrated— was very much to the taste of the Arabs. To a large extent, early Arabic histories and even scientific works are made up of anecdotes intended to entertain as well as educate. They were, of course, about people rather than animals, but then, the animal characters in *Kalila wa Dimna* think and act like humans.

On the whole, the animal stories echo themes from other Arabic folktales. For example, "The Duty of the Host" from the tribes of northern Arabia dwells on the Beduin's appreciation of hospitality. The exposition of human ingratitude in "The Treachery of Man" is the kind of didactic tale that is told in the *kuttab*, or Koranic school. But the animal protagonists of the tales are especially suited to that stock folk subject, the triumph of shrewdness and common sense over mere physical strength: the mouse evading the cat, the ewe the jackal. And that is where the emphasis lies in this collection.

The second important group of literary animal fables in Arabic is that attributed to Luqman al Hakeem, Luqman the Wise. A legendary figure in Arabia before Islam, reputed to be descended from the family of Job, Luqman has a *sura* in the Koran called for him. In it he is honored as a sage and a prophet: "We gave wisdom to Luqman." It was not until medieval times that Luqman became linked to the animal fables. By then he no longer resembled a prophet, but rather an artisan or a slave—sometimes a black Nubian slave. In short, he acquired some of the characteristics of the Greek Aesop. Significantly, a story about him that illustrates his understanding of human nature is identical to one told of Aesop. When his master asked Luqman to place before the guests the best parts of the sheep that had been killed in their honor, he brought out the heart and the tongue. Another time, on being requested to serve the worst parts, Luqman again offered the heart and the tongue.

The earliest surviving manuscript of the fables of Luqman dates from the year 1299. With one exception, its stories correspond to Aesop's fables. Given the interest in the translation of Greek texts into Arabic during the reign of the Abbasid caliphs of the eighth and ninth centuries in Baghdad, an Arabic version of Aesop must have become available then. Since each of these tales ends with a moral, it is understandable how they came to be ascribed to Luqman al Hakeem.

Whatever their origin (Stith Thompson traces most literary animal stories to India and Greece), these fables and anecdotes were quickly assimilated into the Arabic tradition. *The Arabian Nights* opens with the fable of the donkey and the ox. The donkey advises the exhausted ox to feign sickness so that he can rest in his stall. Finding that the burden of the ox's tasks has fallen on his own shoulders as a result, the donkey tells the ox that he overheard their owner talk of taking the sick ox to the slaughterhouse. The ox's recovery is immediate.

Of course, to those who tell a story like "Division of the Prey," and they are many, it makes no difference that the tale is one of Luqman al Hakeem's, nor does it matter that "The Pious Cat" was known in the tenth century. Like the simple Beduin fable "The Duty of the Host," they are told to amuse. And then told again because there is in them a grain of truth to think about.

Both character traits and incidents in the anecdotes that follow are common to the whole culture; only the animals are occasionally regional. For example, it is everywhere considered a sin to waste bread—the staff of life. Children dropping a crust onto the floor are taught to pick it up, kiss it, and touch it to their foreheads as they would the hand of a revered elder, after which they may eat it. So it is not surprising that the tale "How the Monkey Got

His Shape" should have variants in many places. In one the mother who defiles the bread is herself turned into a monkey, and in another she is punished by having her face pressed flat against the moon, where it can still be seen.

A snowballing plot like "How the Fox Got Back His Tail" amuses children everywhere. This one is set in the olive-growing hillsides of the eastern Mediterranean. In a variation told in Morocco, it is a fly who is found half drowning in the milk pan. When the woman pulls off his tail, the fly pleads for it desperately. He explains that he has to go in company with all the males of his tribe to make a formal request for a bride for his brother, and he cannot go without a tail. "Maybe I would feel kindly if you were to bring me a little goat," says the woman, and he is off.

"The Knotter of Tails" was recorded in Jordan, where rough shepherds' coats like the one described in the story hang in the markets. A North African equivalent has the fox promise to make a lion some shoes out of camel hide in return for an adequate supply of young camels. The fox delivers the shoes while they are still damp and advises the lion to put them on and dry them in the sun. The hide shrinks, and the crippled lion punishes the fox just as he is punished in the Jordanian tale.

Northwest Africa, Berber country, is remarkably rich in stories featuring animals. The variety of animals is wider and the plots often more complex. "Father of a Hundred Tricks," a tale of the jackal and the hedgehog, and "How the Animals Kept the Lions Away" are part of a cycle of adventures shared by the same animals. The bear, not found elsewhere except in the Kurdish mountain region of Iraq, appears in a Moroccan version of "Division of the Prey." The hedgehog, not much noticed in other areas, is a main character here; so is the ewe who, championed by the desert greyhound, behaves with a circumspection far from sheeplike.

It is striking that the camel, for whom scholars have found over 160 descriptive terms in Arabic, should play a marginal part in these stories,

while the lion, no longer found except in the Sudan, should retain its importance. It may be that wild or exotic animals make better subjects.

The stars of the tales are the masters of trickery: the fox, who is as sly as Reynard, and the jackal. The jackal lies low in the day and steals sheep at night. In North Africa they say,

> On nights when brother jackal's tail is soaked,
> There's food for his mother and grandmother both.

On stormy nights, when men keep to their tents, he of course has a better chance at the flocks. The hedgehog is seen in Morocco and Algeria as a creature of cunning. It is believed that he can feed off snakes because, having discovered that the wild thyme is "father of ninety-nine remedies," he seasons his poisonous meals with this healing herb. By contrast the lion, though strong, tends to be slow and gullible. The owl, a frequenter of abandoned places and ruins, is regarded as a bird of ill omen and the ugliest of all creatures. That's why the scorpion, meeting the owl on the day that God was distributing heads to the animals, decided to manage without.

Since the animals in the stories are able to talk, they address one another, like their human counterparts, in the polite form, that is, by their oldest son's name rather than their own: Abu Ali or Imm Ali—Father of Ali or Mother of Ali—where Ali is the firstborn son. The jackal is known as Abu Sirhan and the lion as Abu Harith, and the fox is nicknamed Abu l'Hssein (Father of the Little Fortress). In some places these names are the only words for the animal in the vernacular.

The section is rounded with a few tales that are enlivened with rhyme and not overburdened with reason—"The Scarab Beetle's Daughter," "The Tortoise and His Frog Wife," and "Little Mangy One." They come from the nursery, where one first looks for animal stories.

The Cat Who Went to Mecca

Syria

A long time ago the king of the cats went on the pilgrimage to Mecca. When he returned, the king of the mice felt obliged to pay him the traditional visit of congratulations on his safe return as a Hajji, or pilgrim. He said to his subjects the mice, "Etiquette demands that we go to his house and welcome him back formally." The mice were not convinced. "The cat is our enemy; how can we go near him in safety?" The king explained, "Now that he has been to Mecca and become a Hajji, he is no longer free to do what was permitted before. Nowadays he remains at prayer from dawn till sunset, and the prayer beads never leave his hands." The mice were not persuaded. "You call on him and see," they said. "We shall wait here for you."

So the king of the mice set out. He poked his head out of his hole and looked around. There sat the king of the cats, the white cap of a pilgrim on his head. He was praising God, murmuring prayers, and every now and then spitting over his shoulder, first to his left and then to his right, in case the devil was lurking behind to distract him from his devotions.

But no sooner had the king of the cats caught sight of the king of the mice peeping out of his hole than he dropped his rosary and sprang! And but for God the Preserver, he would have bitten the mouse's tail right off.

The king of the mice jumped back into his hole and rejoined his subjects. "How is the king of the cats after his pilgrimage?" they asked. "Let's hope he has changed for the better." "Never mind the pilgrimage," said the king of the mice. "He may pray like a Hajji, but he still pounces like a cat."

The
Woodcutter
Without a Brain

Morocco

Two woodcutters were walking in a thicket when they saw lion spoor on the road. "This is the mark of a lion," said one. "What shall we do?" "Let us go on our way and do what we have to do," said his friend. So they continued along the path and each collected a load of firewood. When it was time for them to return, the first man said, "Let us take another way home, in Allah's name!" "No, this path is shorter," said his friend. The first man said, "I saw lion's spoor on the road and I shall not return that way, by Allah!" And he took a rocky path higher up the mountain.

The second woodcutter returned the way they had come. When he reached the place where they had noticed traces of a lion, he found the lion himself sitting in the middle of the road. "Peace, uncle lion," said the man. "Peace, O son of Adam," said the lion. "What are you doing here?" asked the man. "I am sick," replied the lion, "and I need the brain from the head of a man to cure me. God in His mercy has led you to me and is offering me your brain, praise be to Him." "Listen, O lion," said the man, "for what I am about to tell you is the truth. I am a brainless fellow. Had I the least bit of brain I should not have returned this way. The one with the brain is up there beyond the rocks!"

"God grant you happiness," said the lion and began climbing up the mountain.

Who Lied?

Saudi Arabia

Long ago in the beginning, a Beduin tribe—some say it was the Beni Zeid—was looking for new pasture, having used up all its water and grazing land. To scout the countryside around them they released the crow, the partridge, and the dove. The three birds flew off together. But in a short time the crow was back with the sad news that as far as he could fly, there was only more desert with not a stalk or blade of grass for the cattle to feed on. Later the other two birds returned, and what they had seen was the opposite: lush grazing grounds with plenty of water. "So soft is the grass there," they said, "that a newborn babe treading on it would hurt the blades."

Not knowing which of the two reports was true, the tribe moved to the place the partridge and the dove had described. They found that the crow was the false one, and for that they painted him black as his lie. The dove and the partridge they rewarded, staining the feet of one a festive red with henna and lining the eyes of the other with *kohl*. To this day the dove walks on pink feet and the partridge's eye is ringed with black.

The Hospitality
of Abu L'Hssein

Egypt

Once Abu l'Hssein, the fox, sent word to the raven: "I should feel honored if you allowed me to be your host for a meal!" The raven accepted and the fox busied himself making preparations: boiling camel's milk and flour to make a thick porridge.

When the raven arrived, the fox poured the mixture onto a flat rock and said, "Welcome to you, brother! Enjoy yourself, and may Allah grant you health and more health." The raven tried unsuccessfully to peck at the porridge, unable to catch a single mouthful of food, while the fox lapped the rock clean with his tongue. "So this is the hospitality of Abu l'Hssein," said the raven to himself. But he did not show his true feelings. Instead he invited the fox to return the compliment and visit him for a feast of sweet dates. The fox's mouth began to water, for above all things he relished ripe dates. Only rarely did he eat them, because they grew well out of his reach at the top of the date palms.

At the appointed time the fox appeared at the raven's house. The raven flew up to a date palm and began to knock the finest and sweetest dates down into a dense thornbush which grew below. Then the raven invited the fox to eat his fill: "Let none be abashed but the devil; eat, brother, until you can eat no more!" How eagerly the fox ran round and round the bush trying to pry out at least one date! But the thorns were like needles, and all he got for his pains were torn paws. How enviously he watched as the raven snatched date after date from the spines with his armored claws and strong beak.

Since that time the fox has respected the raven as his equal.

The Monkey Learns
to Weave

Syria

A man who had a monkey wanted to train it to weave at the loom. But even when the man beat it, the monkey refused to learn.

One day the man brought one of his sheep to the loom and, while the monkey watched, pretended that he was trying to teach it to weave. The sheep, of course, did nothing but bleat, which made the monkey laugh. The man drew out his knife and said to the sheep, "If you do not learn, I swear by your young lambs that I shall kill you!" The sheep continued to do nothing but bleat. And then the man did kill it.

At the sight of the blood, the monkey jumped into the pit of the loom and began to toss the shuttle to and fro as fast as he could go. Hence the saying, "Kill the sheep and the monkey will learn to weave."

How the Fox Got
Back His Tail

Palestine

There was an old woman who kept goats. Every evening she would milk her herd and heat the milk pan in the warm ashes at the bottom of the bakehouse for herself and her children's supper. One day Abu l'Hssein, the fox, nosed his way to the milk and cleaned out the pan. When the old woman came for her supper she found not a drop. The next night and the night after that, the same thing happened. "Well," she said to herself, "I'll

wait up and see who's drinking up my little bit of milk every night." She took the cleaver and hid inside the clay bakehouse. She did not have to wait very long, for soon Abu l'Hssein loped in and headed straight for the milk pan. He had scarcely dipped his chin into it when the old woman swung her cleaver and sent his tail flying to the other end of the oven. "Oww! Oww!" he yelped. "Give me back my tail!" "First give me back my milk— then you can have your tail," said the old woman.

So the fox went to the she-goats and said, "Will you give me some milk for the old woman so she'll let me have my tail back?" "Bring us some green twigs to nibble," said the goats. "Then we'll give you milk." So the fox trotted off to the olive grove and said to the olive trees, "Give me some green twigs for the she-goats so they'll give me milk to take to the old woman so she'll let me have my tail back." "Bring us a man who will hoe the earth round our roots. Then we'll give you some twigs," said the olive trees. So the fox went to the day laborer and said, "God keep you, uncle. Will you come and hoe round the roots of the olive trees so they'll give me green twigs for the goats so they'll give me milk for the old woman so she'll let me have my tail back?" "If you find me some shoes first," said the day laborer.

So the fox went to the cobbler and said, "Uncle, please give me some shoes for the day laborer so he'll hoe round the roots of the olive trees so they'll give me twigs to feed the goats so they'll give me milk for the old woman so she'll let me have my tail back." The shoemaker was a decent fellow and let the fox have a pair of worn-out slippers. The fox took them to the laborer, who hoed around the roots of the olive trees, and the olive trees gave the fox some green twigs, and the fox fed the twigs to the goats, and the goats let him have some milk, and he took it to the old woman, and the old woman let him have his tail back. Then the fox sped off, shouting "Oww!"

The Pious Cat

O m a n

A cat was warming himself near a clay brazier which had been left out in the yard to be fanned by the breeze. Above his head a rat suddenly hurried along the edge of the roof. The cat looked up at the sound and exclaimed, "Ya Hafeedh! O Allah our Protector, preserve him!" "May Allah preserve nobody!" snapped the rat, somewhat testily. "Why this interest in my affairs? Am I dear to you, all at once? Best to leave me alone!"

Just then the rat tripped over a waterspout and fell to the ground, where the cat caught him firmly in his claws. "When I said Ya Hafeedh! you became angry and said May Allah protect nobody! Now you see what has come of your blasphemy!" "How right you are, my uncle cat!" said the rat. "I beg you, give me a chance to atone; let me recite the 'Fatiha' one last time before I die! Better still, why don't you pray with me, and let us both say, 'May God bring this affair to a just conclusion!' "

The cat raised his paws in the attitude of prayer, and the rat scampered to the safety of his hole. So the cat was left to scratch his face in remorse.

And now whenever you see a cat rubbing his face, you will know that he is remembering the smell of that rat.

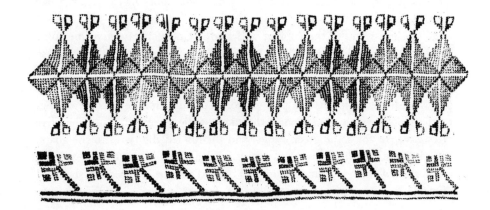

Who Has the
Sweetest Flesh
on Earth?

Palestine

Have I told you, or have I not, why the serpent is the least loved of the creatures of the earth?

Well, when Iblees, the devil, was hounded from heaven and the gates were locked against him, he was not content to obey the will of the Lord. No, he went skulking round and round the outer fence of paradise hoping to find a gap or a hole through which he could steal in again. But the fence was tight and he could not find a way in. So he went to the animals, to each kind in turn, and tried to persuade them to help him return to paradise. But the animals all refused.

At last Iblees came to the serpent. "If I give you the sweetest flesh on earth to be your food, O serpent," he said, "will you help me return to paradise?" The serpent thought and then asked, "What is the sweetest flesh on earth?" "The flesh of the sons of Adam," said the devil. When he heard this, the serpent agreed. "Hide yourself in my right fang," he said, "and no one will see you enter the gates of paradise."

So it was that Iblees returned to paradise and spoke to Eve and brought upon her and Adam and their children to this day all the troubles in the world. Eve thought it was the serpent speaking, but it was the devil hiding in the serpent's fang.

What of the serpent himself, who was the cause of all this evil? Well, he did not receive the reward that had been promised to him. For when he came to claim the sweetest flesh from Adam, this is what happened.

The swallow, who is a pious bird (for does he not make the pilgrimage to Mecca every year and fly south to visit the holy places?), has always been a friend of the sons of Adam, as he was of Adam before them. Just as he likes to build his house in the shadow of our houses now, so in the beginning he liked to stay near Adam. When the serpent came to Adam to take his flesh as food, the swallow heard him. And this is what the swallow said:

"How do you know that the flesh of man is the sweetest food on earth?"
"Iblees told me so," said the serpent. "But Iblees is the devil, and who can
trust his word?" countered the swallow. Then Adam spoke and said, "Give
me a year's respite, O serpent, to sample and test and find out the truth
about the sweetest flesh on earth. I shall send the mosquito on a journey to
every corner of the world, and I shall command her to taste a drop of blood
from every kind of creature that roams the earth. At the end of that time,
when she has drunk every kind of blood, she will return and proclaim before
the assembled animals which is indeed the sweetest flesh on earth!"

The serpent was satisfied with this arrangement, and the mosquito set
out on her long and difficult mission. But neither the serpent nor the
mosquito knew that the swallow was following the mosquito wherever she
went. Only when the time was up and the year had gone did the swallow
meet the mosquito face to face on her way to report to Adam. "Praise be to
Allah for your safe return!" said the swallow to the mosquito, who replied,
"May Allah grant you peace also!" "Have you discovered which is the sweetest
flesh on earth?" asked the swallow. "Yes," said the mosquito. "I am on my
way to tell Adam and the animals that it is man's flesh." "Whose flesh?
I am a little deaf," said the swallow. The mosquito opened her mouth
wide to shout in the swallow's ear when—Frrr!—in a flash of feathers the
swallow dipped his beak into the mosquito's mouth and plucked out her
tongue!

When she came to Adam and he asked about her findings, all the mosquito
could say was "Winnn!" No one understood what she meant. The swallow
spoke up and said, "I am the mosquito's friend, in whom she confides."
And several of the animals bore witness to this, saying, "It's the truth;
wherever you see the mosquito, the swallow is not far away." The swallow
continued, "Before the misfortune occurred which deprived my friend of
speech, she told me that after tasting the blood of every animal in the world,
she found the frog's flesh the sweetest of all." And the snake was given the
flesh of frogs to be its food forever afterwards.

But the snake was not pleased to be deprived of man's flesh, and in her
anger and disappointment she lashed out at the swallow. The swallow was

quick to make his escape, but not quite quick enough, and the snake was able to take one bite out of his tail.

Now you know why the serpent is the most unloved of animals, and also why the swallow's tail is forked.

May Allah keep you whole, and us also!

The Scarab
Beetle's Daughter

Iraq

Once there was a scarab beetle who had a daughter called Khunufseh. When she was fully grown, her mother washed her and dressed her and combed her hair with rose water and set her in the house door in all her finery so that she might be seen.

The first to notice Khunufseh was the camel. He liked her silks and velvets and said, "Cousin, will you marry me?" Khunufseh replied,

> He who has the gold to pay bride-money
> Wins the sultan's daughter sweet as honey.
> Tell me what you'll give me for my dower
> And I'll run inside and ask my mother!

She went indoors to tell her mother about her suitor with the big, big hump and the long, long neck. And this is what her mother said:

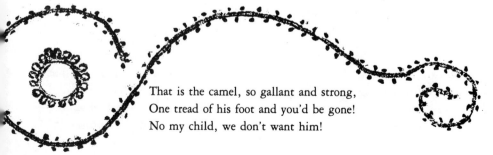

> That is the camel, so gallant and strong,
> One tread of his foot and you'd be gone!
> No my child, we don't want him!

Next to admire Khunufseh and the jewels round her neck was the donkey. He said, "Cousin, will you be my bride?" Khunufseh answered,

> He who has the gold to pay bride-money
> Wins the sultan's daughter sweet as honey.
> Tell me what you'll give me for my dower
> And I'll run inside and ask my mother!

And she went into the house to tell her mother about her new suitor with his deep, deep voice and his long, long ears. And her mother said,

> That is the donkey, so sturdy and stout,
> A kick of his hoof would make you shout.
> No my child, we don't want him.

Finally the mouse scampered by, stopped to look at Khunufseh, and lingered to talk with her. Then Khunufseh ran in to her mother and told her about the dearest, queerest little creature with the slightest, brightest little eyes and the finest, shiniest sleek fur. And her mother said,

> Why, that's your first cousin the mouse,
> Blessings on your union and your house!

And so they were married.

One day Khunufseh wanted to wash clothes. The mouse went to the grocer's shop to find a scrap of soap while Khunufseh carried her laundry to the spring. But just as she reached the water trough, she slipped on the wet stones and fell in.

Luckily a horseman was riding past just then, and Khunufseh called out to him,

> O you, who spur your horse and make him spring,
> And shake his bells and make them ring,
> Spread the news—go tell
> How I slipped and fell
> Into the village well!
> And if by chance you should forget,
> May your feet stick to your carpet.

The rider continued on his way into the village. He stopped at the grocer's shop to buy a sack of sugar and a packet of tea, and Khunufseh and her misadventure slipped from his mind. Only when he rose to go and found that his feet were stuck to the ground and he could not move did he remember the scarab beetle. So he hastened to tell the story of Khunufseh falling into the well, and the mouse, who was gnawing on a cake of olive oil soap, heard him.

Off he raced and did not stop until he came to the well and tried to pull his dear Khunufseh out. But his arms were too short to reach her. So he hung his tail down into the water, and Khunufseh climbed out into safety, and they went home dearer to each other than they had been before.

How the Monkey
Got His Shape

Palestine

In the beginning the monkey did not look as he does today—he was a son of Adam like the rest of us.

Once a woman was baking bread in her clay oven. Her son, a one-year-old boy, was squatting nearby watching as she worked. She was sitting on the floor, arranging her dough on the bottom of the oven, when the child suddenly shat on the ground. His mother cursed him, and having nothing near to wipe him with, exclaimed, "Help me, O Lord!" And God heard her and sent down seven silken handkerchiefs for cleaning her son.

But the woman could not bring herself to use the precious silk. Instead she took a flat cake of warm, freshly baked bread and wiped the child with it. As soon as she touched him with the bread, the boy was changed into a monkey and the place where the loaf had scalded him remained red as blood. So it is to this day. That's why the monkey's face, and his hands too, are like a man's, only deformed.

May God guard us and protect us from such abominations!

King of Birds

Tunisia

Once the lion and the kinglet, that least of birds, were taunting each other, boasting of their strength and courage. "I can take your life with a wave of my paw," said the lion. "I'll break your head over my knee first," retorted the bird. Soon they were challenging each other to test their claims in battle. The lion called all the creatures that walk on the earth and cannot fly, while the kinglet summoned every living thing that travels on wings. So the fighting began.

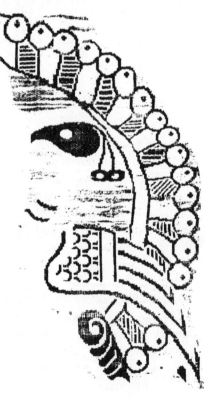

"Attack the lion about the head," the kinglet commanded the mosquitoes and the gnats. And in their thousands they buzzed around the lion's eyes and ears so that he could not see. He stumbled against the foxes and the hyenas, crying, "Let us flee!"

"Charge the cattle," the kinglet ordered the oxflies and gadflies. Soon the camels and donkeys were running in confusion to escape the insects' bites.

Meanwhile to add to the heat of battle, the kinglet carried embers on her tail to shower on the enemy, calling *"Ittfou! Ittfou!* (Put out the fire!)" And it was not long before the lion and his army were routed.

But the kinglet to this day continues to call *"Ittfou! Ittfou!"* And though the tent she lives in is but the size and shape of a coffee cup, we call her the king of birds.

The Duty of
the Host

Saudi Arabia

The mole, the owl, the swallow, the frog, and the moth once pitched their tents in the same place and lived together. One evening as darkness fell, a camel rider came into sight. The animals invited him to be their guest, setting before him what food they had, entertaining him with talk, and offering him the shelter of the guest tent to sleep in.

Came the darkest time of the night, when the morning star had yet to rise and all the creatures were deep in sleep. A robber crept up to the tents, untied the guest's camel, and led it away. Next morning when the camel rider discovered his loss, his wails and cries were so piercing that he woke his hosts.

Mortified, the animals dispersed to look for the stolen beast. The mole searched underground, the owl among the ruins. The swallow flew over the grazing camel herds, the frog dived into the water holes, and the moth went through the carpets and bedding. But nowhere could they find the missing camel.

Such was their feeling of disgrace and unhappiness because a guest suffered loss while under their tent pole, that to this day the moth will throw herself at every fire, saying,

> Rather die by the flame
> Than live with such shame!

∴ ∴ ∴ ∴ ∴ ∴ ∴ ∴ ∴ ∴ ∴ ∴

The Tortoise and
His Frog Wife

∴ ∴ ∴ ∴ ∴ ∴ ∴ ∴ ∴ ∴ ∴ ∴

Algeria

Did I tell you, or didn't I tell you, about the frog who married the tortoise?

One day she said, "O tortoise, I long for a meal of meat!" "You have but to wish, O my soul," said the tortoise. "Bring your basket and let us go down to the *wadi* where the cattle are watered. I'll butcher a cow so that your heart's longing may be stilled." And off they went: the tortoise walking in front and the frog hopping behind him.

They came to the *wadi* and found the cattle drinking. So the tortoise marched up to the nearest cow and seized one of its hind legs with his teeth. Taach! Giving a hefty kick, the cow flung the tortoise into the air so that he landed on his back, helpless to do anything but snort in the manner of angry tortoises, *"Njur! Njur!* (Outrage! Injustice!)"

What did the frog do meanwhile? Well, she stood by and said over and over again, *"Rak mrook! Rak mrook!"* This may sound to you like what any frog might say round a well or stretch of water of an evening, but if you understood the dialect you would know that she was taunting him: "I see you've fallen flat!" And then, since there was not much hope of the meat she had been promised, the frog went home to her own damp hole.

After a while an eddy in the water of the *wadi* lifted the tortoise back onto his feet. Off he pattered as fast as his legs could carry him to rejoin his own dear frog. "Who is that at my front gate?" shouted the frog when she heard him. "It is I, your husband the tortoise," he called down into her hole. "Husband? What husband?" snapped the frog. "If I ever had a husband, our marriage is ended and he can go wherever he wants."

How slowly and sadly the tortoise retraced his steps! His heart was so full of sorrow that it turned upside down. It was painful to see him, and when the donkey happened to pass by, he could not help asking, "What makes my uncle tortoise look so worried and harried, as if his little heart were turning over with grief?" "Can I be otherwise," wept the tortoise, "when I have lost my darling wife, my own dear gazelle? O respected donkey, by your far-famed generosity I beg you to go and bring her back to me."

So the donkey went knocking on the frog's front door. "Who has the temerity to approach the house of a well-born lady without first receiving permission?" asked the frog. "It is I, your uncle the donkey," he said. "I come to appeal to you in the name of the All-Powerful to be reconciled with your husband the tortoise." "You?" said the frog,

> You who bray,
> You who neigh,
> You who feed on rubbish and crusts,
> Who roll on the ground in dirt and dust?

And she began to laugh. The donkey did not wait for more but ran angrily away, while the tortoise went on mourning the loss of his gazelle.

One day the horse noticed the poor tortoise and asked, "What ails father tortoise, that his head hangs pensive and sad as if his little heart were overturned with woe?" "Can I lift up my head as long as my own dear gazelle is gone?" cried the tortoise. "I beseech you as a horse whose pedigree is known, do not disappoint me but go and bring her back to me."

So the horse went knocking at the frog's front door. "Who seeks admittance to the seclusion of the seraglio without sending word ahead to announce his visit?" asked the frog. "It is I, your maternal uncle the horse. I have come to conjure you by your Maker to return to your husband's tent!" "You?" said the frog,

> You who whinny,
> Whose face is skinny,
> Whose mane is nibbled,
> Whose feet are hobbled?

And she began to laugh. The horse did not linger but stamped crossly home, while the tortoise continued to lament his own dear gazelle.

On another day the hen saw the tortoise and asked, "What is the matter with cousin tortoise? Why is he so crestfallen and low-spirited, as if his little heart were overwhelmed with pain?" "Can I retain my reason," wailed the tortoise, "when my own dear love has left me? O daughter of my aunt, let me lean on your kindness; go on my behalf and bring her back to me!"

So the hen went knocking at the frog's front door. "Who intrudes so rudely on a lady who lives in retirement, keeping herself to herself with the greatest propriety?" asked the frog. "It is I, your cousin the hen. I come to ask you in the name of your Creator to put your hand in mine and come back with me to your husband the tortoise." "You?" said the frog,

Who live in a hovel,
Lay eggs and cackle,
Loud as the devil?

Before the frog could laugh, the hen retorted,

My eggs are gems to set in rings,
My flesh is food to give to kings,
None tastes it but the timid bride
And boys when they are circumcised!

Then she stalked off, while the tortoise went on weeping for his lost love.

At last the serpent observed the tortoise's state and asked, "What has happened to afflict you so sorely that you walk as though your heart were hanging upside down?" "O serpent," sobbed the tortoise, "my wife has divorced me and my life is a torment without her. Please bring her back to me!"

The serpent went to the frog's front door. He did not stand on ceremony but slid down into her damp hole without knocking. Quietly but clearly, he hissed,

O frog, you surely know, for you are clever,
My bite is deep: my tooth will pierce your liver!
Gather your clothes and tie them together,
Hurry to the tortoise, your own true lover!

The frog did exactly as the serpent advised her, saying nothing but,

Wait while I wash my robe and hang it on the line,
Wait while I brighten my eyes with a black *kohl* sign.

Then they set out together, the serpent leading and the frog jumping behind him until they reached the tortoise.

How did the tortoise greet the long-lost frog?

Here comes the cause of my lament,
The frog with evil temperament,
Whose face is blotched with bright pigment,
Whose eyes have popped,
Whose ears are lopped . . .

But before he could get any farther, the frog interrupted:

I'll have you know, who speak so bold,
My ears were maimed by rings of gold.

And if my eyes seem prominent,
The reason is my silk garment,
My veil so rich in ornament!

As for you, why so hollow-chested,
Hard-footed, and bony-breasted?

Not to be outdone, the tortoise gave this explanation:

My costly coat of Tunis weave
Hangs full and may the eye deceive.
My boots of finest leather tooled
Your sense of sight no doubt have fooled.

Indeed, the tortoise and the frog were well matched. And without further ado they threw their arms about each other and became lovers again.

There goes my story tumbling down the hill,
While I remain, a guest at your doorsill!

Little Mangy One

Lebanon

Once upon a time three little goats were grazing on the side of a stony hill. Their names were Siksik, Mikmik, and Jureybon, the Little Mangy One. Soon a hyena scented them and loped up. "Siksik!" called the hyena. "Yes sir!" answered the goat. "What are those points sticking out of your head?" "Those are my little horns, sir," said the goat. "What is that patch on your back?" continued the hyena. "That is my hair, sir," replied the goat. "Why are you shivering?" roared the hyena. "Because I am afraid of you, sir," said the goat. At this the hyena sprang and gobbled him right up. Next the hyena turned to Mikmik, who answered like his brother, and he too was quickly devoured.

Then the hyena approached Jureybon, the Little Mangy One. Before the hyena came within earshot, Jureybon began to snort. As the hyena drew nearer, Jureybon bellowed, "May a plague lay low your back, O cursed one! What have you come for?" "I wish to know what the two points on your head are," said the hyena. "Those? Why, those are my trusty sabers!" said the goat. "And the patch on your back, what is that?" said the hyena. "My sturdy shield, of course!" sneered the goat. "Then why are you shivering?" asked the hyena. "Shivering? I'm trembling with rage! I'm shaking with impatience, for I cannot wait to throttle you and squeeze your very soul till it starts out of your eye sockets!" snarled the goat, and began to advance on the hyena.

The hyena's heart stopped beating for an instant; then he turned and ran for his life. But Jureybon sprang after him over the rocks and gored him with his sharp little horns, slitting open his belly and freeing his two little brothers inside.

The Knotter
of Tails

Jordan

One rainy day a jackal passing near the lair of Abu l'Hssein, the fox, saw him running to his hole with a sheepskin between his teeth. The fox spread out the skin, obviously stolen from a tanner's yard, and began to spray it with water. "What are you up to, O Abu l'Hssein?" asked the jackal in astonishment. "Didn't you know," countered the fox, "that for the past two years I have been working as a furrier?" "You, Abu l'Hssein, a furrier?" said the jackal in amazement. "Indeed yes, O Abu Sirhan," said the fox with a dignified air, "I make two fur coats a month to order."

"Tell me," the jackal went on, "would you be willing to make me a fur coat?" "I would consider it a pleasure and an honor!" "How many skins does it take to make one coat?" "That depends on the style you choose. If you fancy a horseman's coat, you need about twenty soft lambskins, while a shepherd's cloak takes ten large skins of fully grown sheep. For a jacket, five sheepskins are enough."

"Can you explain the difference between the coats you mentioned?" asked the jackal. "Well," said the fox, "a horseman's coat is light and ample and lined with felt—it is worn by sheikhs when they travel. A shepherd's cloak, on the other hand, is somewhat rougher and dyed russet red, while the jacket is short, not more than a hand's span below the armpit." "May I ask how much you charge for your work?" said the jackal. "With the generous of heart there is no need to set terms! Whatever your soul should prompt you to offer me will be welcome. But tell me which of the styles you find most suitable." "I wish to have a horseman's fur," said the jackal. "Would five sheep be a fair price?" "May God prosper you," said the fox, "but I shall also have to ask you to provide me with the lambs I need for making the coat. I shall be happy to skin them myself and salt the skins, and I hope that you will be indulgent about the flesh—you see, my guests are many."

The jackal agreed, and every day thereafter he presented Abu l'Hssein with a young lamb. This the fox always solemnly received and dragged into his den, where he promptly ate it. When a month had passed in this way, the jackal came to inquire about his fur coat. "O Abu l'Hssein," he called down the fox's hole, "how is my coat progressing?" "Come back for it in a month, O Abu Sirhan," answered the fox from inside his den.

A month later the jackal returned for his coat. "Have you finished my coat, O Abu l'Hssein?" he asked. "The coat is ready," said the fox. "All that remains to be done is to attach the sleeves. Give me another week." Ten days later the jackal stood outside the fox's den, calling, "Abu l'Hssein! Abu l'Hssein!" "God's blessing upon you!" the fox replied from his hole. "Where are you?" demanded the jackal. "Here I am, God grant you a long life!" said the fox, appearing at his door. "Where is my coat?" the jackal snapped. The fox turned toward his den, but the jackal seized him by the tail and said, "I will not let you go until I have my fur coat!" "I'll ask my son Watawit to bring it out," said the fox calmly, and called, "Watawit!

Watawit! Dig a bit and look around; fetch me the coat of your uncle Abu Sirhan." "I hear no one answering you," growled the jackal. "Let me go for it myself," said the fox, and as he spoke he jumped for his hole. But the jackal held fast to his tail, so that though the fox escaped, he left his tail behind.

"Now you are well marked, O Tailless One," laughed the jackal. "As Allah is my witness, if I so much as catch sight of your maimed form, I shall kill you."

The threat filled the fox with fear. Straining to think of a way to save himself, he devised a trick. He climbed to the top of a pile of rocks, raised his head, and began to howl. At the sound the foxes of the region assembled in their hundreds. "God save us from bad tidings!" they muttered when they saw the disfigured fox. "How did you lose your tail?" "That's nothing!" the fox assured them. "Listen to the news I bring you. In my wanderings I stumbled upon an abandoned vineyard. The vines are heavy with fruit, yet there is no watchman. I propose that we soothe our throats there in the noonday heat. There is ample for all, but you must promise not to yield to greed." The foxes swore to show restraint.

"To make certain that each is fair to his brothers," the fox went on, "I shall tie all your tails together so that none can outstrip the rest." This too was agreed upon. So the fox led the pack to a large vineyard and tied their tails together. The foxes fell upon the quenching fruit and fed until they could barely move. Then Abu l'Hssein lifted his voice in a warning cry:

> Farmer, farmer, see who feasts
> In your vineyard filled with beasts!

In the panic that followed, each fox looked to save his own soul. In a few moments the vineyard was empty except for the bundle of knotted tails which was left behind. And now Abu l'Hssein, the jackal's adversary, was no different from the rest of his kind, and could go about the world without fear again.

How the Ewe
Outwitted
the Jackal

Algeria

A jackal and a ewe once decided to farm together. They plowed their field and they sowed it, and when the wheat turned yellow under the sun, they cut it and trod it to separate the grain from the straw. "Why don't you divide our harvest?" said the ewe to the jackal. "In the name of Allah the Beneficent, here goes," said the jackal. "One share for me, a second share for me, a third for me, a fourth for me, and here is the fifth share for you." "I thought we were partners, each with a right to a half share of the reward for our toil," said the ewe. "We are partners indeed," said the jackal, "but our needs are different. A fifth share should be enough to make you happy— or may Allah withhold all gladness from you and those who got you!"

The ewe said nothing, but when the jackal had divided the grain into two mounds, one large and one small, she said, "Will you wait for me here while I ask the donkey to come and carry my share home for me?" Then she ran to the saluki dog and addressed him thus: "I come to you as a supplicant and place myself under your protection. Will you help redress the wrong that I have suffered?" "How have you been wronged?" asked the saluki. "The jackal invited me to be his partner. We plowed and sowed together, we harvested and threshed together, my hand alongside his hand. But when it came to dividing the grain, he took the greater part for himself and left me with a mere fifth."

The saluki agreed to help. So the ewe took him to the donkey who was to carry her share of the harvest. The dog jumped into one of the donkey's panniers, and the ewe covered him with an empty grain sack.

When they reached the place where the jackal was waiting beside the wheat, the ewe called, "Uncle jackal, come and lift down my little lambs. I brought them to help me load the grain." "A sheep with her young lambs!" said the jackal to himself. "God is showering His blessings down on me. May His will be done!" And he trotted over to the donkey to seize the tender-fleshed lambs. But as soon as he lifted the sacking and saw the saluki with his sharp teeth glinting, he turned and fled. Without pausing to take either one share or two, he abandoned the whole wheat harvest.

And the ewe remarked,

> A female who faces life alone
> Can do little but beat her breast with a stone!

It is said also, "If a man is not content with little, God takes away from him much."

Two Close Calls

Morocco

One day a he-goat was browsing on the mountain side. Toward noon when the sun was high, he came to the mouth of a cave and decided to go inside to rest till the heat of the day was over. But to his horror, when he stepped into the cool shade he found himself face to face with a lion. "I must think of some way to save my life," he said to himself. "What do you want?" growled the lion. The goat stared fixedly at the lion for a while. Then he said, "I am one of the angels of heaven. The Lord of Creation has sent me to kill seven lions and seven hyenas and seven jackals. I was checking to see if your markings fit the description of the animals I must destroy. No, you are not one of them. You are destined to live long. Take your ease here in your cave while I continue on my search." And the goat walked out of the cave.

The lion was shaken by what had passed. When he met the jackal a little while later, the jackal asked, "What's wrong?" "I have just seen a creature sent by God to devour seven lions, seven jackals, and seven hyenas. Luckily it is my destiny to be spared. But you had better be on guard and look out

for yourself!" "What was this creature like?" asked the jackal. "Black," said the lion, "with a long beard and thick, matted hair." "It sounds like a goat," laughed the jackal. "You should taste his flesh—then you would know what a heavenly mouthful it is! Let's go find him."

And off they went, one behind the other, until they saw the goat in the distance. "This time there is no escape," thought the goat to himself, and he began to tremble for his life. Meanwhile the lion and the jackal were closing in on him. When they came within earshot, the goat bellowed to the jackal, "O you son of a cur! Why are you bringing me this lion? I have already examined him and he's not the right one. That's not the lion I asked you to bring to me!"

When the lion heard the goat, he pounced on the jackal and lifted him to the sky and dashed him to the ground till every bone in his body was broken. Then he went away while the he-goat returned to the safety of the tents.

Father of a
Hundred Tricks

Algeria

Once the hedgehog and the jackal went out together to see what they could steal. The jackal boasted, "I know one hundred tricks; we shall eat well today!" The hedgehog spoke more modestly: "I only know one trick and a half, but let us try our luck together."

Soon they came to a grain silo—a grain pit hollowed out of the ground. In they jumped and ate and ate until they were sated and their bellies were swollen. When they tried to climb out, their stomachs weighed them down. Try as they would, they could not reach the opening.

"Come," said the hedgehog, "there's nothing we can do. Let me groom your head; I'll comb your hair for fleas to while away the time." The jackal lowered his head. The hedgehog bent over him and bit him hard in the back of his neck, drawing blood. The jackal roared with pain and reared his head up to the sky. In that instant the hedgehog jumped off his friend's head as if it were a springboard and managed to clamber up out of the pit.

When the hedgehog looked around, he saw the farmer coming across the field. "Here comes the farmer—what are we to do?" the hedgehog called down to the jackal. But the jackal could think of nothing. "You claim you have a hundred tricks, and look at you!" said the hedgehog. "I boast of no more than one and a half, yet I still have half a trick left to help you with." "How can I escape? I feel my destiny is written," said the jackal. "Stretch yourself out at the bottom of the pit and pretend to be dead. The farmer will come and say, 'Look at that infidel, son of an infidel, he has eaten so much mildewed grain that he has blown himself up and died!' Then he will take a swing or two at you with his cudgel, but be patient and don't move. In the end he will take you by a paw and throw you out."

Indeed, when the farmer came he exclaimed at the sight of the jackal, "O unbeliever, son of an unbeliever, have you gorged yourself on my grain?" And he beat the jackal about the head a few times, then slung him out of the silo.

As soon as he felt solid ground, the jackal shook himself and ran off as fast as he could, still trembling from the beating.

On his way he met a wild sow. "Why are your teeth chattering, O Taleb Yusuf?" inquired the sow. "Accursed be the Shaytan, here I am reciting the holy Koran and you say that my teeth are chattering!" grumbled the jackal. "Far be it from me to wish to offend you, Taleb Yusuf," protested the sow, "since you are a Koranic scholar, let me bring you my little ones, so that you may teach them how to chant and recite the holy words." The jackal paused. Then he said, "I have taught generations and will surely teach your litter also, but I have developed my own method. If you agree to it, I shall gladly undertake the guidance of your sons." "What is your method of teaching?" asked the sow. "I find that if my students stay with me for a full week at a time without returning home, their progress is much quicker. If you are ready to leave them with me and come for them only at the end of seven days, I will accept them as my pupils."

The sow agreed, and that evening the jackal led the little wild boars into his den. Each day he feasted on one of their number.

But first he tied a bee's nest into a leather bag. Whenever the sow walked by the opening to the jackal's den, he would shake the bag and disturb the bees. Hearing the buzzing and droning from inside the den, the sow would sigh, "O my joy, O pride of my eyes, my sons are learning to recite the Koran!"

Seven days passed, and the jackal ate every one of the little wild boars. When the sow came for her young scholars, the jackal welcomed her and invited her inside. Then he untied the leather bag, and while the sow was blindly fighting off the bees, he pounced on her and killed her also.

> Our story has traveled from valley to valley.
> Good men have heard it and been merry.
> As for us, God show us His mercy,
> And spare us from the jackal's trickery.

Division of
the Prey

Morocco

Once the jackal, the fox, and the lion agreed to go hunting together. They set out as soon as it was light, and by the time the dew dried they had caught a bear, a partridge, and a hare. When they stopped to rest, the fox said to the jackal, "Why don't you divide the prey between us, uncle?" "In the name of Allah, here goes," said the jackal. And he pushed the hare in front of the lion, dragged the partridge toward the fox, and stationed himself near the bear. "Let everyone enjoy the meal in front of him, and may God give him health and more health!" he said. But the lion growled, "Yours was ever a big-bellied race!" and smacked the jackal with his paw. It tore the skin off his head, and the jackal began to bleed.

"Why don't you divide the spoils then, uncle fox?" said the jackal. And the fox pulled the carcass of the bear over to the lion and said, "This shall be for my master's breakfast!" Next he pointed to the hare lying in front of the lion and said, "This shall be for my master's dinner." Then he brought the partridge and said, "And this shall be for my master when he feels hungry between meals."

The lion, well satisfied, asked the fox, "Who trained you in the law and taught you to divide so justly?" The fox replied, "It was the crown of blood on uncle jackal's head that instructed me, O lion!"

How the Animals Kept the Lions Away

Algeria

Once when a tribe of Beduins moved their camp to a new site, they left behind them a lame rooster, a broken-backed donkey, a sick ram, and a desert greyhound suffering from mange. The animals swore brotherhood and determined to live together. They wandered until they came to an unfrequented oasis, where they decided to settle.

One day when the rooster was flying to the top of a tree, he noticed something important: the opening to a grain silo full of barley. The food was wholesome, and he began to visit the place daily. Soon his feathers became glossy as polished silk, and his comb began to glow like the fire inside a ruby. The donkey, observing the improvements, asked his friend, "How is it that your cap has grown so bright?" The rooster feigned surprise and tried to change the subject. But with the perseverance of his race, the donkey continued to pester the fowl until at last he said, "Very well, I shall show you the reason why my cap has grown so bright, but it must remain a secret between us." The donkey promised to be discreet and the rooster led him to the grain silo.

At the sight of the barley the donkey flung himself into the grain and fed until he could eat no more. Brimming with well-being, he danced back to the others and said, "I feel the urge to sing come upon me. With your permission I shall bray awhile!" The animals objected. "What if a lion should hear you?" they said. "He will surely come and devour us all!" But despite his friends, the donkey could not contain his high spirits. He cantered off by himself and began to bray long and noisily.

Now, a lion did hear the sound and came streaking across the wilderness on his silent feet until he was within one spring of the donkey. Almost too late the donkey became aware of the danger. "Sire," he said, "I see that my fate has been written, but I beg you to do me the favor not to devour me without my friends. It would be more honorable, considering that the animals of this oasis have sworn an oath of brotherhood to live together and die together, if you made an end of us all without exception." The lion conceded the merit of this plea and allowed the donkey to guide him to his friends.

When the other animals saw the donkey leading a lion toward them, they put their heads together and said, "How can we defend ourselves against a lion!" And they made their plans. When the lion came near they all said with one voice, "Greetings and welcome, uncle lion!" Then the ram butted him in his side and knocked the breath out of his lungs, the rooster flew up and pecked at his eyes, and the dog buried his teeth in the lion's throat. The lion died, of course. His flesh was given to the dog to eat, but the animals kept his skin and tanned it.

After that the four friends were able to live in peace for a time. However, soon the donkey was announcing, "I sense that I must bray again!" "Be still, O ill-omened animal!" said the others. But the donkey could not suppress his feelings, and his unmelodious call rang repeatedly in the air.

A second lion prowling that quarter of the desert was attracted to the braying. With water running in his mouth, he hurried to the oasis. Again the donkey invited the lion to kill all the animals of the oasis together, and the lion gladly complied. This time too the rooster, the ram, and the dog put their heads together when they saw the lion approaching and made a plan.

But what they said to the visitor was, "Welcome, may you be a thousand times welcome!" Then the rooster hinted to the ram, "Our guest should be made comfortable and have a carpet to sit on!" The ram trotted into their dwelling and brought out the tanned lion skin. "Be ashamed, O ram!" chided the rooster when he saw him. "Our guest is of a noble tribe. His presence among us is an honor. Do you want to disgrace us by offering him that old, worn-out mat?" Meekly the ram carried the lion skin back into the house and brought it out a second time. This time the dog expressed impatience. "Surely we have a softer carpet than that, O ram! Besides, this one is quite faded." Obediently the ram took the lion skin inside and returned with it a third time. Now the donkey chimed in, "For one of such eminence as the lion, nothing but the finest can serve the occasion! Choose more carefully from among our store!" The ram withdrew into the house, but the lion did not linger further. He jumped to his feet and without bidding his hosts a formal farewell, ran away as fast as he was able.

Although the donkey continued to bray from time to time, no lion was seen near the animals' oasis again.

Suleyman and the Little Owl

Morocco

Suleyman bin Dawood, who ruled over all the animals, was married. His wife said to him one day, "Make me a beautiful carpet and a soft bed out of birds' feathers."

That was in the days when the animals still possessed the power of speech. So Suleyman sent word for all the birds to assemble before him. And in a short time they began to fly in, all shapes and all colors. "Is any one of you missing?" asked Suleyman. "The little owl is not yet here," they told him. "Then I'll wait till she comes before I begin to pluck your feathers."

At last the little owl arrived. "What makes you so late?" asked the king.

"I was delayed, sire," said the owl, "because I was comparing night to day, and stone to clay, and man to maid." The king smiled and asked her, "Which did you find more numerous—the days or the nights?" "I found more day than night," said the owl, "for when the moon is full, the night is light as day." "And what is there more of, O little owl," said the king, "stone or clay?" "There are more stones than clay," said the owl, "for is not a clod of clay as hard as stone?" "Tell me about men and women," said the king. "Are there more men than women?" "No, sire," said the owl. "Women far outnumber men, for when a man submits to the wishes of his wife, what is he but a woman!"

"Then am I—who intend to pluck the feathers off all the birds in order to make a beautiful carpet and a soft bed for my wife—to be called a woman?" asked the king. "It is so," said the owl. "For you may ask your wife's advice, but do not do her bidding."

Then Suleyman addressed all the birds, saying, "Go, my children, each of you fly whither he wills!" So he sent them all away again, and to his wife he spoke thus: "Sooner would I let you pluck out the beard on my chin than allow you to say a word now."

God grant you happiness and to us also!

The Angel Wedding

Morocco

Once the raven said to the tortoise, "Come, I'll carry you on my back and take you for a ride through the sky. Let's fly up and help the angels celebrate a wedding! We'll be back by evening."

The tortoise accepted the invitation and climbed behind the raven's wings. They set off, and when they had been flying for some time the raven asked, "Can you see paradise yet?" "No," said the tortoise. "What about the earth?" asked the raven. "The mountains look like rocks and the rivers like threads of silk," said the tortoise. "What does the earth look like now?" asked the raven after a while. "No larger than one of the round baskets that women carry on their heads to market," said the tortoise. "And now?" "Now it is like a bird's nest," answered the tortoise. The next time the raven asked the question, the tortoise said, "I see nothing except a mist like the blue smoke from a village bake oven."

When he heard this, the raven threw the tortoise off his back so that he fell and fell and fell down onto some sharp rocks. The raven swooped down after him and devoured him until nothing was left except his hard shell.

Such is what befalls him who would feast in heaven!

The Treachery
of Man

Tunisia

Once a traveler crossing a desert arrived at a water hole and eagerly sought to slake his thirst and water his camel. Yet as he leaned over the wellhead he saw that a number of creatures had fallen in and were trapped in the depths. Roaring and bellowing, they begged him to take pity on them and rescue them from certain death. The traveler, a kind man, was moved by their plight. Unwinding the long sash at his waist, he dropped one end of it into the mouth of the well.

First to be rescued was a snake, which hung clinging to the cloth with its fangs. In gratitude for its life, it sloughed off a piece of its skin for the traveler with the words, "If you should ever find yourself in desperate straits, burn this and I shall come to your aid." As it prepared to slide away, it added, "Beware of the son of Adam who is in the well. Leave him where he sits, for no good ever came of him."

Next the traveler pulled out a female rat. She too handed him a token of her thankfulness, a few of her hairs, saying, "Take these, and when you are in need of help, burn them and they will summon me to your side." Before leaving she also warned, "Know that the son of Adam in the well is evil."

The man took heed of these warnings, and when he had saved all the animals from the trap, he prepared to resume his journey. But from the echoing depths of the water hole the son of Adam called out in the most piteous voice, "Will you abandon me to my fate when you have helped all the other creatures? Are we not both sons of Adam and therefore brothers?" The traveler was troubled. He could not in good conscience continue on his way until he had set free the son of Adam like the rest. Only then did he proceed to his destination, the capital of the kingdom.

Arriving in the bustling city, the traveler took a house on a side alley and for some time lived contentedly without further adventures. Then one day the thought occurred to him, "I wonder whether the rat's promise was a true one." He pulled at the stout silk cord that held the leather amulet pouch around his neck and carefully drew out the rat's hairs. No sooner had he set fire to them than the rat stood before him, asking him what he wished. "I wish I owned a king's treasure," said the traveler. "Do as I say and it shall be yours," said the rodent. "As soon as it is dark this evening, leave a basket near the city gate. And tomorrow morning before it is light enough to tell a white thread from a dark one, make sure you bring it home." That very night he left his basket just where the rat had told him. And when he went to fetch it before the next day's dawn, he found that it was full of gold.

For a number of days all went well and the traveler indulged himself like a sultan, spending whole mornings in the public baths and keeping the best tailors and pastrycooks in the city busy with his orders. But in time the king noticed that some of his treasure was missing, and a crier went through the bazaars calling, "Whoever finds the robber of the king's treasury shall have the king's daughter for his bride and half the kingdom as his reward."

Now, in the city there lived a necromancer famed for his shrewdness. When he was summoned to find the lost gold, he hastened to the palace gladly, certain that his skill would win the prize. Asking to be left alone in the king's vault, he looked with patience for an entrance a robber might have used, but in vain. Next he called for straw, and two guards dragged in a mattress stuffed with hay. Setting this alight, the necromancer waited outside the palace buildings. In a while he noticed a thread of smoke curling out of a narrow crack in the ground, and with confidence he declared to the king, "The robber of your treasury was a rat." But the king, thinking this a mockery, was angered. He sent the necromancer to the executioner and the crier on his errand a second time.

Meanwhile news of the necromancer's fate had spread fast through the markets and lanes of the city until it reached the son of Adam who had been saved from starvation in the well. All at once he remembered the rat's words to the traveler, which he had overheard as he sat despairingly below. He ran to the palace and bowed before the king. "You will find the robber of your treasure in such and such a street," he panted. The king's soldiers seized the traveler at his house and, clapping a chain around his neck, threw him into the darkest dungeon.

In the bitterness of his betrayal the man remembered the snake's warning and then the snakeskin in his amulet pouch. With trembling fingers he pulled it forth and burned it. In the next instant the snake was in his cell, asking, "What is your wish?" "Only to escape this prison with my life," said the traveler. "You shall sleep a free man tomorrow," promised the snake, and disappeared under the door of the cell.

That night the stillness of the sleeping palace was broken by cries from the quarters of the king's only son. Running into the prince's chamber, the king stood horrified to see a venomous serpent coiled about the neck of his young child, its head reared in the boy's face. Neither the guards with their strength nor the ministers with their wisdom could think of a way to save the prince. Messengers were sent through the night to the Isawis, who worship God in the desert and live in harmony with its creatures like the hermit Isa. But even they, who handle snakes without fear of harm, were unable to approach this serpent.

Again the city was abuzz with news from the palace. Hearing the prison guards talk among themselves, the prisoner told them, "There is but one remedy against this serpent. Take me to the king and I shall save his son." Without delay the guards brought him before the helpless monarch. "The snake will depart of its own accord," said the prisoner, "but only if you feed it the brain of such and such a one." And he named that treacherous son of Adam. Now it was the turn of the son of Adam to be surrounded by the soldiers. They cut off his head and split it open and took his brain to the king in a dish. As soon as the prisoner placed the dish before the serpent, it loosed its hold on the prince's neck and crept into a fold of the prisoner's robe. In this way he carried the snake out of the palace and set it free.

The prisoner was then married to the king's daughter, and what feasting and celebrating there was!

> Just one mouthful of honey and butter I got,
> Then I ran here to tell you this tale on the spot.

.· .· .·

Famous
Fools
and
Rascals

Stories
of Djuha and
His Kind

··

By far the best known and most popular comic character in Arab folklore is Djuha. Also known as Djawha in Nubia, Djahan in Malta, and Giufa' in Sicily, he seems to have found an audience wherever he was introduced. His adventures are among the sturdiest survivors in the oral tradition and are told even by those who know no other tales. A book called *The Eccentricities of Djuha* is mentioned at the end of the tenth century, and a thousand years later one still hears the words, "Tell us a Djuha story," in coffeehouse and nursery. At the turn of the century the stalls of the booksellers near the gate of the Al Azhar Mosque and University used to sell cheap booklets filled with Djuha jokes as if he were still alive.

Over the centuries a cycle of stories has been attached to Djuha's name. In some, like "Djuha's Meat Disappears," he is a literal-minded pedant. In others he moralizes, as when addressing his coat in "Djuha's Sleeve." Apart from the humor, what endears him to his Arab audience is an originality of outlook coupled with a matter-of-fact canniness about his own interests.

The catch of the tales, of course, is that Djuha is a wise fool rather than the simpleton he pretends to be. The incidents are often of the slightest, but a note is struck which echoes in the mind, and that is what distinguishes Djuha from other tricksters. In "Djuha Borrows a Pot" for example, he hatches an elaborate, even charming, plan to steal his neighbor's property. But it is not so much the trick that is memorable as Djuha's exposure of the neighbor through the trick. "No one should laugh at Djuha on hearing the jokes told at his expense," said Al Suyuti in the sixteenth century. "On the contrary, it would be more appropriate to ask Allah to let one profit from Djuha's gifts as a natural." The quick retort in "Djuha Fries Quails" is also a comment on Djuha's friends. In the stories "Djuha in His Old Age" and "Djuha and the Donkey," there is an absurdity that seems almost reasonable at first hearing, then amuses because it is surreal. Just as a stick standing in water will seem to be bent through refraction, so logic filtered through Djuha's mind veers in an unaccustomed direction, acquiring fresh relevance.

In North Africa Djuha's identity merges with that of Si' Djeha. The two share a large number of stories, yet Si' Djeha can be harsh and even cruel in his mischief—seeming closer to the German Till Eulenspiegel than the quietly eccentric and even philosophical Djuha. Like Djuha, Si' Djeha often begins an adventure as the dupe of his relatives or neighbors but then employs his considerable shrewdness and cunning to take a savage revenge on his enemies. Many of the stories, like "Si' Djeha Cheats the Robbers" and "Si' Djeha's Miracles," take the form of a chain of related incidents rather than of single anecdotes.

The Moroccans claim Si' Djeha as an inhabitant of Fez. They call him Si' Djeha el Fasi and have named a street for him in his hometown. The history of Djuha in the East, however, is more complicated. A Djuha is mentioned in Arabic writing of the middle ages as having lived to be one hundred years old in eighth-century Kufa (Iraq). In 1880 the first modern collection of Djuha stories was printed in Cairo under the title *The Anecdotes of the Khodja Nassreddin called Djuha Al Rumi* [the Turk]. A tomb of supposedly historical Nassreddin Khodja at Akshehir in Turkey is still visited by Djuha fans. This Djuha is said to have once lived at the court of Tamerlane, the Mongol conqueror, who invaded Asia Minor and Baghdad in the fourteenth century.

The number of different Djuhas claimed suggests that a Djuha type was necessary to the Moslem Arabic-speaking world in which his stories are set. In that world he continues to be appreciated today. These trickster stories, short and pithy, needing no adornment, resemble the animal trickster stories that depend on a clever phrase or a shrewd trick. Both travel well, surviving time and distance with little change.

Ben Sikran, son of the drunkard, is a rascal peculiar to the nomadic tribes of North Africa. He is a *taleb*, or student—literally a "seeker." Forsaking his poor, bleak tribal encampment to travel from one mosque to the next, he sits at the feet of the sheikhs, the scholars of Islam, gleaning the intricacies of Koranic law and learning how to interpret the utterances of the prophet.

Forever on the road, always hungry and always penniless, Ben Sikran is a master at scrounging a free meal. When he appears, muffled in his hooded *burnous*, on a doorstep just at nightfall, the householder feels obliged by custom to offer shelter. The thrifty housewife, however, is dismayed. In the ensuing battle of wits between voracious student and wary hostess, the prize—a warm supper—ends under Ben Sikran's belt more often than not.

Young and carefree, Ben Sikran and his fellow students are boisterously high-spirited and given to playing practical jokes. When Ben Sikran spies a well-to-do farmer selling olive oil in sealed sheepskin bottles, he pretends that he wants to buy and asks to taste the oil. Then, with the farmer holding one unplugged sheepskin full of oil in each hand so that he cannot put them down, Ben Sikran pulls the back of his robe over the man's head and hurries on his way. At worst annoying, these adolescent pranks are never really malicious. In one Algerian account, a teacher finally retaliates against his turbulent, cadging students when he invites them to dinner. As soon as he has ushered in the eager guests, he gathers up the shoes they have shed at the door (for no one may bring in street dust where all walk barefoot) and sells them in the *suk*, turning the proceeds into a mouth-watering spread for the students. Whenever they try to thank him, he says, "Eat, for it is yours!" Only as they leave do they discover how literally he has spoken. One day when his studies are done, Ben Sikran may rise to be a judge or a learned sheikh and so bring honor to the name of his tribe. Meanwhile his youthful exploits are forgiven for the entertainment they bring.

With Abu Nuwas we enter the world of *The Arabian Nights.* Here in the company of princes and courtiers, the trappings are luxurious, the adventures sensual and piquant, and a well-worded quip is rewarded with a purse full of gold. Born around 750 in Persia of Damascene parents, Abu Nuwas was the ablest and most famous poet of the 'Abbasid Caliphate in Baghdad. One of the "modernizing" poets of his time, he wrote daringly and lyrically in praise of the pleasures of wine and the love of beautiful young boys. Though he tried to find favor at the court of Harun Al Rasheed, there is no evidence that he was especially successful with the caliph. Instead he was taken up and protected by the influential family of the Barmakids and, soon after their fall, was murdered at a banquet.

In the folk imagination, however, Abu Nuwas has been recast as Harun Al Rasheed's court jester and boon companion. Their escapades as they roam the evening streets of Baghdad in disguise are described in *The Arabian Nights,* but the anecdotes printed here are those that have become part of the oral tradition. Some are told as far away as Zanzibar and Mauritius, where Abu Nuwas is known under the more African-sounding names of Kibunwasi and Banawasi.

As a contrast, Bahlul is the prototype of the learned idiot. A fervent Shiite who lived at the turn of the ninth century, Bahlul was nicknamed *Al Majnun al Kufi,* the Lunatic of Kufa. He was renowned for his lack of understanding of the simplest common sense and became the butt of his less literate fellows' jokes. Bahlul's name has become a noun meaning fool or clown.

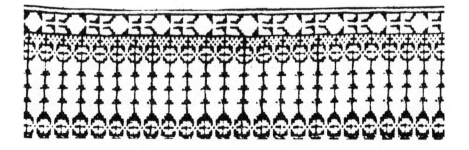

⠒⠒⠒⠒⠒⠒⠒⠒⠒⠒⠒⠒⠒⠒⠒

Djuha and
the Donkey

⠒⠒⠒⠒⠒⠒⠒⠒⠒⠒⠒⠒

Jordan

One day a neighbor came to Djuha's house and asked, "Will you let me borrow your donkey?"

"O best of friends," said Djuha, "much as I should like to be of service and assistance to a man so honorable as you, I regret that my donkey is not here today."

He had hardly finished speaking when the donkey began to bray. "It appears that I am blessed with good fortune and your donkey is here after all," said the neighbor.

"What!" exclaimed Djuha, "are you willing to accept the word of my donkey and to doubt me, a man advanced in years, whose beard is white?"

⠒⠒⠒⠒⠒⠒⠒⠒⠒⠒⠒⠒⠒⠒⠒

Djuha Borrows
a Pot

⠒⠒⠒⠒⠒⠒⠒⠒⠒⠒⠒⠒

Syria

One day Djuha wanted to entertain his friends with a dinner of lamb stewed whole with rice stuffing, but he did not have a cooking pot large enough. So he went to his neighbor and borrowed a huge, heavy caldron of fine copper.

Promptly next morning, Djuha returned the borrowed pot. "What is this?" cried the neighbor, pulling a small brass pot from inside the caldron. "Oh yes," said Djuha, "congratulations and blessings upon your house! While your caldron was with me it gave birth to that tiny pot." The neighbor laughed delightedly. "May Allah send blessings your way too," he told Djuha, and carried the two cooking pots into his house.

A few weeks later Djuha knocked on his neighbor's door again to ask for the loan of the caldron. And the neighbor hurried to fetch it for him. The next day came and went, but Djuha did not return the pot. Several days passed and the neighbor did not hear from Djuha. At last he went to Djuha's house to ask for his property. "Have you not heard, brother?" said Djuha looking very grave. "The very evening I borrowed it from you, your unfortunate caldron—God grant you a long life—died!" "What do you mean, 'died'?" shouted the neighbor. "Can a copper cooking pot die?" "If it can give birth," said Djuha, "it can surely die."

Djuha's Meat Disappears

Egypt

One day Djuha bought three kilos of lamb's meat in the market and took it home to his wife. After explaining to her how he would like to have it prepared for his dinner, he went out again.

Djuha's wife seasoned the meat and cooked it carefully. But it smelled so delicious that she sent for her brother and the two of them feasted on it until nothing was left.

When Djuha came home and asked for his dinner, his wife wailed, "While I was busy in the kitchen the cat ran in and ate up the meat, and now I have nothing to give you for dinner."

Djuha grabbed the cat and set it on the scale, which tipped at exactly three kilos. "If this is the meat," said Djuha, "then where is the cat? And if this is the cat, then tell me where in the name of Allah is the meat?"

Djuha and the Tough Chicken

Egypt

One of Djuha's friends once asked him to share a meal of stewed chicken. Djuha was hungry and went gladly, but when he tried to bite into the meat, he found it too tough for his teeth and contented himself with dipping his bread in the gravy.

Next day the friend said, "Why don't you come and help us finish what was left from yesterday's dinner?" Again Djuha found the chicken too leathery and satisfied himself with bread and sauce. When they had finished eating, Djuha lifted the chicken off the dish and, placing it before him, faced toward the holy city of Mecca and began to pray. "What are you doing?" asked his host in amazement. "I want to recite my prayers in the presence of this chicken," said Djuha, "since its flesh must surely belong to some saint or prophet. Twice it has gone to the fire and yet it remains untouched by the heat!"

Djuha Fries Quails

Egypt

Two friends came to visit Djuha just as he was frying himself some quails. "This dish lacks salt," said one friend after he had picked a bird out of the pan and tasted it. "It also lacks vinegar," said the second friend, biting into another quail. Taking the last quail, Djuha said, "What matter, since now it lacks quails!"

Djuha's Sleeve

Syria

One day Djuha arrived at a banquet in his usual rags, only to be turned away at the door. After changing into his costliest clothes and saddling his mule, he returned to his host's house looking like a man of substance. This time the servant welcomed him respectfully and seated him near the guests of honor. As Djuha reached for a piece of roast meat, his sleeve happened to slip down into the food. "Pull back your sleeve," whispered the man sitting next to him. "No," replied Djuha, "that I shall not do!" Then, addressing his sleeve, he said, "Eat, my sleeve, eat and take your fill! You have more right to this feast than I, since they respect you above me in this house."

Djuha and the Hunter's Gift

Morocco

A countryman who enjoyed hunting once visited Djuha in the city and brought him a hare as a present. Djuha took the hare to his wife, had her roast it in the way he most relished, and invited the hunter to stay and share it with him.

Some days later a man knocked at Djuha's gate. "Who is it?" he called. "A neighbor of your good friend the hunter, who brought you the hare the other day," the man shouted up. Djuha asked him in and let him rest and set a meal before him most hospitably.

Not long after this, another stranger in country clothes called on Djuha. "Who are you?" asked Djuha. "I am a friend of the neighbor of the hunter who gave you the hare." "Welcome, welcome," said Djuha and led him inside. When the guest was comfortably seated, Djuha placed in front of him a steaming bowl of hot water. "What is this?" asked the stranger. "This water was boiled in the very same pot as the hare that my good friend the hunter, whose neighbor you know, brought me," said Djuha.

Djuha and the Basket of Figs

I r a q

One year when Djuha's pomegranate tree bore very large fruits, he chose the three reddest and most perfect and took them to the palace as a present for the emir. And for this he was generously rewarded. Some months later, when his turnip crop proved unusually fine, he filled a basket with the best of his harvest and set out for the palace again.

On the way he met a neighbor, and when he had explained his errand, the man said, "Are turnips any gift for a prince? Shame on you! Something dainty or something sweet is what will please an emir. Take him figs." Djuha was persuaded, and when he arrived at the palace gates he had a basket of figs over his arm.

This time, however, the prince happened to be angry, with a frown on him that would frighten a hero. Far from rewarding Djuha for his pains, he ordered his servants to pelt him with his own figs and chase him out. But every time a fig hit the mark, Djuha would cry out, "May Allah reward you with His blessings, dear neighbor!" or "God grant you many sons and abundant riches, dear neighbor!" The prince's curiosity finally overcame his anger, and he asked Djuha why he was saying such things.

"Sire," replied Djuha, "I was bringing you a basket of the largest turnips you have ever seen, white and sweet as apples, but my neighbor told me that figs would be a better gift. Should I not thank the man who saved my life? Had my basket been full of turnips, every bone in my body would be broken by now!"

The prince laughed and, regaining his good humor, sent Djuha home with a purse of gold.

Djuha in His
Old Age

Egypt

When Djuha grew to be an old man, his friends began to admonish him with regard to his welfare in the next world. "You would do better to turn your thoughts to prayer rather than joke all the time," they said. "You should spend your days in serious meditation and in studying the Hadith." "I have not neglected the utterances of the prophet," retorted Djuha, "I am sure that none of you has ever heard the Hadith of Ikrimah."* "Tell it to us," said his friends. "The learned Ikrimah," began Djuha, "says that according to Ibn Abbas, who had it from the prophet himself, there are two qualities which can ensure happiness for the faithful both in this world and the next." "Tell us what they are," said his friends eagerly.

"Ikrimah forgot one," said Djuha, "and I have forgotten the other."

---

* One of the *tabi'un*, successors of the prophet. A slave in the house of Ibn 'Abbas, Ikrimah is one of the main transmitters of the Koran according to Ibn 'Abbas.

⋰ ⋰ ⋰ ⋰ ⋰ ⋰ ⋰ ⋰ ⋰ ⋰ ⋰

Si'Djeha Cheats
the Robbers

⋰ ⋰ ⋰ ⋰ ⋰ ⋰ ⋰ ⋰ ⋰ ⋰ ⋰

Algeria

One day Si' Djeha was riding the fine white mule his father had left him when he died. As he rode, he happened to meet four men, robbers by profession, leading a hollow-sided little donkey to market.

"Si' Djeha!" they called. "You are mad to risk your life on that mule! What if you should fall? You would break your head dropping from that height. Look, we have a neatly built little donkey here, a safer animal by far."

"What you say is true, by Allah," said Si' Djeha.

"Ha! But what will you give us for the exchange?"

"Do I owe you anything?"

"Si' Djeha, have some shame," said the robbers, "here we are saving your life, and you begrudge us fair payment."

"What you say is right," said Si' Djeha. "Tell me what I should give you."

"What does the amount matter among generous men? But since you are dear to us, we will content ourselves with one hundred silver pieces." So Si' Djeha dismounted, paid the money, and rode the puny little donkey home.

When she saw him tethering the donkey in the yard, Si' Djeha's mother shouted to him, "Where is your father's mule, child?" "I was afraid that if I fell off its back, I might get killed and leave you with no one to look after you. So I exchanged it and one hundred pieces of silver for this donkey."

"May Allah forgive you your foolishness," sighed his mother. "If you don't show a little more sense, we shall surely be ruined."

When the next market day came round, Si' Djeha decided to take his donkey to town. But before he went, he glued a few gold coins under the donkey's tail. As he entered the *suq* he met the four robbers again. "Greetings, O my benefactors, may Allah increase your fortunes!" he hailed them. "I praise God and thank Him every hour for causing me to make your acquaintance." "Why, O Si' Djeha?" asked the robbers. "Because of your donkey, of course! The thorny cactus is sweet inside, but who would have guessed that an ordinary donkey, no different from any other except for his lankness, drops nothing but gold coin!" "A thing not to be believed!" said the robbers, and they walked alongside Si' Djeha to the stable where he had tied the donkey. There they saw for themselves the gold pieces on the animal's flanks, and they bit their fingers in remorse.

They began to blame each other and quarrel in whispers. Then they cried, "May Allah reward you with nothing but good, Si' Djeha, if only you will let us have our donkey back! Take your mule and the hundred pieces of silver." But Si' Djeha refused. The men begged him again and offered him more silver. At last when they promised to return the mule with two hundred pieces of silver, Si' Djeha consented. "Be sure to feed him well, and spread rugs beneath him to catch the gold," he said as they led the donkey away.

The first of the robbers to have the use of the donkey ran home, took his sickle down, and cut a whole field of grass. Bringing the fodder into the stable, he covered the floor with matting and locked the donkey in for safety. All night long the donkey feasted, and in the morning the robber found his carpets full of dung. He was ashamed to seem a fool, so he said nothing to the second robber except, "Enjoy your fortune, brother!" The second robber and the third suffered as the first robber had, and they too remained silent. When the fourth robber turned on them angrily and accused them, "You have taken the gold and left me nothing but the dung!" they realized that they had all been tricked and swore to take their revenge.

Now Si' Djeha was expecting to hear from the four men. He bought two roosters and a hen and asked his mother to fry them in butter and steam a dish of couscous to go with them. When the meal was ready, he put it in a covered bowl and buried it in the earthen floor of his house. "Four men will come to visit me," he told his mother, and he gave her careful instructions what to do when they came.

Sure enough, before midday the four robbers came marching up to Si' Djeha's door. "Welcome, O my benefactors!" said Si' Djeha on his doorstep. "You should have sent word that you were intending to honor me thus. Then I might have had time to prepare for you as you deserve. But never mind. I have my Hoe of Hospitality, and it will save me from disgrace." Then men were curious to know what he meant, and forgetting what they had come for, followed him into the house.

When the guests had been seated for a while, Si' Djeha called, "Mother, I have visitors today; bring me my Hoe of Hospitality." And his mother came in and handed him an old garden hoe as if there were nothing odd about his request. With the robbers watching him attentively, Si' Djeha began to dig at the earthen floor. In the glancing of an eye he uncovered

the dish of chicken and couscous. "Come favor us with your company!" he invited his guests, and the fragrance of warm chicken broth filled the room.

"Whenever I am surprised by company," explained Si' Djeha after they had eaten, "I never need worry about being unprepared and ill-provided as long as I have this Hoe of Hospitality. Whether my cupboard is full or empty, I know that this tool will enable me to entertain as a good host should. You yourselves saw that the food it brings me is the best." The robbers agreed that, praise be to Allah, they had indeed eaten well. Then one of them uttered the thought that was in all their minds. "Si' Djeha, how much would you sell this useful hoe for?" "It is not for sale," said Si' Djeha shortly. But although he tried to turn the conversation to other things, the robbers kept returning to the hoe. And eventually Si' Djeha parted with it for one hundred silver pieces.

"My wife's brother is coming to eat with me tomorrow," said one of the robbers on the way home. "Let me have my turn first." But next day, though he dug until he plowed up the whole floor of his house, he found no covered dish and no warm meal. On top of that, he was despised by his brother-in-law for being a miserly host.

The other three robbers were as disappointed in their expectations of the hoe. When the last of them threatened to take his partners to court for eating all the food and leaving him nothing, they showed him their ruined houses to prove that they too had been duped. "This time we must not let Si' Djeha escape us," they vowed.

But this time too, Si' Djeha was ready for them. "I think I shall go and weed the sesame," he said to his wife early in the morning. "If my four friends should come to see me again, send them out to the east field—that's where I shall be working. And as soon as they go, run to the butcher's shop, buy some spring lamb, and help my mother prepare a banquet for our noon meal." Then he picked up his tools and left the house. In the yard there was a sack holding two hares that Si' Djeha had trapped. Before leaving, he took one of them and carried it inside his robe, resting on his belt.

Very soon afterwards, the four robbers knocked on the door, talked to Si' Djeha's wife and followed him to his field. "Ho! Si' Djeha!" they called as soon as they could see him. "Come here, we have some things to discuss with you." "He who doesn't work doesn't eat," Si' Djeha shouted back to

them. "I cannot stop, brothers." "Our errand is pressing; take a rest," they said when they drew near. "Very well," said Si' Djeha, "but let me send word to my wife to prepare some food for us—it will soon be time to eat." The robbers looked around in astonishment. "Whom do you mean to send?" they asked. "I have a messenger right here," said Si' Djeha, pulling the hare out of his bosom. And as they looked on in disbelief, he set it on the ground, saying, "Go find your mistress and tell her to cook a dish of tender lamb's meat, since we have guests this noon." In a flash the animal disappeared into the thornbushes at the edge of the field.

"Do you expect a hare to carry a message?" the robbers asked, laughing. "My father trained him," replied Si' Djeha, "and I am so used to him that I couldn't do without him, especially when I am out here in the fields." And he led the doubting guests to his house, where they found everything hospitably prepared down to the ewer and bowl for them to wash their hands in rose water. "That hare is certainly a good servant," murmured the robbers. "That he is," said Si' Djeha bringing the second hare in from the yard and patting its neck. "He's a good worker and cheap to feed." "Would you consider selling him?" asked the robbers. "How can I do without him?" said Si' Djeha. "I have neither son nor daughter to send on errands." "Name your price," urged the robbers. And in the end Si' Djeha let them buy the hare for one hundred silver pieces.

"This time," said one of the robbers as they set out on the road home, "this time let us not basely suspect each other. Let me send the hare to my house with a message for my wife to cook supper for all four of us, so that we can all try our new messenger at the same time." "That's the best plan," said the others as they watched the hare leaping across the fields before them.

But when they came to the first robber's house toward evening, they found that his wife had not even lit her cooking fires. "What is the meaning of this neglect?" the first robber asked his bewildered wife. "Didn't I send instructions with our new messenger for you to have a meal ready when we arrived?" "What messenger?" said the wife. At this the robbers turned on their heels, cursing, and retraced their steps to Si' Djeha's house with murder in their hearts.

When they reached Si' Djeha's doorway, a sight met their eyes that left them rooted where they stood, their mouths dry with horror. Si' Djeha was shouting angrily at his wife with a knife raised in his hand. While they watched, the woman fell to the ground with blood on her dress. Forgetting their own troubles, the robbers could only gasp and ask him why he had done this evil deed. "How else can a man control the sour temper of his wife? All I asked for was a glass of water, but she refused me!" Then to their amazement, Si' Djeha touched his wife's wound with the knife and she raised herself up. Standing meekly before him, she asked her husband what he wished. "Brew coffee for our guests," he said, frowning. As soon as she left the room, the robbers questioned Si' Djeha. "What is this miracle that we have witnessed?" "Have you never heard of the knife that kills and brings back to life?" "Never!" said the four men together. "I would not part with it for half the kingdom," declared Si' Djeha. "Every man married to a quarrelsome wife should have one!"

The robbers soon saw proof of the virtues of this singular tool. Wearing a fresh gown, her eyes modestly on the ground like a bride of one month, Si' Djeha's wife carried in a tray of coffee flavored with cardamom. Before they finished drinking the coffee, the robbers had succeeded in buying the knife off Si' Djeha for one hundred pieces of silver.

Each in turn used it in his home and discovered just how magical it was. All four robbers were soon tried for murder and never bothered Si' Djeha again.

How Si'Djeha
Staved Off Hunger

Algeria

Once Si' Djeha was traveling across a stretch of desert. His throat was parched and his belt was slipping way below his hips, for it had been many hours since he had eaten. At last, in the distance, resting in the slim shadow of a rock, he saw another traveler eating his midday meal. Si' Djeha's spirits rose, and in no time he was squatting in the shade beside the traveler.

"Where do you come from?" asked the man.

"From your very own village," said Si' Djeha accommodatingly.

"May your news be good news, brother," said the man.

"As good as you could wish for," Si' Djeha assured him.

"Tell me about my wife Umm Othman."

"Plump and healthy as a duck."

"And Othman, my son?"

"In the coffeehouse beating his friends at backgammon."

"And the camel?"

"So fat it will surely burst."

"How about my dog?"

"Watchful as ever."

"And the house?"

"Like a fortress."

Satisfied, the man fell silent and returned to his meal. Si' Djeha waited hopefully, but the man did not invite him to share the food. Then suddenly Si' Djeha jumped up.

"Where are you off to in such a hurry?" asked the man.

"I must return to the village. Since your dog died, the robbers have become quite a plague."

"My dog dead?"

"Yes."

"How did he die?"

"He must have eaten too much of the flesh of your camel."

"My camel dead?"

"Yes."

"How did it die?"

"It tripped over Umm Othman's tomb."

"My wife dead?"

"Yes."

"How did she die?"

"Of a broken heart over Othman's death."

"My son dead?"

"Yes."

"How did he die?"

"He was buried in the rubble when the house collapsed."

At that the man began to tear his hair and roar as if he were mad and ran off to the village as fast as he could.

Meanwhile Si' Djeha drew back his right sleeve, invoked the name of Allah the Merciful and the Compassionate, and reached for his dinner.

Si'Djeha and the Qadi's Coat

Tunisia

One day Si' Djeha was strolling on the outskirts of the town when he came upon the *qadi* snoring under a tree, working off his last wine-drinking bout. So deeply sunk in sleep was the judge that Si' Djeha was able to pull his fine new woolen cloak off him without making him stir.

When the *qadi* woke up and saw that he had been robbed of his costly coat, he sent his men to search for it. They soon recognized it on Si' Djeha's back and dragged him to court. "How did you come to possess so fine a cloak?" demanded the *qadi*. "I saw an unbeliever grossly drunk with the stink of wine upon him lying asleep under a tree. So I spit on his infidel beard and took his coat. But if your honor claims the cloak, it is only just that you should have it back." "I have never seen this coat before in my life," hissed the *qadi*. "Now be off with you, and take the coat along too."

Si'Djeha's Miracles

Libya

When Si' Djeha was young, his was the task of driving the family's cows to pasture on the mountainside. He himself owned one small calf and no more. Yet of all the herd this calf was the best-fed and by far the fleshiest.

One day Si' Djeha's relatives sent him on an errand into the town. When he returned they said to him, "Your calf looked so fat and inviting that we couldn't hold ourselves back. While you were away, we butchered it and feasted on it." And they smacked their lips to show him how delicious it had been.

"Let me have the hide, at least," said Si' Djeha. He took it to the market and stood all day holding it up for sale. But he got no more than a penny for it. "What use is one meager penny?" said Si' Djeha to himself, but he punched a hole in it and threaded a length of red string through it and turned homeward.

On the road ahead of him walked two men. Suddenly they stopped and bent down as if they had found something on the ground. When Si' Djeha caught up with them, he saw that they had a small coffer full of gold coins which they were dividing between them. *"Salaam!"* said Si' Djeha. And when the men looked up angrily and demanded, "What do you want here?" he dropped his own penny among the gold without their noticing. "I want to know how two men can be so shameless as to divide other people's property between them," said Si' Djeha. "It was God the All-Bountiful who placed this treasure in our path! It is ours," protested one of the men. "I tell you that it belongs to me," insisted Si' Djeha. "How can we be sure that you speak the truth?" asked the men. "I keep a penny threaded on red string among my gold to remind me that but for the blessings of Allah, I would be a poor man," said Si' Djeha. The men looked among the coins and found the penny. "You are right, by Allah," they said. "Let's divide the gold three ways!" "No," said Si' Djeha, "you take half and I'll keep half." And he tucked his share into the bosom of his *burnous* and continued on his way.

Si' Djeha's relatives were amazed. "Where did you find such wealth?" they asked. Si' Djeha laughed. "Can't you guess? That's what I got for the hide of my calf." "We want to be rich also," said the relatives to one another. And they killed their cows and skinned them. "Don't rub salt into the hides," advised Si' Djeha. "I'll tell you when they are ready for sale." The relatives were hanging upon Si' Djeha's words by now, and they left their hides to rot in the sun until the maggots began to hatch on them. "Now you can take them to market," said Si' Djeha. When the cobblers and leather workers saw the stinking hides, they cried, "Do we look like simpletons, that you think you can cheat us?" And they fell upon Si' Djeha's relatives with sticks and drubbed them till they could hardly hobble home.

"You have ruined us, Si' Djeha!" they wailed when they came within earshot, but he laughed at them. "Did you truly believe, by Allah, that men would pay gold for unclean hides?" They said nothing, just seized him, pushed him into a sack, and tied it up firmly. "He'll be the death of us if we don't get rid of him first," they whispered. And they carried him down to the sea to drown him.

Since Si' Djeha was young and his body well-filled-out, he was heavy on his bearers. By the time they reached the shore they were tired and puffing loudly. When they saw a shepherd grazing his sheep beside the waves, they stopped and demanded some milk. The man tilted his goatskin bottle for each in turn and they drank. Then they rested awhile, leaning their heads on their elbows, and soon they had all dozed off to sleep.

The shepherd meanwhile began to round up his flock. Noticing the bulging sack on the sand, he poked it with his crook, wondering what was inside. "Leave me in peace!" growled Si' Djeha. The shepherd started back in fright. "What are you—man or spirit?" he asked. "And whoever you are, what are you doing in this sack?" "I am a man like you, brother," said Si' Djeha, "but I am more fortunate. They are taking me to read the Book of Fate to find out what is written for me and what God hides from the eyes of men." "O that I could see it too!" said the shepherd. "There is room for only one man in the sack," said Si' Djeha, "and I cannot forgo this chance."

The shepherd continued to sigh and exclaim at Si' Djeha's good fortune, until at last Si' Djeha allowed himself to be persuaded. "May I be forgiven for such folly," he said, "but never mind, brother, you may go in my place. Untie the knot." Then when he had packed the shepherd securely into the sack and bidden him farewell, Si' Djeha began the walk back to his village, slowly driving the sheep before him.

In time Si' Djeha's relatives sat up from their rest. They lifted the sack and heaved it into the sea. Then they hurried home across the fields to celebrate their deliverance. The women were clapping and singing when, just before dusk, they saw Si' Djeha entering the village with a large flock of ambling sheep. "Here comes Si' Djeha, and he is far from dead!" cried the women. Now they all crowded round him and inquired, "Where did you find so many sheep?" "Beneath the waves of the sea," said Si' Djeha. "I discovered that the sea hangs suspended from the sky, and under it lie great grazing grounds covered with numberless herds of cattle and sheep." "Tell us how we can get cattle for ourselves," they begged him. "There is nothing to do except tie your children up into sacks as you did me and throw them into the water. By sunset they will lead your flocks home to you."

Next day Si' Djeha's relatives did as they had been told and waited. The sun set and no children returned. It grew dark and still no children appeared. "When will our children come back?" they asked. "Surely you didn't believe that sheep and cattle graze under the sea!" said Si' Djeha. The grieving parents dragged him a long way into the desert far from the paths of men and tied him to a tree and left him. "If he is not eaten by the wild beasts, he will die of thirst," they said.

Hardly had they left from here than a horseman came riding from there. It was the *caiid*, an ancient man. He had been to visit the bey in Tunis, and it happened that his way home lay past this tree. He stopped in astonishment when he saw Si' Djeha and exclaimed, "How came you to be bound in this way, so far from any house or town?" "Huss! Do not disturb me, I beg you," said Si' Djeha sharply. But the *caiid* was more accustomed to be obeyed than to do what others told him, and he was curious. He put his question once more. "Do not talk to me," Si' Djeha rebuked him, "or I'll return to my former state." "Why, what were you before?" asked the *caiid*. "Almost one hundred years old," said Si' Djeha, "and so bent I could only look upon the ground with what was left of my sight. But they tied me to the tree of Sidi Abdel Kader, the holy man, and look how I have changed already!" "Is it really so?" asked the *caiid*. "You can see with your eyes that it is!" retorted Si' Djeha. "And it will be so with any aged man who wishes to regain his youth. He has but to tie himself to this tree and stand in silence." "Let me try it," said the *caiid*. Si' Djeha appeared to hesitate then said, "I do not wish to grow much younger. You may loosen my bonds."

Eagerly the *caiid* prepared for his turn. But Si' Djeha stopped him, saying, "First take off these rich clothes; a simple shirt like mine is best between the tree and you." So the *caiid* removed his traveling cloak and his robe and laid aside his sash and fine turban. Putting on Si's Djeha's shirt he stood against the tree while Si' Djeha fastened the knots tightly. "Remember, for the miracle to take place you must not utter a word," said Si' Djeha. Then he began to don the *caiid*'s finery. When he was dressed he mounted the *caiid*'s horse and, humming a song to himself, turned its head toward home.

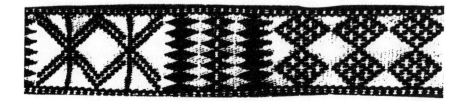

.· .· .· .· .· .· .· .· .· .· .· .·

Ben Sikran
Improves
the Couscous

.·. .·. .·. .·. .·. .·. .·. .·. .·. .·. .·. .·.

Algeria

Once when Ben Sikran was traveling to a distant mosque to study under a learned sheikh, he had to cross a barren plain. All day long he walked without meeting another human being, but as night fell and he was beginning to feel cold and hungry, he came upon a Beduin tent. "Let me stay with you tonight," he said to the owner. "I will not trouble you, as I need no food. All I want is protection from my enemies."

The man led Ben Sikran into his tent and went to tell his wife. She was squatting in front of her cooking pot preparing a dish of plain couscous. She complained crossly: "There's hardly enough for the two of us!" "But I can't very well chase a man from my door when he needs protection," said her husband, "and besides, he says he won't want any food."

Nevertheless, once they were seated together the Beduin could not refrain from being hospitable. He asked Ben Sikran what he would like for supper. "Nothing," said Ben Sikran. "I told you I wouldn't need anything. One thing I cannot abide is dried salt meat. Put dried meat into a dish of couscous and you can be sure I will touch neither one nor the other. I have never been able to eat it."

"Well, praise be to God for protecting us from his appetite," muttered the woman to herself as she took a sheepskin pouch and shook two or three lumps of dried meat from it into the pot of couscous. Then she went out to milk her cow. Ben Sikran, who was dying of hunger by now, stole over to the sheepskin pouch, emptied the best part of it into the stew on the fire, and stuffed some cakes of dried cow-dung fuel into the pouch to fill it out. Then he crept back to his place.

When the woman returned to the tent, there was a rich smell of meat gravy. She looked into her pot and saw that the stew was bubbling to the brim with meat. She ran to check the sheepskin bag, but it was bulging full, as before. "Husband," she called, "this student of the holy Koran has brought us luck. Our hearth has been blessed! Look—the pot is overflowing with meat and the pouch is still full!"

Before serving her husband, she pushed the dish toward Ben Sikran, who plunged both hands into it and ate heartily. "I thought you said you did not touch dried meat," murmured the woman." "Ah, but this is no ordinary meat," said Ben Sikran, wiping his mouth. "Praise be to Allah—it is extraordinarily good!"

When Ben Sikran
Owed Money

Algeria

One day Ben Sikran was wandering through the marketplace when he passed a man selling dried figs. He tasted one of them and found it sweet as honey, so he asked, "How much do you ask for a basketful of figs?" They agreed on a price, but then Ben Sikran added, "Only do me a kindness so God may show you kindness, too: let me owe you the sum until next market day." The man agreed, and Ben Sikran went off with the load of figs.

When the next market day dawned, Ben Sikran rubbed his face with nettles till it was swollen and unsightly. Then, leaning on a staff, he limped into the marketplace looking as if he were at death's door. He searched out the fig seller and, gasping and pausing for breath at every word, he asked him, "Have you seen that scoundrel who sells dried figs? He was here last market day." "Why do you want him?" replied the fig vendor. "If I were to tell you the terrible story, you wouldn't believe me," said Ben Sikran. "Tell me all the same," said the man. "Everyone in my village who tasted the figs I bought off him has died except for me. And look what a state I'm in! Before I die, I want to find him and take him to court."

"No," said the fig vendor, "I've never seen him."

Ben Sikran's Hunger

Algeria

One evening on his travels Ben Sikran ran out of provisions far from any town or village. Spying a Beduin tent in the distance, he hurried toward it goaded by hunger. "A guest stands at your door, may God bless you!" he called into the tent. The Beduin came out and welcomed him most hospitably. The Beduin's wife, however, was not so pleased. She had been on the point of spreading her risen dough on the clay griddle to bake it and did not have enough for three. Sighing, she dug among the embers of her fire and hid the dough in the hot ashes where it could bake out of sight. "All guests are welcome," she said, "but to our shame we have no food to offer this night."

Ben Sikran, who had watched her bury the dough, sat with his host and entertained him with tales of his travels. Soon he said, "I feel cold; let me sit near the fire." "Give him a blanket!" said the Beduin's wife suspiciously. "Look; I can hardly close my fingers," said Ben Sikran. So the Beduin invited him to draw near to the hot embers. Stretching his legs comfortably and warming his hands, Ben Sikran went on with his talk.

"We are three brothers," he said, "and when our father died he left us a piece of land hardly bigger than a sheepskin. How were we to divide it? We began by pacing it, so many paces from here to here." As he spoke he demonstrated by tracing three furrows with his stick through the middle of the ashes in the fire. "But my younger brother did not think it was just. So we measured the land with ropes from there to there." He poked his stick through the ashes in the other direction. "This time my oldest brother was dissatisfied. So we mixed it all up between us." Here he stirred the ashes thoroughly round and round.

"May God upset your stomach as you have upset my yeast dough!" wailed the Beduin's wife in anger.

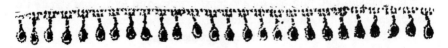

Abu Nuwas and the Fur Cloak

Tunisia

One day when Harun Al Rasheed, the caliph of Baghdad, was in a particularly good humor, he decided to grant a handsome present to his companion, the poet Abu Nuwas. That week a caravan had arrived from central Asia with a load of costly furs, and from it the caliph chose a cloak of rich, soft sable. Abu Nuwas was delighted with the gift and, throwing the new cloak over his shoulders, strolled through the streets of Baghdad.

By and by he passed under the house of one of the ministers. The minister's wife, looking down through the slats of her shuttered casement, saw him and could not help noticing the fine fur he was wearing—just the kind of fur, as it happened, that she had been longing to own. Without delay she sent down a maidservant to invite Abu Nuwas up.

When Abu Nuwas had been offered refreshments, the minister's wife asked him about his fur. "It was a gift from the caliph," he told her. "Then you cannot make me a gift of it," said the minister's wife. "If you allow me to rest by your side awhile, it could be done," said Abu Nuwas. "Wish me joy of it then," the minister's wife replied, pulling the fur off Abu Nuwas's shoulders.

But later when Abu Nuwas had risen from the lady's bed and was leaving the house, he began to worry that Harun Al Rasheed might ask where his gift had gone. Standing halfway down the staircase, he called up to the servants for a drink of water. And when he had drunk, he dropped the cup onto the stone steps to break it.

Shortly afterwards when the minister came home, he found Abu Nuwas sitting halfway up his stairs with tears falling down his cheeks. "What has happened, Abu Nuwas, to make you weep on my doorstep?" he asked. "I troubled your people for a drink of water," sobbed Abu Nuwas. "And just because I broke this cup, they have confiscated my new fur cloak."

The minister summoned the servants to reprimand them. "But that's not what happened, Abu Nuwas is confused . . ." began the maidservant, when Abu Nuwas interrupted. "Maybe in my foolish way I am unable to explain properly. Since your memory is better, please tell your master exactly what happened to my cloak."

The maidservant lowered her eyes and ran off to fetch his fur cloak from her mistress.

Abu Nuwas and the Caliph's Queen

Syria

Once Abu Nuwas asked Harun Al Rasheed for permission to take one donkey from every husband in the kingdom who proved to be afraid of his wife. Some time later the caliph was sitting in a palace window when he saw a cloud of dust on the horizon. Soon he made out Abu Nuwas driving a herd of donkeys toward the cattle market. "What is this, Abu Nuwas?" he asked. "This is the sad state of your kingdom, sire," said Abu Nuwas. "Did you not give me leave to demand one donkey from every man who fears his wife?

"By the way, on my journey I saw a girl with cheeks like pomegranates and breasts like marble. I immediately thought of you . . ." "Shhh!" whispered the caliph. "Queen Zubeida is sitting behind that screen—she will hear you!" "Sire," said Abu Nuwas, "from the men of your land I have taken one donkey; for the king the fine is two donkeys—and make them white ones."

Abu Nuwas Travels
with the Caliph

Iraq

Once Abu Nuwas was called early in the morning to accompany Harun Al Rasheed on a journey. Since there was no time for him to breakfast before starting, he took a handful of dates to eat as he rode. Not wanting to offend the caliph by eating in his presence, Abu Nuwas turned his head away and tried to consume each date surreptitiously.

Harun Al Rasheed, however, saw what Abu Nuwas was up to, and whenever Abu Nuwas succeeded in slipping a date into his mouth, the caliph would ask him a question. Abu Nuwas was obliged to duck his head and spit the date out in order to reply. Unable to enjoy a single mouthful, he rode the whole way suffering fierce pangs of hunger.

That evening in the *khan* where they were to rest overnight, Abu Nuwas noticed that Harun Al Rasheed had retired to his quarters with a beautiful fair-skinned slave girl from the Caucasus. Just as she was about to recline with him, there was a knock on the door. "Who is that?" he demanded irritably. "It is I," said Abu Nuwas. "You asked me as we rode today about the pedigree of your friend's horse, and I have just remembered the answer." He gave him the details.

Hurrying him out, the caliph returned to the girl and had just succeeded in slipping his arm around her waist when there was another knock at the door. "Who is it this time?" he shouted angrily. "It is I," said Abu Nuwas, "I have just found out the answer to your question today about the owner of the land we were riding through." And so it went throughout the night.

Long before dawn the caliph had given up all hope of pleasurable sleep and roused his companions to make an early start. Seeing Abu Nuwas's mare saddled and ready, he vented his rage by slicing off the animal's lips with one swing of his sword. Abu Nuwas saw what happened and, passing behind the caliph's horse, lopped off its tail.

"I wonder why is your horse grinning so broadly?" asked the caliph as soon as Abu Nuwas drew abreast of him. "She is laughing at your horse's tail, sire," retorted Abu Nuwas.

Abu Nuwas and the Hundred Eggs

Syria

Once as a joke on Abu Nuwas, Harun Al Rasheed gave a hundred eggs to the hundred members of his court and ordered each to put one on his chair and sit down. In a while Abu Nuwas made his appearance and sat down with them. The caliph spoke and said, "I wish each of you to lay an egg for me this morning." And each of the courtiers did produce an egg except for Abu Nuwas. For a moment he was at a loss. Then he threw back his head and began to crow, loud and shrill. "What is the matter with you, Abu Nuwas?" asked the caliph. "O master and protector, with a hundred hens in this chamber don't you need at least one rooster?"

For his quick answer, Harun Al Rasheed rewarded him with a hundred coins of gold.

Bahlul and the Sweetmeats

Iraq

Once Bahlul was included among the guests at a sumptuous banquet in the house of a wealthy merchant. Among the delicacies that were offered was a dish of Damascene nougat. "What is this?" asked a fellow diner. "I don't know," said Bahlul, "but I have heard people say that the most exquisite thing on earth is a bath. This, I think, must be a bath!"

The Wise Man and Bahlul

Palestine

There once was a villager who fancied himself as a man of learning to be ranked among the scholars of renown.

One day he set out to the next village to see if there were others as wise and as well informed as he.

He settled into the coffeehouse and began to display his learning. The villagers, who were no scholars, did not find his highbrow conversation to their taste. So they sent for Bahlul, the village simpleton, and seated him near the stranger. "Now they can instruct each other to their heart's content," they said.

The learned stranger began by lifting his forefinger and pointing it to the sky as if to declare, "There is no god but Allah!" Bahlul did not hesitate, but pointed two fingers to the sky. "Here is a man after my own taste," thought the stranger. "He not only understands my sign but signals back, 'And Allah has no equal!'"

Next the stranger raised his palm by way of saying, "God created the heavens above." And Bahlul responded by lowering his palm toward the ground. "O ho!" thought the stranger, "he is following my meaning closely— he is telling me 'And God created the earth below!'" Pulling an egg out of his pocket, he placed it before Bahlul to signify, "God created the living from the dead." When Bahlul produced a small chick from the folds of his robe, the learned stranger was delighted. "This is a true scholar," he said

to himself. "Now he is reminding me that God, to Whom all praise and exaltation, also makes the dead from the living!" And feeling well satisfied with this exchange, the man left to continue his search.

The villagers had been watching all these antics and now, laughing, asked Bahlul what he thought of the scholar. "Oh" said Bahlul, "he thinks himself much cleverer than he really is. He began by threatening to gouge out my eye with his bare finger, but I let him know that if he dared to try it, I would blind him in both eyes. Next he raised his hand to show me how he could send me flying into the air. But I made it clear that a blow from my fist would soon take him to the fires of hell from which there is no return. At last he thought he could make fun of me and pulled an egg out of his pocket, but I topped him there, too, with my chick. He knew he had met his match; that's why he slipped off so quickly."

Bahlul and the Owl

Morocco

When Bahlul was young he lived with his mother. She was a poor woman who had very little besides her son and one goat. A day came when she had no more money and nothing left in the house to eat. "Come, my son, may

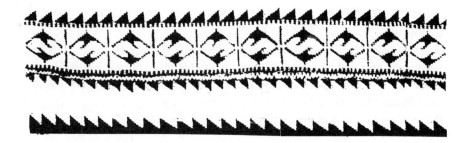

Allah protect you and prosper you," she said. "Take the goat to the market in town and sell her so that we can buy a mouthful of bread to put in our mouths."

Bahlul led the goat out of the village. Soon he came to a deserted place where he saw an owl perched on a rock. "Uh-huh!" called the owl. "Did you wish to buy my goat?" asked Bahlul. "Uh-huh!" "Have you got ten dinars to pay for her?" asked Bahlul. "Uh-huh!" "Then she is yours; may she bring you good fortune!" said Bahlul. He waited to be paid and finally asked the owl for his money, but the owl only repeated its call, "Uh-huh!" "If you want me to come for the money tomorrow, I'll return then!" said Bahlul, and ran home.

"How much did you get for her?" asked Bahlul's mother when she saw him without the goat. "I agreed to wait till tomorrow for my ten dinars," said Bahlul. "Why, who did you sell her to?" asked the mother. "To a bird who says 'Uh-huh!' He promised to have the money ready tomorrow." "You'll get neither money nor melons from an owl, my child," said Bahlul's mother. "We'll not see the ten dinars tomorrow or at apricot harvest, may Allah forgive you your foolishness!"

Next day Bahlul returned to the lonely spot and found the owl perched on the same rock. "I have come for the price of my goat," called Bahlul, but all the owl would say was "Uh-huh!" At last Bahlul picked up a stone and flung it at the bird, which fluttered off into a narrow opening between two large boulders. Bahlul chased after it and found himself in a cave. On the ground in front of him stood an earthenware jar full of gold pieces. "I'll take what you owe me," said Bahlul to the owl, and counted out ten gold coins.

"Where did you find these, my son?" asked his mother. "I followed the bird to his cave and took what he owed me from his store of gold." "Can you find the place again?" "Yes," said Bahlul. "Will you take me there tomorrow?" "Gladly," said the boy.

Before she went to sleep that night, Bahlul's mother boiled a potful of chick-peas and another of broad beans and tied them into a sack. As soon as it was light she woke her son, and the two of them set off for the owl's cave. When they reached it Bahlul's mother scrambled over the rocks, climbed into the cave, and gathered up all the golden treasure into the skirt of her robe. In a short time she and Bahlul were on their way home again. While they walked toward the village, Bahlul's mother kept throwing handfuls of the boiled chick-peas and broad beans into the air. As they showered down Bahlul went darting after them and stuffed them into his mouth.

Then while his mother carefully dug a hole in the floor of their house to bury the pot of gold, Bahlul spread the good news to all he met. "My mother has found a treasure!" he told the villagers happily. "Where did she find it?" they asked. "Among the rocks out that way." "When did she find it?" "Just before it began to rain peas and beans."

At this the villagers smiled knowingly and shook their heads.

Live long and live well, and may peace be with you.

∴ ∴ ∴

Good Men
and
Golden
Words

Religious Tales
and
Moral
Instructions

∴

*G*eometric designs to decorate mosques, calligraphy to write the word of God, and music to chant the Koran represent art put to its best use. Islam has been stern in its view of sculpture, poetry, or painting which might distract the believer from the practice of religion. In the same spirit, the sheikh in his turban who drills his students in the Koranic verses would prefer that young and old listen to the stories in this section, which were created to teach and improve, rather than to the frivolous tales in the rest of the book.

"A Father's Advice," "We Two Against Fortune," and "Tests of Friendship" are serious, fatherly, "I told you so" stories. In each case a son disregards his elder's wise warning to his own cost. They have about them a ring of Friday, the Moslem Sabbath, when the weekly sermon is given after noon prayers, and all the adult males pray together in the mosque as a community. On Friday the father of the family does not go to work and can see more of his children. For in general boys and girls are raised by the women of the family, staying together until adolescence, after which they go their separate ways.

There is more fancy and humor in some of the shorter stories like "If God Wills," "God Disposes," and "God Will Provide." Even these wittier tales, however, reinforce the same important message: never forget that God is greater than His creations.

The common ground of Islam and Christianity should not be overlooked. The prophets of the Bible are also the prophets of the Koran. One of the *suras* of the Koran is called "Mariam" for the Virgin Mary. In it is an account of the Nativity. Mary leans against a date palm when her labor pains begin. As soon as she has given birth there is a miracle. "He who was below her" comforts Mary, telling her of the stream that God has made to flow at her feet and the ripe dates that the tree will shower down on her.

Since the beginning of Islam, Jews and Christians have lived among Moslems as "people of the book" with no interference in matters of religion. There are Christian tribes among the Beduins and sizable Christian Arab populations in many countries: for example, the Copts of Egypt and the Maronites of Lebanon. The homespun legends about Adam and Moses and Lot are appreciated by Christian and Moslem listeners alike.

The cult of good men believed to be close to God and able to intercede for their fellows is widespread, especially in Egypt and North Africa. Their tombs, inside plain domed shrines with a few surrounding trees, are tended

by their adherents, village women who take comfort in the saints' guardianship. "The Protection of the Prophet Hanun" is a story of a humble miracle effected through such a folk cult figure.

If God Wills

Palestine

Near here used to live a man who had no time for religion. All his life he neither prayed nor fasted. He never even invoked God's name or said "*Inshallah* (if God wills)" before doing anything. On fine days he plowed and hoed his land and when it rained he worked at his loom.

One night he said, "O woman, it looks as if the weather is clearing. I think I'll finish my winter sowing tomorrow. See that the seeds are ready and pack a couple of loaves and a handful of dried figs in my leather bag. I want to make an early start."

> Sabbah
> Rabbah
> Start with the day
> And win rich pay!

answered his wife, "but let us see what tomorrow brings." "There is no wondering about it," he said. "If the day dawns clear I'll plow and if it is rainy I'll finish the cloak that is on my loom." "For once, O man, say 'If God wills.' " "If God wills or if God doesn't will, it will either rain or turn fine tomorrow. If it is fine I'll plow and if it rains I'll finish weaving." Well, the woman picked over the seeds for sowing and kneaded her dough. Then she and her husband laid down their heads and slept.

Before it was light next morning, the wife was already up. She had just prepared her oven for baking when someone knocked loudly at the house door Her husband unlocked it and found a Turkish soldier on the doorstep. "Omniscient God and Protector! What have we here?" asked the weaver. "Are you Abu Hasan?" asked the soldier. The man said that he was. "Step

out then. You are to walk me to town. I don't know how to get there alone,"
said the soldier. "But, sir, today I am busy. I have no time to spare. . . ."
"Busy or not busy, lead the way."

The man was about to refuse when the soldier dealt him two or three
blows with his crop to speed him on. So he hitched up his belt and trotted
ahead of the Turk like a saluki hunting dog. Without a pause or a word
they continued in this way until they arrived at the town. "May God see
you safely home, my friend," said the soldier. The man turned on his heel
and under a shower of rain began the long walk home. When he finally
reached his house, it was dark. He banged on the door and his wife called
out, "Who is it?" "Open the door, woman! It is I, if God wills, your
husband, if God wills!"

Don't Count
Your Chickens

Egypt

In a small village of mud-brick houses on the banks of the Nile lived a poor
young peasant. One day, tiring of his miserable lot, he resolved to leave
home and seek his fortune. With borrowed money he bought himself eight
hundred new-laid eggs and a large, round basket to carry them in. His
merchandise on his arm, he carefully stepped down to the river and waited
for a northbound sailing boat to take him to Cairo.

Then as he sat in the shade of the sail and sped over the cool water, he
began to daydream. "As soon as I reach Cairo I shall go to the poultry
market and sell my eggs. With the price of the eggs I shall go to the weavers'
bazaar and buy some fine striped cotton cloth and bring it back to the village.
The women will crowd round the brightly colored material and buy it up
to sew robes for their families. I shall earn enough to pay back my creditors
and buy myself a ewe. I will pamper my ewe until she gives birth to two
lambs, and then I shall sell her and her young and buy myself a water-

buffalo cow. When the water buffalo calves, I shall have two water buffaloes to sell. They will bring me the price of a servant to do my work. Then I shall be able to say, 'Come, boy! Go, boy! Hurry now! Run!' And if he is stubborn I shall kick him, like this . . ."

And with his mind dwelling on his future fortune, he gave a kick that sent the basket of eggs at his feet sliding off the deck and into the Nile. The water swallowed it up in an instant, while he was left with nothing, not even a dream.

God Disposes

Iraq

Once a man went to the mosque to pray. He took off his shoes and prepared to wash at the row of waterspouts where the men make their ritual ablutions. There he noticed that while the water was gushing strongly from some of the spouts, it merely fell in drips from others. "I wonder why that is," the man murmured to himself. Then God spoke in his ear, saying, "These streams of water represent the fortunes of mankind." "Which is my spout, then?" asked the man. "This one here," said God, "from which the water is falling drop by drop." As soon as God left him, the man took out an awl and drove it into the mouth of the spout, meaning to widen it. But instead he found that he had blocked it completely, and indeed, thereafter he felt that his luck was gone.

This man, a weaver by trade, worked from day to day and from job to job. One day he would have money enough to eat and one day not. On the day that his spout was blocked, he sat at his loom and began to weave furiously, throwing his shuttle to and fro. As he flung it with his right hand, he would say, "With my eye I saw it." And when he returned the shuttle with his left hand, he would say, "With my own hand I stopped it."

Now, his loom was set up in a shed under the king's palace. The king's daughter heard him chanting, "With my eye I saw it and with my own

hand I stopped it." Not knowing the story, she thought he had spied her doing something that he should not have seen. So she had a goose killed, hid thirty dinars in its belly, and sent it to the weaver. The poor man considered such a treat too fine for a pauper like himself, and without even looking inside, sold it for two dinars.

Then he went back to his loom, resuming his refrain. The next week the king's daughter killed another goose, stuffed it with thirty dinars, and sent it to him. The man was as hard up as ever and could not bring himself to eat such a luxury. So he sold it again, this time for just one dinar.

The third week the princess sent him yet another goose stuffed with dinars, and it went the way of the others. And all this time the man continued chanting his song, "With my eye I saw it and with my own hand I stopped it." At last the king's daughter asked her father to do something about the weaver. So he was summoned to the palace, and the king asked him to explain the meaning of his words.

The weaver told his sad tale from beginning to end. Then the king comforted him and said, "God has deprived you, but I shall make you rich." And he gave him a sack full of gold. Overjoyed, the weaver heaved the sack onto his shoulder and went out. But as he left, God caused him to trip on the doorstone. He stumbled and fell, hitting his head on the stone and in a very short time he died.

Then God spoke these words to the king: "When I made him poor, you wished to make him rich. Now that I have killed him, can you make him live? In days to come, whenever you see a piece of meat in a man's hand, say, 'He deserves it,' and if you see a man begging in rags, say, 'He deserves no more than this.' "

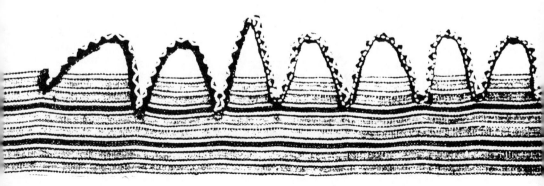

The Truth

Syria

A king once ordered that whoever told a lie should pay a fine of five dinars. The crier went through the city announcing the command, and people began to avoid each other, fearing that they might speak an untruth. Meanwhile the king and his *wazir* disguised themselves and wandered about the marketplace to see the effects of the decree.

They paused in front of the store of a rich merchant—though who is rich beside Allah? The merchant invited them in and served them coffee, and they passed the time pleasantly in conversation. "How old are you?" they asked. "Twenty," said the merchant. "What are you worth?" "Seventy thousand." "How many children do you have?" "One, by the grace of God."

When the king and the *wazir* returned to the palace, they checked the records and sent for the merchant. "How old did you say you were?" "Twenty." "That will cost you five dinars. And how much are you worth?" "Seventy thousand." "That will be another five dinars. And how many sons do you have?" "One, by Allah." "Pay another five dinars." "First prove your case against me," said the merchant. "You are an old man—sixty-five years old, according to the books—and yet you claim you are only twenty!" "The years I enjoyed and in which I found happiness are but twenty—of the rest I know nothing." "Then what about your vast wealth, so large that it cannot be counted or calculated, while you admit to seventy thousand only." "With those seventy thousand I built a mosque. That is my fortune—the money I dedicated to God and man." "Well, do you deny that you have six sons?" they asked, and named them one by one. "No, but five are godless drunkards and adulterers. Only one, may God look kindly on him, is upright and good."

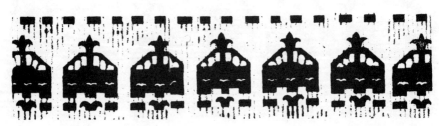

"You have spoken well, O truthful one," the king admitted. "No time is worth remembering but that which was passed in bliss; no wealth worth counting but that spent for the cause of God and man; and no son worth mentioning unless he is pious and good."

A Father's Advice

Iraq

There was and there was not a man burdened with years who saw the Angel of Death, snatcher of souls, hovering near. He summoned Ali, his only son, to his side and said, "I have no wealth to leave you when I die, my child, only a few words of advice. And yet if you take them to heart they can be worth more than gold to you and make yours a happy and carefree life. Never share a secret with your wife. Never become intimate with a servant of princes. Never marry into a richer house than your own." Not long afterwards the father died and, sad to say, before the days of mourning were done his son had forgotten everything he had been told.

Years passed, and Ali's younger sister grew old enough to draw suitors to his door. When a man whose herds grazed as far as the eye could see brought bride-money, Ali was only too happy to give her to him. Now that Ali had a marriage tie to the wealthy cattle owner, he was included in a banquet given by one of the sultan's ministers. O how flattered and delighted was Ali to be the friend of one who ranked so high! He starved his family to be able to entertain the minister and did not rest until they had exchanged the pledge of brotherhood.

One day his father's dying words came into Ali's mind. "How mistaken my old father was," he thought to himself. "My sister is living in comfort, and I may enter the minister's house whenever I wish." He paused. And then he said, "But let me test the truth of his advice."

Next morning before it was fully light, he stole into the royal gardens and caught the sultan's pet gazelle. Then he killed a suckling lamb, brought it to his wife, and whispered in her ear, "Don't tell, but today I was lucky and trapped the sultan's gazelle." While the lamb was yet cooking on the fire, the palace crier disturbed the midday quiet with his message: "A rich reward to the finder of the king's gazelle!" Ali's wife stirred her pot and said nothing.

But not very long afterwards, Ali happened to raise his voice in anger at his wife. Yielding to the promptings of her temper, she sent word to the palace that her own husband had stolen the sultan's gazelle and slaughtered it for their noontime meal. The sultan's minister, Ali's well-placed friend, promptly knocked at Ali's door with an armed guard to take him before the sultan. "Are we not friends, and have we not pledged brotherhood?" pleaded Ali. "I do not know who you are," said the minister. "How can you be my brother?" And he took Ali in chains to the palace. There the sultan commanded Ali to bring fifty camels in payment for the stolen pet before three days passed, or else he would lose his head.

"Who will help me now?" thought Ali. "Allah has showered blessings on my youngest sister's husband, and he is renowned for the herds he owns that graze wherever one casts one's eye. Surely he will show me kindness in my trouble." But when he rode to his brother-in-law's house and told his tale of woe, the cattle owner's face hardened like flint and would have blunted an axe. Ali's sister pleaded with tears on her cheeks, but all that her husband would consent to give was one old male goat from his flocks.

Now, Ali's older sister had long been wed to a poor goatherd. Her life was hard and her children fed on bread and onions. Ali set out to ask her for help, although he had little hope of success. "If my wealthy brother-in-law will give no more than one goat, can a poor herdsman who finds it hard to feed his children produce fifty camels?" said Ali to himself. And the world seemed to dwindle in his eyes till it felt no greater than the crack in a mud wall that a viper nests in.

Yet when he reached his older sister's tent near the pastures where her husband tended his master's animals, his coming was hailed like a holiday. They shared a meal and as they talked together afterwards, his brother-in-law said, "I see trouble sitting on your brow. Speak, and let your heart feel lighter." Ali told all that had happened. Then his sister's husband smiled and said, "You are like my own eyes to me, and would I not protect my eyes from hurt?"

Early next morning the goatherd stood nearby on the crest of a small hill and cried in all directions "Haihum!" This is the rallying cry the tribes use before a raid. From every side the camel herders and goatherds came in answer. When Ali's brother-in-law told of the danger that threatened his wife's brother and his children's uncle, the men spoke as one. "Rejoice!"

they said, and each brought a camel from his own animals. When Ali awoke, he saw fifty camels tethered outside and knew that his poor sister's husband had saved his life.

So on the evening of the third day, with a string of fifty camels behind him, the wealthy brother-in-law's goat to the right of him, and the sultan's pet gazelle to the left of him, Ali appeared before the sultan. "What does this mean?" said the sultan. And Ali explained to him the whole story in all its details: how he had told a secret to his wife to test his father's advice, and what he had learned in his dealings with the minister and his two sisters' husbands. The sultan, as astonished as he was delighted by the tale, ordered the fifty camels returned to Ali laden with gold and costly gifts. And so Ali left the sultan's presence thinking on the depth of his father's dying words and the wisdom they contained.

May you live long and live well.

The Protection
of the
Prophet Hanun

Palestine

There are two shrines west of the town of Bir Zeit: one to Nabi Hanun and the other to Nabi Sair, both children of our lord Jacob, peace be on him.

Now, there was a good piece of hard, flat ground near Nabi Hanun which a peasant used as a threshing floor. Whenever the man came to thresh his wheat in the morning, he found that the heap of winnowed grain from the day before had been trodden on and scattered about. Finally one day he went into the prophet's sanctuary and said: "O prophet of God, father of blessings and merit before Allah, I am your neighbor, under your mantle and protection. If it is you, O Nabi, who is disturbing my grain, I'll be happy to move elsewhere. But if it is someone other than you, let him die, O Nabi, through your will." Thus he prayed and then went home.

The next day when he returned to the place, he found a flight of partridges lying dead among his grain. They it was who had been scattering his wheat in the night!

Lot and the Devil

Palestine

When Lot sinned, he asked his uncle Abraham, "What must I do so that my transgressions may be forgiven me?" Abraham gave him a staff and said, "Plant this in the ground and water it with water from the River Jordan. But as you fetch water, should you meet anyone who asks you to quench his thirst, give him freely of what you carry and throw away what is left. Then return to the river for fresh water to give your plant. When it blossoms and bears leaves, you will know that God has forgiven you."

Now, this was no ordinary stick. One of the angels who visited Abraham and ate in his tent had carried it. Then Sarah found it and tossed it on the fire, but as it began to burn it had filled the air with such perfume that she had plucked it out of the flames and hidden it away. Now Abraham gave it to Lot.

Lot did as he was told and planted it, then took a waterskin down to the River Jordan. But the devil, knowing that Lot sought forgiveness for his sins, devised a way to hinder him. Disguising himself as a traveler, he waited by the side of the road and begged for a drink. Lot was filled with pity and poured him as much water as he needed. Then he returned to the Jordan for more. Again the devil waylaid him and asked for water. Lot gave him what he had and retraced his steps again. So the devil continued until Lot was weary and his legs weak from walking. God now took pity on him and blinded the devil to prevent him from finding Lot. At last Lot was able to water the staff, and straightway it burst into leaf and blossomed. And Lot felt easy in his heart, for he knew that God had shown him mercy.

Justice

Syria

One day the kings of the world met together and said, "Let us find out about these Moslems and how they govern. Do they rule justly?" Napoleon, who was among the kings, said, "Yes, let us test them with some trick and see if we can catch them out." So they called one of their ministers and gave him a fine black stallion. "Take this horse," they said, "to Istanbul, the city of the Ottoman sultan. The sultan can tell one pedigreed horse from another, and he will want to buy it. Do not sell it. If he seizes it from you by force, then appeal to their Koranic tribunal, the *shari'a* court."

Taking the stallion, the minister went off. He arrived in Istanbul and rode the black horse in front of the sultan's palace. The sultan sent for him and said, "Will you sell me your horse?" "It is not for sale," said the minister. The king persisted. "I'll give you several horses for it. I'll give you whatever you ask for." "Even if you were to offer me one hundred thousand dinars, I would not part with it," said the minister.

One month passed, two months passed, and every day the minister continued to parade on the black stallion in front of the sultan's palace. And every day the sultan, seeing that matchless steed, made the minister an offer.

The courtiers and the people of the city tried to persuade the man to let the sultan have his wish. But he would only say, "I cannot give up my horse."

Well, the sultan could endure no more and sent his soldiers to force that stallion into the royal stable. The minister went straight to the *shari'a* court and complained to the *qadi*. The *qadi* took him to the courthouse and sent word to the palace. In swept the sultan past the minister, who was sitting near the door, and

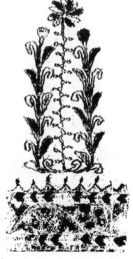

walked to the center of the hall, where he took a seat beside the *qadi*.

The *qadi* began. He said to the minister, "State your claim against the sultan." "Tell me first," said the minister, "does your Koranic law rule that the sultan may sit near your lordship in the place of honor, while I must crouch here by the door where every man that enters kicks off his shoes?" The *qadi* ordered the sultan to stand next to the minister and went on, "What is the accusation?" The minister said, "The sultan has taken my stallion. I want neither money nor horses in its stead. I only want my own horse back."

"Does he speak the truth?" the *qadi* asked of the sultan. "Yes, that is what happened," said the sultan. "And you do not wish to sell the horse?" asked the *qadi*, turning to the minister. "No, not if he were to offer me all his kingdom," said the minister.

Then the *qadi* gave judgment: he ruled that the sultan must return the stallion to its owner. The sultan nodded his turban with approval. "Justly spoken," he said. "Had you ruled otherwise, O *qadi* of the court, I would have cut off your head with this sword!" "And had you disregarded the decision of the *shari'a* court, O sultan," said the *qadi*, "had you broken the law of the Koran and made light of my judgment, I should have let this viper destroy you and turn you to ashes." And he lifted the corner of the mat on which he sat and revealed the snake in a bag beneath it.

We Two
Against Fortune

Saudi Arabia

They speak of a prince who had an only son. The boy grew up and became old enough to need a wife. His father advised him: "My son, when you marry, choose the girl who says, 'You and I must face fortune together!'—not she who claims, 'I am your fortune. In me you face your destiny.' " The boy asked for a sheikh's daughter. The father arranged the match, and when they were about to be wed the prince asked his bride, "What do you say about fate?" "I am your fate. But only time will tell," she told him. So he left her and asked for the hand of another girl. "What do you think about fortune?" "I am your fortune. But only time will tell," she said. He sent her back to her father and looked for a third, and a fourth, and so on.

The last girl gave him the same reply as those who had come before, but she was beautiful and the boy's heart clung to her. He went to his father and said, "Father, this girl says that she will face fortune at my side, and I want to have her." "May she bring you blessings, O my son," said his father. They got up and called the preacher, and the boy and the girl were married— may the same be true for all who need it. The prince was old in years. One day when his son was not there, he called his son's wife and went with her to the pool in the garden. He drained the water out of it and in its bed uncovered a trapdoor. This he lifted, revealing a cave underneath. He took the girl down and showed her seven piles of treasure, the gold heaped on the gold, the silver on the silver, the pearls on the pearls, and so on. And he told her that his son and his son's riches were in her trust.

Go day, come day, the prince died. His son's wife took a lover. And when she was sure of her paramour she said to her husband, "O son of good people! Before was before. Then we could depend on God and your father's wealth, but now on whom can you rely? Why don't you go and look for some job of work? Move yourself and prove yourself." The boy asked, "Did my father say anything before he died?" "Not a word," said his wife.

From place to place the prince's son went hiring himself out as a day laborer. And every night he would come home dirty and spent like a burnt-

out wick. One day a friend of his father's saw him working at a building site. He said, "O son of princes, have you no sense of your own worth, that you hire yourself out by the day? Your father's wealth is enough to see you through, and your children, and your children's children." "I have no knowledge of it," said the boy. "And there is my poor wife like one who has cut off her hand and sits in the gutter begging from those who pity her." "Go," said his father's friend, "pick a quarrel with her, beat her, and divorce her."

The boy went home, trouble sitting between his eyes. "What is the matter with you?" said his wife. "Your face is enough to turn one's luck!" "It would be a stroke of fortune to see you laid low!" he said. From him a word and from her a word, until he hit her and she screamed, and he divorced her and she went off, home to her people.

When she was gone, the friend of his father came and let the water out of the pool, took him down into the secret vault, and showed him his father's wealth lying there untouched. The boy loaded the treasure into wooden chests and moved to the friend's house. Then he filled the pool with water as it was before and sent the crier to announce to the people that the house was for sale.

That cursed woman, his former wife, said to her lover, "Buy it!" She was thinking of the gold and silver under the garden pool. And he did what she said and bought it for one hundred thousand dinars—fifty thousand of his own and fifty thousand that he borrowed. Then he married her.

Well, she emptied the pool and opened the entrance to the cave and went down with her husband to show him the treasure. She stretched out her hand, and what did she touch? Nothing but stone walls. So this husband of hers began to blame her and shout at her and beat her. And he divorced her and put the house up for sale. "Buy it back!" said the friend to the prince. And he bought it for fifty thousand dinars, making a tidy profit. Then he married the daughter of his father's friend, returned the money to the cave where it belonged, and lived in peace.

Unhappy is the man whose wife sides with fortune against him for his house is ruined!

The King Who
Changed His Ways

Syria

Long ago there lived a king who oppressed his people and taxed them cruelly. In his lust for riches he resented any man who appeared to rival him, and he would soon find a way to confiscate that man's property. At length the whole kingdom was reduced to penury. Yet even so the king was not satisfied.

One day he chose a beautiful slave girl from those who served in the palace. He had her dressed in robes of the finest cloth, then called the crier and ordered her taken to the marketplace and offered for sale at one lira. But no one was left in the city who possessed even one lira, and the crier stood for many hours offering the girl in vain.

A merchant's son who saw the girl longed to buy her. He went to his mother—since his father was dead—and said, "I shall fall sick if I cannot have that slave girl. Won't you buy her for me?" "I have nothing, my child," said the mother. "We put the last lira that we had into your father's mouth when he was buried." Then her sinful son went to the cemetery and dug up his father's grave, and with the gold that had been buried with his father he bought himself the girl.

The king, anxious to see who among his people was able to buy the girl, had the youth brought before him and ordered him to tell where he'd found the money. "I dug it out of my father's grave," said the boy. When the king sent his soldiers to check this statement and found that it had been so, he was filled with remorse at the harshness of his rule. He did not rest until he had called all his subjects to the palace that very day and distributed his accumulated wealth among them.

The king's entire life changed, until indeed he became known for his compassion. He even presided over the court of law in person to see that justice was done. Once when word reached him that a poor man had been prevented from coming into his presence with a grievance, he had a bell hung above his head with a rope that hung down into the street. Thus at the pull of a rope, anyone could have the king's ear.

Now, in that kingdom there lived a bird. She had built her nest in a tall tree, but when her brood hatched, a thick snake attacked her young and devoured them before they could fly. The bird had heard of the king's kindness, so when she next laid her eggs and the chicks were about to hatch, she flew to the palace and perched on the king's bell rope. The guards who went to see who wanted an audience with the king reported that they found no one, except a bird fluttering a short distance and landing. "Follow that bird, for it may be that she has a grievance too," ordered the king. And so they ran behind her until they reached her tree, arriving just as the snake was about to swallow the newly hatched chicks. They were able to kill it in time, and when they brought this news back to the palace, the king was filled with joy. "I can now die in peace," he said, "for if in the past my oppression reached the dead under the ground, now my compassion has become such that it eases the lot of the birds in the air."

If you are asking about the present Turkish government, its injustice has already reached the dead in their graves, and of justice there is none for the people on the ground, let alone the birds in the air.

The Virgin Mary and the Goats

Palestine

As the Virgin Mary was fleeing with the Holy Child, she sought a safe place to lie down and sleep one night. Coming to a sheepfold, she hid among the ewes who were penned in there. The ewes let her take shelter in their midst without betraying her presence, making no restless movements nor uttering a sound. "May God protect you as you have protected me," said Our Lady when she resumed her journey the next morning.

The following night she crept among a herd of goats, who at once began to bleat. "May God forevermore expose your shame as you exposed me this night," said the Virgin. Straightaway the goats' tails, which till then had hung down like those of other animals, lifted and curled upwards. And since that day all goats walk with their shameful parts uncovered for all to see.

The Virgin Mary and the Plowmen

Palestine

When the Virgin Mary, peace be on her, was on the flight to Egypt with her son in her arms, she passed by some plowmen making furrows in their field. She said to them, "Though today you are only sowing, before the sun rises tomorrow morning your field will be ready to harvest. But remember, if anyone comes this way and asks about me, say, 'She was here just as we were getting ready to plant these chick-peas.' "

Indeed, when the Beni Israïl, who were after the Virgin, came to the place on the very next day, these same plowmen were busy harvesting chick-peas. The Beni Israïl asked, "Has a woman carrying a child passed your way recently?" The plowmen replied, "By God, such a one did go by, but that was when we were digging the furrows to sow this crop." "O ho," said her pursuers, "that must have been some time ago. How will we catch up with her now?"

Tests of Friendship

Syria

There lived a wealthy merchant who had but one child, a son. When the boy was fifteen years old, he was befriended by a group of lazy good-for-nothings. Every day they would take him to the taverns and houses of ill-repute, and by evening the boy would have spent a sizable sum entertaining his companions. At length his father said, "My son—may Allah look favorably on you—these friends of yours are children of shame. Tomorrow when I am gone they will waste all your wealth and leave you poor as a Gypsy." "No, father, they are the truest friends a man can have." "Will you let me test them, then, and show you their real worth?" "Yes indeed," said the boy. "Very well. Go to the market and buy a sheep, a large one, and invite those of your companions you trust most to sup with you tonight."

When the boy had brought the sheep, the merchant proceeded to butcher it and daub the walls with its blood. Then he spoke to his son: "My child, you claim you have twenty friends, and you believe that in the world there are none more loyal. For myself, I can count on the friendship of only three men, one an intimate friend, affectionate and true, another only half a friend, and the third merely an acquaintance. Let us see which of us is the more fortunate."

At sunset the boy's companions arrived at the house and were welcomed in. The father led them into the room that was smeared with blood and said, "Look! My son brought a man home and they quarreled and he killed him. You—may Allah add to your days—are my son's friends. Will you carry the corpse to the river and throw it in?" They refused and fled the house. Each found his way by a different route to the palace and the presence of the pasha. Each said, "In such and such a merchant's house they have killed a man, and I have come to bring you news of it."

So much for the boy's friends. As for the merchant, he called his servant girl to bring him fat and almonds and pistachios. She lit the fire and heated the butter, then stuffed the sheep with rice and nuts and stewed it until it was done. She wrapped it in one hundred loaves of the leather-thin *saj* bread, rolled it up in a silken sheet, and tied it at each end so that it resembled a corpse in its shroud.

Just then there was loud knocking at the door. The merchant opened it and found the pasha and a hundred soldiers with him. They seized the merchant, shouting, "Where is the body?" "In there, may Allah have mercy upon me!" When they saw the place awash with blood and a corpse on the floor, they bound the merchant and clapped a chain around his neck and dragged him off to the execution place.

On the way they passed the shop of the merchant's acquaintance. When the shopkeeper saw the merchant in chains, he ran out and asked what crime he had committed. "He is a murderer," answered the guard. The shopkeeper appealed to the pasha: "Sire, will you accept a quarter of all I possess and let this man free?" But the pasha refused.

Meanwhile the merchant's second friend, seeing the procession, came to

the pasha. "Sire, will you take half my property in exchange for this man's life?" But still he refused.

The merchant's best friend was a grocer. When he saw the soldiers dragging his friend through the streets, such was his dismay that he went into his store and began to throw the fat into the rice bin and tip the oil into the cheese vat. Then tearing at his beard, he ran to the pasha demanding to know. "What has this unfortunate wretch done?" "He killed a man." "No, no, it was I who killed him," cried the grocer. "Cut off my head and give my property to the victim's family; only let the merchant go free." "But we found the corpse in the merchant's house," said the pasha. "Yes, I threw it there during the night," said the grocer. "Very well," said the pasha, "loose the merchant's bonds and take the grocer to the executioner, instead."

When the merchant had been set free, he addressed the pasha: "Sire, Allah is compassionate and in no haste. Stay the execution for one hour, and untie the corpse to see who it is." "It shall be done," said the pasha. When the corpse had been brought before the pasha and unwound they discovered not a dead body but a sheep stuffed with rice and stewed in butter. "This looks like a banquet more than a beheading," said the pasha. "But what does it mean?" And the merchant replied, "I'll tell you my tale as soon as you bring back my friend the grocer."

When the prisoner entered the pasha's presence as a free man again, the merchant began. "Sire, I am a very rich man and my young son has fallen into bad company. Every day he spends five gold liras on these companions. I have tried to warn him, saying, 'My son, they are robbers; they pretend to be your friends but all they want is your money. When that is gone they will desert you and forget your very name.' But he has insisted that they are the best of friends. So I played a trick to teach my son the truth. I killed this sheep and stained the walls with blood. I asked the boy to invite his friends, and when they came I said, 'Look, my son has killed a man. What should we do?' They did not pause but ran to accuse us before your highness. As you led me through the streets in chains, however, my few friends proved their loyalty, each according to the love he bore me."

"Call your son," said the pasha. And when the boy arrived, he asked him to name his friends. These he arrested and reprimanded for their faithlessness, but to the merchant he gave fifty liras, praising him for his wisdom.

The Bones of
Father Adam

Palestine

Once there was a woodcutter. Every day he would go up into the thick scrub above his village, cut a load of brushwood, and bring it back to sell. For ten or twelve years this was how he lived. Then he grew tired of it. "I don't want this work. I don't like this trade," he said. "I'll go and cut a load of kindling, and then I shall look for the bones of our father Adam, who brought all this pain and trouble upon us, and burn them up." Off he trudged, gathering twigs into a pile.

But God sent an angel to him in the shape of a man. The angel asked, "What are you doing here?" "I am collecting wood, sir, to burn up the bones of our father Adam," said the woodcutter. "What has our father Adam done? How has he wronged you?" "But for him, there would be no weariness in the world." "And if someone were to free you from all work? What would you say?" "I should thank him a thousand thanks!" "Then I shall take you to a garden where you can eat to your heart's content without doing a stroke of work. One thing only you must remember: no matter what you may see in the garden, you are not to speak a single word."

The angel struck his palms together, and the woodcutter found himself in an orchard filled with every kind of fruit. For three or four days he feasted happily. Then he noticed a man walking through the trees, cutting off the green boughs and leaving the dead wood. "Do I say something, or don't I?" the woodcutter asked himself. "That son of accursed parents is trying my patience. By God, I'll tell him. You there!" he called aloud. "What is it?" asked the man. "Don't you know the right way to do that is to break off the dead wood and leave the green?" "Have you been here long?" asked the man. And before the woodcutter knew it he was back in the thicket with his ax.

He began to beat his breast with two stones, wailing, "What have I done! What have I done!" Again the angel appeared to him. "What happened?" he asked. The woodcutter begged him, "Take me back to that place!" "Didn't I tell you not to speak?" "I promise I shall not say a word this time," said the woodcutter. So the angel clapped his hands together and the woodcutter returned to the garden. All went well for three or four days, until he saw a gazelle running and an old man in his nineties hobbling after it. "Only God is All-Knowing! What is this I see?" the woodcutter said. "That gazelle is springing from one boundary wall to the next, while this greybeard is puffing after it a step at a time. Should I speak or not, I wonder. I can't help but say something. Old man!" he called out, "that gazelle is darting before you like lightning. When will you give up and stop dragging after her?" "Have you been here long?" asked the old man, and the woodcutter looked around and saw that he was in front of his woodpile again.

He beat his breast and moaned. The angel came to him and said, "What is it now?" "Please have some pity and take me back!" said the woodcutter. "And this time, may I be cursed if I speak again!" The angel clapped his hands and the woodcutter returned to his place in paradise. He had been there only three or four days when he saw four men struggling to move the millstone of an oil press. They would all lift on the same side, and it would fall onto its other face. "Should I tell them, or not?" the woodcutter said to himself. "These men are senseless. I have to tell them. You, there! If you want to carry the millstone, you have to lift it from all sides." "Have you been here long?" they asked him and in an instant the woodcutter found himself back in the thicket. "What misery! What a load of trouble!" he wept, plucking at his beard and beating his breast. The angel asked, "What is wrong?" "I beg you . . ." began the woodcutter. "It is no use," said the angel. "Your father Adam only sinned once. You have committed sin upon sin upon sin. Your place shall be here among the firewood until the end of your days."

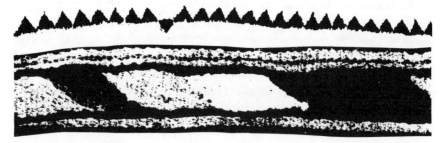

How Moses Died

Syria

When Moses was nearing his end, God sent down the two Angels of Death, Munkar and Nkir. They were digging in the ground and had just finished making a grave when Moses happened upon them. "May you work in good health, O flower of men," he greeted them. "The best of health to you also, O dearly beloved. Tell us, who are you?" they asked him. "I am Moses, who speaks with the Lord, praise be to Him and exaltation," said Moses. "But what are you doing here?" "We, best beloved, were sent by Him Whom all praise and exalt, to dig a grave for a man. But we do not know what size the sons of Adam are, and how large to make the grave." "But I am a son of Adam myself," said Moses. "Why don't you make the grave my length and width?" "Well, here is the shaft we have been digging," they said. "Will you try it and see if it is large enough?"

So Moses lowered himself into the grave and stretched himself out, and it fit. Then, as he was sitting up in order to get out, one of the angels handed him a flower, saying, "Smell this rose." Moses sniffed it and found that it was sweet. Then he fell back lifeless into the grave, with neither a twitch nor a tremor of hand or foot. The angels buried him and burned incense over him, and then winged their way back to heaven.

The prophet of the Lord mentions that Moses' grave is in the heights east of Jericho, but to this day no one knows exactly where.

Four Men and
One Miracle

Saudi Arabia

They say that four men were traveling once through the open country. They were a carpenter, a tailor, a jeweler, and a student of the Koran. Night overtook them near a wood of tamarisk trees, and they decided to sleep in the wood. But since it was known that a lion lived nearby, the men decided to divide the night into four watches so that each would spend three hours watching for the lion while the others slept.

The first shift fell to the carpenter. To while away the time, he picked up a piece of wood and began to chip at it and carve. By the time it was the tailor's turn to watch, the carpenter had made a statue of a girl.

The tailor admired the carpenter's statue and decided that it needed some clothes. So, molding mud from the ground, he dressed the wooden girl. Then it was time to wake the jeweler. The jeweler saw at once that the statue needed some finery, and he made earrings and necklaces for it out of small stones.

Finally the student of the Koran sat up for the last watch before dawn. He looked at the statue of wood with its clothes of mud and jewels of stone and said to himself, "I do not have any skill of my own like my friends." It was then the time for morning prayers. The student made his ritual ablutions, unrolled his prayer mat, and prayed. "O Lord," he said, "I cannot carve wood, nor can I sew, nor can I make jewelry. But I beg you, Lord, to turn this wooden statue into a real girl." And the statue sat up and began to talk. It was a living girl.

When it was light, the other men woke up and saw that the dead branch had become a girl; her clothes of mud had become robes of green velvet, and the pebbles round her neck gold pendants. And they began to quarrel over her, each shouting that she was his by right. They almost fell to blows, but decided to take their case to court for settlement. When they explained what had happened, the sheikh of the Koranic law said, "Though you, O carpenter, carved her out of a branch, and you, O tailor, sewed her clothes of mud, and you, O jeweler, fashioned baubles of stone for her, she would never be alive if the student had not prayed to his Creator to breathe life into her. She is his, and you have no share in her."

> So the seeker found what he was looking for,
> The lover married the one he was longing for.
> May everyone who is sitting here
> Be well and happy all through the year.

God Will Provide

Libya

Once there was a man who had many children but no work. Sometimes he was able to hire himself out, but one day he would earn and ten days he would go hungry. At last he said, "Let me go out of the village; maybe I can find something to do in the countryside." Off he went, but he was still hunting for work when night began to fall.

Where should a penniless man like him sleep in the night? He saw a cave and thought it would make a good shelter. As he climbed up to the cave's mouth, he saw a blind owl perched on a stone with its beak hanging open. Gnats and moths and insects would fly into its mouth until it was full, and then the bird would close its beak and swallow. For a long time the man sat watching this in amazement. At last he said, "Will the Almighty and the All-Knowing, Who provides for the blind owl in her cave, not make provision for a son of Adam?"

He returned to his house, climbed onto the sleeping platform, lay down on his mattress, and refused to move. The next day he would not go to work. Instead he stretched himself out and said, "The Lord will provide."

After the man had gone back to sleep on his bed, there was a knock at the door. When his wife opened it, two rough-looking men on the step asked, "Have you a donkey for hire?" The man's wife said that she did but inquired what they wanted to load him with. They had some vegetables to take to the market, they told her. So she gave them the donkey and they saddled it, bridled it, and led it off.

They took the donkey to a third man, their partner, who was guarding a treasure all three had discovered. Now they began to divide it so that each could take one-third of it home. Filling the donkey's saddlebags with gold, they covered the coins with turnips and radishes. Soon all that remained was the golden crock in which the treasure had been stored. Who should have it? The three men began to fight, first beating each other and then pulling out their knives and stabbing until all three fell down dead on top of the golden crock.

The donkey, seeing that he was free, trotted home. When he reached the gate of the house yard, he began to knock his head against it. The man's wife opened both panels of the gate to let in the animal with the bulging saddlebags. She shouted to her husband, still dozing on the bed, "Come and see what Allah has provided! Enough turnips to feed the children for a week!" The man came down happily, saying, "Let us look at the gift from Him Who provides for the blind owl." And they began to unload the vegetables when—O Lord!—they uncovered the gold.

They spilled all the gold coin onto their bed. Taking a handful, the man ran out and bought meat and fat and sugar and tea, and they all went to bed sated, happy, and content.

Say, "Praise be to Allah!"

∴ ∴ ∴

W·i·l·y
W·o·m·e·n a·n·d
C·l·e·v·e·r M·e·n

Tales of
Wit and Wisdom

⁚

I n the *sura* of Joseph in the Koran, Potiphar's wife, when she hears that the women are whispering slyly about her attempted seduction of Joseph, invites them to eat with her. Just as they take up their knives to cut into the food, she calls Joseph to wait at the table. "And when they saw him they so admired him that they cut their hands saying, 'God save us! This is no mortal; he is no other but a noble angel.' 'So now you see,' she said."*

That is the kind of woman Potiphar's wife was. No wonder her husband had said, of her false accusation against Joseph, "This is of your women's guile; surely your guile is great." The two words "guile" and "slyness" used in describing the women's doings in this passage of the Koran have become associated with a class of story in which women successfully trick and deceive men.

The story called "Women's Wiles" in this collection is widespread and a model of the type. Exploiting her female charms, the heroine goes to extreme lengths to prove her claim that women are quicker-witted than men. Another frequently told story, "The Old Woman and the Devil," an episode in what is sometimes a chain of linked "old woman" tricks, makes the same point. In most tales, however, it is an assumption, requiring no proof, that women are mistresses of intrigue. The short tale "The Chain of Truth" has at the end, as a kind of QED, the quotation from the *sura* of "Joseph" about women's guile.

Islam brought great improvements to the situation of the women of the time. For a start, it prohibited female infanticide, till then an acceptable form of population control. In marriage and divorce it gave women guarantees of financial protection. By limiting polygamy to four equally loved legal wives, it bettered the status of children and their mothers. It granted women freedom to manage their own finances independently of their husbands and relatives—property rights not to become law in Europe until well over a thousand years later. Above all, the prophet's own treatment of women believers and his wives (the first of whom, Khadija, was a wealthy widow with caravans trading with Syria) showed a respect beyond their function as wives and mothers. In compiling the early history of Islam from recollections of descendants of the companions of the prophet, the testimony of women was accepted as readily as that of men. Poetry and letters by women of that era suggest a degree of education as advanced as that of the men.

* From *The Koran Interpreted: A Translation* by Arthur J. Arberry (New York: Macmillan, 1964).

The dictates of custom rather than religion, and a convention in which the honor of the family rests on the moral conduct of its women, has resulted in the severe seclusion of Moslem women in most parts of the Arab world. The Koranic prescription for modesty, addressed to both sexes, has been applied to women with a fervor that has in many places muffled them in cloth, leaving only their eyes uncovered. After puberty women may associate only with men of the family and close relatives. Social activities outside the house are strictly segregated and freedom of movement is inhibited. Even within the home, women are required to withdraw demurely from sight at the entrance of male visitors.

Women the world over, still battling for equal rights, enjoy a story of a woman making a fool of men. How much more piquant the pleasure of such a tale when told in the women's quarters! Stories of women's wiles are among the cycles of tales told by Arab women, though appreciation of the two cited above does not depend on gender.

One of the places outside the home permitted to women was the public bathhouse, or *hammam*. It was a clean, often marble-lined building clouded in warm steam and smelling of olive-oil soap scented with mastic, where the women could meet their friends and exchange intimate gossip while scrubbing each other's backs with loofah. Shocking confessions like those recorded in "The Gown in the Bathhouse" might well be imparted while cooling and resting in the bath keeper's room.

The *hammam* is also an ideal setting for intrigue, and the legitimate excuse of a trip to the *hammam* provides a good opportunity to plan a meeting with a lover arranged through a conniving maid. Bathhouses are things of the city, as are the tales of guile. For the plots to succeed, a certain amount of anonymity is necessary. It is therefore not surprising that a large number of such stories are found in Cairo and Damascus. The stock character of the scheming old woman would not do as well if she did not have a labyrinth of covered *suqs* into which to disappear. When she has ordered the wooden chest, the size of a man, which locks from the inside (a standard property in these stories), she needs to steer the porter carrying it through the noisy *suq* of the coppersmiths beating patterns into shining metal trays, past the pungent alleyway of the spice vendors with their sacks of green cumin, yellow turmeric, and red sumac, round by the narrow booths of the jewelers until the man doesn't know where he is when she finally knocks at a door three steps up a dark archway. For the merchant's wife in "The Old Woman and the Devil" to believe in the devout old woman who needs to say her prayers, or the first wife in "The Gown in the Bathhouse" to spy a youth who is a stranger from her roof, the setting has to be a large town or city.

In the literature on *The Arabian Nights,* Cairo is presented as the fountainhead of stories of intrigue and of merry thieves. "The Judgment of the *Qadi*" was recorded in Cairo a hundred years ago, but in fact the taste for such knavery goes back much farther. Herodotus tells of King Rhampsinitus, who so admired the ingenious robber who stole from his treasury that he rewarded him with his daughter for a wife. "This man has outwitted all the Egyptians," he says, "and the Egyptians are the cleverest people in the world." Arabs still look to Cairo and the Egyptians for inventive humor and entertainment.

There are no famous wily women, only nameless types: the schemers, usually old women and midwives; the sharp-witted daughters, like "The Clever Minister's Daughter," "The Sultan's Camp Follower" and the caliph's daughter in "The Weaver's Dream"; and the bold young wives who will not be snuffed out by heavy veils or contained within windowless walls.

Complementing the tales of deceitful wives are those of husbands who catch them out, like the man in "A Lion the Color of Yellow Silk." But these are neither as numerous nor as entertaining as the first, since it is the success of the underdog that gives spice to a tale. The three Mohammads in the story of the same name are as sharp as the clever daughters, except that theirs is quickness of observation rather than wit. This is a popular and still current folk story, though it is traceable to *The Arabian Nights.* Most appealing are the bold and brassy young men, like the youth in "A Tall Tale" and the good-humored husband in "When Twice as Many Is Half the Trouble."

To balance the section a few stories are included at the end in which the women triumph through their simplicity rather than guile.

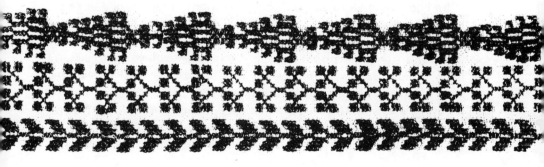

⠒⠒ ⠒⠒ ⠒⠒ ⠒⠒ ⠒⠒ ⠒⠒ ⠒⠒ ⠒⠒ ⠒⠒ ⠒⠒ ⠒⠒

A Tall Tale

⠒ ⠒ ⠒ ⠒ ⠒ ⠒ ⠒ ⠒ ⠒ ⠒ ⠒ ⠒

Palestine

There was and there wasn't, O Ancient of Days, a king who had one daughter. She was of such astonishing beauty that when she reached the age to be married, suitors thronged her father's court. Yet whenever the king mentioned marriage to her, she would say, "I shall be wed only to the man who can tell me a story whose beginning is impossible and whose end is untrue." News of the challenge spread and many were the princes who took it up. Time and again a suitor would begin in the traditional manner of storytellers with the words, "Let us profess that Allah is One and has no equal." And there and then the princess would send him on his way, saying, "A story that is lies from beginning to end is no place for the profession of the unity of Allah!" So it went on until one day a handsome and quick-witted youth came before her and said, "I shall tell you a tale to fulfill your heart's desire." And when she had invited him to sit before her, he began:

"Before uttering an untruth, I crave forgiveness from Allah Who alone is All-Knowing.

"When my grandmother gave birth to my grandfather, I was a child old enough to walk and run. So she called me and said, 'Take these two pennies, my child, and fetch me eggs and cumin so that we can celebrate the cutting of your grandfather's navel cord.' I ran to do her bidding and bought the eggs and the spice and put them in my pocket and hurried home. But on the way I stumbled, and one of the eggs dropped to the ground and broke, and out hopped a chick carrying a load of firewood on his back. I unloaded the wood off him so that I could ride him home, but found that the skin of his back had been rubbed raw. Filled with pity, I sat by the side of the road and wept.

"Then a man passing by comforted me and gave me a date stone, saying, 'Roast this stone and crush it and rub it into the wound on your chicken's back.' I did as he advised me and all at once a date palm laden with red and yellow dates began to grow from the chicken's back. 'It would be wrong to pass by such sweet fruit without tasting it,' I said to myself, and shinned up the palm. At the top I found a date grove so vast that a harvester beating the fruit down from one tree could not hear his fellow's blows at the next.

Between the trees the earth was so rich and black that I plowed it and sowed sesame seeds. After the seeds were ripe, I gathered them into sacks but found an ant stealing one sesame seed. When I seized an end of the seed and tried to pull it away, the ant held on tight. As I tugged on my side and he on his, the seed broke and out of it spilled a stream of sesame oil. I jumped into it and swam until I reached your presence!"

The princess laughed and was married to the handsome storyteller, according to the laws handed down by the prophet.

> Now the bird has taken flight.
> I wish you peace and goodnight.

Seven Cauldrons
Bubbling

Lebanon

One day a woman went out to the wool market to sell the yarn she had spun. A man asked, "How much do you charge for your yarn?" and she told him. "I don't need yarn," said the man, "but I've heard that you have three daughters. I have no one. I am lonely and want one of your daughters for my wife." The woman could see that he was a man of substance, whereas she had nothing. So she gave him one of her daughters.

The husband and his bride reached the man's house. He knocked at the door and the maidservant said, "Who is it?" And he answered, "I." So she unlocked the door and stood on the doorstone like death's sister, her face yellow as sulfur and her voice hollow as a well. "I have brought you a mistress," said the man.

The wife sat down and the husband said to the servant, "Come." She came and he said, "Bring me the sack." She brought him a sack and out of it he picked three chick-peas. He offered one to the bride and one to the maidservant, and one he kept for himself. "Every day I shall give you three of these," he told his wife. "One for your breakfast and one for your lunch and one for your supper."

The seventh day came, and the wife said to her husband, "It is time for me to go to the bath." He replied, "Prepare your clothes and take the maid to carry them. Here is a penny to give to the keeper of the bath; be sure to bring back the change."

She went to the bath and washed, and when she was finished she gave the penny to the woman who kept the bath. "My husband says he wants his change," the wife said. The *hammamjiyeh* who looked after the bath shouted, "A curse fall on your parents and on his! What do you mean by giving me a miserable penny? And you want change too, do you?" And she snatched the girl's towel and the bundle with her clothes and chased her away. The girl went to her husband, crying. "What is wrong?" he asked. "They took my towel and my things and chased me out of the bath," she wept. He frowned a frown, took her down to the cellar, and hung her by her feet until she died.

He returned to the mother and said, "And how are you? How is your luck, how is your fortune?" "It is as Allah wishes," she answered and inquired after her daughter. "She is at peace and resting," he said, "and wants nothing except her sister to visit her." So the woman called her second daughter and said, "Take her with you; let her see her sister and stay and keep her company awhile." And so the man took the sister home with him and did with her as he had done with the first.

Then the man went to the mother's house a third time and said, "Your two daughters are happy and contented sitting in the house. They only ask for their sister." But the youngest daughter objected. "I don't want to go with him. Why are you sending me away?" When her mother insisted, however, the girl said, "Tell him I need three days to get ready." For three days she cooked. After preparing *kebab* meat on skewers and vegetables stuffed with rice, she packed the food into a chest and took it with her when she accompanied the man to his house.

He knocked at the door and from inside the servant called, "Who is it?" And he said, "It is I. I have brought you a mistress." When the servant unlocked the door, she was doubled up as if the knots of her body had each been loosened so that she was hardly able to walk. The man told her, "Bring me the sack." And when the servant had brought it, he picked out nine chick-peas and said, "Here are three for you and three for me and three for the maidservant." "Why such extravagance?" the girl complained. "One each is enough!" And the man said, "You are the woman I have been seeking! You must become my bride!" But as soon as he left the house, the girl pulled out her chest and set the food between herself and the servant, and they ate and ate. The servant girl gorged herself, resting only to say, "What a clever mistress I have!" And then she went on eating. When the man came home, the servant said, "Who is it?" and he remarked, "Her voice is stronger. Her mistress's housekeeping has given her health."

When seven days had passed, the girl said, "I want to go to the bath." He gave her a penny, but she murmured, "Why a whole penny? Half a penny will do!" And he was overjoyed and cried, "You are the light of my eyes! You are the soul in my body!"

Now the food that the girl had brought was eaten up. So what did she do? She begged a lump of tar off a caravan passing by the house and stuck it on the end of a long stick. She went to the cellar, which was filled with heaps upon heaps of money, and poking the stick through the bars, she fished out the coins that stuck to the tar. So she was able to send the maid for food and the two of them lacked nothing.

One day a group of the man's acquaintances cornered him and said, "Many's the time we have invited you to our houses. Now it is your turn to invite us." "Why not?" said the man. He went to the *suq* of the butchers and asked the price of meat. They told him, "The kilo goes for ten." "Ten!" he screamed. "Are you telling me that meat costs so much?" And he fled without buying. Next he went to the vegetable *suq* and priced the okra. They told him, "A kilo for five." "Five for a kilo of okra!" he shouted. "O people, how can it be so much?" He walked the length and breadth of the *suq* and could not bring himself to buy anything.

Then the man saw an ignorant boy with a sparrow in his hand and asked, "Will you sell me your bird?" The boy agreed, but even so the man held back and wondered which was more, the value of the bird or a coin worth a *qursh*. The bird or the *qursh*; the *qursh* or the bird? In the end he bought the bird and took it home. He said to the girl, "Here is a bird for the dinner for my friends. Prepare one side as a roast in the oven and the other side as a stew." "As you say," she answered.

Off he went, and she left the house close on his heels. Down to the *suq* she hurried, and bought and bought of everything there was for sale: rice, meat, vegetables, bread. She bought stewing pots and hung them over the fire and heaped the wood high. A smell of saffron frying in butter filled the house.

The man came home, and looked around. "Where does all this food come from?" he said.

> Seven cauldrons bubbling,
> Seven stewpots brimming,
> Is it all with the flesh
> Off one little starling?

And after that his tongue ceased speaking and he was struck dumb. But he went on pointing his finger at the pots and the cauldrons on the fire until the anger in him pressed violently on his soul, squeezing it till his heart burst and he died.

And so the guests and the girl and the maid sat down and ate, and invited the poor of the quarter besides. The house and the yard and all that was in it, including the treasure in the cellar, now belonged to the girl, and she brought her mother to live with her.

> We were with them then,
> Now we are back again.

Women's Wiles

Syria

There was a merchant, a very rich merchant—though no riches equal Allah's—who kept a store. Above it he had hung a sign which read, "Men's Wits Beat Women's Wiles." One day the master blacksmith's daughter passed through that part of the *suq*, a beautiful girl who had drunk her fill of mother's milk. She saw the sign and it angered her. She was so determined to teach the shopkeeper a lesson that all night long she tossed and turned on her mattress, forming a plan.

In the morning she dressed herself in her finest gown, braided her hair and arranged herself with the greatest art, and went straight to the merchant's store. "Good morning, O my uncle," she greeted him. "A morning to bring happiness from Allah," replied the merchant. "God keep you happy," said the girl. Then suddenly she burst into tears. The merchant was astonished. "Tell me why! Speak!" But the girl only cried the harder. The merchant became alarmed. "Tell me what you need, only please stop crying," he said. "You are making my heart burn like fire! Whatever you want done, I'll do it." The girl sighed, "If only that were possible!" "Let me know what it is, at least," said the man.

Well, dear listener, at that the girl lifted her head and, looking the merchant full in the face with two eyes that shone like polished mirrors, asked, "Do you see any fault in my eyes?" When she put this question, staring up at him like a doe, the merchant began to feel a little faint. "Allah has not graced the gazelle with more beautiful eyes than yours," he said. And his mouth was dry. "Then what is wrong with my arms?" she asked, pulling back her sleeves. When he saw her neatly turned arms, pale and smooth like peeled cucumbers, the merchant lost his senses. "Is crystal finer or marble whiter than this, O Lord?" he asked. With the tears still falling down her face, the girl lifted the hem of her gown. "What blemish do you see in my feet?" she asked. Now the poor man was quite overcome. "My eyes have seen nothing daintier. Only do not cry," he begged. Sobbing bitterly, the girl pulled off her headcloth, uncovering hair that hung down in thick ropes, black and shining. "Is anything amiss with my hair, then?" she asked. "It is perfect," said the merchant. "There is no silk in my store as fine."

Then at last the girl began to tell him this story. "I am the qadi's daughter," she said, "and whenever a suitor comes to my father to ask for my hand, my father tells him, 'My daughter is bald; my daughter is lame; her eyes are crossed; her limbs are crippled.' Who would want to marry such a person! Of course, they leave. A woman needs protection and marriage is her shelter. Now I don't know what to do." When he had heard this tale, the merchant said, "Tomorrow I myself shall go to your father and ask for you. Whatever he says, I shall reply, 'I am willing,' and 'I do not complain.' Now there is no reason for you to be sad." So the girl left him.

When the merchant closed his shop and went home that night, sleep fled before him and thoughts of the girl's beauty filled his mind. When the day dawned, he smoothed his whiskers and dressed with care, and as soon as it was the proper hour for calling, he hastened to the qadi's house. When they had exchanged their greetings and were sitting face to face, the merchant said, "I have come seeking kinship with your honor. I ask for your daughter in marriage." The qadi put him off, saying, "Have I a daughter?" But the merchant said, "I know for certain that you do." "But she is squint-eyed," said the *qadi*. "I'll marry her!" cried the merchant. "She is lame," said the *qadi*. "I have no objection!" answered the merchant. "She is crippled," said the *qadi*. "I shall not complain," insisted the merchant. In the end the *qadi* said, "Can you pay her bride-money? It is ten thousand dinars." The merchant paused, and remembering just how beautiful the girl was, said, "It is less than she is worth." And so the *qadi* finally agreed to the match.

Now began the preparations for the wedding. The paper was written that "a well-born bride was bound in marriage to a groom of good family." All that remained was for the bride to be taken from her father's house to the bridal chamber in her husband's house, for the night of the entering and the unveiling. Pacing forward and backward, the merchant awaited the wedding procession with impatience.

Who was that knocking at his door? It was a hired porter bent in two under the weight of a huge covered basket. "This is from the *qadi*'s house,"

he announced. "This must be her linen," said the merchant, and told the man to carry it up the stairs. To himself he thought, "Why not take a look and see what she is bringing with her!" He raised the cover of the basket, and what do you think he saw? A girl exactly like the squint-eyed cripple that the *qadi* had described: not one deformity, not one blot wanting! "Who are you?" asked the merchant. "I am your bride, the *qadi*'s daughter." "How can you be? When you came to my store, you were like a full moon on the night of the fourteenth!" he cried. He left her in her basket and sat thinking. Then he lay on his bed and wondered, "What have I done, that that beautiful daughter of sin should want to play a trick like this on me!"

Next day he was back in his store. He sat with his head in his hands, and in a little while the master blacksmith's daughter came by. "May your day be glad!" she said. When he saw who it was, the merchant said, "May Allah not gladden yours! What have I done to you that you should make me fall so low?" The girl pointed to the sign above the store and said, "Whose wits, do you think, are sharper now?" "Is that what prompted your revenge?" asked the man. "Is that not enough? If you want me to help you out of this calamity, all you need to do is change your sign," she said, and went.

Wasting not a minute, the merchant took down his board and wrote in letters of gold, "Women's Wiles Beat Men's Wits." When the girl saw the new sign next day, she smiled. "Now I'll gladly help to save you from your present trouble," she said. "What you must do is this. Go to the Gypsy camp on the edge of the town and invite some twenty tinkers to bring their pipes and drums and come to your house in the evening. Tell them it is your wedding and that you want to celebrate with much noise and laughter. Let them wish you well and call you 'cousin.' You must also invite the *qadi* to be your guest at supper. When he asks, 'Who are these rough and noisy folk?' say, 'Honored uncle, he who denies his origins has none to boast of. These men are my cousins, for I am of Gypsy stock. But as you know, God has looked kindly on me, praise be to Him.' When he hears this news, he will surely demand a divorce."

The merchant did exactly what the blacksmith's daughter told him to. In the evening as he and the *qadi* sat together after their meal, a band of Gypsies suddenly burst into the house blowing their pipes, beating their drums, dancing and singing. They embraced the merchant and kissed his beard, shouting "God bless your match, O cousin!" Puzzled by all this movement, the *qadi* asked, "What does this mean, O my son?" The merchant said, "You have heard them, uncle, they are my cousins, coming to wish me well. He who disowns his ancestors has something to hide. I am what I am, and I have a *qadi* for a father-in-law, praise God!"

The *qadi* was enraged. "You never told me this before the marriage. I never would have given a daughter of mine to a tribe of Gypsies! You must divorce her—speak the words and I'll stand witness." "Had you asked me, I should have told you," said the merchant. "I value our kinship far too highly and I do not wish for divorce." "If I pay you back the bride-money, if I refund the expenses of the wedding?" said the *qadi*. But the merchant still refused. In fear and desperation the *qadi* finally said, "I shall pay you twice the sum you spent!" This time the merchant was persuaded. The *qadi* took his daughter home, and the merchant slept in peace the whole night through.

The first thing the merchant did when he woke up next morning was to go to the master blacksmith's shop. "I have come to ask for your daughter," he said. "I am willing to pay any sum you ask for her marriage settlement, but on this condition, that I see her first." "Has it ever happened that a man looked at his bride before the wedding?" the man objected. "I'll give

you a thousand dinars above her price if you let me see her," said the merchant. Hearing this offer, one of the blacksmiths looked up from his work and said, "Why not, O uncle? Is your daughter lame or bald, that you are afraid?" So the master blacksmith took the merchant home with him. He called to his daughter to bring in coffee. When she saw who sat with her father, she laughed and asked him the purpose of his visit. He told her, "To be quite certain that I am not tricked a second time."

So the notables of the town were assembled and the wedding of the merchant and the master blacksmith's daughter was celebrated amid great feasting and rejoicing. And the bride and the groom lived in happiness as pure as gold of twenty-four carats.

The Judgment
of the Qadi

Egypt

Once there was a bird catcher. Every day he went out after birds and waterfowl and sold them in the *suq* of the city. One time he caught a nice fat goose and decided that this one was for his own pleasure. He took it to the bakehouse, and the baker said, "What a good plump bird! It will take some time to roast. Come back after an hour."

Soon the *qadi* went walking past, sniffing the scent of the roasting goose. "What is this smell, brother?" he asked. And the baker said, "A goose, your honor, that I am baking for the bird catcher." "Listen to my opinion," said the *qadi*. "Why don't you bring it to my house as soon as it is ready, and we can both dine off it." "And what do I say to the owner?" "You can tell him that you were taking the goose out of the oven when it suddenly bit you and flew out through the door." "Doesn't he know that roast geese don't fly?" "If he is not satisfied, let him take you to the *qadi*. Believe me, you have nothing to worry about."

When the bird catcher came for his meal, the baker said, "What an unlucky day! And all because of you and your goose!" "Why so, brother?" "When it was good and done and I was bringing it out of the oven, it bit my hand and flew out the door!" complained the baker. "Are you mad?" said the bird catcher. "Since when do cooked geese fly? The truth is, you are nothing but a swindler and a thief, and this is a case for the *qadi*!" And he marched him off to court.

They had hardly walked the length of the street when a woman crossed their path. Seeing the bird catcher holding the baker by the collar so tightly that he was almost strangled, she said, "Leave the poor man alone!" She tried to separate them. In the scuffle the baker fell against her belly—which was high, for she was pregnant—and she miscarried. Now the woman's husband raged, "This is a matter for the courts! You have murdered my son!" And he seized the other side of the man's collar, and he and the bird catcher pulled the baker to the *qadi*'s house.

Just as they were passing in front of the Coptic church, the priest came out. Taking pity on the baker's state, he said, "Brothers, forgive him; do not do violence to him." All the while, the baker was fighting to free himself from the two men. Suddenly he wrenched his arm so forcefully that, accidentally knocking against the priest's eye, he blinded him. So now the priest joined the husband and the bird catcher and, holding the right-hand sleeve of the baker's gown, helped to drag him to the *qadi*.

An old man with a white beard rode by on his donkey. Looking down on them all, he said, "Lah! Lah! Have a heart, O people!" The baker turned to him for help, grabbing his donkey by the tail. But the donkey's tail came away in the baker's hand, and the old man spoke from the other side of his face. Jumping off his donkey, he clutched the baker's left sleeve and, with the priest and the husband and the bird catcher, hauled him towards the *qadi*'s court.

In front of the door of the mosque, hard by the *qadi*'s house, the baker quickly ducked and escaped into the crowd of people praying. The others were right behind him. Up the minaret steps he pelted, with the others on his heels. When he reached the top, he panicked: he jumped. And where did he land but on the back of a man who was bowing himself in prayer. He broke the man's neck, of course, and killed him. The dead man's brother, who had been praying by his side, sat on the baker till the others came. Then all five men, the brother and the old man and the priest and the husband and the bird catcher, took the baker before the *qadi*.

"Is anything troubling you, O people?" said the *qadi*. The bird catcher spoke first and told his story. The *qadi* cleared his throat and said, "Are you saying that geese don't fly?" "I am not a fool, your honor. I am saying only that roast geese, baked till they are brown and savory, are unable to fly." "Are you a Moslem?" asked the *qadi*. "Yes, your honor," said the man. "Do you believe that God is Almighty?" asked the *qadi*. "Yes, your honor." "Then why do you deny, O blasphemer!" said the *qadi*, "the truth of the holy Koran when it says that God can bring life even to bones that are decayed!" And he fined him ten dinars for his blasphemy.

Next the woman's husband explained his case. The *qadi* shook his turban from right to left. "It is a serious crime indeed to take the life of the innocent. The baker shall make just retribution. Come, O baker: take this woman home and return her to her husband only when she is pregnant, and in the same month as when you hurt her." "Wait, your honor," said the husband. "Maybe I do not need any more children after all." The *qadi* let him go, but not before he had fined him ten dinars for refusing the judgment of the court.

Now it was the turn of the priest. The *qadi* frowned on the baker and said, "Does not God say in His book, 'an eye for an eye and a tooth for a tooth'? Prepare yourself, O baker. But this is a Coptic priest, and a Moslem eye is worth two Christian eyes. Bestir yourself, O baker, and take out his other eye, so that he may get justice and blind you in one eye." The priest said, "Wait, your honor, I will be happy to forgo my rights and stay as I am." So the *qadi* sent him out, not forgetting to fine him first.

Then the brother of the dead man made his accusation. "Is there a worse crime than killing a Moslem as he kneels in prayer?" said the *qadi*. "Justice must be done! Those who have been wronged must be compensated! Go, O baker, and sit in the mosque, and let the dead man's brother jump from the top of the minaret onto your back. God grant him sweet revenge!" The plaintiff's mouth was dry. "Wait, your honor," he said. "Though it is my right, I am content to give it up." "First give up ten dinars in payment of your fine," said the *qadi*. And the man went out.

The old man with the white beard who owned the donkey had been listening all this while. Slowly he began to edge his way out of the courtroom. When he was near the door, he heard the *qadi* call, "Isn't it your turn next?" So he ran out of the building, shouting, "Your honor, my donkey was born without a tail!"

The Talking
Turkeys

Syria

Once when the sultan was sick, he did not leave the palace for thirty days. Finally he recovered and felt well enough to step out. Now, it happened that a sly old woman saw him and hurried into the women's reception hall to congratulate the queen on her husband's regained health.

As she was sitting in the queen's presence, the old woman noticed that there were about a hundred turkeys in the courtyard outside the window. So she said to the sultan's wife, "O queen of our time, can these birds of yours talk?" Naturally, the queen said, "No." "If you let me have them for sixty nights, I'll teach them to speak in seven tongues," said the old woman. The queen agreed to have the birds trained. "But," said the old woman, "I shall need provisions to feed them. One hundred sacks of flour, one measure of nuts, one measure of sugar, and so much of this and so much of that." The queen agreed. She gave the order, and they brought what the old woman had asked for.

When the sixty days were almost past, the old woman went to the queen looking very distressed. She said, "These birds of yours are saying strange things, and much as I beat them they will not change their song." "What are they saying?" asked the queen. "They say: 'Tsk! Tsk! The sultan's daughter has a lover!'" said the old woman. The queen now looked distressed. "Kill them at once," she said. "And whatever you do, don't bring them back to the palace!"

The old woman obeyed the queen. She kept the turkeys in her house, dining on them herself and cooking some of them for her son's wedding feast.

The Weaver's Dream

Iraq

O you who love the prophet, say,
"God bless him and grant him salvation!"

There was or there was not a caliph who sent his crier through the city to proclaim, "Let those of you who are present inform those who are absent that none may kindle a light tonight by order and command of the caliph." The sun set and the caliph and his minister went down into the town in disguise. They wandered up and down the streets and markets, and all was dark. Only when they came to an outlying *suq* did they see a lamp lighting a weaver sitting at his loom.

"Peace!" they said. "On you be peace!" the weaver greeted them in return. "Did you not hear the caliph's crier say that no light may be lit tonight?" they asked. "What do I care for the caliph?" said the weaver. "Will he be sending me food tomorrow if I don't weave and earn my living tonight?" "Why not work in the daytime rather than at night?" asked the visitors. "Because I do as I please," said the weaver, and returning to his bench, he hummed and sang to himself as he wove. The visitors sat down next to him and eventually the weaver's head fell upon his work in sleep, but they did not move. The man started in his sleep and awoke. "What, are you still here?" he asked. "Such a strange vision—I must have been asleep and dreaming." "Tell us your dream," said the caliph. But the weaver did not wish it, and the two men left him.

The next day dawned. Two soldiers came for the weaver, and each seized him by one shoulder and brought him before the caliph. "Peace!" said the caliph. "On you be peace," the weaver replied. "You who did not mind the crier's words and lit your lamp last night! Do you know who the men were that came and sat next to you as you worked?" "No, by Allah, I saw two men like other men," said the weaver. "It was I with my minister," the caliph informed him. "Now will you tell me your dream?" "My dream has gone where dreams go," said the weaver. "But did you summon me because of my dream or my light?" "Throw him into the dungeon," ordered the caliph. "Let his daily ration be one can of water and a crust of bread!"

But the weaver was not subdued. He sat in his prison and cupped a hand behind his ear and loudly sang all the odes and songs that he could sing so well. Now, the domed room of the caliph's only daughter was built over the dungeons, and she could hear the weaver's melodies every day. Soon she asked her father whom he was keeping in the prison. "It is a young man called Mohammad, a weaver," the caliph replied. So she sent her maid for a mason and, when he bowed before her, saying, "I am here for you to command!" she asked, "Can you carve me a secret passageway down into the dungeon?" "May my head and eyes be forfeit if I don't," he said.

After it was dark, the princess told her maid, "Go and wake Mohammad the weaver." The maid took a lantern and descended into the prison. "Who are you?" asked the weaver when he saw her standing over him with a lighted torch in her hand. "I serve the caliph's only daughter. She says, 'Let him come up now, now, immediately.'" "My lady, I and the caliph's daughter are as like as 'come' and 'go.' What have we to do together? She must be planning some mischief for me." So the maid returned and reported, "He said, 'I and the caliph's daughter are as like as a rose and a weed; what have we to do with each other?'" "Go tell him that if he does not come quickly, I shall have him hanged tomorrow." This time when the maid came for him, Mohammad put himself under the protection of Allah and followed her.

The caliph's daughter smiled. "Welcome, a thousand welcomes! The bath is ready and the water is hot and here is a shirt for sleeping in." Sweet syrups were poured into glasses and the food was served in all its colors and varieties. Our friend the weaver set all five fingers working, thinking to himself, "I'm like the beggar shivering in the cold who stumbled on a heap of gold!" When he had satisfied his appetite and washed his hands with rose water, the princess said, "Now let me hear some of your songs." And he sang for her till the middle of the night. Then she put a sword into the

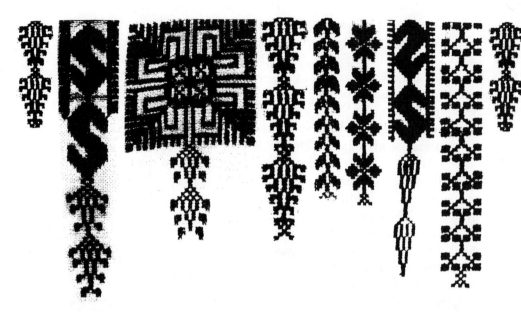

middle of her bed and invited him to sleep beside her. So they slept like that, with the sword between them, until the maid brought them tea and sugared quince in the morning. The weaver returned to his cell, but every night thereafter he climbed up to the princess's room as before. Every week when the caliph called for the weaver and asked about his dream, the weaver said, "I shall not speak." "Look how he flourishes on his diet of bread and water," observed the caliph. "His cheeks are like a rose!" "O caliph, it is not my food that makes me thus. My vigor comes through the blessing of God," said the weaver. And down to the dungeon he went again.

You should know that there was a neighboring sultan who liked to get the best of his rival the caliph whenever he could. One day he sent two apples of one size and one color with a riddle written on them: "Which is this year's and which is last year's fruit? Guess correctly and you shall have five of our provinces to add to your kingdom." The caliph sent for every wise man in the land, but none could guess. The princess said, "Mohammad, only you are left to guess the riddle. My father will come to you and say, 'I shall give you a house and I shall give you a wage if you tell me which is this year's and which is last year's fruit.' Tell him, 'If Allah lets me guess the truth, all I want you to give me is the princess your daughter.' " "But what if I fail to guess?" asked the weaver.

"Oh, but I shall tell you the secret of the riddle," said the princess. "Last year's apple is dry and light and it will float in water, but this year's apple will sink to its middle and dance. Go, and trust in God."

Not one hour passed before they came for the weaver and said, "Rise up; the caliph wants you." As soon as the caliph saw him enter, he said, "Tell me your dream, O weaver." "Have you called me, O caliph (may your life be long and your days be happy) to ask about my dream or about something else?" returned Mohammad. "Perhaps the dungeon suits you," said the caliph. "By Allah, that it does," said the weaver. "All the same, I offer you a house with a compound around it and a monthly salary brought to your door if you can take these apples and guess which is this year's and which is last year's fruit." "If Allah permits me to guess the truth all I want from you is the princess your daughter as my wife." A flush of anger darkened the caliph's face, and the weaver added, "It is as you wish. Do not give me the princess and I shall not guess." Here the *wazirs* bent round the caliph and whispered, "You will lose five provinces!" So the caliph agreed to the terms. "For the gift to be sure and certain, it must be solemnized with a reading of the Fatiha prayer like other marriage contracts," insisted the weaver. So the sweet drinks for the onlookers were prepared, and the Fatiha was read, and the contract was written out, and everyone present stood as witness.

Mohammad had said, "Bring me two basins full of water." And he placed one of the sultan's apples in one basin and one in the other. On the apple that hung deep in the water and danced he wrote, "This year's apple," and on the one that floated high he wrote, "Last year's fruit." And the caliph sent the apples back to the sultan, and the sultan gave him the five provinces that were the prize. And Mohammad the weaver? Well, he was thrown back into his dungeon.

Seven days went by, and the sultan challenged the caliph a second time. He sent two mares of the same height and color and equal in beauty of proportion, with the message, "Guess which is the mother and which the foal, and you win ten provinces of my land." The caliph asked everyone in his kingdom, but no one knew the answer. Then the *wazirs* said, "Do not tire yourself with searching. Let him who guessed the apples also guess this riddle of the horses."

The princess again warned Mohammad. "Early tomorrow, when my father will call for you," she told him, "say, 'I shall not guess until you settle a sum on my bride.' " "And if I cannot guess?" asked Mohammad. "I shall tell you the answer," said the princess, and explained what he must do to solve the riddle.

He hadn't been back in his prison one hour before he was told to go up to the caliph. "Speak, and tell us your dream!" was the first thing the ruler said to him. "Have you brought me here to recount my dream or for some other purpose?" asked Mohammad. "I want you to tell me which of these two mares is the mother and which the daughter," said the caliph. "I am willing to guess this riddle, but first you must settle a dowry on the princess, who is my bride." The caliph looked vexed, but his *wazirs* hastened to say, "You gave him your daughter and we were witnesses. Why refuse the dowry at the risk of losing ten provinces?" So the caliph complied with Mohammad's wish.

"Bring me barley," said the weaver. "Clean it and husk it and pour it into two nose bags. Tie the bags to the necks of the two mares and let them be ridden for one hour." When the men brought back the mares after their ride, Mohammad went up to the first one and saw that her heart was calm, resting in its place, that her flanks were dry and her nose bag empty. On her bridle he wrote, "This is the foal." As for the other mare, her heart was throbbing and her neck bathed in sweat, while a quarter of her barley was left uneaten. "This is the mother," wrote Mohammad. Then the mares were returned, and the sultan signed over ten provinces to the caliph, adding that he wanted to meet the guesser.

"The sultan has requested your presence!" the princess informed Mohammad. "He will surely test you further. But I know his wiles and will tell you how to save yourself. Take my thimble and my needle, these scissors, and a bag of sand." And she furnished him with all the necessary knowledge.

The caliph ordered, "Accompany the weaver to the bath. Have the wardrobe master measure his size and clothe him in fine stuffs." And with music preceding and a crowd of the city people and the caliph following behind, Mohammad was escorted to the ship on which he was to travel.

When Mohammad arrived in the sultan's country, he was met with drums and pipes and joyful clamor. The sultan stood on the bank with his soldiers and the *wazirs* and his pashas and the emirs. For a week there were banquets and entertainments, and in every house Mohammad was welcomed as an honored guest. On the eighth day the sultan said, "I should like us to walk about a little and keep each other company while we take the air." "I am willing," said Mohammad. Their steps led them some way from the palace near a black hill. Pointing to it, the sultan asked, "Could you cut me a cloak out of that hill?" "Yes," said Mohammad, "and while I am doing that, here is some sand. Will you spin me some thread out of it to sew the coat with?" And he gave the sultan the bag of sand he had brought from the princess. Mohammad walked about for a while. Then he returned to the sultan and asked, "Have you finished making the thread?" "How am I to spin thread out of sand?" complained the sultan. "And how am I to cut a cloak out of a rocky hill?" asked Mohammad. The sultan laughed and told him "I want you among my kin: you may have my daughter for your bride."

From the early morning of the next day, the guest halls of the palace were opened to receive the well-wishers. The drums began to sound, and the whole city was invited to celebrate the giving of the sultan's daughter to Mohammad. "I shall not marry her here, but in my own country," said Mohammad. So all the things that a wife takes from her father's house to her husband's house were made ready, and Mohammad and his bride traveled to the caliph's city. There amid much rejoicing, Mohammad was married in the same week to both the sultan's daughter and the caliph's daughter.

One day Mohammad was sitting with one bride on one knee and the other on his other knee. The caliph entered, saw him thus, and laughed a great laugh. "Now you must tell me your dream," he said. "Yes," said Mohammad, "now I shall tell you my dream on the night you and your minister sat next to me. As I slept, I dreamed that I had the sun on my right shoulder and the moon on my left shoulder. And so it has come about. Here is your daughter, as golden as the sun, and the sultan's daughter, as radiant as the moon. Praise be to God."

May you live long and remain well.

The Cure

Syria

An old widow had only one son. When he grew to be a man she found him a bride, but she was jealous of her daughter-in-law and began to complain of imaginary sicknesses. Every day she would nag her son and say, "Bring me the doctor, my boy. Let the doctor come." The son did nothing for a while, but eventually he gave in and went to fetch the doctor. While he was out, the widow washed herself and lined her eyes with *kohl*. She put on her best gown and wound a sash of silk about her waist. She donned a velvet vest and her daughter-in-law's wedding headdress and placed an embroidered kerchief over it. Then she sat and waited. When the doctor arrived and asked for his patient, the son showed him in and said, "There she is. It is my mother. Since the moment I was married she has been grumbling like a hen, and not one day has brought her joy or pleasure." "This lady needs a husband," said the doctor. "But she is my mother!" "Yes," said the doctor, "and she needs a groom." "She is over ninety years old! Surely she can't be thinking of marriage again!" "You are wrong, my son," said the doctor. "As often as her skirts are lifted by the wind, the thought of a bridegroom enters her mind." "Sir," said the son, "If she had wanted a husband, she could have married long ago. Why don't you examine her and see what is the matter with her." "I have already told you what is wrong." At this the old woman sprang up from her corner and said to her son, "My boy, may you find favor in the sight of God, do you fancy yourself a greater expert than the wise doctor?"

When Twice as Many Is Half the Trouble

Palestine

A man from a village near here had a wife who was very contrary. One day he decided to plow around his fig trees, which grew on a rocky slope outside the village. His wife had not yet baked bread that morning, so he said to her, "I am going up to the grove. Bring me my breakfast as quickly as you can." Then he went to do his plowing. Well, the morning passed, noonday prayer time came and went, and the afternoon waned, and still his wife had not shown her face. The poor man's girdle was slipping halfway down his hips for lack of nourishment. It was not till the end of the day as he was about to unyoke his oxen that his wife finally appeared.

As she came within earshot he called to her, "Bring the dish over to me." "No, let's stay over here, near this stump," she answered. A little later he asked, "Did you bring the water jar?" "I did not have time to fill it," she said. Well, after the poor man ate what there was to eat, he got up to go home. "Will you bring me my coat? It is hanging on that tree," he said.

"I will not bring it," she said. "I'm not going back for it either, by God," said the man angrily, and he hurried back to the village.

Without saying a word to his wife, the man went straight to the men's gathering place and sent for his kinsmen. When they had all come, he said, "Cousins, I live under the protection of God and you, my relatives." "O Abu Hasan, you are welcome, we are here to help you," they said. "O my cousins, my wife, may God forgive her, has done so and so and so. I need bride-money so that I can take another wife." The cousins gave him the money he asked for, one slapping down three hundred, another four, one a thousand even, and so on. The man knotted the coins into his kerchief and, accompanied by his kinsmen, went to the house of the oil merchant, who had a young daughter just the right age for marriage. The merchant agreed to give his daughter, and that night in her father's house she became Abu Hasan's second wife.

Next morning, dressed in an embroidered silk gown, her arms and feet ornamented with patterns in henna dye, the gold coins of her wedding headdress jingling with every step, the new bride followed her husband home. Driving his yoke of oxen before him and with his new wife following behind, Abu Hasan went to finish his plowing. He set her to work in the field, and the young bride had just begun to weed the grape vines growing between the fig trees, when Abu Hassan's first wife came into the orchard. Not knowing what had passed the night before, she said to the oil merchant's daughter, "What are you doing in my husband's field? Are you trying to take over?" "I am doing nothing wrong, sister," said the bride. "He is my husband as well. Last night he slept in my bed." When she heard this, the first wife was filled with terror. Was he going to divorce her?

Just then Abu Hasan turned to the bride and said, "Hand me my coat. It is hanging on that fig tree over there." Off she went, running lightly on her toes. But the first wife, biting on the front hem of her gown to give her legs more freedom, raced her to it. At the same moment the two women caught hold of the coat and struggled, each wanting to be the one to carry it back. With his eyes laughing and singing a love song the while, Abu Hasan unsheathed his knife and cut his coat down the middle. "That is the end of you," he said to his coat, "but of my problems too!"

The Gown in
the Bathhouse

Egypt

Three women, merchants' wives, went to the *hammam* together to bathe. As they were washing they noticed hanging up in the bathhouse keeper's room a gown with gold thread woven into the cloth. When they had finished, one of the women said to the *hammamjiyeh*, "Will you sell me that gown?" Her friend said, "No, sell it to me. My eye has been on it from the moment I entered the *hammam*!" And the third told them that she too had been admiring it and wanted to buy it. The *hammamjiyeh* did not know which of the three to sell it to, and in the end she said, "I'll tell you who should get the gown. Let each of you tell me about a trick she has played on her husband, and I'll make a present of the dress to the one whose scheme was the most successful!" So they sent for tea and sat down together.

The first lady said, "When I was a new bride, my husband was so afraid I might deceive him that he built a house with no windows onto the street. Every day when he left for his warehouse, he locked the front door and took the key with him. One day I was weary to the end of my nose with this life, and I longed to trick my husband as no one had ever been tricked before. I pushed all the furniture in the room against the wall and climbed up to the loft and out on the roof. As I was gazing down into the alley at all the passersby going and coming, I caught sight of a handsome young man who looked merry. I called, 'How are you, O youth?' 'Wishing to pay compliments to the mistress of my heart and the light of my eyes,' he replied, and he was smiling. 'Open your door so that I may come and visit you.' I explained to him how carefully my husband locked me in every day, and he said, 'Never mind! I'll find a way.' In a very short while he had knotted rope into a ladder, shinned up the outside wall, and climbed onto the roof. He sat with me from morning until noon and after.

"Just before midafternoon prayers, my husband came home with a watermelon under each arm. I went down and said to him, 'This is no supper. We need meat. People eat melon to sweeten their mouths after food.' He went out, locking the door, and down to the *suq* to find meat. Then quickly

I climbed back onto the roof and instructed the youth to bring me three fishes from the shop and go, since my husband was coming home. He did what I asked, and I took the fishes, made a slit in the side of one melon, and stuffed them into it. Soon I heard the rattle of the lock. My husband walked in with meat and eggs for his supper, but I said, 'I don't feel like cooking. Look, it's after sunset already.' 'Give me the melon, then,' he said. 'I'll eat that.' He cut open the melon, and there were the fishes inside. 'O Lord our Protector!' I cried. 'What is this?' And he said, 'Wife, since when do fishes grow inside melons!' Then I praised God, saying, 'Glory to the Creator for all His creations!'

"Well, the next day at noon my husband brought home some of his fellow merchants. They rested awhile, then my husband called to me in the kitchen, 'Wife, fry us some of the fish we found in the melon we cut open last night.' And I said to him in a low voice, 'Hss! Be silent; are you not ashamed! Whoever heard of fishes inside watermelons?' 'But you were with me when we took the fish out of the melon, O my wife!' 'O, it must have been a dream,' I said. He called for the second melon and cut it open, and of course there were no fish inside. Without going on too long, say I made some lunch for the men, who were happy to still their bellies.

"When they left, my husband came to me and said, 'Swear that you will tell the truth: were there or were there not fishes in the melon we cut open yesterday?' And I said yes, that there had been. 'Then why did you deny it in front of my friends?' he asked. 'Because I didn't want them to think that you were mad, O my husband, for it has never happened that fish grew inside melons!' I replied. 'How did the fish get into yesterday's watermelon, then?'

" 'I'll tell you a story,' I said. 'There was a man who was so afraid his wife would deceive him that he built a house with no windows onto the street. And every morning he locked the front door and took the key when he went out. But his wife found a way to bring a friend into the house, and it was he who bought her the three fishes. This is a warning to you, O husband, who fear the wiles of women! This is but the least of my schemes!' And since that day he has not done anything against my wishes.

"This is the trick I played on my husband. Was it successful?" the woman asked of the bath keeper when she finished.

"Let us hear what your friends have to tell, then we will judge it," said the bath keeper, and the second woman began. "My husband's trading was with another city and often he was obliged to undertake long journeys, leaving me alone in the house. The children of Adam are sinners, and in his absence I took a lover. One day my husband returned much sooner than

I expected. My lover and I were in the middle of eating when we heard him at the entrance door. What were we to do? Without thinking, I opened my big chest and pushed my lover in. I had just banged the lid shut when my husband walked into the room.

" 'Welcome and twice welcome!' I said. 'You have come as if by appointment! The food is on the table and two healths to you!' He sat down and tore off a piece of bread to dip into the dish—when what did he see? He saw that the food had been touched on both sides of the plate. 'Two hands have dipped into this dish,' he said, anger reddening his face. 'Who was eating with you, wife?' I swore that there was no one, but he searched the house and opened the chest, and there was my lover in all his height and breadth. 'Fine,' said my husband, locking the chest with my lover inside it, 'I am going for some porters to carry this chest to the governor's palace. Then we shall see what you have to say.' No sooner had he left than I opened the chest with another key and let my lover out. In his place I put a baby donkey that I bought off a shepherd who was passing in front of the house.

"Soon my husband appeared with two porters, who loaded the chest on their shoulders. We all went to the palace, and my husband spoke to the governor: 'The earth belongs to God—praise be to Him!—and the government to the sultan! The one who is in this chest was with my wife. I caught him! What is to be done?' The governor ordered the men to open the chest, and there was the young donkey, which began to bray. 'A curse on you!' said the governor to my husband. 'Is this a mockery of our government, or are you out of your senses?' And then he said to me, 'Is he mad? Shall we take him to the madhouse?' And they began to tie chains about my husband's neck. 'I swear by Allah I shall never accuse you of anything again!' cried my husband with tears in his eyes, for now he was almost dead with fright. So I said to the governor, 'O my master, if you will bear witness to this oath and protect me if he breaks it, I am willing to take him home. He only suffers these mad seizures every few years.' So they ordered my husband to be freed, and he has been like wet clay in my hand ever since. How do you judge this for a trick?"

The bathhouse keeper was astonished, but she said, "Let us listen to the last one." And the third woman took up the tale. "Once when my husband was tired and feeling limp as a wick in the lamp, unable to stand on his feet, he closed his warehouse—he was a leather merchant—and came home to rest. I was here in the bathhouse getting ready to receive my lover, having cooked and prepared for him a sheep's stomach, which was what he liked to eat. Good. Not finding me in the house, my husband pulled down the bedding so that he could stretch himself out. He gave the mattress a tug, and down it came, and the pot with the sheep's stomach too, for that is where I had hidden it. 'In Allah's name, what have we here?' he said, uncovering the pot. Now the smell of spices filled his nose. He tasted the food. 'This is delicious, by Allah,' he said. One bite and another bite, and soon he had eaten the whole thing.

Wait a bit, and his stomach began to ache. Aach! What a pain! That's how I found him—the bedding spread on the floor and my husband twisting himself and groaning from the pinching of his belly. 'What happened?' I asked him, and he told me. 'Don't say that you ate what was in the pot, man!' I cried. 'That was a special medicine for pregnancy.' 'Lah! Lah! Lah!' said my husband, moaning. 'Now, don't worry!' I said. 'As soon as you are delivered, you will feel no more pain!'

"And I left him and ran to the midwife. Folding ten dinars into her palm, I said, 'Find me a two-day-old infant. The reason I need it is such and such and such.' Early next morning, in she came to my husband. 'God's name be upon you, brother,' she said, 'this is nothing to be afraid of. If Allah wills it, it may be a boy!' She lifted the covers and placed the child under him and pinched the baby to make it cry. 'Yih! God give you joy in your son! God keep him well for you!' she said, and began to trill lululey as women do when a boy is born.

"But my husband, he was so filled with horror and shame at what had happened to him that he crept out of the house and fled the city, not daring to show his face. So I brought my lover to live beside me, and for five years, eating and drinking, we were happy and carefree. Then one day, when I was sitting in the window, whom do I see in the distance, walking toward the house? My husband! Running and running, I went out from the back of the house, rounded up the street children, and said, 'This shilling will be yours if you do this and this and this.'

"As soon as my husband came near the children, they began to fight and hit each other. Naturally my husband tried to make peace and separate them.

But the youngest said, 'If I were a little bigger, I should have shown them! But I was born the year that the leather merchant became pregnant and gave birth to a boy.' 'Is that story still traveling the rounds?' said my husband, and he turned about and went back the way he had come. The boys got their shilling, and here I am, as happy as a woman can be. What do you say to my trick?"

Then the bathhouse keeper said, "I am not selling the gown to any one of you—you are all daughters of sin, and your tricks make the brain whirl till it is dizzy!" So she played them the worst trick and took down the gown and put it into her own chest and kept it for herself.

A Lion the Color of Yellow Silk

Iraq

A man got married and was living happily when—God keep us from bad news—his friend came and told him, "O my brother, I have heard the people talking. They say that your wife is not faithful." "People like to tell lies, brother," replied the husband. "I am only repeating what I have heard," said the other. "I speak only out of concern for you, brother; what benefit can it be to me?" Then he went on, "But why don't you find out the truth for yourself? Tell your wife that you have to travel to the city, but come back and hide where you can watch what she does in your absence." And that is what the man did. His wife packed food for his journey and he went out, shutting the house door behind him.

When the coast was clear, he quickly crept back into the yard and hid. Soon he heard his wife send the servant out to her lover who was a cloth merchant. "Tell him to bring a length of yellow silk cloth and come," she said. The merchant came running, and the woman entertained him and sent him away, throwing the silk over the rope on which she hung her clothes.

Next the woman sent the maid to her lover who was a poultry farmer.

"Tell him to bring a brace of plucked pigeons and come," she said. The man arrived in a very short time, carrying his present in his hand. The woman entertained him and sent him away, putting the two birds into a bowl on the shelf.

Finally the servant girl received orders to go to the woman's third lover, who kept an eating house. "Tell him that I am in the mood for a dish of ground meat broiled on the spit." The man soon appeared with a basketful of skewers of ground meat *kebab*.

As soon as the eating-house keeper left, the husband came out of his hiding place. "Oh," said his wife, "are you back so soon, O father of my children?" "Yes, by Allah, O mother of my sons," said her husband. "I had hardly got beyond the last houses of the village when I met a lion the color of the yellow silk hanging with your clothes. Had I not been as light-footed as the two birds in the dish on the shelf, I should have been reduced to minced meat—like the *kebab* on the skewer in your basket."

As soon as she heard these words, the woman's limbs stiffened and her face became the color of saffron. "What are you saying, husband?" she cried. "I am saying that I have found you out. I was hiding in the yard while you were feasting and entertaining." And he pulled out his dagger and stabbed her to death.

The Sultan's Camp Follower

Iraq

In one of the furthest provinces of the land there lived a saddlemaker with his three daughters. He owned his house and his shop and lived off what he earned through his skill. In time he saved one hundred gold coins. When he thought about where to hide them, he decided to sew them into the saddle that he was stitching.

One day a mountain herdsman came to buy a saddle. Only after the man had left did the saddler realize that he had given him the saddle with the gold in it. What could he do? Nothing. So he kept his grief in his heart and said not a word to anyone. However, from that time, as he worked and tooled his leather, he hummed these words:

> It has gone and I'm to blame.
> What it is I cannot name.

A year later the same herdsman brought the saddle back to the saddler's shop and said, "It is worn in some places. Can you patch it for me?" The saddler was overjoyed and promised to have it ready the next day. Without losing a moment, he cut the seams, shook out his hundred pieces of gold, and began to sing,

> Long ago it left me,
> What it is I'll not betray.
> Now again it's found me,
> What it is I'll never say.

And thereafter, this became the saddler's song while he worked. One day when the sultan rode through that part of the *suq*, he heard the tune and puzzled over it. So he called the saddler and asked him its meaning. The saddler's only answer was to sing, "I'll never say!" The sultan questioned him once, twice, and a third time, but received the same reply. Then the ruler grew angry. "How many daughters do you have?" he inquired. "Three, *maulana*," said the saddler, with proper respect. "Then I wish to see them pregnant before the palace gates tomorrow morning," ordered the sultan. "They are virgins, *maulana*," said the saddler, "How can virgins be pregnant?" "If I do not see them pregnant tomorrow morning, I shall cut off your head," said the sultan, and rode away.

Sunk in care, the saddler walked slowly to his house. His youngest daughter noticed how dejected he was and asked the cause. "My child, the sultan has commanded me to bring you and your sisters to him pregnant, or he will have my head!" said her father. "That is a simple request, Father. Buy me three earthenware water jars, and I shall show the sultan how virgins can be pregnant." When he did as she said, she tied one jar round her own waist under her gown and bade her sisters do the same. And in this guise the three girls filed past the palace gate the next day.

"How many months are you with child?" the sultan asked the eldest girl. "Three, *maulana*," she told him. "And what do you crave?" "Cucumbers steeped in brine," said the girl. Then he put his question to the middle sister, and she said, "Six months, and what I crave is eggplant pickled in vinegar." When it was the turn of the youngest daughter, she told the sultan, "This month is my month, and I have a longing for fish roasted under the seven seas." "How can fish be roasted under the sea?" protested the sultan. "In the same way that a virgin can be pregnant!" replied the girl.

The sultan said nothing and sent the girls home. But on the following day he summoned an old woman who served as a marriage broker and handed her a purse of one hundred gold liras. "Go to the saddler's house and ask for the hand of his youngest daughter," he commanded.

The old woman slipped two of the gold coins into her own pocket and set off on her mission. It was the youngest daughter who opened the door when she knocked. "I want to speak to your mother," said the old woman. "My mother has gone to change one into two," said the girl. "Then let me have two words with your oldest sister," the old woman said. "She has gone to change black into white." "And your middle sister?" "She is plucking roses." "At this time of year there are no flowers," said the old woman, "but here is a purse that the sultan has sent you; take it." When the youngest daughter had examined the contents, she said, "Ask the sultan this: when a man makes a present of a lamb, does he cut off its tail?"

The old woman returned to the sultan and reported everything that the girl had said, though she understood nothing of it. She added that the saddler's daughter was mad; but the sultan was wiser. "To change one into two," he said, "means that her mother is a midwife and went to assist at a birth. To change black into white means that the sister is a ladies' maid and has the skill of removing body hair. And to pluck roses in the winter means that the other sister is a needlewoman and embroiders roses in silk.

This is no madwoman but a girl fit to be a sultan's wife! You may keep the gold pieces you stole from my purse, but do not steal again, for that was the meaning of cutting off the lamb's tail." The old woman slipped away in fear and shame, and the sultan did what was necessary to make the saddler's youngest daughter his wife.

But the sultan's bride became his wife only in name, for while she awaited him in the bridal chamber, he was off to war. He sent word that he must lead his armies to the land of Siin in far-off China. Before the wedding night he was gone.

The saddler's daughter did not mourn or wait for her husband's return. The next day she assembled an army of her own, changed her clothes to those of a man, and rode after the sultan. Setting up her tents not far from his camp, she faced him across a river as if she were an enemy. In the evening she sent a messenger challenging him to a game of chess. To while away the time he played, and she won his dagger off him. They played again, and this time the sultan won and asked for his dagger back. But she said, "I have a Kurdish girl in my camp, a virgin; let me send her to you this night instead." The sultan agreed, never suspecting who the chess player really was.

That night the girl put on her women's robes and let down her perfumed hair and took herself to the sultan's tent. At dawn she left him and in her man's disguise led her army home again. Nine months later she gave birth to a boy and called him Siin.

After two years the sultan rode back victorious from the wars, but he did not linger many days. He came to his wife's chamber only to say, "I must go beyond the land of Siin to Masiin. I promise that we shall be man and wife on my return."

Once again the girl, wearing the clothes of a man, followed her husband with an army of her own. And as before, she camped nearby and passed an evening with him at chess. This time she won his prayer beads of precious amber. And when he won the second game and asked for their return, she said, "I own a Kurdish slave who has only known a man once. She is beautiful, and I am ready to let her sleep with you tonight." The sultan was willing, and the girl spent the night in the sultan's tent as before and disappeared with her army next morning. This time when she gave birth to a son, she called him Masiin.

The sultan's army returned laden with spoils after more than a year, and still the sultan thirsted for further victories. Without resting he told his bride, "I have decided to travel west to the land of Gharb. This will be my last campaign and I shall be your husband when I return."

A few days later, the saddler's daughter prepared her army and set out for the land of Gharb. She camped opposite the sultan's tent and invited him to try and beat her at chess. She won the first game and took his headcloth, and he won the second game and accepted the favors of her slave. Once more she adorned herself in women's finery and shared the sultan's bed, then dressed herself as a man and guided her soldiers home. When her time came, she gave birth to a girl, to whom she gave the name of Gharb.

Three years passed, and then the sultan turned toward home. But this time he did not approach the bridal chamber, for he had decided to marry his father's brother's daughter, as is the custom, and abandon the saddler's daughter. Sheep were slaughtered for the banquet, and the notes of the horn and the throbbing of the drums began to sound in celebration of the coming wedding between the sultan and his cousin.

Now the saddler's daughter could not sit still. She called her three children and dressed them carefully. She gave the eldest the sultan's dagger to carry, slipped the amber prayer beads round the second son's neck, and tied the sultan's headcloth round her daughter's hair. Then she taught them to sing this song:

> We're going to the sultan's wedding
> To join the feast and laughter!
> Who in the palace will be guessing
> That we are his two sons and daughter?

Holding each other by the hand, the three children lisped the verse as they were brought into the sultan's presence. When he heard the words they were chanting and saw one boy carrying his own dagger, another wearing his precious amber prayer beads, and a little girl wrapped in the cloth he used to wear on his head, he asked, "Who is your mother?" They led him to the saddler's daughter, and the sultan immediately understood all that had happened in the long years while he was absent. He said,

> After all the eating and drinking,
> Even after the deed has been done,
> Draw a line both black and winking
> Of wedding *kohl* though the hour has gone.

And he sent his cousin back to her father and at last married the saddler's daughter, the mother of his three children.

> So there we left them, and home we came.
> And then we never saw them again.

The Woman Whose Husband Went to Mecca

Palestine

A man once left his wife and his son Mohammad and went on the pilgrimage to Mecca. His absence was long, but after three or four years he finally returned. His wife ran out and kissed his hands. He gave her dates and henna dye, which he had brought from Mecca, and called his son Mohammad. The boy came running, and his father fed him sweet dates. Whereupon another boy came running and said, "What about me?" The man said, "Wife, who is this child?" "Why, this is your son, who was born after you left," said the woman. "But didn't I leave you with Mohammad still sucking at your breast?" "No," she said, "this second boy is yours from the night before you set out on the Hajj." "Good," he said, "but what about this one?" and he pointed to a third child." "This is his brother, who came after him." "O you daughter of accursed parents!" said the man. "I'll grant that the second is mine, but where did this dwarf come from?" She began to explain, stammering and stumbling over her words, when she was interrupted by an infant's cry from the cradle.

The man's blood rushed to his face and his frown was terrible. "Well!?" he shouted. "O this poor little thing is still in swaddling bands," she said. "Surely you are not going to count him against me too!"

The Three
Mohammads

Tunisia

A wealthy merchant lay on his bed and, knowing that death was near, called his three sons to his side. Now, all his days he had been a man who fasted and prayed and stood in fear of his God, and when each of his sons was born, he had named the child Mohammad. The three Mohammads came to kiss their father's hand, and the merchant spoke to them about his will. "Mohammad shall inherit," he said, "and Mohammad shall inherit. But Mohammad shall not inherit." Then he turned his face and died.

For seven days the boys mourned their father, and for another seven days respect held back their tongues and no word was said about inheritance. But then they argued, and they asked who was the Mohammad who must not inherit. Although they were each cleverer than the next, they could not solve the riddle. In the end the sheikh advised them to seek the judgment of the *qadi*, whose years and wisdom had made him famous among judges.

So the three brothers set off walking to the *qadi*'s court. When they had gone halfway they stopped at a grassy place to rest. "A camel rested here who had no tail," said the oldest brother, looking around him. "A one-eyed camel," said the second brother. And the third said, "It was laden with fat on one side and something sweet on the other."

They continued their journey, and soon they saw a man advancing with a camel stick in his hand. "Have you lost your camel?" they asked. "Yes, not an hour ago it broke away!" said the man. "Was it missing its tail?" asked the first brother. "Yes, yes," said the man. "And blind in one eye?" asked the second. "Yes, that is my camel!" said the man. "Was it carrying fat on one side and a sweet load on the other?" asked the third. "Indeed yes, a load of boiled butter and date syrup! Tell me where it is, and may Allah reward you." "May God restore it to you," said the oldest brother. "We have not seen your camel." "O shameless ones, you have stolen my camel; how can you deny it?" wailed the man. "I shall accuse you before the *qadi*." "That is where we are going at this moment," said the brothers.

"Come with us and let us lay the matter before him." Of course the man consented.

In the time four men arrived at the *qadi*'s door. After greetings, business: the *qadi* asked what brought them. "These three young men have stolen my camel!" the owner cried. When he repeated all that happened, the *qadi* said, "In justice and rightness, you should give the camel back to its owner." "As God is our witness," said the brothers, "we have not stolen it nor do we have it now." "Then how were you able to describe my beast to me just as it is—tailless and one-eyed and carrying fat and syrup?" shouted the camel owner. "Yes," said the *qadi*, "how can you know that a camel has no tail if you have not seen it?" "Well," said the oldest brother, "on our way to consult your honor on a difficulty of our own, we came to a place where the grass grows high by the side of the road and said, 'Let us rest our feet.' Seeing that some of the grass was flattened in a certain way, I knew that a camel had rested there. But where a camel's tail switches from side to side and pushes down the grass, the blades stood tall. So I guessed that on this animal there was no tail."

"And in what way could you tell that it lacked one eye?" the *qadi* asked. "Where the camel had rested," the second brother said, "on one side the grass was cropped to the ground and on the other it remained untouched. This made me think that the camel could not see the rich pasture on that side."

The *qadi* was satisfied but asked further, "How did you know what was packed in the saddlebags of the camel you never saw?" The third brother said, "There were ants in hundreds in one place, and they like what is sweet. In another place there were flies, which are drawn to rich and greasy food. So I concluded that the camel must have spilled something fat and something sweet when it got up."

"Go look for your beast, and may Allah open the way before you," said the *qadi* to the camel owner. "God gave these youths such wits that they can recognize a thing in all its details without even seeing it." Then he gave his attention to the brothers. "Rest this night in my house as guests, and tomorrow you can tell me of the matter that brought you here," he said.

A lamb was butchered and a meal was cooked, and the three brothers sat down to eat. Their host the *qadi* meanwhile hid in a curtained doorway out of sight, listening to what his clever guests might say. After a while he heard the oldest brother complain, "This meat is dog's meat and cannot be eaten!" And the next one added, "As for the woman who cooked our meal, she is in the days of her uncleanliness!" "What do you expect, when our host is a bastard," said the youngest brother. "Hush," whispered the others,

"Do not insult the *qadi*!" "A bastard and a son of shame," the youngest brother repeated.

Without a sound the *qadi* left his hiding place. He seized his servant and demanded, "How can you disgrace the house and put dog's meat, of all impurities, before our guests!" "By your life, we did not," said the servant, "Ask the shepherd who killed the lamb." The shepherd was called, and he said, "It was a suckling lamb we killed this night, by Allah, but when it was born the ewe died, and I put it with a nursing bitch to suck." The *qadi* was astonished. He hurried into the kitchen to find the cook. "Are you in the days of a woman's uncleanliness?" he asked her, and she admitted that it was so.

By now the *qadi* was anxious and worried. He entered his mother's quarters. Grasping her by the throat, he held his dagger before her eyes and said, "Tell me the truth about my father, or I shall kill you now!" Life is dear, and the woman spoke as follows: "There was a peddler who brought his wares to the house door. It was written that I should falter from the straight path. How could I escape my fate? I grew big from him and brought you into the world, may God forgive me."

The *qadi* turned on this side and on that all the long night. Next day he met the youths and said, "Now, my sons, speak, What is the difficulty that you cannot solve with all your cleverness?" And they told him: "When our father was on his deathbed he said to us, 'Mohammad shall

inherit, Mohammad shall inherit, but Mohammad shall not inherit.' Being all three named Mohammad, we do not know which one he wanted to disinherit."

"While I turn your problem in my mind, will you answer some questions I have?" said the *qadi*. To the brother who had complained of the meat, he said, "What made you say yesterday at dinner that the dish before you was dog's meat?" The youth replied, "The muscles of the leg were larger and harder than a lamb's, like those of an animal that had to run to keep pace with its dam." Of the other brother who had complained of the cook, the *qadi* asked, "How did you guess that the girl who cooked the food was unclean?" "Because there was no seasoning in our meal," said the second youth, "and a girl in her days cannot tell the salt from the sweet."

The *qadi* said nothing for a while. Then he turned to the youngest brother, the one who called him a bastard and a son of shame, and said, "Mohammad and Mohammad your older brothers shall inherit, and you shall not." "Why so?" asked the youth in surprise. "Your father willed his wealth to his true sons, the sons of his loins," said the *qadi*. "And it is a thing well known that only one who is himself a bastard can recognize a fellow bastard."

The Chain of Truth

Iraq

In the days when streams flowed in the *wadis* and breezes blew on the hills, when the grey-haired women huddled together and gossiped, in those days there lived a man and his wife. The woman was very beautiful. Everyone said so. She was also very cunning. She had a lover, who came to visit her whenever her husband stepped out of the house.

Weeks passed, and months. Things continued as they were. At last the husband began to have some doubts. He asked his wife a question or two. She blew up in his face. What was he suspecting? She wept such tears. How unbearable to be accused! She swore by her own life and the soul of her mother—may she rest in peace!—that she was as pure as milk and innocent as the babe in swaddling bands—no one had dared to come near the hem of her gown!

But the husband wanted to be absolutely certain in his own mind. He said, "Get yourself ready for travel, O woman! Tomorrow we shall go to the hill of Qaf. There we can discover what is true and what is false. At the top of the hill a chain hangs down from heaven; whoever touches it and swears falsely is burned to ashes as if struck by a thousand bolts of lightning." "You but have to say it," and his wife.

Yet no sooner had he turned his back and shown her the breadth of his shoulders, than she ran to her lover and informed him that the story was thus and thus and thus. As luck would have it, the lover owned a stable and earned his living renting donkeys and mules to those who needed them. "When my husband comes looking for a couple of donkeys today," said the woman "be sure to offer him a better price than all other stables." This he did, and the husband rented from him not knowing that the man was the lover of his wife.

The husband said to the woman, "I have two donkeys. We start in the morning early. The owner of the stable will come with us to care for the animals." And off they went, all three of them, the lover riding a mule. Up one hill and down the next, they reached the neighborhood of the hill of Qaf. Then the woman cried, "Ach! O my mother!" and she slipped from her saddle, fell onto the road, and lay in the dust with her skirts up to her waist and all her nakedness bared.

The shame of it!

She cried and she wept, and she scolded her husband, "But for you and your eternal fussing I should never have ridden this donkey or fallen off its accursed back, shaming myself before this stranger! Now tell me where to go and hide my face!"

They rode on, the woman's shoulders still shaking with her sobs. When she had climbed to the top of the hill, she held the chain of truth in her hand. And while her husband watched, she swore by all that is holy and terrible that she was a modest woman and a chaste wife, screened and protected from the eyes of men. No man had seen her nakedness save her own husband and the stable owner riding the mule beside him.

And then? And then they rode back, all three of them, as happy and contented as you could wish.

But God in his wisdom pulled up the chain from the hill of Qaf, because he saw that women knew how to evade its punishment. For such is their cunning—terrible cunning indeed!

> May you stay healthy
> And I continue strong!

Idle Ahmad

I r a q

There was and there was not, in times long forgot, a youth named Ahmad. His neighbors and those who knew him called him Et-Tanbal, the idle one, because all day long he sat in the house with his hands hanging by his sides. His mother would rage and rail at him to go find something to do, but her words struck him with no more force than empty air. "If only you'd work like other people," she scolded. "Then you would earn some money and I could find you a wife—who would bear me a grandson to gladden my heart a little." But the most Ahmad would do in the way of exertion was to pick up his prayer beads and listen to them clicking while they slipped between his fingers.

One day as Ahmad's mother was frowning on her son as he sat, a thought came into her head. "Ahmad, instead of sitting here playing with your beads, why don't you take yourself off to the mosque, where the stones are cool in the shade of the wall, and set yourself up as a dervish? You have the beads already; all you need is a large turban. And then you can sit all day. And whenever someone comes to you for advice, just say whatever happens to be on the tip of your tongue. Maybe God will take some pity on me and make one of your prophecies come true."

So Ahmad twisted a bulky turban around his head and sat in the portico of the mosque, rocking to and fro with the beads in his hand and moving his lips silently. Thinking he was magnifying the name of Allah, people took him for one of the holy men inspired by God, and the women especially would come and sit near him and ask him to tell their fortune. One would want to know whether her husband loved her or was yearning for a second wife. Another would ask if the child she was bearing was the male her mother-in-law wanted, or merely a girl. A third wondered whether she was barren or would some day, through the mercy of God, feel her belly rise with child. To each Ahmad would whisper the answer she most wished to hear. And every now and then one of the women would return joyfully and say, "Your words are as true as gold; I have a son!" or "I am with child!" and press a coin in his hand. In time Ahmad Et-Tanbal became known as Ahmad Ed-Darwish, Ahmad the Dervish, and his reputation spread until one day it reached the highest ears in the land, those of the sultan himself.

On that day the sultan's jeweled ring, costly beyond price, was lost. Servants searched the palace inside and out, but it did not reappear. Seeing the sultan grieving over his loss, one of the courtiers said, "There is a man of the people of Allah, a dervish who sits in the mosque. He can see and foresee things that are not visible to other men. Maybe he can find your ring."

Word was sent to Ahmad. "What can the sultan want with me, unless he needs my advice as a dervish?" thought Ahmad, troubled. "And if he finds me out—may Allah the Mighty and Merciful protect me from the headsman's sword!" When he reached the sultan's palace he was welcomed as if he truly were a wise man, and he trembled all the more as the sultan began to explain. "This morning as I prepared to wash myself for the dawn prayers," said the sultan, "I placed my ring on the edge of the garden pool. When I reached to put it on again, it had disappeared. Searching we have searched, and looking we have looked, and have not seen either ring or its shadow. Only you, who are able to discern what is hidden from the uninspired, can help us. We grant you three days to find the ring." Ahmad walked back to the mosque fervently repeating the name of Allah and all its attributes, not daring to think what would happen when the three days had passed and he had not found the ring.

Next day among the crowd that gathered around the dervish was a servant from the palace. As he bent close to Ahmad and kissed his hand, he whispered, "In the name of the Almighty and the All-knowing, save my life! It was I who stole the sultan's ring, and when you tell him he will cut my head off." "You are safe," said Ahmad. "It is a simple matter for me to protect you, but I need to know whether there are ornamental birds in the palace gardens." "Yes," replied the servant, "peacocks and ducks and parrots." "Good," said Ahmad. "All you have to do is hide the stolen ring in a lump of dough and feed it to a plump young duck on the day that I go before the sultan—but first mark the bird with a touch of henna dye above its bill. Your head will be safe."

So three days passed, and when the time came, the sultan asked for his ring. "I shall give it to you as we take a turn in the royal garden," answered Ahmad. As they strolled past the pretty birds that stood in the shade, Ahmad pointed to one and said, "Let me sup off that duck, stuffed with nuts and spice and saffron rice, and I promise you that your ring will come to light." Indeed, no sooner had the palace cook cut into the bird's craw than his eyes were dazzled by the many-colored light glancing off the jewels in the sultan's ring. Ahmad not only stayed to sup off roast duck with the sultan, but was rewarded with a purse of gold and escorted home as a well-loved and honored man.

Now that Ahmad the dervish became known as the finder of the sultan's ring, many came to ask his help, and many were the coins that he knotted into his sash each day. Thus he lived, a happy and carefree man—until one morning the palace guards opened the palace treasury and saw that it had been robbed. At once the sultan said, "Bring the dervish!" So once again Ahmad shivered with fear as he went to the palace. "This time the truth will be discovered," he thought, "and the sultan shall have my head!" And when he heard that the sultan's treasure was missing, he knew that the days of his life would soon be counted out. "Grant me forty days in a matter as important as this. I need time for my meditations and time for my recitations," pleaded Ahmad with despair. Leave was given him, but on condition that he did not depart from the palace.

How frail and doomed his life seemed now, as he sat locked into one of the palace rooms. At sunset a servant silently brought him his evening meal. "There goes one of the forty," said Ahmad, dejectedly counting off the days left to him in this world. Hearing the words, the servingman hastened to the servants' quarters and announced, "The dervish is as knowing as the people say. Already he has discovered our crime. With my own ears I heard him say as I left his room, 'There goes one of the forty!'" For the robbers of the treasury had been forty of the palace servants. One of the accomplices said, "Let me take his food to him tomorrow and hear what he says. We must be certain."

It was near sundown when the second thief carried Ahmad's ration in to him on a tray. "So this is the second of the forty!" sighed Ahmad hopelessly. "There is no doubt left," said the second thief to the other servants. "It is as our friend reported. Hardly had I set down his evening meal than I clearly heard him say, 'So this is the second of the forty!' " And each evening a different man of the forty would go to Ahmad's room, and every day increased their awe of the dervish's powers and mutiplied their fears for their own lives.

At last, on the thirty-ninth day, they could endure their silence no more. All forty of the guilty servants entered Ahmad's room, and the leader spoke: "We kiss your hands and we kiss the hem of your cloak and ask God to lengthen your days and make them prosperous as we place ourselves at your mercy and beg for your protection." "May God forgive me," said Ahmad, modestly and in some surprise. "What is your tale, gentlemen?" "As you well know," said the thief, "it was we who stole the sultan's treasure. We have come to beg you not to betray us. We are your servants to do with as you please." Ahmad's head seemed to spring wings, so light and joyful did it feel at this moment. But he answered solemnly, as befits a holy man, "Bury the sultan's treasure forty paces from the palace gate, and I shall keep your secret and you shall keep your heads."

On the next day, when the sultan and his court waited on Ahmad's words, he said, "Bring your gardeners and come with me." Then he led them forty paces beyond the palace gate and ordered, "In the name of Allah, dig!" And soon the chest containing the stolen treasure was uncovered. The sultan gave Ahmad gifts and gold in plenty, and further said, "Wish, and you shall have it!" "I wish to return to my house," said Ahmad. With drums and music he was escorted home, and there he offered prayers in gratitude for God's mercy and blessings. Soon afterwards his mother found him a wife, and let him lay aside his dervish's turban.

And he lived happy and content,
That is how we left him and went.

⠒ ⠒ ⠒ ⠒ ⠒ ⠒ ⠒ ⠒ ⠒ ⠒ ⠒ ⠒

The Clever
Minister's Daughter

⠒ ⠒ ⠒ ⠒ ⠒ ⠒ ⠒ ⠒ ⠒ ⠒ ⠒ ⠒

Syria

A king once wanted to test the sharpness of his minister, the *wazir* who stood on his right. He said, "Here are three questions:

> What is the most precious of all stones?
> What is the sweetest of all sounds?
> What, after God, gives us life?

Then he said, "Bring me the answers by tomorrow morning or I shall have your head."

The minister went home, his face yellow as wax. His daughter came out to meet him, and said, "Are you ill, O my father?" "No," said the minister, "but unless I find the answer to the king's three questions by tomorrow morning, I shall die." "You, who are the king's first minister, who stands on his right, are frightened by three questions? Tell them to me; maybe I can find the answers." And he told her. His daughter listened, then said, "It is not difficult. Tell the king: the most precious of all stones is the millstone, the sweetest of all sounds is the call to prayer, and the most life-giving after God is water." And so with the help of his daughter, the minister escaped with his life.

But the king wanted to challenge his *wazir* further. He gave him a tray made of gold that held a golden sculpted hen and her golden chicks, all pecking seeds of pearl. "Guess the worth of this golden hen with all her train, and you may keep it," he said. "If you fail to find the answer, you lose it and your head." The minister immediately went to repeat the king's riddle to his daughter. "Don't worry, Father," she said. "When the king questions you, say,

> More than the golden hen with all her train—
> More than your minister with all his brain—
> Is the worth of a shower of April rain.

Astonished at his minister's wit, the king thought of a new way to trip him up. He gave the *wazir* a lamb and said, "Can you feed me a supper off this lamb and earn me money with this lamb, yet bring it back alive to me tomorrow morning?" This time the poor minister went home with the lamb in his arms and despair in his heart.

His daughter laughed to hear his troubles. She said, "Geld the lamb and I can do it easily." When he had done so, she cut up the gelded parts and roasted them on a skewer over the fire. Next she sheared the lamb's wool and sold it in the market for ten pennies. In the morning she sent her father off with the skewer of meat in one hand and the price of the wool in the other and the lamb trotting on the end of a rope behind him.

The king was impressed. "I shall not ask any questions again," he said, "except this last. How did you find the answers to my riddles?" The minister felt some fear, but also pride. He confessed that it was not he but his daughter who had solved the riddles. The king gave a shout of delight and said, "That is the very woman I have been looking for to be my wife."

And so the first minister continued to stand at the king's right shoulder, and now he was also father of the queen.

The Rose in the Chest

Iraq

There was a man called Hakim Mustafa, the governor of a town, and he was known for his cleverness and munificence and also for his great pride. He had married his uncle's daughter, and Allah the Almighty had blessed him with one child, a girl called Wardah (which is the same as Rose). Wardah grew up in a house of wealth and importance in the town. She had only to ask and her father would indulge her. But when she was not yet twenty years old, her mother died. Now, when Hakim Mustafa had to travel on the business of governing, and was gone for ten days and more at a time,

Wardah had only her devoted servant Qurunfula, or Carnation, to keep her company.

Living in the same town was a handsome youth called Mohammad. One day when Mohammad was walking past the governor's house, the door to the courtyard chanced to be open and he caught a glimpse of Wardah. One glance at her beautiful face was enough to make him mad with love for her.

Though Mohammad was not wealthy or well-born, he was cunning and alert above the generality of men. So he thought of a scheme to make Wardah desire him in her turn, by which he might the more easily win her and make her his wife. He called three of his servants and instructed them: "Let one of you carry a piece of ewe's-milk cheese, and another of you lean on an uncut length of sugarcane as a staff, and the third hold a ripe pomegranate in his hand. Go thus to the house of Hakim Mustafa and stand under its windows. Then let the man with the cheese say to his companions, 'Whom do you know with a skin as fair as this ewe's-milk cheese?' And let the other two say, 'Young Mohammad's body is as white and as smooth, if not more.' Let the man leaning on the length of sugarcane say, 'Is there any man in the town as tall as this cane?' To which the other two are to answer, 'Your cane is almost the same height as Mohammad.' Finally let the man holding the pomegranate ask, 'Whose cheeks does this pomegranate most resemble?' And let the others say together, 'Mohammad's cheeks are as red as your pomegranate.' "

The men did go and stand near the windows of Hakim Mustafa's house, and they spoke the words they had been coached to say. Furthermore, it did so happen that Wardah overheard them, and without even seeing Mohammad, she began to feel as if he had been kneaded into her heart. "Qurunfula!" she called to her servant girl, "go to the carpenters' *suq* and tell the master carpenter to build a chest large enough to contain me with comfort." Not long afterwards the carpenter's apprentices delivered the finished chest to Wardah's house. "Qurunfula!" called Wardah, "I shall lock myself into this

chest. I wish you to pay a porter to carry it, with me inside, to the house of the youth Mohammad, and to ask the youth to keep the chest for you in the room where he sleeps."

The servant followed her mistress's orders. She knocked at Mohammad's gate, and when he came out to see who wanted him she said, "In this chest is a thing of great value. Can you keep it for me for a few days while I go on a journey? Maybe it would be safest in the room where you sleep at night." And Mohammad agreed to what she asked.

That evening when Mohammad prepared himself for sleep, he noticed that some of the food on his supper tray was missing. So the next evening when the servant brought in the meal on its tray, Mohammad hid himself to see who was touching his food. What he saw was Wardah noiselessly stepping out of the chest and creeping to the tray to eat.

He sprang out of his hiding place, took her in his arms, and said, "I have prayed for you to the heavens and now I have found you on earth!" She too confessed her love for him and called him, "O son of my uncle!" which is no different from saying "O my husband!" He kept her in his room well hidden even from his servants and they spent all the hours of the day and the night with each other. For such was their love that Mohammad could not bear to be parted from Wardah even for one minute. When seven days had passed in this fashion, Wardah unclasped one of the golden anklets on her left foot and bound it about Mohammad's ankle as a sign that she would always be his. Only now could Mohammad feel sure of Wardah, and he left the house to go about his work.

But the seventh day was also the day on which Qurunfula had arranged with Wardah to collect the chest from Mohammad's house. While he was out, the maid came and took the chest from his servants and brought her mistress home again.

Fate willed that Wardah should conceive. After her months were counted out, she gave birth to a son whom she named Saiid, or Happy. When the baby was one week old she placed him inside a basket and covered him with roses. She said to Qurunfula, "Take this basket over your arm and cry, 'Fresh roses! Fresh roses!' outside Mohammad's door. If he buys them, leave the basket with him and come back to me."

Mohammad bought the basket of roses without recognizing Qurunfula as the woman who had brought him the chest. And great was his astonishment when he felt something alive and moving inside it. He lifted the flowers and found a baby boy more beautiful than any rose. What was he to do now? As he was asking himself this question, Qurunfula returned disguised with white hair and said, "Word has come to us that there is a newborn child in your house. My daughter's child died in the night, and she would gladly nurse your boy without charge." Mohammad, unaware that the child was his own, agreed, and the baby was taken back to Wardah.

What of Hakim Mustafa? What did he say? Wardah bought a baby's cradle and told her father that Qurunfula had found a child abandoned by the side of the road. She said that she wished to give it comfort and show it kindness. Pleased to see such generosity in his daughter, Hakim Mustafa welcomed the beautiful child into his house.

Now to bring him news of his foundling child, Mohammad had hired a little girl to go and come between him and the infant's wet nurse. The girl would sit and watch Wardah rocking the boy and singing him to sleep, and soon she learned the words of Wardah's favorite lullaby:

> Sleep, darling of those nights
> When each hour held a day of delights,
> And a young lover handsome and bold
> Wore his lady's anklet of gold.

Not long afterwards the girl sang them as she worked in Mohammad's hearing. When he asked where she had learned them, he knew from her answer that the child was his child and the wet nurse no other than his own love. So he summoned his neighbors and all the men in his family, and together they proceeded to Hakim Mustafa's house to ask for his daughter Wardah's hand. But Hakim Mustafa, proud of his wealth and his birth, refused to let his only daughter marry a man of such humble means and small consequence. "Permit me to say one word in your ear," said Mohammad, and he spoke softly: "The pheasant wandered from your house to ours; the chicks she has hatched belong to your house and ours."

Then Hakim Mustafa knew that his daughter had met Mohammad and the child was theirs, and he agreed to the wedding. So after long parting, there was much rejoicing.

The Old Woman
and the Devil

Palestine

An old woman and the devil placed bets to decide which of them was more skilled at sowing discord and creating sorrow. The devil claimed that he was a master at setting people against each other, but the old woman insisted that her skills were unsurpassed. "Deeds rather than boasts will prove the point," said the devil. "Come with me."

So together they went to the bazaar and stood before a butcher's stall. Presently a man came to buy meat. When the butcher had weighed the piece the customer had chosen, the man refused to take it, saying "You short-weighted me, though God commands an honest scale." "Are you accusing me of cheating?" shouted the butcher. "Are you calling me an unbeliever who holds God's word as nothing!" Here the devil fanned the quarrel, goading them to curse and insult each other until the butcher struck the man with his cleaver, leaving him dead on the spot. As the butcher was being hauled off the jail, the devil turned to the old woman and said, "Observe my power: in one instant I have destroyed one soul and and dispatched another to prison."

"Follow me," said the old woman, "before we make our judgment." Accompanied by the devil, she went to a cloth merchant and said, "I need a length of cloth for a dress, a fine piece, the best you carry. I have a shameless son who keeps a mistress—may God curse them both—and he must take a present whenever he goes to visit her. Now, I have been a God-fearing woman all my life and I know this is a sin, but I beg the Lord, Who fathoms all secrets, to forgive me. I have no choice; unless I do as my son says, he beats me and curses me and threatens to drive me out of the house."

"There is no power or strength except in God," intoned the merchant, and added, "God tests the believer through his own nature, his property, and his family. You may look to Him for a just reward for your sufferings." As he spoke, he picked out a beautiful piece of Aleppo cloth for her. She paid its price and tucked the material under her shawl.

Then the old woman made her way straight to the cloth merchant's house and knocked at the door. When the merchant's young wife opened it she said, "The time for the afternoon prayer is almost up, my child, and my house is a long way off. Would you let me say my prayers in your home?" The young woman welcomed her in and spread a prayer mat for her in the bedroom. Then she returned to her kitchen, where she was preparing her husband's meal. When she was alone, the old woman hid the piece of cloth in the clothes basket. And after praying she thanked the wife and left. "Let's see what happens now," she said to the devil, and they waited for the cloth merchant to return.

As soon as he came home, the merchant slipped off his coat and was about to put it away in the clothes basket when he noticed a length of Aleppo cloth like the one he had sold that morning. Turning it over in his hands, he saw it was the very same piece. Stunned, he ran to his wife and began to beat her and accuse her of adultery. The poor woman screamed and wept and swore on her faith that she was innocent, but he continued to beat her. Finally he sent her back to her parents, still sobbing over her miserable fate.

"Am I your equal?" the old woman asked of the devil. "You have succeeded in coming between man and wife," he asknowledged. "Now watch the superiority of my powers," said the old woman.

Next day she returned to the cloth merchant's store. "On my way home yesterday, I mislaid the piece of cloth I bought off you," she said. "I didn't want to miss the afternoon prayer and knocked at a door in the city. A kind young woman let me pray in her room, and I left my package there. Now I cannot find the house again, being a stranger in this place." The merchant stumbled into the back of his shop and returned with the length of cloth. The old woman snatched it from him, asking, "How did you find it?" "It was my home you prayed in yesterday," said the merchant, closing up his store so that he could go and bring his innocent wife back from her parents'.

The old woman turned to the devil. "Whereas you cannot repair the damage you have done, I have brought peace between these two again," she pointed out. "Now what do you say?"

"I concede. You old women are wilier than the devil himself!"

The Girl Outwits
Three Men

Palestine

A rich man decided one year that he would go on the pilgrimage to Mecca. His wife said to him, "I too have wished to be a pilgrim, and it is only proper that I travel with you." "And I will be useful to you on the way; take me, O Father," said his son. And he agreed that they could both accompany him. "What about me?" asked his daughter. The man answered, "My child, you are young and tender and the road to Mecca is a long and weary one." No matter what the girl said, he would not let her go. "The house is well stocked, my dear, and your needs provided for," said the father. "I have asked the sheikh in our mosque to keep an eye on you. Should you crave fresh food—a lemon or a radish from the market—he will bring it for you. You need not leave the house." And the man set off with his wife and his son.

Now, despite his promise to look after her, the sheikh forgot all about his friend's daughter until one day, as he was climbing the steps of the minaret to recite the call to noonday prayers, he looked in the direction of the rich man's house and saw her through the window. She was braiding her hair, hair as dark as the night, against which her white arm gleamed like a sword. After that he could think of nothing else.

The sheikh hurried through his prayer call and stumbled down the steps to get to her house as fast as he could. Standing under her windows, he called out her name. She answered from inside without showing her face. The sheikh tried again: "Give me a basket and I will fetch whatever you need!" Down came a basket on the end of a string; of the girl he caught not a glimpse. When he returned with the supplies, which were heavy, he found only the string and no one at the window, not even the end of a finger.

Annoyed and disappointed, the sheikh stayed away a few days but was eventually drawn back to the foot of the girl's wall. "I am here, my child. Do you need anything from the shops?" She told him in detail and lowered her basket as before. And neither going nor coming was the sheikh's eye brightened by a sight of the girl. He returned next day with hope in his heart but came away unrewarded. Seeing no way to soothe the pain that was burning in him, he went to the old matchmaker, a woman both cunning and shrewd. "My problem is thus and thus and thus," he told her. "Is that all?" she said. "Leave it to me and you shall meet her face to face."

First the old woman made her way to the rich man's house and knocked at the door. "Will you help a lonely soul without family or friends?" she said. "If God wills, I want to go on the pilgrimage and this is the time. But I have a chest full of things (you know the saying, my child: 'Without money put away on her shelf, a woman alone cannot live by herself')—I have clothes and some jewels and the gold I have saved. Will you keep it safe while I am gone? I shall bring you a present when I return, and if I do not come back, you may keep the chest and its contents for yourself." The girl agreed.

Now the old woman went to the carpenter for a chest. She had him build it the length and width of a man and fit it with a lock that opened from inside. When it was delivered to her house, she sent for the sheikh. She packed him inside and called a porter to carry it on his back to the rich man's house. Once it was there, she fussed and she worried over the safety of her treasures and what would happen to them in the night. At last the girl grew impatient and said, "I'll put it right next to my bed." The woman left then, and the girl locked the door behind her.

In the evening and late into the night when people are in their houses and no foot ventures beyond the door, the girl sat up reading the Koran and praying for the safety of her family. Suddenly she heard a noise. Ziq! The lid of the chest began to open, and sitting up inside it was the sheikh— O Lord protect us! A man in the girl's room, and it was the middle of the night.

The girl was quick-witted and well-bred. She said, "Welcome to you, O teacher, it is long since you honored our house with a visit." And she kissed his hand respectfully. Then slowly, very slowly—O Lord preserve us and keep us whole in moments of danger!—she brewed him the customary cup of coffee. But the sheikh sat as if on hot embers and tossed back the cup with one swallow. "It is late," he said. "Roll out the bedding so that we may lie down." The girl did not move, so he said, "No one will see us, and as soon as your father returns I'll ask him for your hand." "Let us play a game of chess," said the girl. "If you win, all that you wish for shall be yours. If I win, you will let me do to you what I wish." They played and it was the girl who won. Up she jumped and snatched a rope that was hanging on the wall. She tied up the sheikh from top to toe, pushed a turnip into his rump—right up to the leaves—and threw him out of the window into the street.

Was he bruised and did he curse! There in the ditch he lay helpless, dreading that someone would recognize him in his preacher's turban.

Just then a man came by, an early riser carrying a load of things to market. "Who lies there?" he asked. "It is your master the sheikh." "Lah! Lah! Lah! What has befallen you?" "It is God's will and the decree of fate," intoned the sheikh, "and your destiny is to be the one to untie my knots as quickly as you can!" The man loosened the rope and the preacher hurried home. He sat groaning on his doorstep until his wife woke up and asked, "What ails you?" "I was out late and fell into the ditch in the dark," he said. "Now rub my back with oil." Which she did.

The next day a messenger arrived in town with the good tidings that the pilgrims had returned safely from Mecca and their boat had put into port. That rascal the sheikh no sooner heard this than he wrote a letter to the girl's father. While the rest of the family was away, the letter said, his daughter had turned their home into a house of shame; anyone wishing to go up did so and was received by the girl. The sheikh sent the letter with the grape growers who take their harvest to the coast to sell. When the girl's father opened it, his face turned black as destruction. He turned to his son and he said, "Your sister has brought dishonor to our house! Nothing but her blood will wash it clean. Go to the town, kill her, and bring me her blood in a jar."

When the brother knocked at the door and called, "Open; it is I, your brother!" the girl sprang down to let him in and greet him with the traditional lululey, the trill by which the women give sound to their joy. "Wait," said her brother, "until we have gone and met our father." She fell into step behind him, and he led her far from town and deep into the wilderness beyond the plowed fields. On and on until the girl was tired and

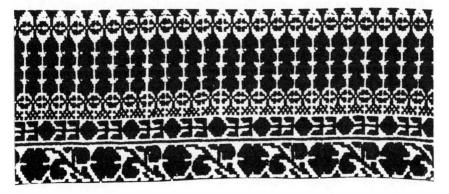

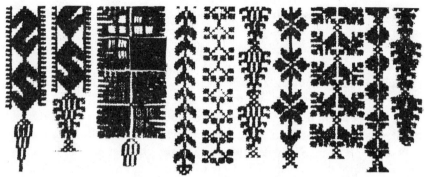

said, "Brother, I must rest." She leaned her head against his knee and fell fast asleep. When he saw her like this, the Compassionate One moved his heart, and he said, "I cannot kill her—I must let her live." Putting a stone under her head where his knee had been, he left her. The jar he filled with the blood of a stray dog.

When the cold night air began to pinch her, the girl awoke. She called to her brother but heard not a whisper or a sound in reply. What was she to do? She followed where her face led her, farther and farther toward the desert, until finally she came to a tree and said, "I will be safer if I climb up and hide among the branches."

At the foot of the tree was a small spring, where a prince of the Beduins liked to bring his prize red mare to water. When he let the horse go down to drink the next morning, she reared, startled by the reflection of the girl in the water. The prince looked for the cause of her alarm and discovered the girl crouched above him in the tree.

"Are you human or one of the Djinn?" he asked her. And she said, "I am a woman like any other, but I am a mere thread in your cloak and ask for your protection." The prince replied, "The protection of God shields you and us all." So she slid down from the tree, and he lifted her onto the back of his horse. Placing his sword chastely between them, he rode home to his camp.

His mother looked after the girl as if she were her very own child, for she saw that this was a beauty most rare. She fed her on sheep's brains and the tenderest of foods. When they talked they spoke, as women do, of weddings and birthings and death. And the prince's mother began to say more and more of marriage, for she wanted a wife for her son. "God has commanded that men should court and take in marriage," said the girl. "There is no dishonor, and for a woman marriage is her protection." In a short time she became the wife of the prince, and when three years had passed she had borne him three sons.

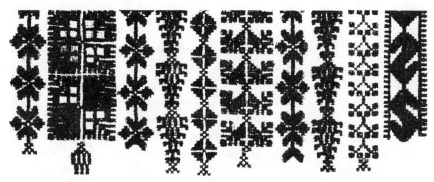

One day when the prince returned from the hunt and his wife came out to hold his horse's bridle, he saw that she had wept. He swore that he would not dismount until she had revealed the cause of her tears. So she told him her tale and said that the thought of her parents was making her heart ache.

Thereupon the prince saddled three camels and loaded them with gifts, the kind that are heavier in worth than in weight. And together they began the journey toward the town. But they had hardly progressed beyond sight of their tents when the men of a neighboring clan came galloping towards them. They said, "We've turned to you in great need, O Prince. We beg you to ride with us and make peace between our tribes." The prince was unable to deny them, and placing his wife and her children in the care of his uncle, he left.

It was the uncle now who led the camels laden with gifts. And as he rode, his thoughts dwelled on the fair-skinned girl with hair like black ropes who sat in the litter on the camel before him. A devil whispered and whispered in his ear until he was unable to hear the commands of the Compassionate, though they are clear. He sent the camel drivers with the pack animals ahead on the road. Then he halted the girl's riding camel by the side of a stream and invited her to rest.

The prince's uncle sat by her side and said, "No one sees in this place; we are far enough from the road. And if you refuse me my wish, I shall kill the child in your lap!" Strong as a woman can be, she remains but the daughter of Adam's rib. The uncle struck down all three of her children, and there was nothing she could do. When he turned on her, she said, "There is no refuge from the decree of God! But first let me wash and say a prayer." He gave her a pitcher, and he tied a rope to her arm. But when she had walked a short way, she fastened her bracelets to the rope and knotted its end to a tree. Then she fled as fast as she could run. Whenever the uncle pulled at the rope, he heard the bracelets jingle. "She is still bathing," he said. Time passed. He went in search of her and saw that she was gone.

"How could I ever find her in this darkness?" he said. So he climbed into the litter and continued on his way.

The girl ran and she ran through the night until it was light. She found herself on the seashore. A soldier bathing there caught sight of her face and was overjoyed. He began to shout to her to stop. "I have no way to escape you," said the girl. "Your strength is greater than mine. But if anyone should see me with you, he will kill you and take me for himself. Let me wear your coat so that I look like a man, and help me up onto your horse." The soldier agreed to her plan, but as soon as she was in the saddle she kicked the horse's side and rode off, leaving the soldier to follow on foot. The man, deciding that he had met one of the Djinn, thanked God and praised Him for letting him escape with his life.

The girl rode and rode all the way to her parents' town, where the camel drivers had brought the camels laden with gifts and the prince's uncle had followed and her own husband had just arrived. She went into the coffeehouse in her man's clothes and sat in a corner offering coffee to every man who came.

Now, her brother's wedding was to take place that very night, and the men who were invited said to the bridegroom, "Why don't you bring to your feast the generous stranger who has treated everyone to coffee?" And so the girl entered her father's house in the guise of a youth. And when the eating and drinking were done, her father said, "O stranger, now is the time for talk and amusement. Why don't you tell us your tale?" She looked around the room, the hall where the men were being entertained, and saw her father, her brother, and the sheikh (who was there to read the prayer), as well as her own husband and her uncle who had come with the gifts. She began her story and recited it to the end. Then she turned to the prince and said, "This is my husband. Now tell them: how did you find me when you took me to be your wife? Speak the truth, and may God destroy you if you lie." The prince said, "She was a maiden with the seal of her maker upon her, I swear."

Then her father understood the facts and cried to the wedding guests, "Whoever loves virtue and respects the holy laws, bring fire and a load of wood!" And all the people set to work, piling wood as high as a house. They tossed the preacher and the prince's uncle into the fire and burned them to death. Then every man went back to his home.

The bird it has flown,
My tale it is done,
Goodnight, everyone!

The Boy Who
Heard the Dew
When It Fell

Morocco

They say that a man lived in a house with his sister. One day the sister found a dried grape on the ground, a raisin. She picked it up and popped it into her mouth. At that moment a serpent slid out of a hole in the wall. "That raisin was mine," he said. "Give it to me or I shall bite you." "I'll buy you a whole sack of raisins tomorrow," said the girl. The snake said, "No! I don't want any raisins but that one." However, the girl had already eaten it. "I shall have to kill you," said the snake, "unless you take me for your husband." Well. She took the serpent as her husband, and in time she gave birth to a child: a little boy whose ears were so sharp that he could hear the dew when it fell. So they called him Smemi' an-Nada, Little-Hearer-of-the-Dew-When-It-Falls.

Now, the girl hated her brother. She said to the serpent who was her husband, "Hide in the waterskin, and when my brother comes home I'll ask him to pour me a drink of water. As he reaches for the skin, bite him and kill him!" The little boy Smemi' was listening, and he heard every word that his mother had whispered.

The man came home. His sister said, "You are not less in worth than I am, brother, but will you please get up and pour me a drink of water?" Before he could move, the boy Smemi' said, "You are tired, uncle, stay seated. I shall bring her the water." And he looked into the waterskin and saw his father coiled up like a round cake, and he said, "What are your intentions? Do you really want my uncle dead?" The serpent said, "The warm wind from the east oppressed me, and I came to the coolness of the water bag."

This time the sister had failed, so she told the serpent, "Go lie in the padded quilt and I'll ask my brother to take it down to the river to wash it. Then you will have a chance to bite him and kill him." But when she asked her brother to wash the bedding, Smemi' said, "Uncle, you take the

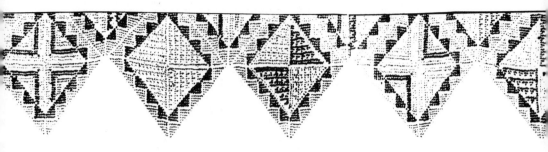

sticks and I'll bring the quilt. Let us wash it together, you and I." And he carried the quilt with the serpent inside it and laid it on the wet stones by the river. Then he and his uncle began to beat out the dirt with sticks until they had beaten the serpent to death. They brought back the bedding and the serpent, who had been torn into seven separate pieces, and gave them to the sister.

"Come, brother, let me pour out your stew so you can eat," said the sister, having cooked the poisonous snake meat with the rest. "Only if you take the first bite," said her son. What could she do? She ate and she died.

Then Smemi' spoke to his uncle: "See how my mother and father plotted to kill you? See how I brought about their deaths? Let us travel about the world together, you and I, wherever God sends us." And they set out and wandered until they reached a fig tree that grew where two roads parted.

"Let this be our meeting place," said the boy. "And whoever comes back when the tree is bearing and does not find the other, will know that his partner is dead. Go along this road and God be with you, but beware of the bald man and do not befriend him." So one went east and one went west.

The uncle did meet a bald man who said, "Will you work for me and pasture my sheep?" "A bald man's flocks I cannot pasture," said the uncle, and turned from him. But the bald one covered his head and spoke again, saying, "Will you be my shepherd for a wage?" The uncle then said yes. "There are two conditions," said the man, "and if you accept them you may have the work. First, every day you must catch seven fledglings for my seven sons to play with. And second, if my hound who follows the sheep reaches the tent before you, she may eat your food and hers; but if you get there first, you may eat her food as well as your own."

The man agreed, and next day he led the sheep out to grass. He was kept so busy looking for fledglings and running after the baby birds, however, that the hunting dog went to the tent and ate his dinner and hers. Yes.

The poor man came back and went to sleep without food. And the following day he led out the sheep and caught the birds, and again the hound ate his dinner as well as hers. And so it went on until he died of hunger.

Well. Smemi' an-Nada came to the fig tree and saw that it was bearing. He said, "My uncle has died; let me follow the road he took."

The bald man stopped him too, and said, "Will you pasture my sheep?" And the boy said, "No." Well, the bald man covered his head and offered him the job once more, and Smemi' agreed. Then the bald man explained his conditions. "I accept," said Smemi', "and I have a condition of my own. Let us work together, but whoever of us becomes angry with the other first, let his head be cut off." "Good," said the bald man.

So Smemi' went to the tent and led out the sheep with the hound following after. Time after time the dog would try to slink off to the tents, but the boy whistled her back. Meanwhile he caught six little birds and an adder. The adder he put into a leather bag.

When he brought the sheep home in the evening, the seven children came out to meet him and he distributed the six little birds among them. But the seventh child cried, "Where is my little bird?" "In my bag," said Smemi'. And the boy ran to pull it out and was bitten by the adder and died.

The father found him dead. "O bald one," said Smemi', "are you angry?" "No, no!" said the bald man, because he did not want to give Smemi' the right to cut off his head.

Next day Smemi' brought back five little birds and an adder, and one of the boys was left without a bird. He too cried for a pet of his own, and Smemi' told him to look in the bag, and the snake bit him and killed him. And so it went until only one of the bald man's children was left: a fat little boy nicknamed Kharouf, which means lamb.

One day guests arrived. The bald man said, "We must offer them a meal of meat. Kill me a lamb from among the sheep." Smemi' called to the man's son, "Come and help butcher a lamb!" And the boy came, and Smemi' cut his neck with the butcher's knife. "What have you done?" said the bald man. "You told me to butcher a *kharouf* and I have!" said Smemi'.

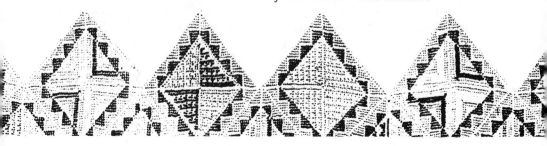

Next day when Smemi' had gone to pasture the sheep, the man said to his wife, "Let us put the boy between us when we go to sleep tonight and take our revenge." "Yes," she said, "when he is asleep I shall pinch you; then you can wrap your belt round his neck and strangle him. Did he not put an end to all our children?"

Smemi', who could hear the dew when it fell, listened to them all the way from the pasture. Pretending to be ignorant of their plan, he closed his eyes that night and waited for the man and his wife to fall asleep. Then he rolled the wife into the middle of the bed and pinched the man, who bound his belt tightly round his wife's neck and killed her.

In the morning when the man pulled the blanket off his wife's face to tell her that Smemi' was dead at last, there was Smemi', well and unharmed, looking back at him. "O Smemi', are you alive, then?" said the man. "Yes," said Smemi', "and you, are you alive, O bald one?" "Yes," said the bald man, "but not for long, unless you leave my tent." "I am ready to go!" said Smemi'. "Go," said the man, "and may God make the road away from here a smooth one."

When One Man
Has Two Wives

S y r i a

A man had two wives and both loved him, though one was young and the other old. Whenever the man lay down to sleep with his head on the young wife's knees, she would pluck the white hairs from his head so that he should appear youthful. And whenever he rested his head in the older wife's lap and slept, she would pluck out the black hairs from his head so that he should be white-haired like herself. And it was not long before the man was bald.

Such is the origin of the saying, "Between Hannah and Bannah, vanished are our beards."

Just Deserts

A man lost all his wealth and accustomed himself to live modestly. Fortune continued to punish him, and at last came a day when nothing was left in the house to eat and nothing to sell for the cost of a meal. The man sat thinking in despair, then called his wife. "O woman," he said, "go borrow the price of a plump fowl from our neighbor. Then spice it with saffron and season it with cardamom and cook it till it is brown." "How can we think of indulging ourselves like princes?" said his wife. "This is not for us, though we are starving," said her husband, "but a gift to take to the caliph." When the bird was ready, he set it on two flat loaves of bread and hurried to the palace.

"Make way for the caliph's dinner," he cried to the guards who stood in his way, and he was ushered directly into the royal presence. The caliph was sitting in conference with his minister of the right shoulder and his minister of the left shoulder. "Peace be on the prince of the faithful," said the man. "Here is a dinner for you and your advisers." And he spread his cloak on the ground, set the dish on it, and began to tear the fowl into portions. All the while, the water in his mouth ran like a fountain. First he placed the head of the bird on a piece of bread and, bowing low, offered it to the caliph. "Eat, and two healths to you, O ruler of our time!" Next he broke off one wing and gave it to the minister who stands at the right shoulder and then the other wing for the minister who stands at the left shoulder. And with the fury of a wild beast he ate up the rest of the chicken himself.

"What is this you have done, O my son?" asked the caliph. "O prince and ruler of the faithful, may Allah lengthen your days," said the man, "you are the head and the chief of all men in the land. This minister stands at your right hand and that minister at your left. We, the rest of your subjects, have no importance. Was it not only right that I should divide the fowl according to our stations?" The caliph laughed and gave the man a purse of five hundred gold coins.

Now he could run to the market and buy all that his house was lacking in rice and fat and sugar and tea, and again he could live as a wealthy man. The neighbors whispered. Was it not yesterday that he had gone supperless to sleep? Finally the boldest woman of the neighborhood asked the man's wife how the change in their fortune had come about. And the wife told her story.

Back to her husband the woman raced. "Listen to this tale," she said. "Our poor neighbor presented a cooked chicken to the caliph and was rewarded with a purse of gold. Why don't we do the same?" The man said, "Good." He went to the market and bought seven hens and had them cooked with rice and gravy. He arranged them on a copper tray and paid two porters to carry them before him.

"What is this?" asked the caliph." "A meal for the prince of the faithful," said the man, and he set three hens before the caliph and two each before the two ministers. "Are you saying that the ruler has more greed than those he rules?" asked the caliph. The man stammered and did not know what to answer. So he was given five hundred blows with a stick and sent home to his wife.

Next day the caliph's wife, the lady Zobeida, went to the bath. She heard a woman say, "May Allah send a sickness on our caliph and strike him blind!" "Why curse the prince of our time?" asked the lady Zobeida. "Judge for yourself whether I am right or not," said the woman. "A man takes one meager hen to the caliph and receives five hundred pieces of gold. My husband offers him a platter of seven hens on mounds of rice and he is beaten till he bleeds. The caliph is not just, and that is why I curse him."

"O master of wisdom and ruler of the age," the lady Zobeida said to the caliph later, "why do you reward the man who brings you one bird and punish his fellow who brings seven? The women in the *hammam* are complaining and wonder at your judgment." Her husband replied, "Let us fetch the two men so that you may judge for yourself, O mother of the faithful, whether I was right to do as I did, or whether you are right to be angry."

The first man, who had been poor and hungry, was summoned to the palace. He found the caliph with the lady Zobeida and his favorite Ja'far. "Will you be able to divide these eggs justly between us three?" asked the lady Zobeida, placing five eggs in his hands. The man was thoughtful for a while. Then he returned three of the eggs to the caliph's wife and gave one each to the caliph and his favorite. "Why so?" asked the caliph. "I was seeking justice and a division that would be equal, O prince of the faithful," said the man. "You and Ja'far have already been provided by nature with two eggs each. Counting the one I gave you, that makes three. In fairness, I had to bestow on the lady Zobeida, having none herself, three eggs, so that each of you is now in possession of an equal number." The caliph was pleased at his solution and rewarded him as before.

The other man, no wiser than before, offered the caliph three eggs and Ja'far and the lady Zobeida one each. He too was repaid as before, and went moaning home to his wife.

"Do you see, O mother of the faithful, that it is the wit of the first man and not his hen that I rewarded with gold?" said the caliph. "Clever men are few, while flatterers we have in plenty and need not encourage."

Live in peace and without pain!

The Simple Wife

Palestine

A man once married a girl who was so good-looking that she could say to the moon, "Set, that I may shine in your place." But—what a calamity—her brain was like the weight of two walnuts on a camel's back. Still, the man was happy with her.

As the month of Ramadan drew near, to save himself the trouble of going to market while he was fasting, the man brought something home every day. He began to lay in stores: one day a measure of rice, another day a jar of fat or a sack of sugar. As he carried each thing into the house he would tell his wife, "This is for Ramadan. That is for Ramadan." Soon the house was crowded with the stores of food.

One day two camel drivers leading a string of five or six camels were passing by the man's house. As chance would have it, the halter of one of the camels slipped, its foot became tangled, and the animal began to limp.

The camel driver who was following the string of animals noticed this and called to his friend in the lead, "Ramadan! Ramadan! Tie up the camel's rope."

When the wife heard the name Ramadan, she looked out of her window and asked, "Which of you is called Ramadan?" "I am, O my mistress," said the camel driver at the head of the caravan. "For God's sake," said the woman, "it's about time you came for your things! We can't move around in our own house any more without tripping over your property. Come, my man, and take it away." "That I shall, by Allah!" said the camel driver. "Look, I have brought all my camels to pick up the stuff." And he made the camels kneel at her door and asked the woman to show him his things. "Everything in this room is yours," she said. Asking no questions, the camel driver and his friend loaded their caravan and went on their way.

At sunset when the husband came home, his wife said to him, "What a relief! Ramadan came and took his things away today." "What things?" asked the man. "All the stores you said were for Ramadan," she answered. "I meant the month of Ramadan, woman, may destruction strike your house! May God destroy all brainless women."

The Woman Called Rice Pudding

Palestine

Once upon a time there was a woman named Kanfusheh. One day a dervish passed her house looking very important and wearing round his neck a huge rosary made of the spouts off clay water jars strung together like beads. "What do you have for sale?" she asked as soon as she saw him. "Names," he said. "How much does a name cost?" "Three hundred piasters." She had just that much money and gave it to him. He then handed her a clay spout from his necklace and said, "Wear this round your neck—from now on your name shall be Rice Pudding."

At sundown Kanfusheh's husband came back from plowing and called, "Kanfusheh! Come and unload the donkey." But she did not go out. "Hey, Kanfusheh! Where are you? Hey, Kanfusheh! Answer me!" But she remained where she was. "What's the matter with you?" her husband asked. "I am not called Kanfusheh any longer," she said. "My name is Rice Pudding." "Where did you get such a name?" "The name peddler passed by, and I bought it from him for three hundred piasters." "Don't tell me the few piasters we had set aside for the tithe are gone?" He reached into the basket where they kept their money and found that it was empty. "Where did the name peddler go?" he asked. "In that direction," she told him, pointing down the road. Her husband threw down his stick and said, "You will never see my face again unless I find someone as stupid as you are. Only then will I come back to you." And so he left.

For many days he traveled the road, and whenever he met anyone he would ask, "Are you the name peddler?" and the answer was always "No." By and by he saw a woman forking manure. "Where are you from?" she asked him. "From hell," he said. "By your father's life tell me, did you see my parents there?" "Of course I did," he answered. "How are they?" "Miserable!" he told her. "Are you going back?" she asked. "Of course," he said. "Please, will you do me a favor and take them my present?" "I'll do it, but first let me see what you want to send them." The woman showed him some butter, her husband's coat, and some money. He agreed to take the things and went on his way.

When this woman's husband came home and ate his meal, he decided to go to the men's coffee-house. "Hand me my coat," he said. "I sent it to my father in hell," she told him. "You whose parents should have been burned before you were born! Why did you do such a foolish thing?" And he began to scold her. But she said to him, "You son of a shameless woman! My poor parents are miserable in hell, and you owe them much. Did you not eat at their table? Had they not done you favors?" "Well, what else did you send?" he asked, and she told him. "With whom did you send all this?" "With a man who was going that way." Sighing, the man mounted his horse and set out after his possessions.

Further down the road, when Kanfusheh's husband saw this man approaching on horseback, he wrapped the butter, the money, and the coat in his own cloak, hid the bundle under a stone wall, and waited. As the man rode up, he asked Kanfusheh's husband, "Sir, have you seen a man carrying a coat and a pouch of butter?" "Yes, a man just as you describe did pass this way." "Can I catch up or is he too far ahead?" "Well, you might if you get off your horse and go on foot." "Why do you say that?" "A horse has four legs to manage, and by the time it gets all of them moving, you'll be far behind. You'll get there more nimbly on your own two feet." So the man got off his mount and said, "Will you look after my horse until I come back?" "All right," said Kanfusheh's husband. As soon as the man was out of sight, he loaded his things onto the horse's back and rode away in the opposite direction. And when he reached his own home, he shouted, "Rice Pudding, I am back!"

She Who Understood Best

Palestine

There was a man who was deaf. So was his wife and his daughter, and also his mother. On the feast day at the end of Ramadan the man went to the market to buy a whole lamb for his family to eat in celebration. On the way he met a friend who had lent him a small sum of money. "A happy new year to you, Abu Ali!" said the friend. And Abu Ali replied, "By Allah, the All-Knowing, on this holy feast day can you think of nothing but claiming your debts? Do people celebrate or worry about what they owe on a day like this? I have no money; I cannot pay!"

And with that the deaf man returned to his house. "What happened? Why have you come back without buying anything?" asked his wife. "I met our friend, a curse on both his parents, and on a day of feasting he began to ask for his money back—he has no sense of shame or decency!" "If you could not find a whole lamb, you might have brought home some meat from the butcher's without coming to ask me first," said the wife.

The wife went to tell her daughter. "My dear, your father can't make up his mind what to buy us to celebrate the feast." "Mother, why are you and my father worrying about my husband?" said the daughter. "Whether he is a young man or a greybeard, I'll consent. After all, isn't marriage a girl's protection?"

The girl went to her grandmother and said, "Grandmother, my father and mother are asking me whom I would like to marry!" "Oh dear!" said the grandmother. "Is no one left to raise the price of girls but me? I am not marrying, by Allah. I swear I will not stir from the seat by this fireplace!"

∴ ∴ ∴

∴ *How This Book Was Put Together* ∴

Though there were thick iron bars in the windows and solid stone walls in the room where we slept as children, and often there were six and even ten of us, visiting cousins and second cousins, crowded on the mattresses on the floor, Hamda, the servant girl, never failed to make us shiver with fright. She could sniff, mmmppph! through her large nostrils in such a way that as we stared in the dimness of the kerosene night-light, she turned into the giant who smelled that there was a tasty human morsel hiding in his house. Six-year-old blood ran cold at her account of the hairy-faced Ghoul whose hot red eyes could burn. So night after night we pestered her for "one more story"—just to feel again the delicious prickle down our spines. Then, having married, she disappeared from our childish lives.

Hamda could neither read nor write and she may well have believed in the terrible creatures she told of. As long as we listened to her we were half convinced, but we moved on to seek other thrills in books (Arabic translations of the voluminous adventures of the French detective Arsène Lupin were the vogue) and we do not retain her tales. In looking for the stories in this collection I returned to where I had last heard them, to rural Palestine, on what is now called the West Bank.

In the Middle East, links of family and guest-friendship, the focus of so many of the tales, are a powerful network in private life. I had but to hint at my quest and, with my tape recorder, I was led along stony paths on foot and up distant hills on donkeyback to men and women who still know the stories Hamda used to tell. Flinging back the iron doors of a musty and little-used reception room, the whole family, with bright-eyed children giggling behing their hands, would file in and perch on the stiff furniture to listen with me. Then, when a tray of sweet, hot tea in tinkling glasses had been passed round, they would all sit patiently to hear the stories once again while the teller listened to the tape.

Interest in preserving the local culture is particularly strong on the West Bank as the status of Palestine continues to be the subject of international deliberation and the identity of a separate Palestinian Arab people is called into question. There is a lively folklore department in the university at Bir Zeit, and I am much indebted to Dr. Abdullatif Barghouthi, who let me look through countless stories recorded in manuscript by his students, and whose book *Hikayat Jan min Bani Zeid (Djinn Stories of the Benizeid)* is a mine of information on the subject of the Djinn.

In nearby Al-Bireh the division of folklore and social research of the In' ash al Usra Society, directed by Samiha Khalil, publishes a quarterly journal which includes one or two folktales in each issue. In Jordan Nimr Sirhan, who has written and edited several books on folk stories and songs, has been publishing the *Encyclopaedia of Palestinian Folklore* since 1977. I am grateful to all three folklorists and to Nabil Alqam, a writer on folklore, for generously giving me their time and attention and for sending books and tapes of folktales to me in New York to help in putting together this collection for English readers.

Nearly seventy-five years ago, Jiryis Abu Yusif Mansur, schoolteacher and notable of Bir Zeit, invited Hans Schmidt, a German working at the Deutsches Evangelisches Institut für Altertumswissenschaft in Jerusalem, for a visit. On hearing that his guest was interested in the oral tradition of the region, Mansur, with characteristic hospitality, arranged meetings with all the best raconteurs in town. He took down their words as they spoke, and that winter the two men produced a German translation of the narratives. Later Mansur was persuaded to transcribe his Arabic texts into Latin letters. On returning to Germany Schmidt, helped by Paul Kahle, published a carefully annotated two-volume edition of the folktales of Bir Zeit. These books are prized by the local students of folklore today because they preserve the speech, with all its idiosyncrasy, of a society as yet unaffected by the outside influences of radio or journalism.

In reviewing the source material for the part of the Arab world best known to me, I found that beyond my own early memories and the tapes I had made, there was a considerable body of current folk texts published in Arabic by specialists interested in the colloquial language. There were also some splendid texts in a vigorous language from a time when listening to the spoken word of one's fellows was one of the major entertainments and reading a rare occupation.

Thanks to Mansur's sensitive understanding of Hans Schmidt's interest and to his position of influence in his hometown, the texts in the Schmidt-Kahle volumes are among the best in style of any oral narratives available in Arabic. *Modern Arabic Tales*, a collection of stories from Jerusalem published in Arabic script in 1905 by Enno Littmann, are pale beside them. Not that Littmann was less able than Schmidt, but he was not as fortunate in his guest-friendships, and the source he relied upon happened to be less gifted than the Bir Zeit talkers. For me the Schmidt-Kahle texts set the standard, and I have drawn on them for stories or parts of stories in almost every section of this book except for the tales in "Famous Fools and Rascals."

Of the modern specialist periodicals on folklore in Arabic, the monthly folklore magazine *Al-Turath al Sha'bi (Folk Heritage)* published in Iraq and edited by Lutfi al-Khouri is an impressive source for the richest and most diverse folk texts. The tenth issue of its 1972 volume, which is devoted to the folktale in Iraq, contains a wide range of tales, anecdotes, and articles on storytelling. Referring to this publication alongside the much earlier texts, such as those collected in Bruno Meissner's *Neuarabische Geschichten aus dem Iraq* of 1903 or Albert Socin's *Der arabische Dialekt von Mosul und Mardin* of 1904, to name but two of many sources, the student of folklore is in possession of a respectable sampler of stories from that country.

Arabists and grammarians from Europe and the United States were busily recording oral narratives in almost every Arab country at the end of the last century and the beginning of this. Though they were most prolific in the countries of the eastern Mediterranean and in Iraq, Egypt, and Morocco, they ventured into the hinterland of Yemen and even chased an Arabic dialect in Zanzibar. They continue to do so today, as seen, for example, in the work of Bernhard Lewin in Syria. But now a new generation of Arab scholars who are interested in their own heritage provide texts of the current oral tradition.

The stylistic quality of the texts varies widely according to the talent of the narrators. I read and reread hundreds of stories and folktales in searching for material suitable for this book, and only rarely did I happen upon a number of delightful texts in the same collection. Gaetan Delphin's *Recueil de textes pour l'étude de l'arabe parlé* published in Algeria in 1891, is particularly enjoyable. It may be that animal fables and anecdotes about rascals are appealing subjects, but one guesses from his introductory remarks that Delphin was an enthusiast concerning the Arab way of life. His hosts among the goat-herding nomads no doubt were quick to sense this and responded by helping him as best they could. A number of the stories they told him are in the sections on animal stories and on famous fools. Another arresting work is Johann Gottfried Wetzstein's *Sprächliches aus den Zeltlagern der syrischen Wüste (Spoken Language of the Tent Sites of the Syrian Desert)*, 1868. A drought in the 1860s having driven the 'Aneza and Beni Khalid tribes to the outer edges of the desert and within riding distance of Damascus, Wetzstein was able to visit them. There is a leisurely, almost epic quality in the texts he recorded, and they provided this collection with the Beduin story of "The Boy in Girl's Dress."

In the last thirty years a number of collections have been published in Arabic for the general reader. Some, like Karam al Bustani's *Hikayat Libnaniyya (Lebanese Folktales)*, Beirut, 1961, and Abdel Karim al Jahiman's *Min Asatirna al Sha'biyya fi qalb Jazirat al Arab (Folk Legends from Saudi Arabia)*, first appearing in 1967, though rendered in classical Arabic, because of the sheer number of stories they include, are valuable in providing an idea of the stories current in Lebanon and Saudi Arabia respectively. Closer to the colloquial is Ahmad Bassam Sa'i's *Al Hikayat al Sha'biyya fil Latakiyya (Folktales from Latakiya)*, Damascus, 1974, and Nimr Sirhan's *Al Hikayya al Sha'biyya al Filistiniyya (The Palestinian Folktale)*, Amman, 1969.

My task has been to locate as many texts of oral tales as possible, both old and new, and sift through them carefully for stories representative of what has been told in the Arab world over the last hundred years. From these I have chosen the ones most likely to interest the English reader. An invaluable guide had been Ursula Nowak's doctoral dissertation, *Beiträge zur Typologie des arabischen Volksmärchens*, Freiburg im Breisgau, 1969. After an introductory essay, Ms. Nowak presents some five hundred stories in briefest schematic plot outline, typed and classified, with citations of sources for parallel versions of each story; a useful tool for a prospector.

Having read through many hundreds of stories published between the 1860s and the present, my bias in making choices has been in favor of style over plot. At best the good storytellers are few and far between. And since my intent is to introduce the English reader to the Arab folk heritage which has been important to me, I have opted for stories which seem to demonstrate either the skill of the speaker or some characteristic folk trait or custom. I have been encouraged in this leaning by the discovery that there are more regional similarities than differences in the plots and subjects of the stories. Thus if a story was recorded in Yemen, Morocco, and Syria and the best-told version is Syrian, I have decided in favor if it even if I did not have any sample for this collection from Yemen. In many cases there were several texts for a story, and if the imagery for the hero's courage and beauty in one version was forceful while his adventures were lamely told, I combined two texts to produce one satisfying story. The provenance of each story indicates where it or its main part was recorded; this does not mean that the tale is more typical of that place than another.

The bibliography at the end lists the sources of the texts from which the collection was made up. In every case except three, I have worked from texts in Arabic, sometimes in dialect. Everywhere I have benefitted from the scholarly notes and information of the original editors. Being unwilling to encumber this collection with annotation in the back, I have provided information necessary to understanding the stories either in the introductions to each section or the narratives themselves. Even though I was unable to find an Arabic text for three tales, I was reluctant to exclude them: "The Duty of the Host" appears in Alois Musil, *Manners and Customs of the Rwala Bedouins*, New York, 1928; "Who Lied?" in Stephan H. Stephan's "Palestinian Animal Stories," *Journal of the Palestine Oriental Society*, 1923. The source for "Who Has the Sweetest Flesh on Earth?" is J. E. Hanauer's *Folklore of the Holy Land*, London, 1907.

After the storytellers who are nameless and the scholars and folklorists whose names are listed, my greatest debt is to the New York Public Library. I wish to thank the staff of the Oriental Division in Room 219, and especially Chris Filstrup, for their help and the miles they have trudged in the stacks to bring me yellowing volumes of obscure journals. For a project like this, the Public Library is an ideal source. Most of the stories in this collection were already on its shelves, though dispersed in journals, bulletins, books, and grammars published in every corner of the Western and Arabic-speaking world over the span of a century and more. Indeed, having looked in the Middle East in vain for some pamphlets (printed seventy years ago for popular entertainment) as a possible source of Djuha stories, I eventually found a number of them on microfilm in the library's Schiff Collection.

Once, having offered to show a visiting Arab folklorist the sights of Manhattan, I arranged for us to meet in the Library. But then, seeing the card catalogue of the Oriental Division, the visitor said, "Please—leave me here!" And no wonder, for there it is, an Aladdin's cave requiring neither password nor magic lamp.

∵ ∵ ∵

Abul Fadl, Fahmi. *Volkstümliche Texte in arabischen Bauerndialekten.* Münster, 1961.

Artin-Pacha, Yacoub. *Contes populaires inédits de la Vallée du Nil.* Paris, 1895.

Bauer, Leonhard. *Das Palästinische Arabisch.* Leipzig, 1913.

Barghouthi, Abdullatif. *Hikayat Jan min Bani Zeid* [Djinn Stories of the Benizeid]. Jerusalem, 1979.

Bergsträsser, Gotthelf. *Neuaramäische Marchen und andere Texte aus Ma'lula.* Leipzig, 1915.

Al Bustani, Karam. *Hikayat Libnaniyya* [Lebanese Folktales]. Beirut, 1966.

Campbell, Charles Grimshaw. *Tales from the Arab Tribes.* London, 1949.

———. *From Town and Tribe.* London, 1952.

———. *Told in the Marketplace.* London, 1954.

Delphin, Gaetan. *Recueil de textes pour l'étude de l'arabe parlé.* Algiers, 1891.

Dulac, H. M. "Contes Arabes en dialecte de la Haute Egypte." *Journal Asiatique,* January 1885, pp. 6–38.

———. *Quatre contes Arabes en dialecte Cairote.* Mission Archéologique Française au Caire, 1881–4, fasc. 1.

Al Jahiman, Abdel Karim. *Min Asatirna al Sha'biyya fi qalb Jazirat al Arab* [Folk Legends fron Ɪudi Arabia]. Beirut, 1967.

Jahn, Alfred. *Die Mehrisprache Südarabiens.* Kais. Akad. Südarabien Exped Bd. 3. Vienna, 1902.

Levi-Provençal, Evariste. *Textes arabes de l'Ouargha.* Paris, 1922.

Lewin, Bernhard. *Arabische Texte im Dialekt von Hama.* Beirut, 1966.

Littmann, Enno. *Modern Arabic Tales, Arabic Text.* Leiden, 1905.

———. *Arabische Beduinerzählungen.* Strasbourg, 1908.

Löhr, Max. *Der vulgararabische Dialekt von Jerusalem.* Giessen, 1905.

Loubignac, Victorien. *Textes Arabes des Zaers.* Paris, 1952.

Meissner, Bruno. *Neuarabische Geschichten aus dem Iraq.* Leipzig, 1903.

———. *Neuarabische Geschichten aus Tanger.* Leipzig, 1906.

Moulieras, Auguste. *Contes Kabyles en dialecte de Zouaua.* Paris, 1892.

Nowak, Ursula. *Beiträge zur Typologie des arabischen Volksmärchens.* Freiburg im Breisgau, 1969.

Oestrup, Johannes. *Contes de Damas.* Leiden, 1897.

Panetta, Ester. *L'arabo parlato a Bengasi.* Rome, 1943.

Prym, Eugene, and Socin, Albert. *Der neu-aramäische Dialekt des Tur Abdin.* Göttingen, 1881.

Reinhardt, Carl. *Ein arabischer Dialekt gesprochen in Oman und Zanzibar.* Berlin, 1894.

Sa'i, Ahmad Bassam. *Al Hikayat al Sha'biyya fil Latakiyya* [Folktales from Latakiya]. Damascus, 1974.

Schmidt, Hans, and Kahle, Paul. *Volkserzählungen aus Palästina.* 2 vols. Göttingen, 1918 and 1930.

El-Shamy, Hasan. *Folktales of Egypt*. Chicago, 1980.

    Sirhan, Nimr. *Al Hikayya al Sha'biyya al Filistiniyya* [The Palestinian Folktale]. Amman, 1969.

Socin, Albert. *Zum arabischen Dialekt von Marokko*. Leipzig, 1893.

————. *Der arabische Dialekt von Mosul und Mardin*. Leipzig, 1904.

Socin, Albert, and Stumme, Hans. *Der arabische Dialekt der Houwara des Wad Sus in Marokko*. Leipzig, 1894.

Spitta-Bey, Guillaume. *Contes arabes modernes*. Leiden, 1883.

Stevens, Ethel Stefana. *Folktales of Iraq*. London, 1931.

Stumme, Hans. *Tunesische Märchen*. Leipzig, 1893.

————. *Märchen der Schluh von Tazerwalt*. Leipzig, 1895.

————. *Märchen aus Tripolis*, Leipzig, 1898.

Al Turath al Sha'bi [Folk Heritage]. Monthly. Iraq, 1969.

Al Turath wal Mujjtama' [Heritage and Society]. Quarterly. Al Bireh, 1975.

Weissbach, Franz. *Beiträge zur Kunde des Irak Arabischen*. Leipzig, 1908.

Wetzstein, Johann Gottfried. *Sprächliches aus den Zeltlagern der syrischen Wüste*. Berlin, 1868.

.: .: .:

∴ *About the Author* ∴

Inea Bushnaq was born in Jerusalem, and educated
there and in Damascus and London. She has a degree
in classics from Cambridge University, and has
translated works from both French and Arabic, including *The Arabs in Israel, Betrayal at the Vel d'Hiv*,
and contemporary Arabic short stories. She lives in
New York City.